DYNAMITE ENTERTAINMENT PRESENTS

BATTLESTAR
GALACTICA
SEASON ZERO

VOLUME I

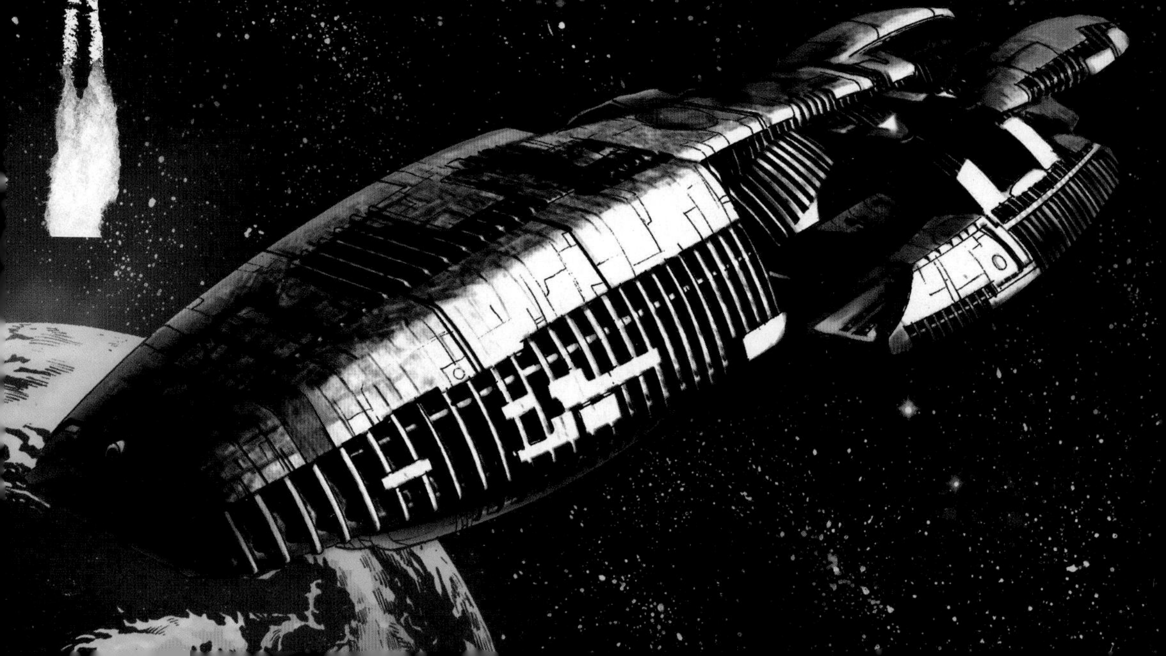

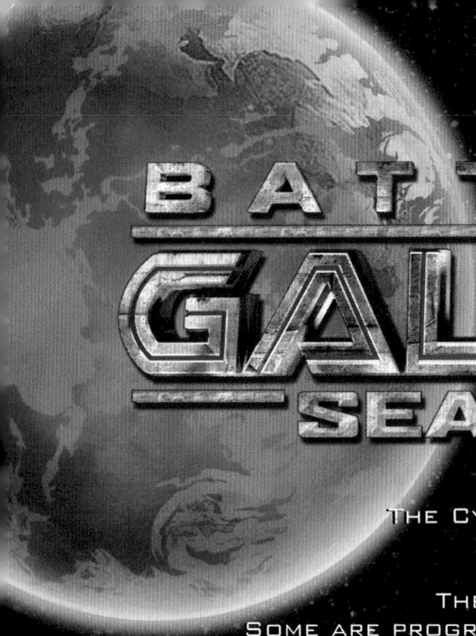

BATTLESTAR GALACTICA™ SEASON ZERO

THE CYLONS WERE CREATED BY MAN...
THEY REBELLED...
THEY EVOLVED...
THEY LOOK AND FEEL HUMAN...
SOME ARE PROGRAMMED TO THINK THAT THEY ARE HUMAN...
THERE ARE MANY COPIES...
AND THEY HAVE A PLAN.

SET APPROXIMATELY TWO YEARS BEFORE THE CYLON DECIMATION OF THE TWELVE COLONIES, THIS STORY FOLLOWS COMMANDER ADAMA AND CREW AS THEY TAKE ON THEIR FIRST MISSION ON BOARD THE BATTLESTAR GALACTICA.

STORY BY:
BRANDON JERWA

ART BY:
STEPHEN SEGOVIA (ISSUE 0)
JACKSON HERBERT (ISSUES 1-6)

COLORS BY:
INLIGHT STUDIO (ISSUE 0)
ADRIANO LUCAS OF IMPACTO STUDIOS (ISSUES 1-6)

LETTERS BY:
SIMON BOWLAND

SPECIAL THANKS TO:
RON MOORE & CINDY CHANG

COLLECTION DESIGN BY:
JASON ULLMEYER

COLLECTS ISSUES 0-6 OF BATTLESTAR GALACTICA: SEASON ZERO BY DYNAMITE ENTERTAINMENT.

DYNAMITE ENTERTAINMENT
NICK BARRUCCI • PRESIDENT
JUAN COLLADO • CHIEF OPERATING OFFICER
JOSEPH RYBANDT • DIRECTOR OF MARKETING
JOSH JOHNSON • CREATIVE DIRECTOR
JASON ULLMEYER • GRAPHIC DESIGNER

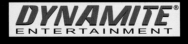

DYNAMITE® ENTERTAINMENT
WWW.DYNAMITEENTERTAINMENT.COM

First Printing
Direct Market ISBN-10: 1-933305-81-9
Direct Market ISBN-13: 9-718933-305813
Mass Market ISBN-10: 1-933305-24-X
Mass Market ISBN-13: 9-718933-305240
10 9 8 7 6 5 4 3 2 1

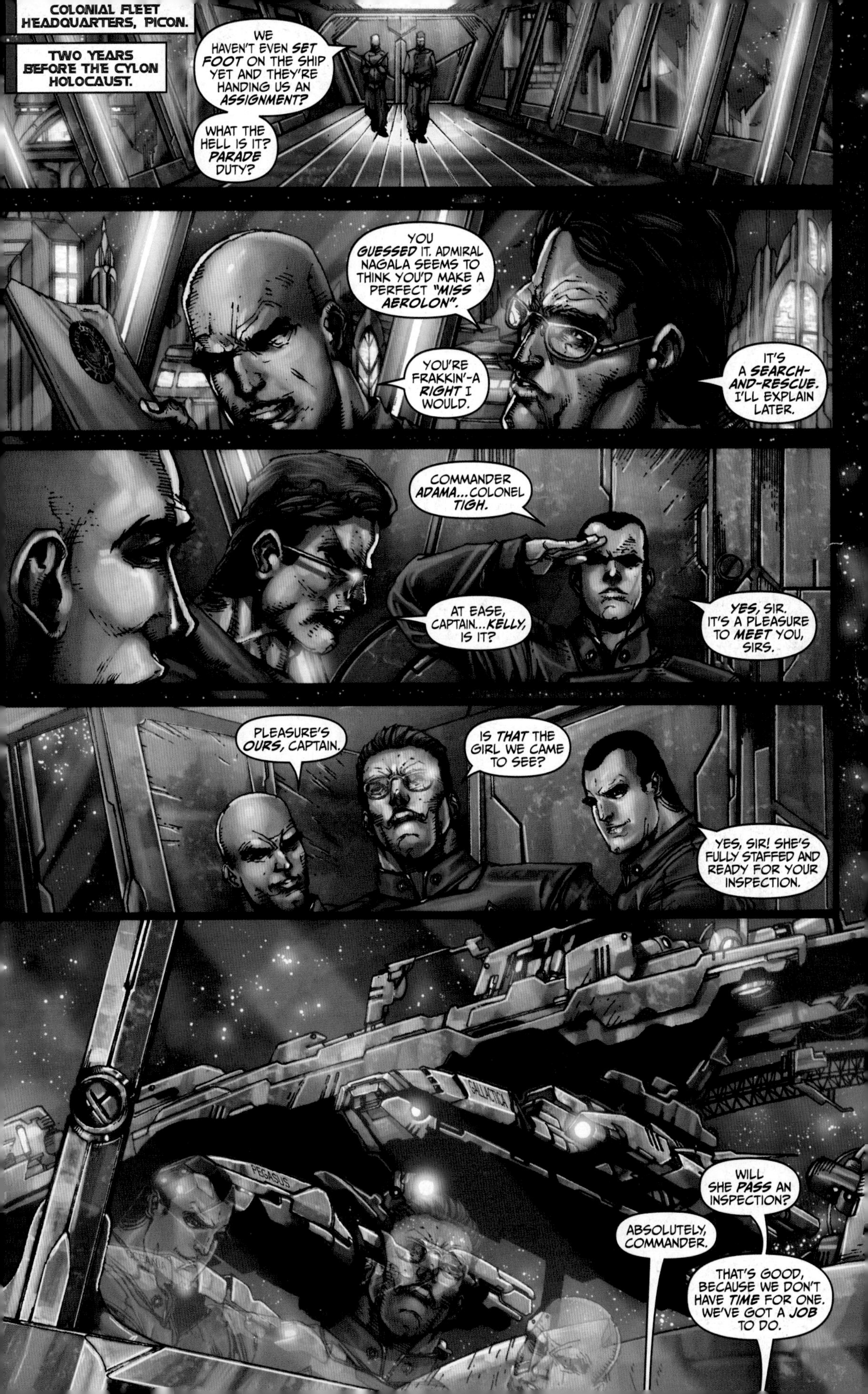
COLONIAL FLEET HEADQUARTERS, PICON.
TWO YEARS BEFORE THE CYLON HOLOCAUST.
WE HAVEN'T EVEN SET FOOT ON THE SHIP YET AND THEY'RE HANDING US AN ASSIGNMENT?
WHAT THE HELL IS IT? PARADE DUTY?
YOU GUESSED IT. ADMIRAL NAGALA SEEMS TO THINK YOU'D MAKE A PERFECT "MISS AEROLON".
YOU'RE FRAKKIN'-A RIGHT I WOULD.
IT'S A SEARCH-AND-RESCUE. I'LL EXPLAIN LATER.
COMMANDER ADAMA... COLONEL TIGH.
AT EASE, CAPTAIN... KELLY, IS IT?
YES, SIR. IT'S A PLEASURE TO MEET YOU, SIRS.
PLEASURE'S OURS, CAPTAIN.
IS THAT THE GIRL WE CAME TO SEE?
YES, SIR! SHE'S FULLY STAFFED AND READY FOR YOUR INSPECTION.
GALACTICA
PEGASUS
WILL SHE PASS AN INSPECTION?
ABSOLUTELY, COMMANDER.
THAT'S GOOD, BECAUSE WE DON'T HAVE TIME FOR ONE. WE'VE GOT A JOB TO DO.

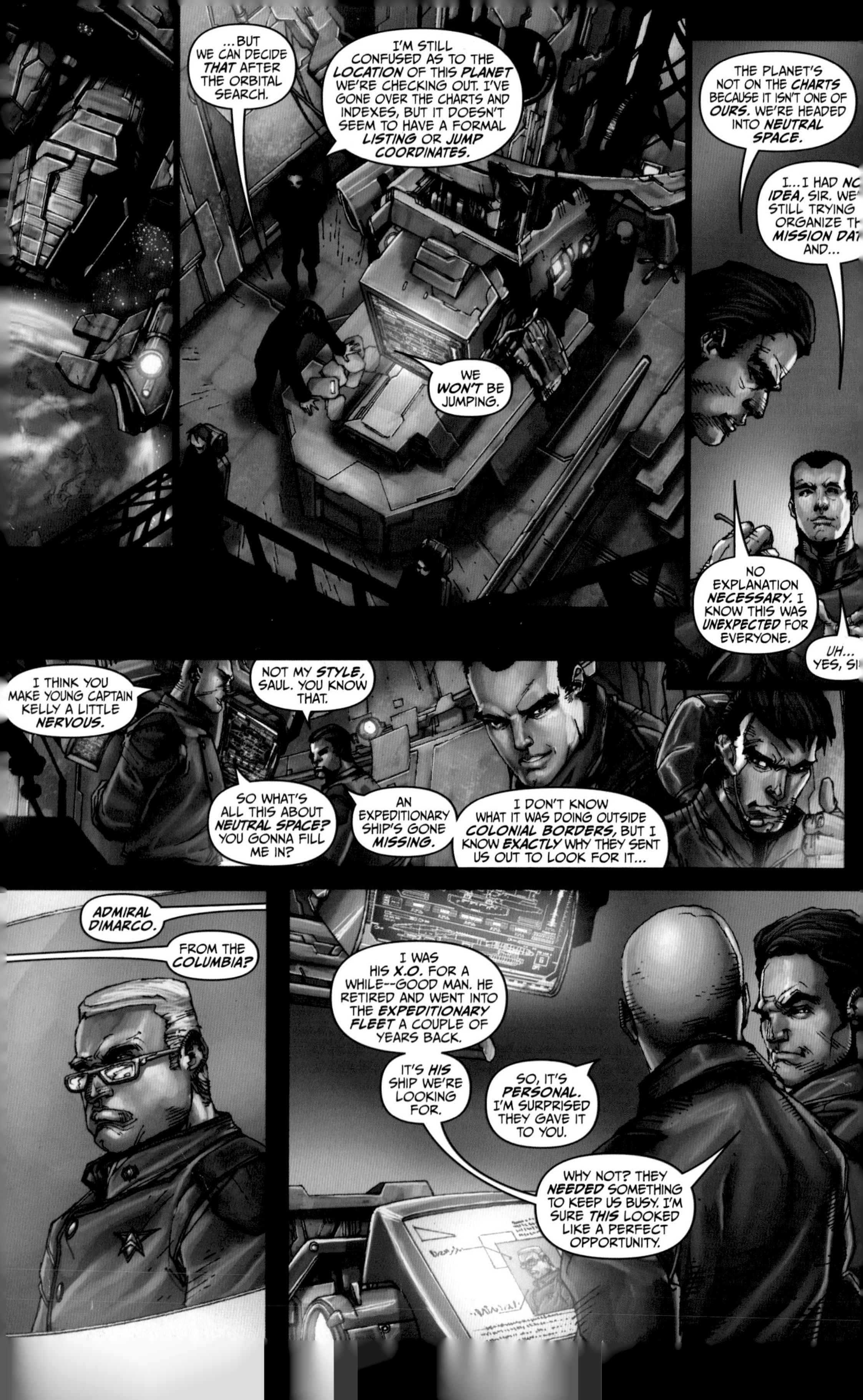

...BUT WE CAN DECIDE THAT AFTER THE ORBITAL SEARCH.
I'M STILL CONFUSED AS TO THE LOCATION OF THIS PLANET WE'RE CHECKING OUT. I'VE GONE OVER THE CHARTS AND INDEXES, BUT IT DOESN'T SEEM TO HAVE A FORMAL LISTING OR JUMP COORDINATES.
WE WON'T BE JUMPING.
THE PLANET'S NOT ON THE CHARTS BECAUSE IT ISN'T ONE OF OURS. WE'RE HEADED INTO NEUTRAL SPACE.
I...I HAD NO IDEA, SIR. WE'RE STILL TRYING TO ORGANIZE THE MISSION DATA AND...
NO EXPLANATION NECESSARY. I KNOW THIS WAS UNEXPECTED FOR EVERYONE.
UH... YES, SIR.
I THINK YOU MAKE YOUNG CAPTAIN KELLY A LITTLE NERVOUS.
NOT MY STYLE, SAUL. YOU KNOW THAT.
SO WHAT'S ALL THIS ABOUT NEUTRAL SPACE? YOU GONNA FILL ME IN?
AN EXPEDITIONARY SHIP'S GONE MISSING.
I DON'T KNOW WHAT IT WAS DOING OUTSIDE COLONIAL BORDERS, BUT I KNOW EXACTLY WHY THEY SENT US OUT TO LOOK FOR IT...
ADMIRAL DIMARCO.
FROM THE COLUMBIA?
I WAS HIS X.O. FOR A WHILE--GOOD MAN. HE RETIRED AND WENT INTO THE EXPEDITIONARY FLEET A COUPLE OF YEARS BACK.
IT'S HIS SHIP WE'RE LOOKING FOR.
SO, IT'S PERSONAL. I'M SURPRISED THEY GAVE IT TO YOU.
WHY NOT? THEY NEEDED SOMETHING TO KEEP US BUSY. I'M SURE THIS LOOKED LIKE A PERFECT OPPORTUNITY.

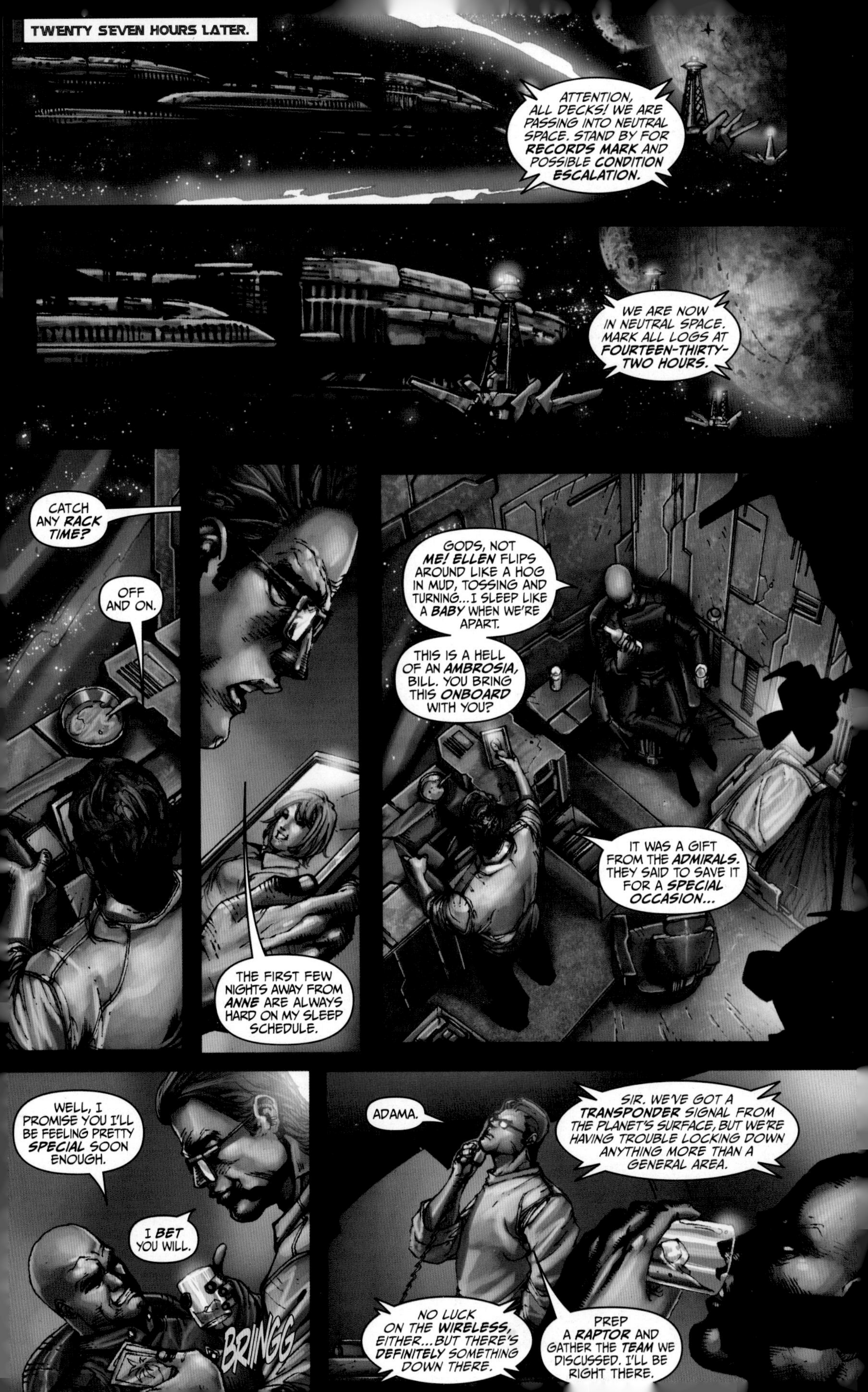
TWENTY SEVEN HOURS LATER.
ATTENTION, ALL DECKS! WE ARE PASSING INTO NEUTRAL SPACE. STAND BY FOR RECORDS MARK AND POSSIBLE CONDITION ESCALATION.
WE ARE NOW IN NEUTRAL SPACE. MARK ALL LOGS AT FOURTEEN-THIRTY-TWO HOURS.
CATCH ANY RACK TIME?
OFF AND ON.
THE FIRST FEW NIGHTS AWAY FROM ANNE ARE ALWAYS HARD ON MY SLEEP SCHEDULE.
GODS, NOT ME! ELLEN FLIPS AROUND LIKE A HOG IN MUD, TOSSING AND TURNING...I SLEEP LIKE A BABY WHEN WE'RE APART.
THIS IS A HELL OF AN AMBROSIA, BILL. YOU BRING THIS ONBOARD WITH YOU?
IT WAS A GIFT FROM THE ADMIRALS. THEY SAID TO SAVE IT FOR A SPECIAL OCCASION...
WELL, I PROMISE YOU I'LL BE FEELING PRETTY SPECIAL SOON ENOUGH.
I BET YOU WILL.
BRIINGG
ADAMA.
SIR. WE'VE GOT A TRANSPONDER SIGNAL FROM THE PLANET'S SURFACE, BUT WE'RE HAVING TROUBLE LOCKING DOWN ANYTHING MORE THAN A GENERAL AREA.
NO LUCK ON THE WIRELESS, EITHER...BUT THERE'S DEFINITELY SOMETHING DOWN THERE.
PREP A RAPTOR AND GATHER THE TEAM WE DISCUSSED. I'LL BE RIGHT THERE.

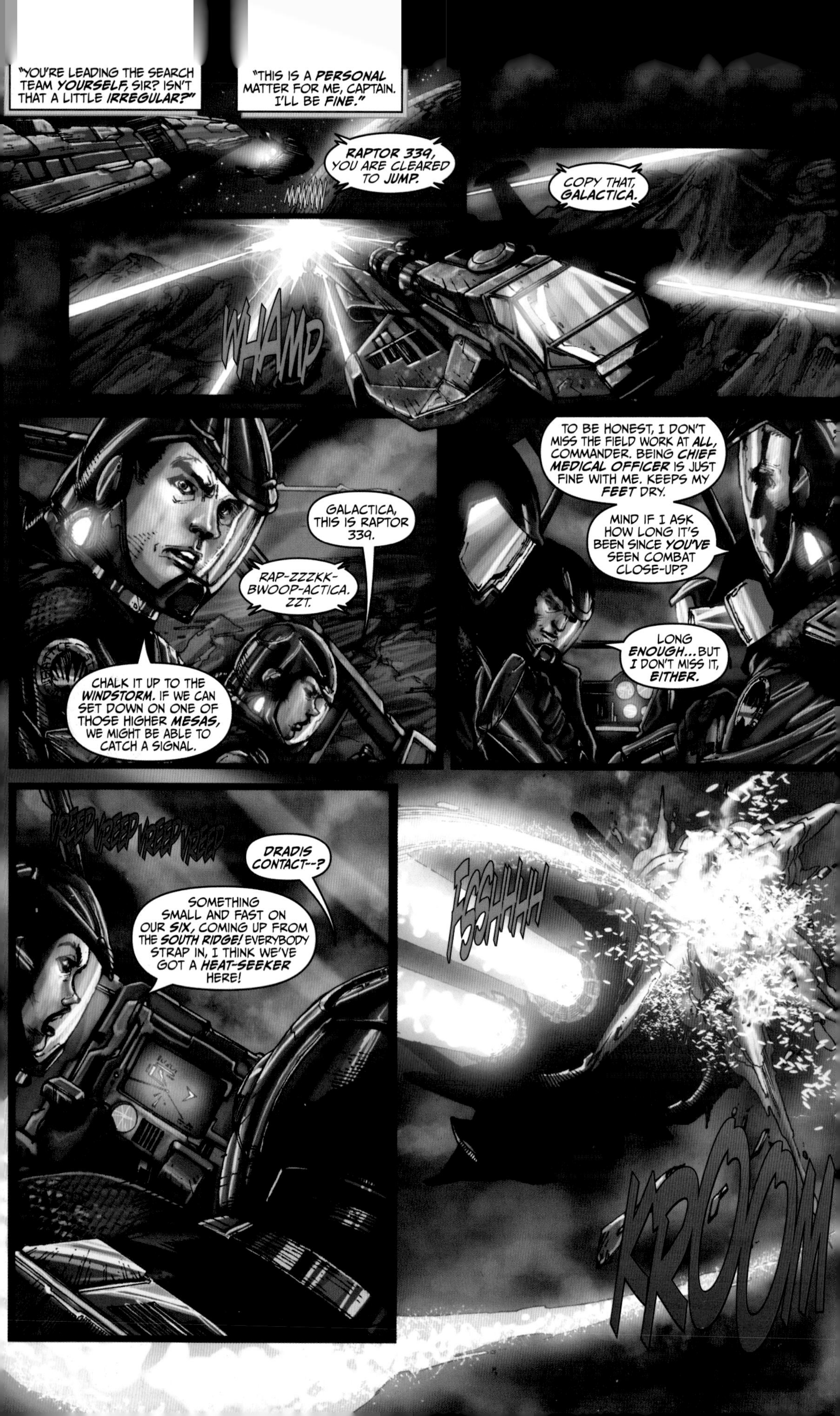
"YOU'RE LEADING THE SEARCH TEAM YOURSELF, SIR? ISN'T THAT A LITTLE IRREGULAR?"
"THIS IS A PERSONAL MATTER FOR ME, CAPTAIN. I'LL BE FINE."
RAPTOR 339, YOU ARE CLEARED TO JUMP.
COPY THAT, GALACTICA.
WHAMP
GALACTICA, THIS IS RAPTOR 339.
RAP-ZZZKK-BWOOP-ACTICA. ZZT.
CHALK IT UP TO THE WINDSTORM. IF WE CAN SET DOWN ON ONE OF THOSE HIGHER MESAS, WE MIGHT BE ABLE TO CATCH A SIGNAL.
TO BE HONEST, I DON'T MISS THE FIELD WORK AT ALL, COMMANDER. BEING CHIEF MEDICAL OFFICER IS JUST FINE WITH ME. KEEPS MY FEET DRY.
MIND IF I ASK HOW LONG IT'S BEEN SINCE YOU'VE SEEN COMBAT CLOSE-UP?
LONG ENOUGH...BUT I DON'T MISS IT, EITHER.
VREEP VREEP VREEP VREEP
DRADIS CONTACT--?
SOMETHING SMALL AND FAST ON OUR SIX, COMING UP FROM THE SOUTH RIDGE! EVERYBODY STRAP IN, I THINK WE'VE GOT A HEAT-SEEKER HERE!
FSSHHH
KROOM

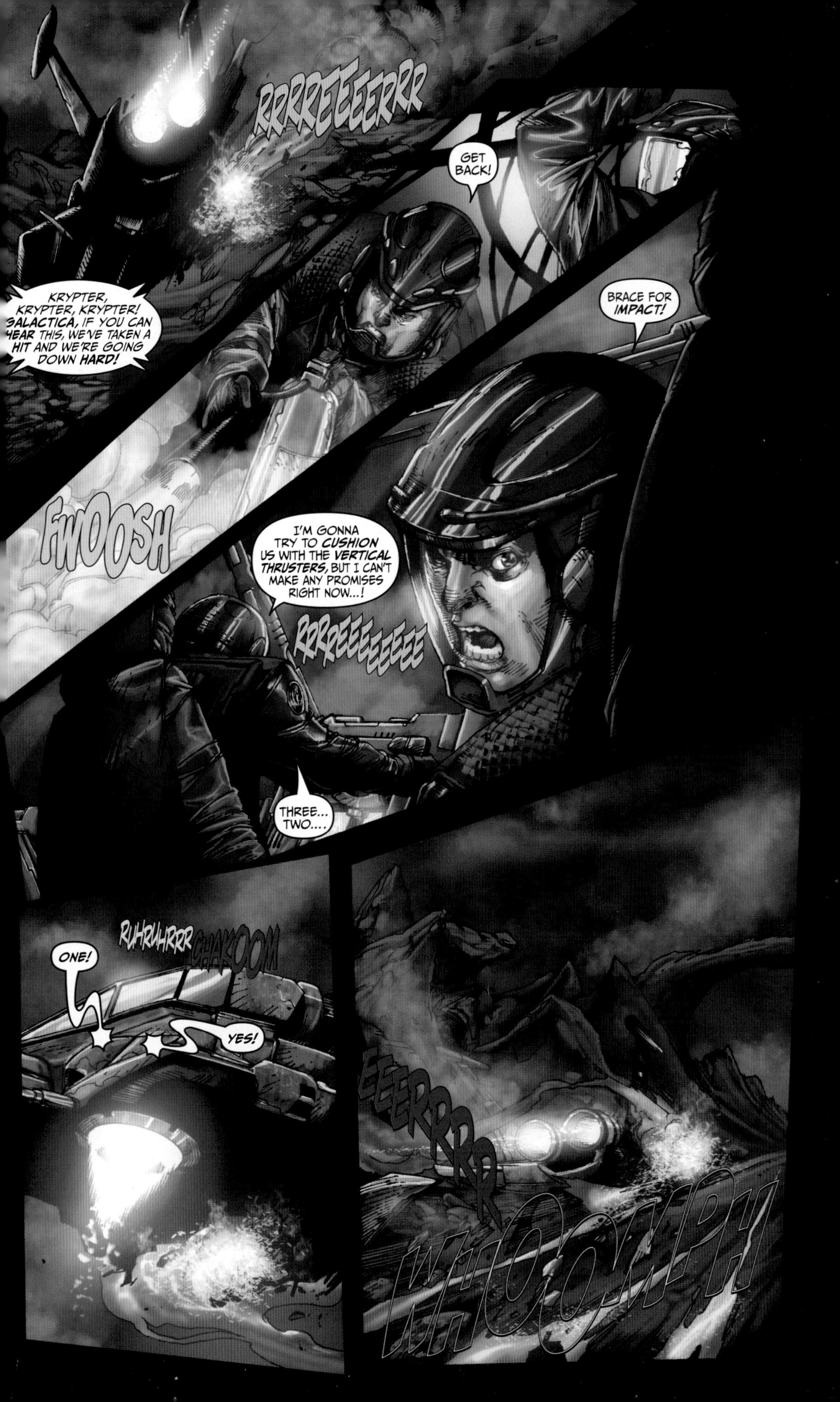
RRRREEEERRR
GET BACK!
KRYPTER, KRYPTER, KRYPTER! GALACTICA, IF YOU CAN HEAR THIS, WE'VE TAKEN A HIT AND WE'RE GOING DOWN HARD!
BRACE FOR IMPACT!
FWOOSH
I'M GONNA TRY TO CUSHION US WITH THE VERTICAL THRUSTERS, BUT I CAN'T MAKE ANY PROMISES RIGHT NOW...!
RRREEEEEEEE
THREE... TWO....
RUHRUHRRR
CHAKOOM
ONE!
YES!
EEERRRRR
WHOOMPH

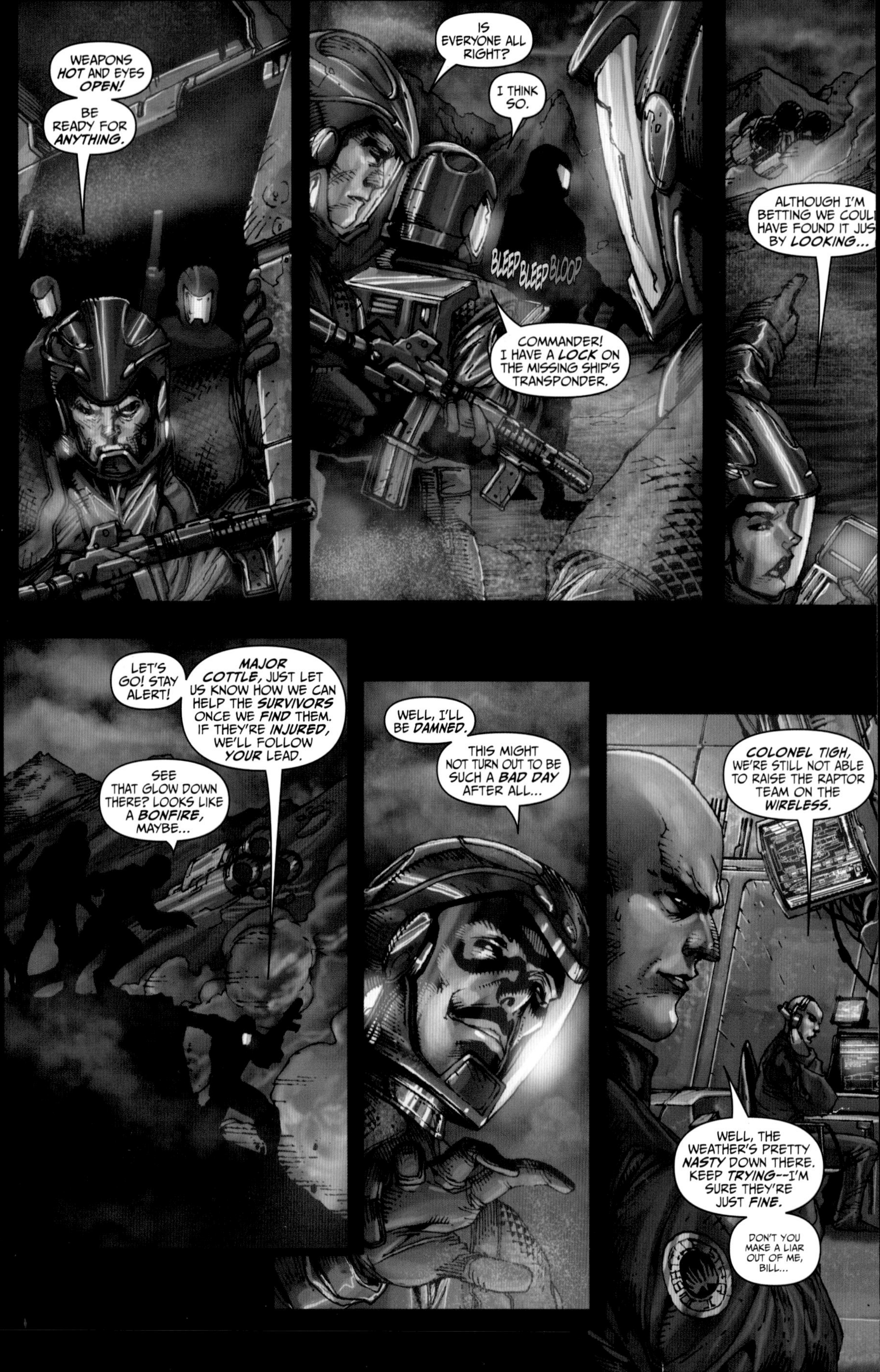
WEAPONS HOT AND EYES OPEN!
BE READY FOR ANYTHING.
IS EVERYONE ALL RIGHT?
I THINK SO.
BLEED BLEED BLOOP
COMMANDER! I HAVE A LOCK ON THE MISSING SHIP'S TRANSPONDER.
ALTHOUGH I'M BETTING WE COULD HAVE FOUND IT JUST BY LOOKING...
LET'S GO! STAY ALERT!
MAJOR COTTLE, JUST LET US KNOW HOW WE CAN HELP THE SURVIVORS ONCE WE FIND THEM. IF THEY'RE INJURED, WE'LL FOLLOW YOUR LEAD.
SEE THAT GLOW DOWN THERE? LOOKS LIKE A BONFIRE, MAYBE...
WELL, I'LL BE DAMNED.
THIS MIGHT NOT TURN OUT TO BE SUCH A BAD DAY AFTER ALL...
COLONEL TIGH, WE'RE STILL NOT ABLE TO RAISE THE RAPTOR TEAM ON THE WIRELESS.
WELL, THE WEATHER'S PRETTY NASTY DOWN THERE. KEEP TRYING--I'M SURE THEY'RE JUST FINE.
DON'T YOU MAKE A LIAR OUT OF ME, BILL...

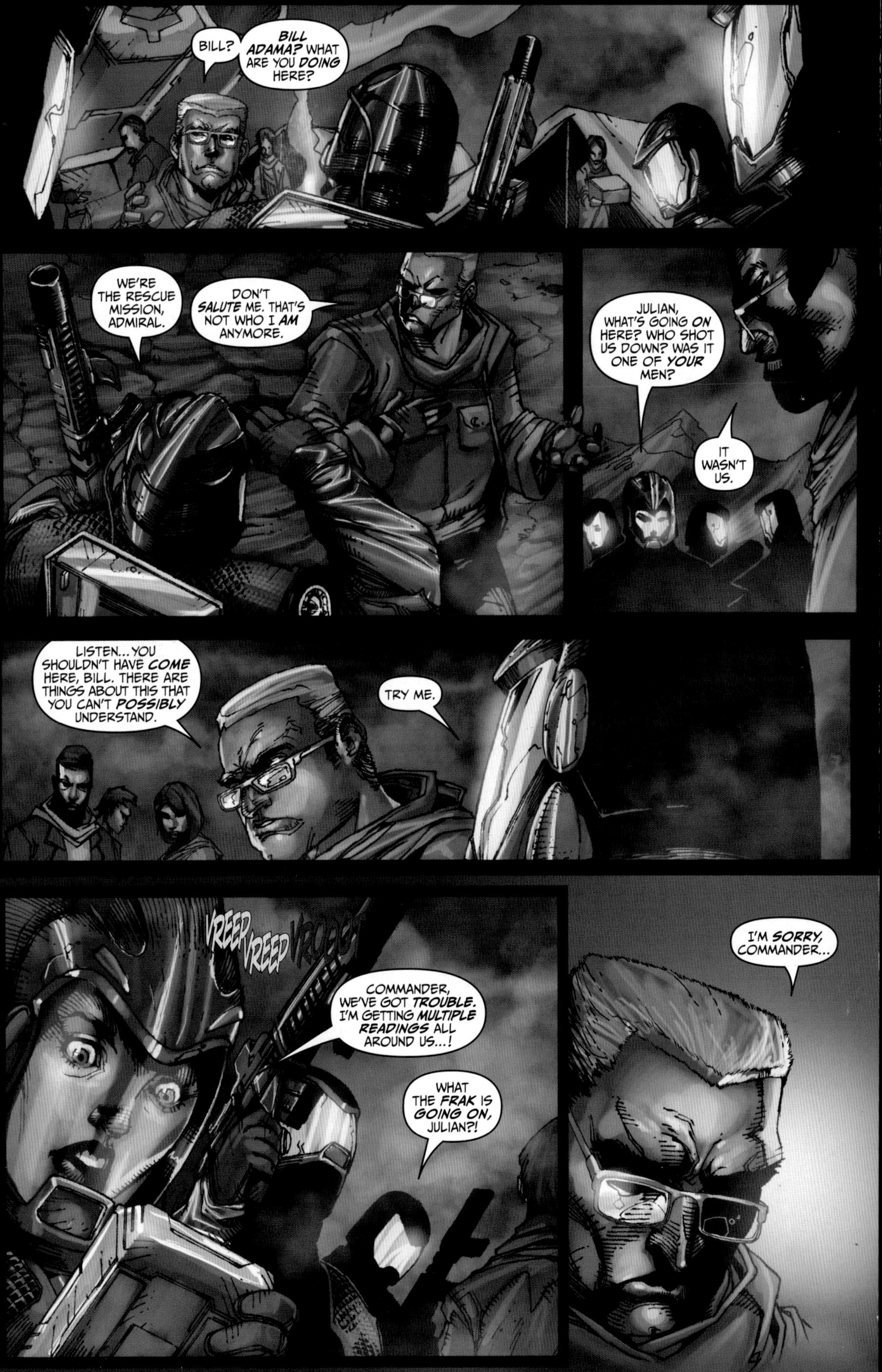
BILL?
BILL ADAMA? WHAT ARE YOU DOING HERE?
WE'RE THE RESCUE MISSION, ADMIRAL.
DON'T SALUTE ME. THAT'S NOT WHO I AM ANYMORE.
JULIAN, WHAT'S GOING ON HERE? WHO SHOT US DOWN? WAS IT ONE OF YOUR MEN?
IT WASN'T US.
LISTEN... YOU SHOULDN'T HAVE COME HERE, BILL. THERE ARE THINGS ABOUT THIS THAT YOU CAN'T POSSIBLY UNDERSTAND.
TRY ME.
VREEP VREEP VROOOT
COMMANDER, WE'VE GOT TROUBLE. I'M GETTING MULTIPLE READINGS ALL AROUND US...!
WHAT THE FRAK IS GOING ON, JULIAN?!
I'M SORRY, COMMANDER...

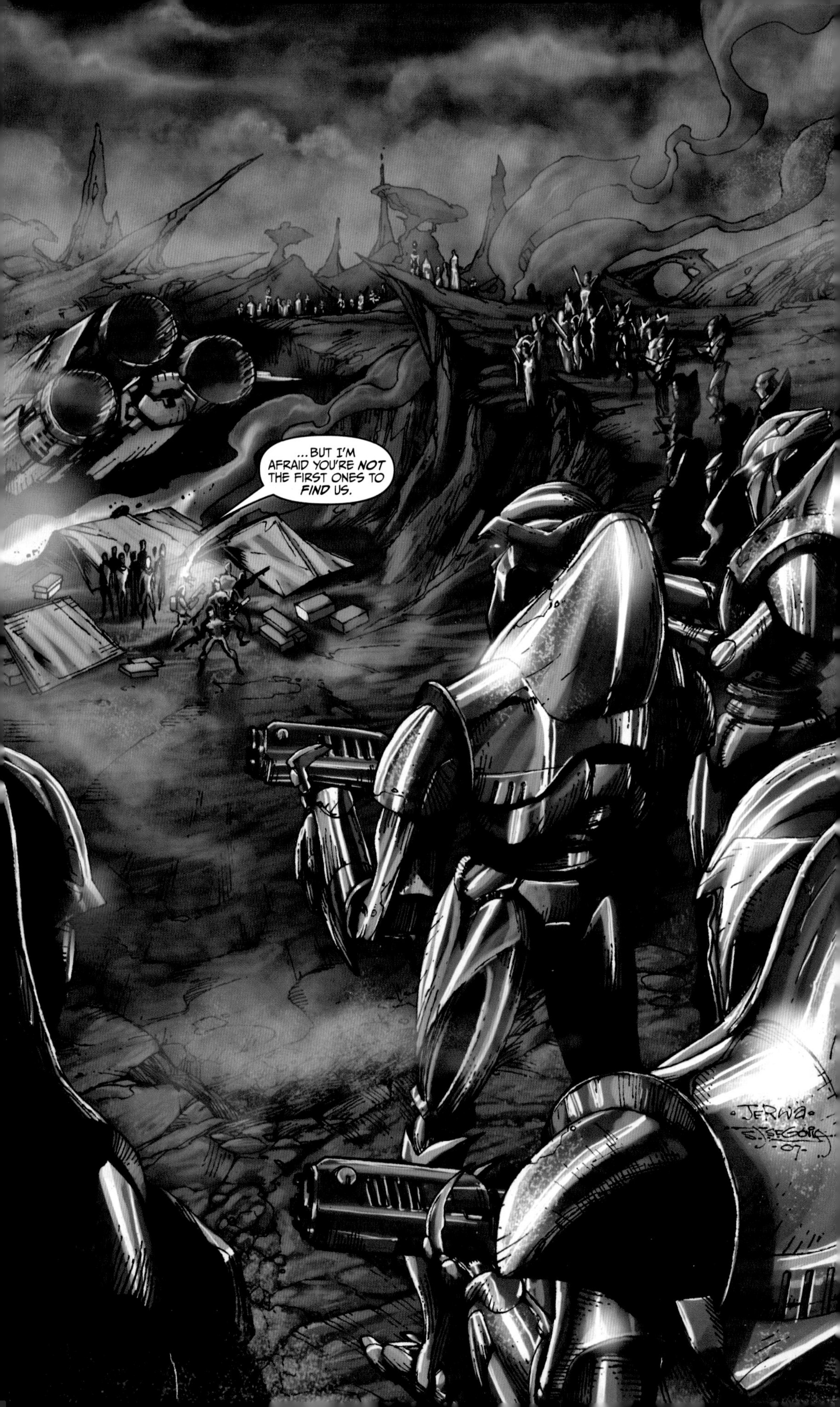
...BUT I'M AFRAID YOU'RE NOT THE FIRST ONES TO FIND US.

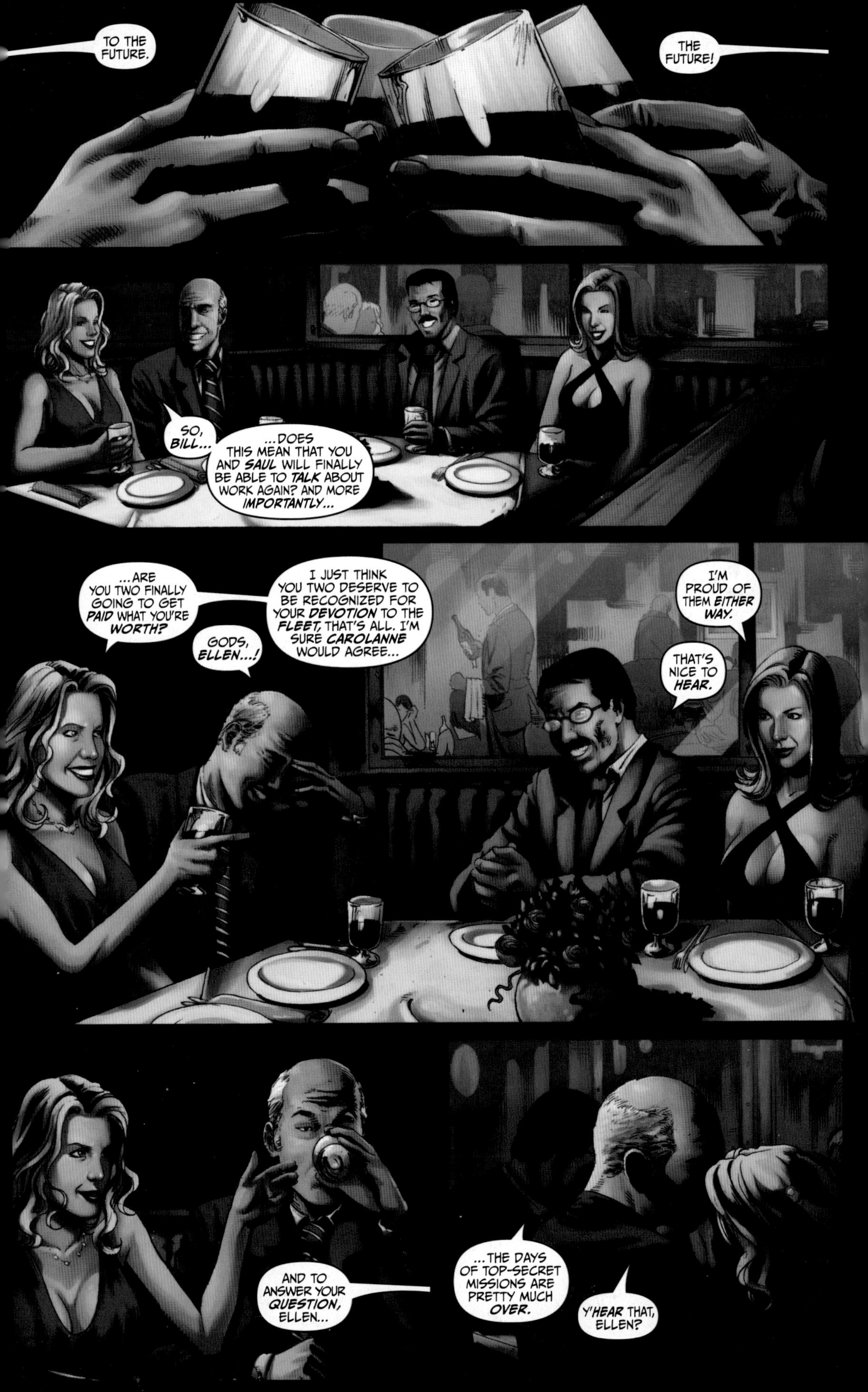

TO THE FUTURE.
THE FUTURE!
SO, BILL...
...DOES THIS MEAN THAT YOU AND SAUL WILL FINALLY BE ABLE TO TALK ABOUT WORK AGAIN? AND MORE IMPORTANTLY...
...ARE YOU TWO FINALLY GOING TO GET PAID WHAT YOU'RE WORTH?
GODS, ELLEN...!
I JUST THINK YOU TWO DESERVE TO BE RECOGNIZED FOR YOUR DEVOTION TO THE FLEET, THAT'S ALL. I'M SURE CAROLANNE WOULD AGREE...
I'M PROUD OF THEM EITHER WAY.
THAT'S NICE TO HEAR.
AND TO ANSWER YOUR QUESTION, ELLEN...
...THE DAYS OF TOP-SECRET MISSIONS ARE PRETTY MUCH OVER.
Y'HEAR THAT, ELLEN?

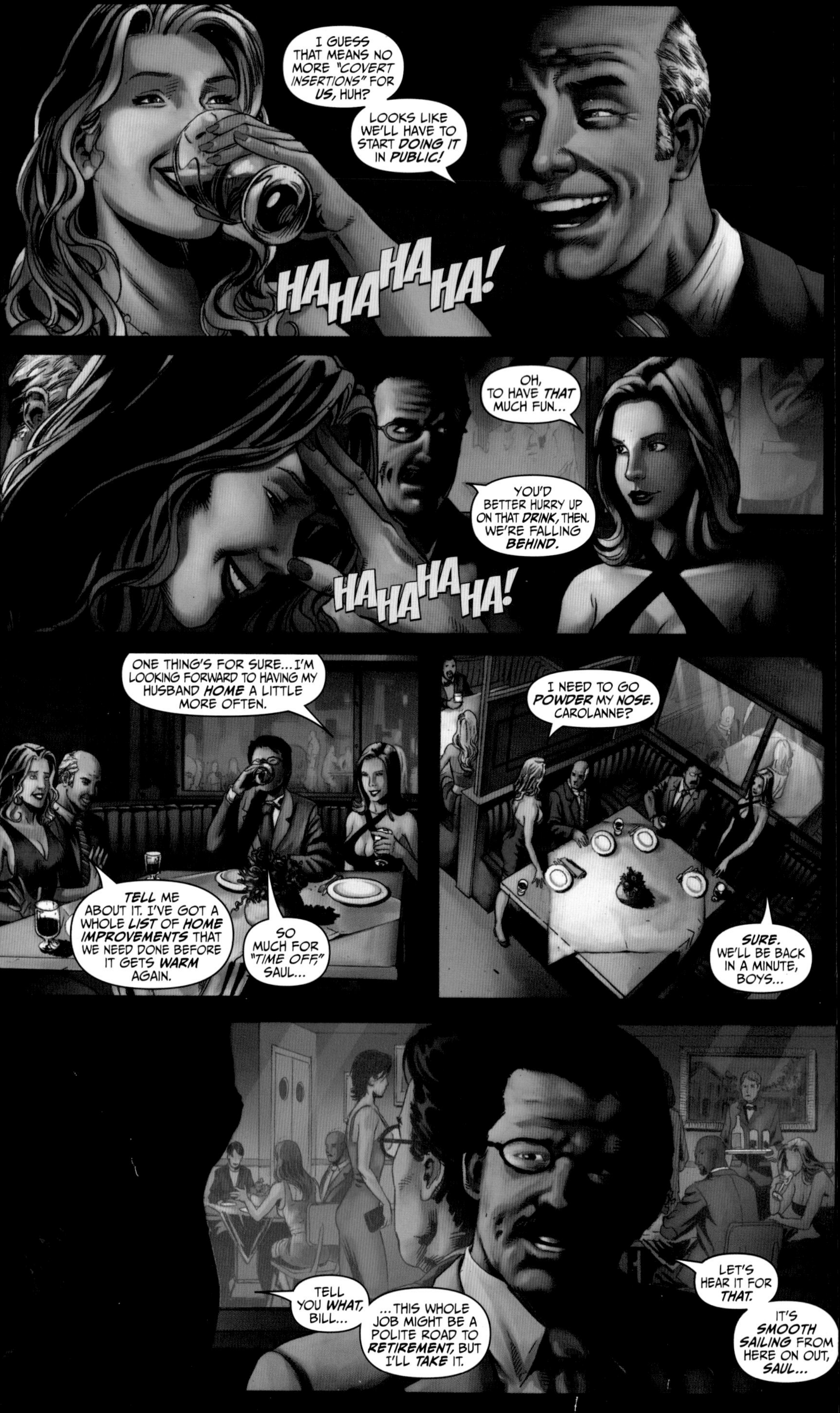
I GUESS THAT MEANS NO MORE "COVERT INSERTIONS" FOR US, HUH?
LOOKS LIKE WE'LL HAVE TO START DOING IT IN PUBLIC!
HAHAHAHA!
OH, TO HAVE THAT MUCH FUN...
YOU'D BETTER HURRY UP ON THAT DRINK, THEN. WE'RE FALLING BEHIND.
HAHAHAHA!
ONE THING'S FOR SURE... I'M LOOKING FORWARD TO HAVING MY HUSBAND HOME A LITTLE MORE OFTEN.
TELL ME ABOUT IT. I'VE GOT A WHOLE LIST OF HOME IMPROVEMENTS THAT WE NEED DONE BEFORE IT GETS WARM AGAIN.
SO MUCH FOR "TIME OFF," SAUL...
I NEED TO GO POWDER MY NOSE. CAROLANNE?
SURE. WE'LL BE BACK IN A MINUTE, BOYS...
TELL YOU WHAT, BILL...
...THIS WHOLE JOB MIGHT BE A POLITE ROAD TO RETIREMENT, BUT I'LL TAKE IT.
LET'S HEAR IT FOR THAT.
IT'S SMOOTH SAILING FROM HERE ON OUT, SAUL...

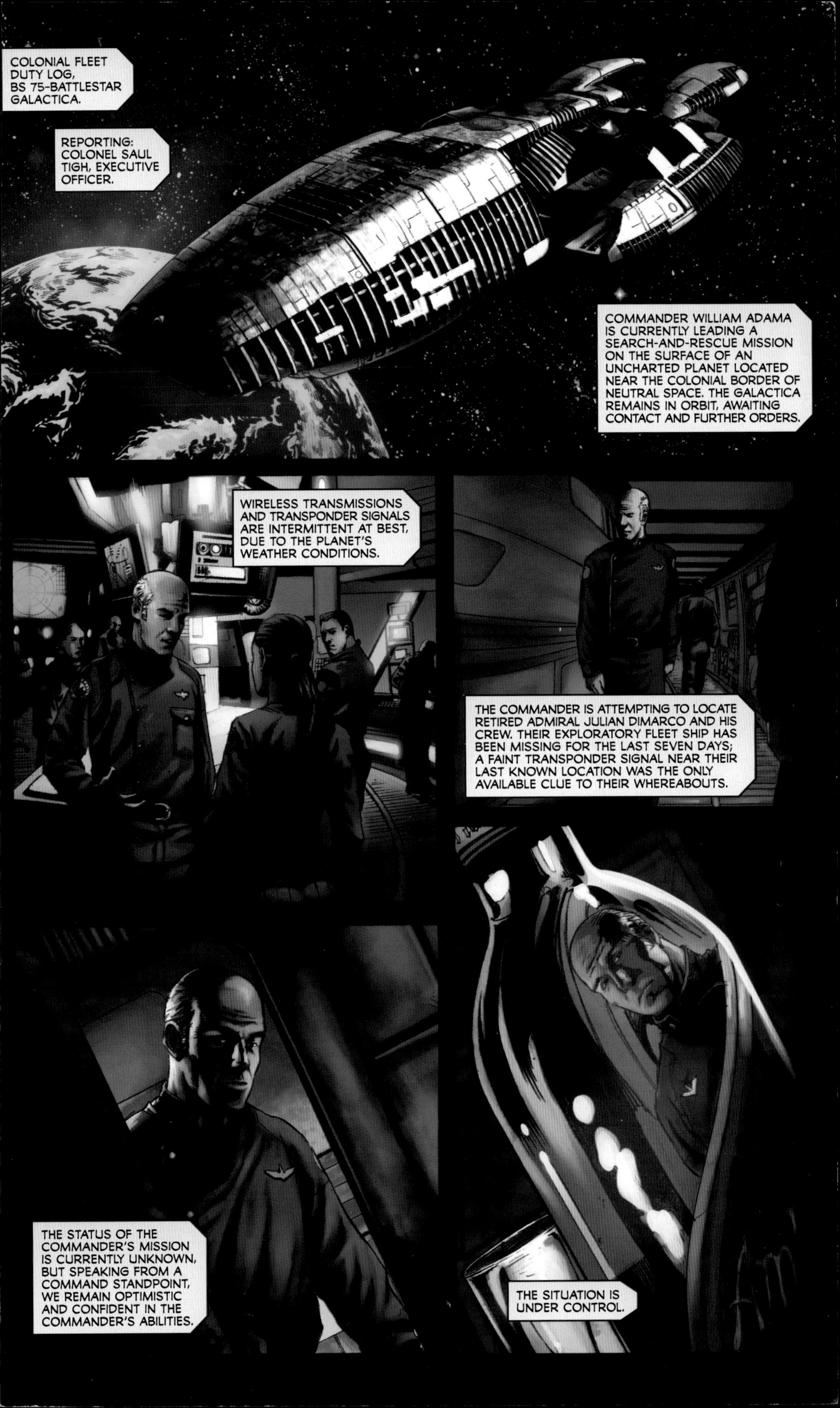
COLONIAL FLEET DUTY LOG, BS 75-BATTLESTAR GALACTICA.
REPORTING: COLONEL SAUL TIGH, EXECUTIVE OFFICER.
COMMANDER WILLIAM ADAMA IS CURRENTLY LEADING A SEARCH-AND-RESCUE MISSION ON THE SURFACE OF AN UNCHARTED PLANET LOCATED NEAR THE COLONIAL BORDER OF NEUTRAL SPACE. THE GALACTICA REMAINS IN ORBIT, AWAITING CONTACT AND FURTHER ORDERS.
WIRELESS TRANSMISSIONS AND TRANSPONDER SIGNALS ARE INTERMITTENT AT BEST, DUE TO THE PLANET'S WEATHER CONDITIONS.
THE COMMANDER IS ATTEMPTING TO LOCATE RETIRED ADMIRAL JULIAN DIMARCO AND HIS CREW. THEIR EXPLORATORY FLEET SHIP HAS BEEN MISSING FOR THE LAST SEVEN DAYS; A FAINT TRANSPONDER SIGNAL NEAR THEIR LAST KNOWN LOCATION WAS THE ONLY AVAILABLE CLUE TO THEIR WHEREABOUTS.
THE STATUS OF THE COMMANDER'S MISSION IS CURRENTLY UNKNOWN, BUT SPEAKING FROM A COMMAND STANDPOINT, WE REMAIN OPTIMISTIC AND CONFIDENT IN THE COMMANDER'S ABILITIES.
THE SITUATION IS UNDER CONTROL.

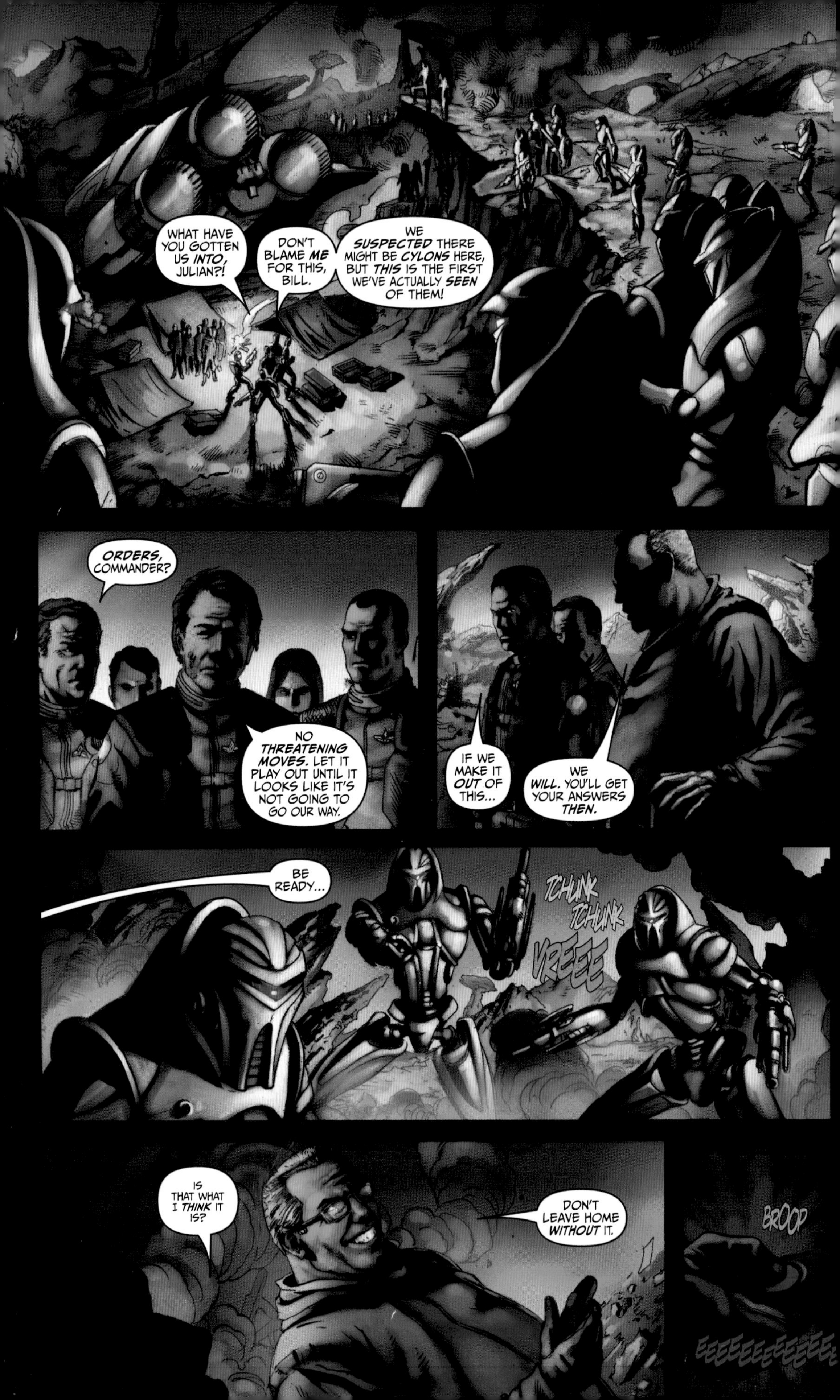
WHAT HAVE YOU GOTTEN US INTO, JULIAN?!
DON'T BLAME ME FOR THIS, BILL.
WE SUSPECTED THERE MIGHT BE CYLONS HERE, BUT THIS IS THE FIRST WE'VE ACTUALLY SEEN OF THEM!
ORDERS, COMMANDER?
NO THREATENING MOVES. LET IT PLAY OUT UNTIL IT LOOKS LIKE IT'S NOT GOING TO GO OUR WAY.
IF WE MAKE IT OUT OF THIS...
WE WILL. YOU'LL GET YOUR ANSWERS THEN.
BE READY...
TCHUNK TCHUNK
VREEE
IS THAT WHAT I THINK IT IS?
DON'T LEAVE HOME WITHOUT IT.
BROOP
EEEEEEEEEEEEE

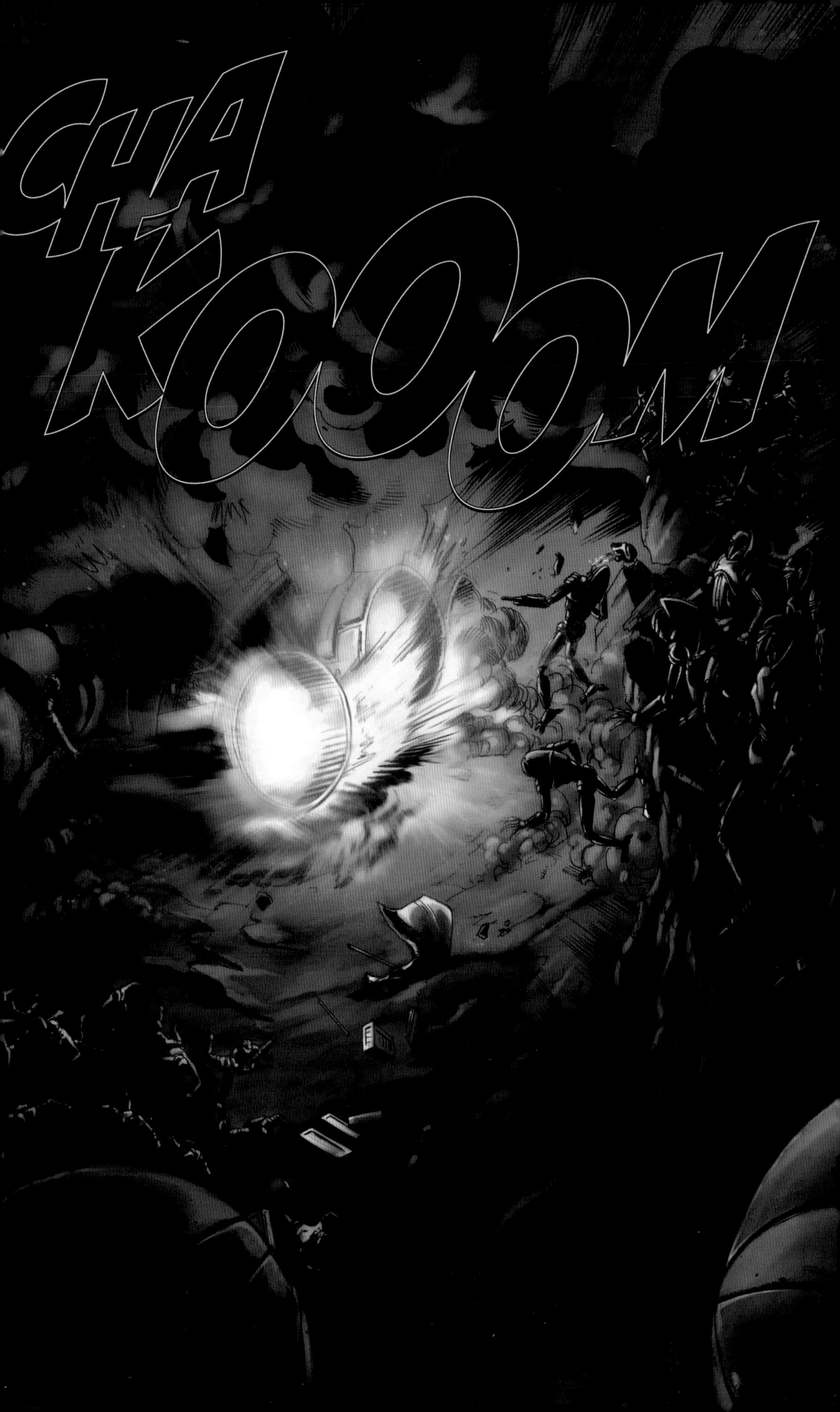
CHA KOOOM

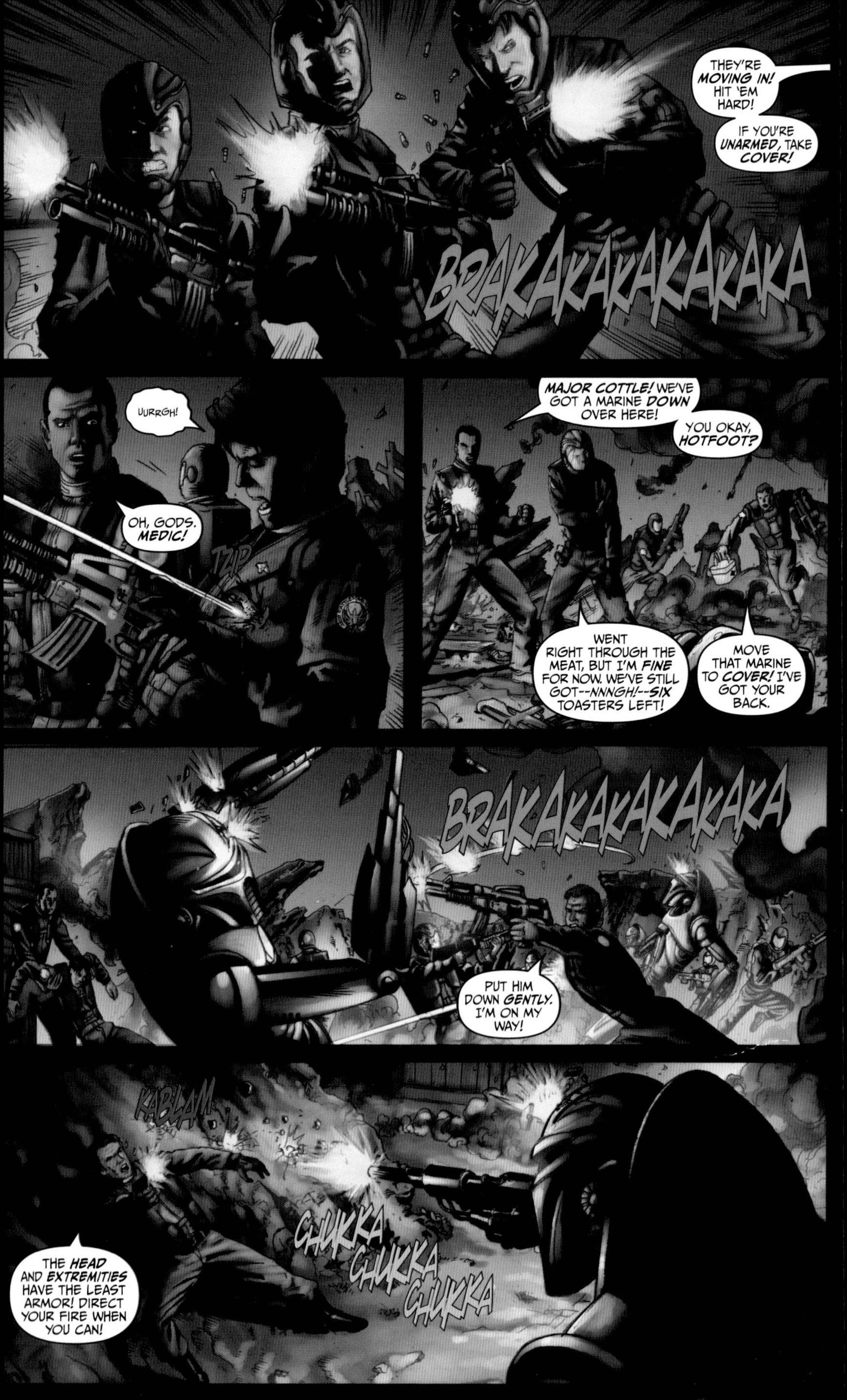
THEY'RE MOVING IN! HIT 'EM HARD!
IF YOU'RE UNARMED, TAKE COVER!
BRAKAKAKAKAKAKAKA
UURRGH!
OH, GODS. MEDIC!
TZIP
MAJOR COTTLE! WE'VE GOT A MARINE DOWN OVER HERE!
YOU OKAY, HOTFOOT?
WENT RIGHT THROUGH THE MEAT, BUT I'M FINE FOR NOW. WE'VE STILL GOT--NNNGH!--SIX TOASTERS LEFT!
MOVE THAT MARINE TO COVER! I'VE GOT YOUR BACK.
BRAKAKAKAKAKAKAKA
PUT HIM DOWN GENTLY. I'M ON MY WAY!
KABLAM
CHUKKA CHUKKA CHUKKA
THE HEAD AND EXTREMITIES HAVE THE LEAST ARMOR! DIRECT YOUR FIRE WHEN YOU CAN!

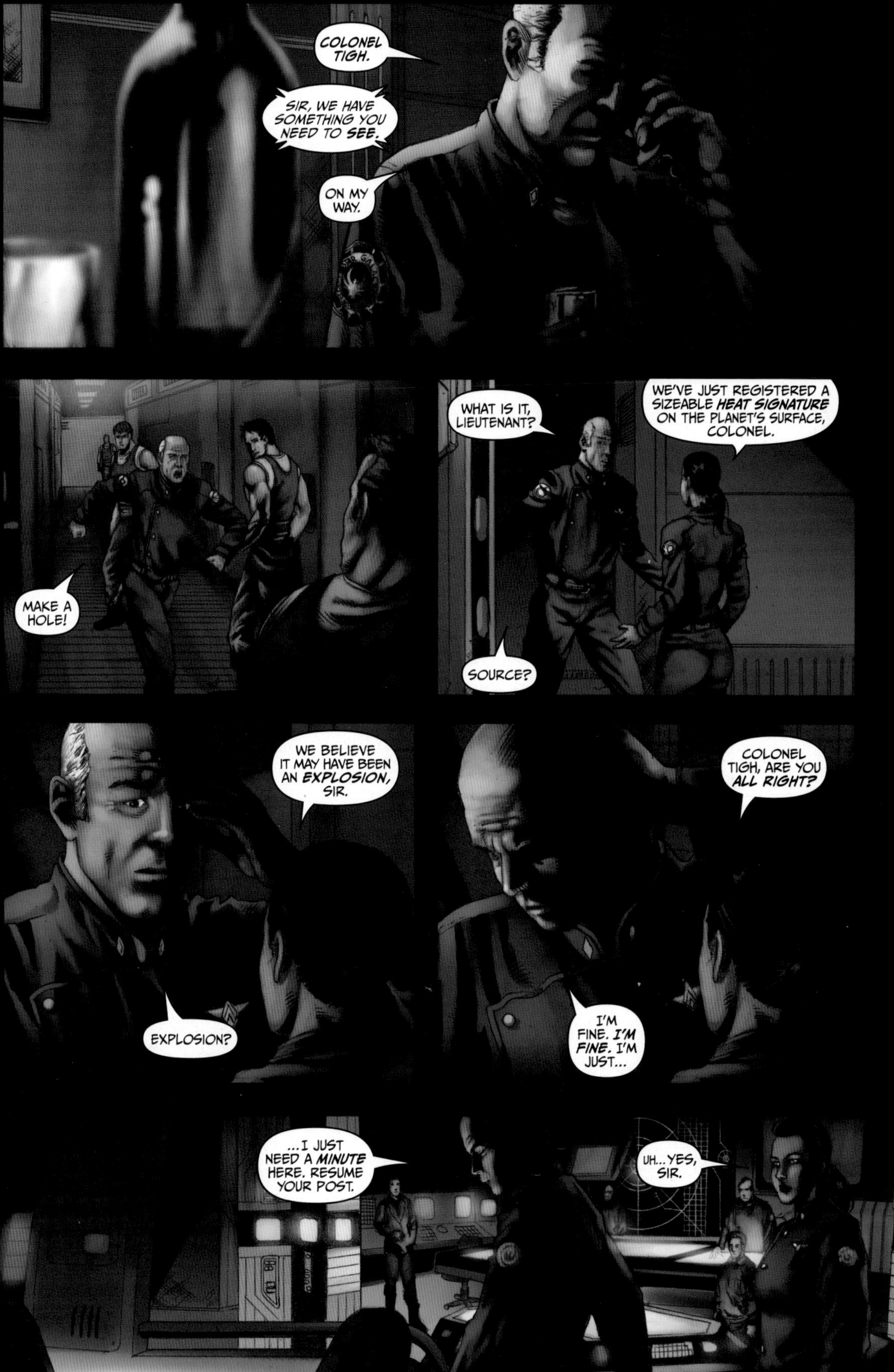

COLONEL TIGH.
SIR, WE HAVE SOMETHING YOU NEED TO SEE.
ON MY WAY.
MAKE A HOLE!
WHAT IS IT, LIEUTENANT?
WE'VE JUST REGISTERED A SIZEABLE HEAT SIGNATURE ON THE PLANET'S SURFACE, COLONEL.
SOURCE?
WE BELIEVE IT MAY HAVE BEEN AN EXPLOSION, SIR.
EXPLOSION?
COLONEL TIGH, ARE YOU ALL RIGHT?
I'M FINE. I'M FINE. I'M JUST...
...I JUST NEED A MINUTE HERE. RESUME YOUR POST.
UH... YES, SIR.

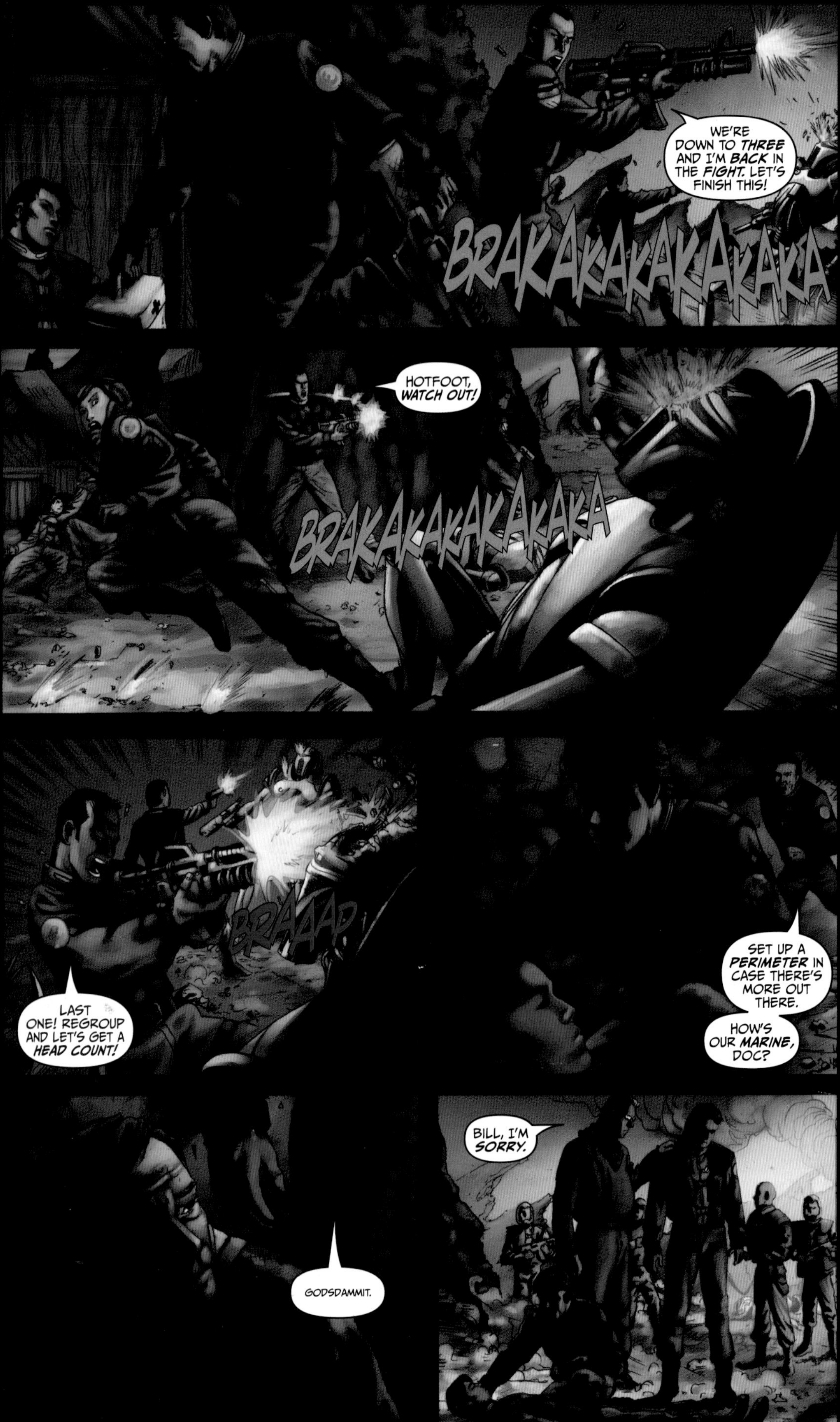
WE'RE DOWN TO THREE AND I'M BACK IN THE FIGHT. LET'S FINISH THIS!
BRAKAKAKAKAKAKA
HOTFOOT, WATCH OUT!
BRAKAKAKAKAKAKA
BRAAAP
LAST ONE! REGROUP AND LET'S GET A HEAD COUNT!
SET UP A PERIMETER IN CASE THERE'S MORE OUT THERE.
HOW'S OUR MARINE, DOC?
GODSDAMMIT.
BILL, I'M SORRY.

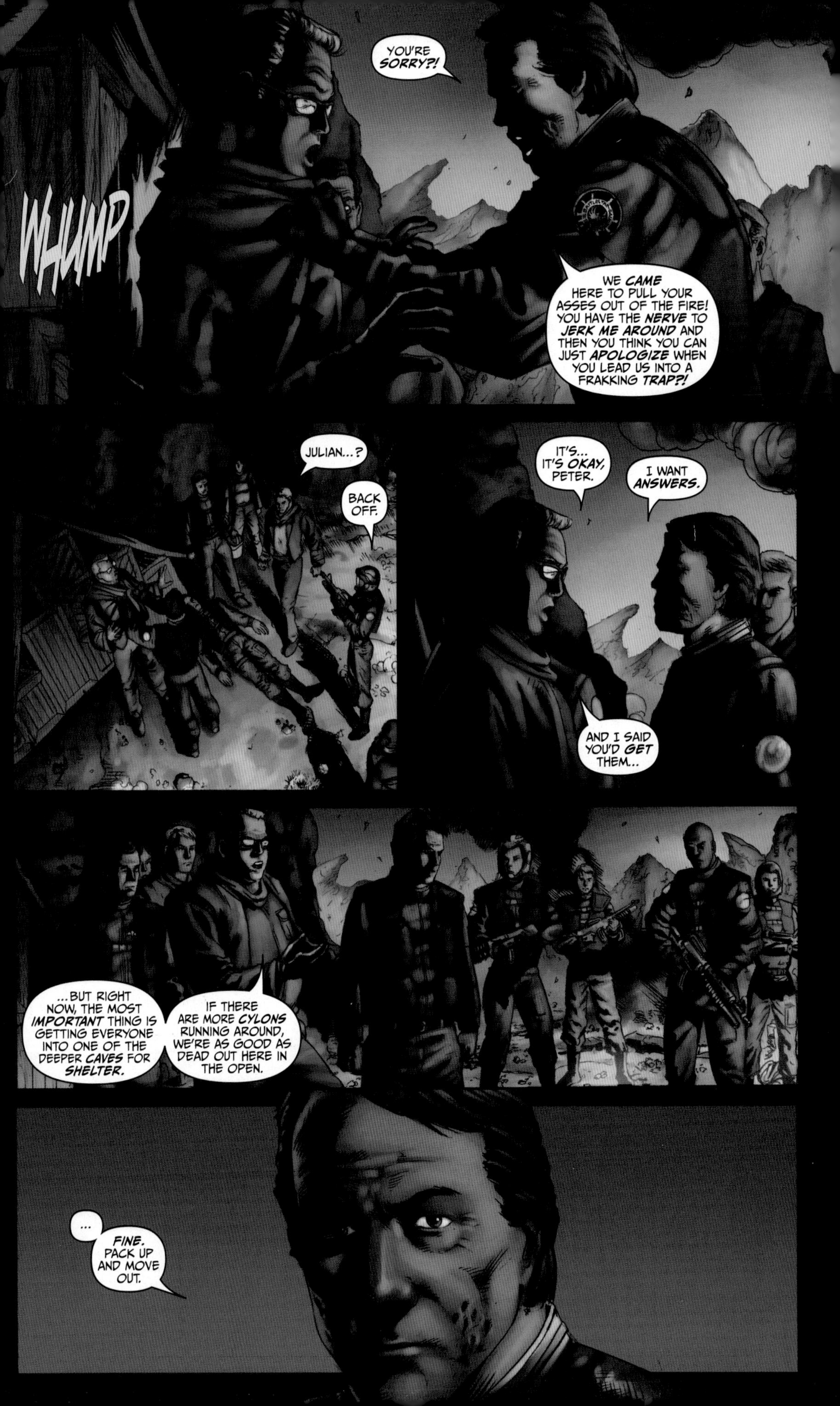

YOU'RE SORRY?!
WHUMP
WE CAME HERE TO PULL YOUR ASSES OUT OF THE FIRE! YOU HAVE THE NERVE TO JERK ME AROUND AND THEN YOU THINK YOU CAN JUST APOLOGIZE WHEN YOU LEAD US INTO A FRAKKING TRAP?!
JULIAN...?
BACK OFF.
IT'S... IT'S OKAY, PETER.
I WANT ANSWERS.
AND I SAID YOU'D GET THEM...
...BUT RIGHT NOW, THE MOST IMPORTANT THING IS GETTING EVERYONE INTO ONE OF THE DEEPER CAVES FOR SHELTER.
IF THERE ARE MORE CYLONS RUNNING AROUND, WE'RE AS GOOD AS DEAD OUT HERE IN THE OPEN.
... FINE. PACK UP AND MOVE OUT.

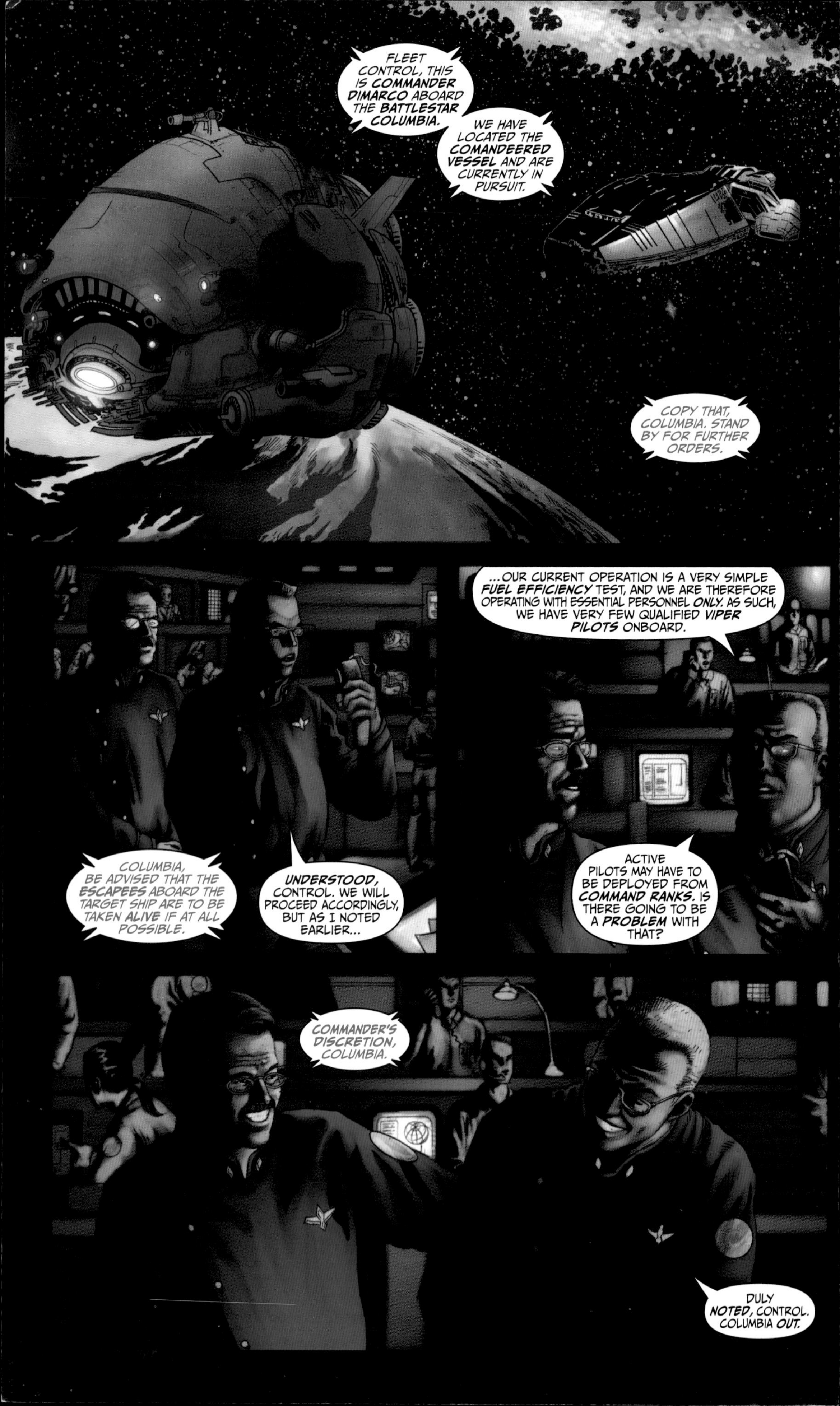
FLEET CONTROL, THIS IS COMMANDER DIMARCO ABOARD THE BATTLESTAR COLUMBIA.
WE HAVE LOCATED THE COMANDEERED VESSEL AND ARE CURRENTLY IN PURSUIT.
COPY THAT, COLUMBIA. STAND BY FOR FURTHER ORDERS.
COLUMBIA, BE ADVISED THAT THE ESCAPEES ABOARD THE TARGET SHIP ARE TO BE TAKEN ALIVE IF AT ALL POSSIBLE.
UNDERSTOOD, CONTROL. WE WILL PROCEED ACCORDINGLY, BUT AS I NOTED EARLIER...
...OUR CURRENT OPERATION IS A VERY SIMPLE FUEL EFFICIENCY TEST, AND WE ARE THEREFORE OPERATING WITH ESSENTIAL PERSONNEL ONLY. AS SUCH, WE HAVE VERY FEW QUALIFIED VIPER PILOTS ONBOARD.
ACTIVE PILOTS MAY HAVE TO BE DEPLOYED FROM COMMAND RANKS. IS THERE GOING TO BE A PROBLEM WITH THAT?
COMMANDER'S DISCRETION, COLUMBIA.
DULY NOTED, CONTROL. COLUMBIA OUT.

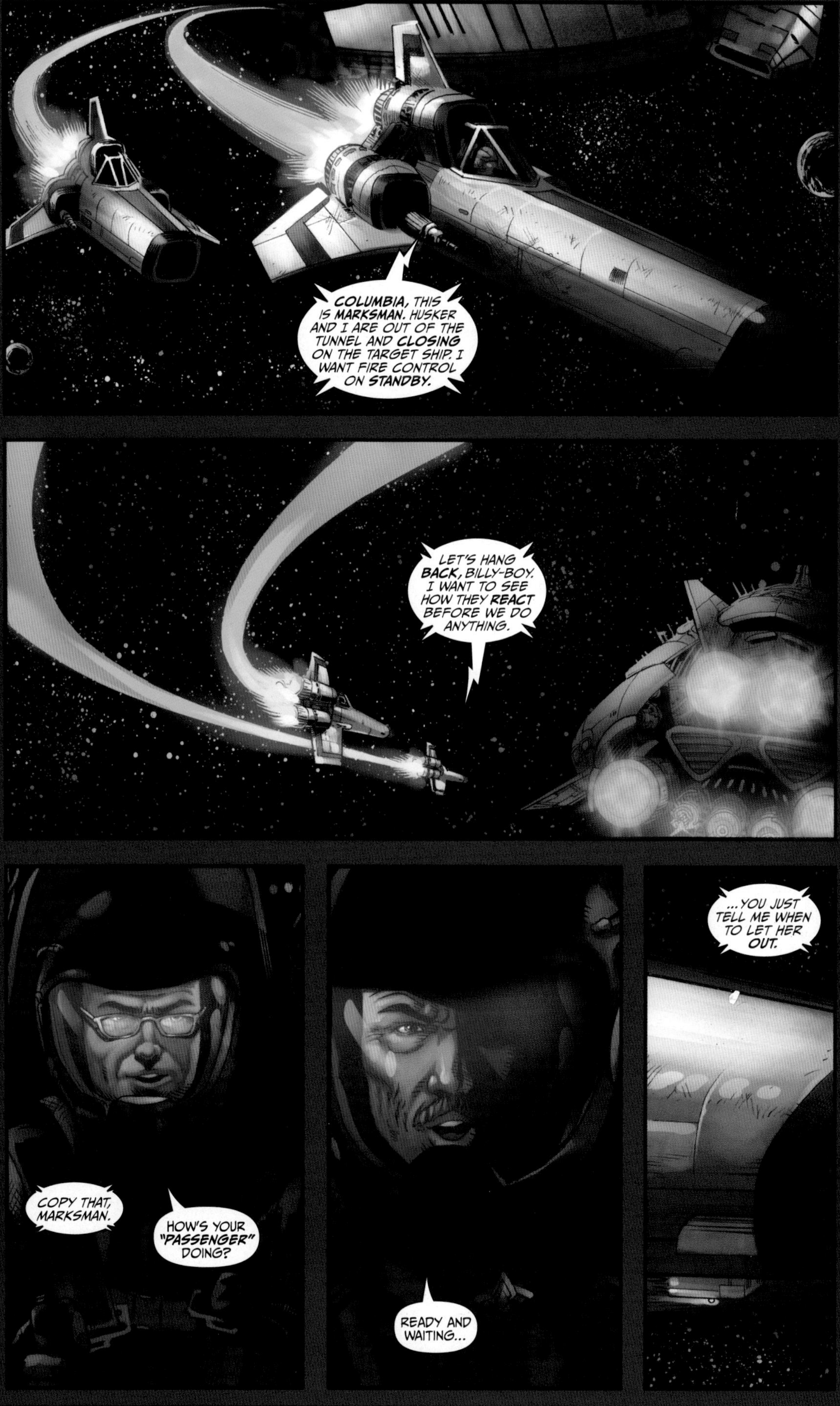

COLUMBIA, THIS IS MARKSMAN. HUSKER AND I ARE OUT OF THE TUNNEL AND CLOSING ON THE TARGET SHIP. I WANT FIRE CONTROL ON STANDBY.
LET'S HANG BACK, BILLY-BOY. I WANT TO SEE HOW THEY REACT BEFORE WE DO ANYTHING.
COPY THAT, MARKSMAN.
HOW'S YOUR "PASSENGER" DOING?
READY AND WAITING...
...YOU JUST TELL ME WHEN TO LET HER OUT.

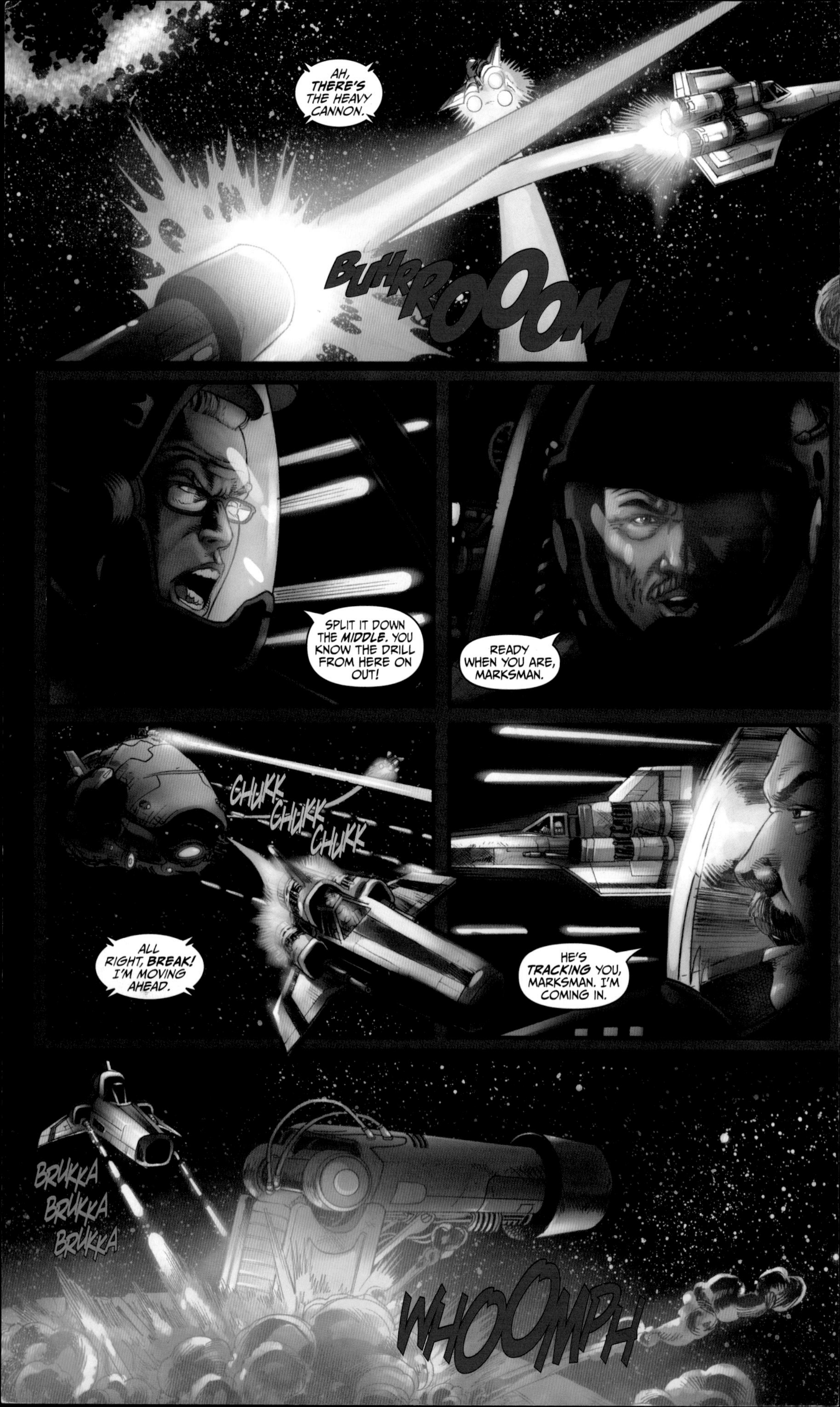
AH, THERE'S THE HEAVY CANNON.
BUHRROOOOM
SPLIT IT DOWN THE MIDDLE. YOU KNOW THE DRILL FROM HERE ON OUT!
READY WHEN YOU ARE, MARKSMAN.
CHUKK CHUKK CHUKK
ALL RIGHT, BREAK! I'M MOVING AHEAD.
HE'S TRACKING YOU, MARKSMAN. I'M COMING IN.
BRUKKA BRUKKA BRUKKA
WHOOOMPH

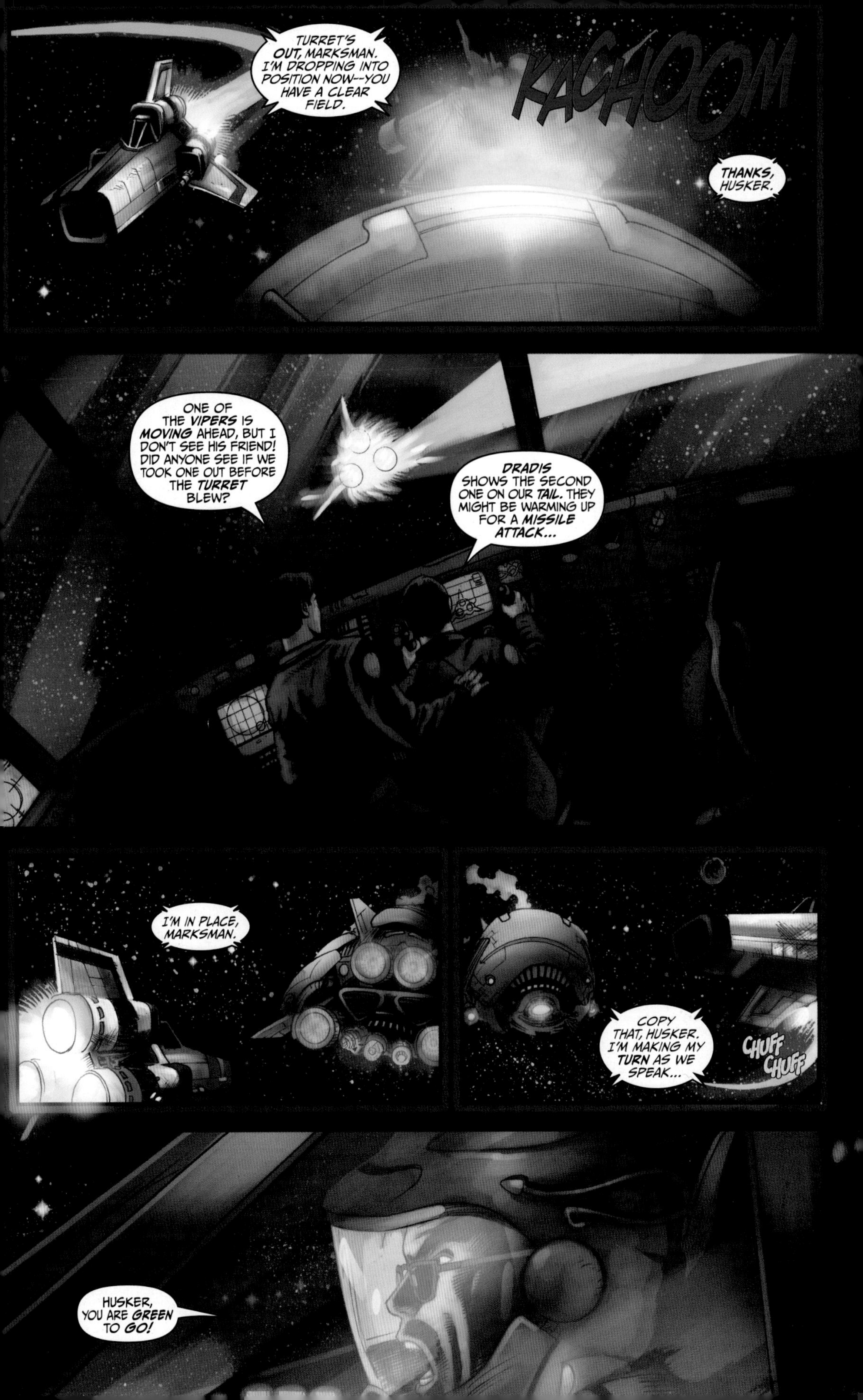
TURRET'S OUT, MARKSMAN. I'M DROPPING INTO POSITION NOW--YOU HAVE A CLEAR FIELD.
KACHOOM
THANKS, HUSKER.
ONE OF THE VIPERS IS MOVING AHEAD, BUT I DON'T SEE HIS FRIEND! DID ANYONE SEE IF WE TOOK ONE OUT BEFORE THE TURRET BLEW?
DRADIS SHOWS THE SECOND ONE ON OUR TAIL. THEY MIGHT BE WARMING UP FOR A MISSILE ATTACK...
I'M IN PLACE, MARKSMAN.
COPY THAT, HUSKER. I'M MAKING MY TURN AS WE SPEAK...
CHUFF CHUFF
HUSKER, YOU ARE GREEN TO GO!

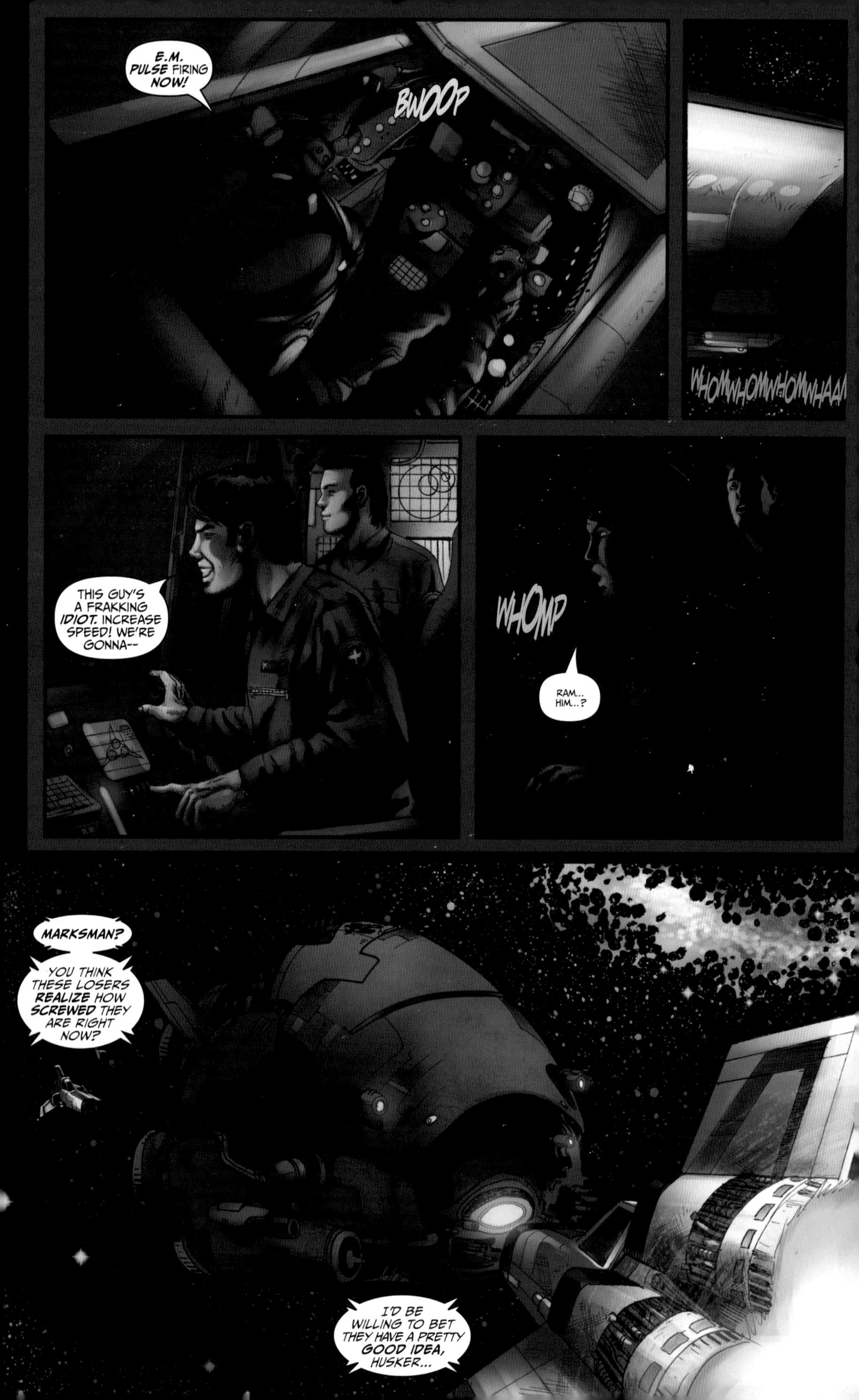
E.M. PULSE FIRING NOW!
BWOOP
WHOMWHOMWHOMWHAAM
THIS GUY'S A FRAKKING IDIOT. INCREASE SPEED! WE'RE GONNA--
WHOMP
RAM.. HIM..?
MARKSMAN?
YOU THINK THESE LOSERS REALIZE HOW SCREWED THEY ARE RIGHT NOW?
I'D BE WILLING TO BET THEY HAVE A PRETTY GOOD IDEA, HUSKER...

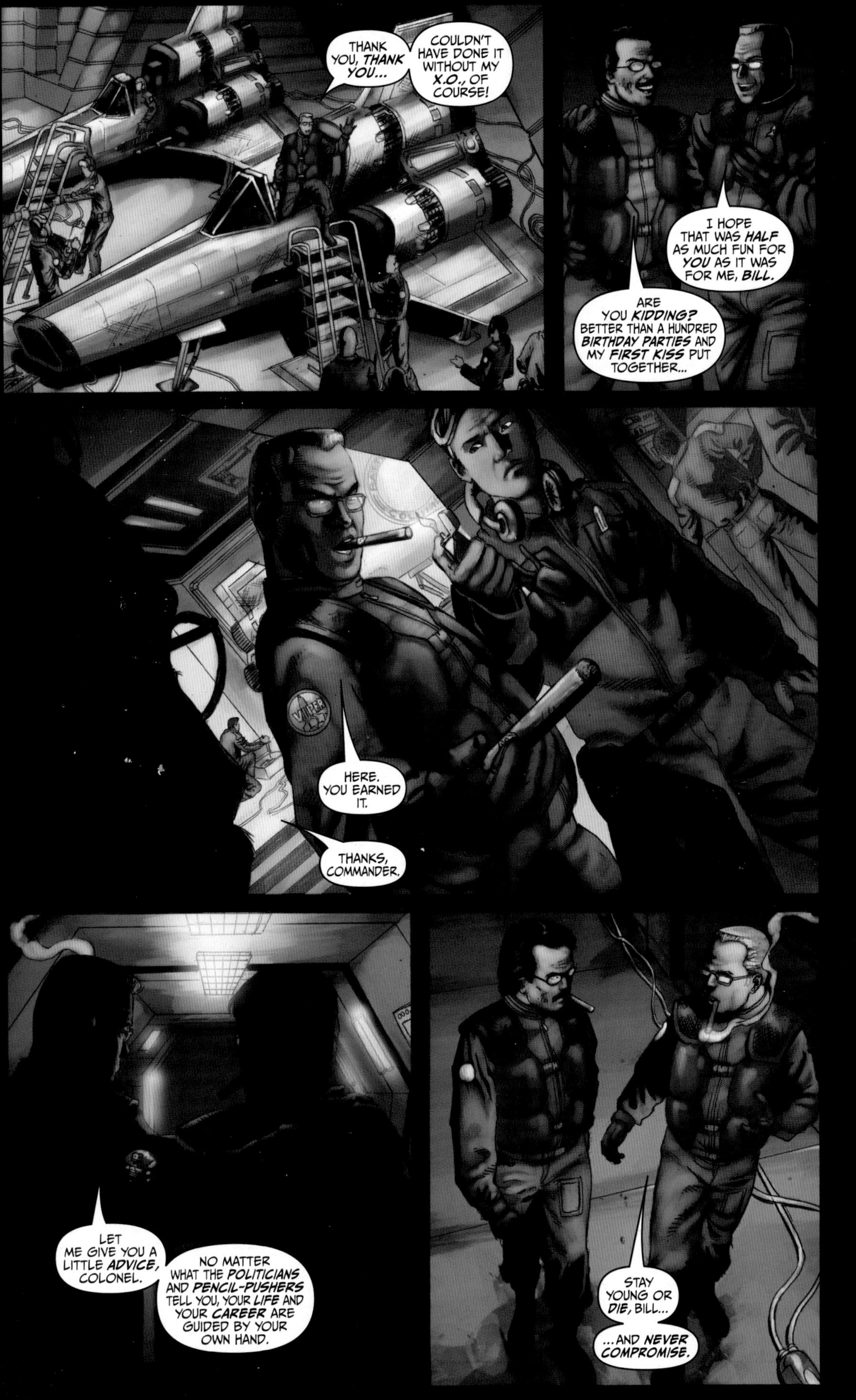

THANK YOU, THANK YOU...
COULDN'T HAVE DONE IT WITHOUT MY X.O., OF COURSE!
I HOPE THAT WAS HALF AS MUCH FUN FOR YOU AS IT WAS FOR ME, BILL.
ARE YOU KIDDING? BETTER THAN A HUNDRED BIRTHDAY PARTIES AND MY FIRST KISS PUT TOGETHER...
VIPER
HERE. YOU EARNED IT.
THANKS, COMMANDER.
LET ME GIVE YOU A LITTLE ADVICE, COLONEL.
NO MATTER WHAT THE POLITICIANS AND PENCIL-PUSHERS TELL YOU, YOUR LIFE AND YOUR CAREER ARE GUIDED BY YOUR OWN HAND.
STAY YOUNG OR DIE, BILL...
...AND NEVER COMPROMISE.

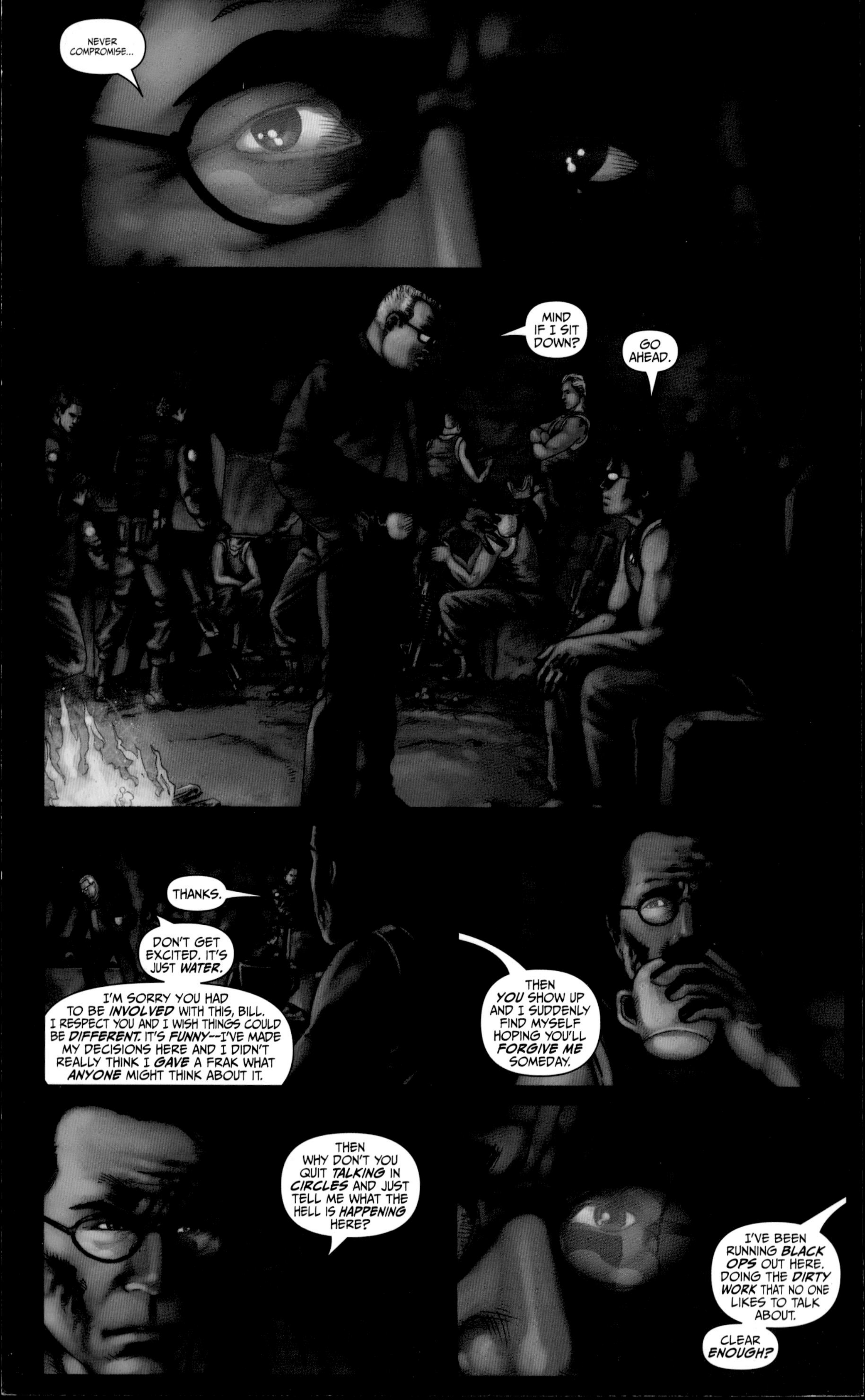
NEVER COMPROMISE...
MIND IF I SIT DOWN?
GO AHEAD.
THANKS.
DON'T GET EXCITED. IT'S JUST WATER.
I'M SORRY YOU HAD TO BE INVOLVED WITH THIS, BILL. I RESPECT YOU AND I WISH THINGS COULD BE DIFFERENT. IT'S FUNNY--I'VE MADE MY DECISIONS HERE AND I DIDN'T REALLY THINK I GAVE A FRAK WHAT ANYONE MIGHT THINK ABOUT IT.
THEN YOU SHOW UP AND I SUDDENLY FIND MYSELF HOPING YOU'LL FORGIVE ME SOMEDAY.
THEN WHY DON'T YOU QUIT TALKING IN CIRCLES AND JUST TELL ME WHAT THE HELL IS HAPPENING HERE?
I'VE BEEN RUNNING BLACK OPS OUT HERE. DOING THE DIRTY WORK THAT NO ONE LIKES TO TALK ABOUT.
CLEAR ENOUGH?

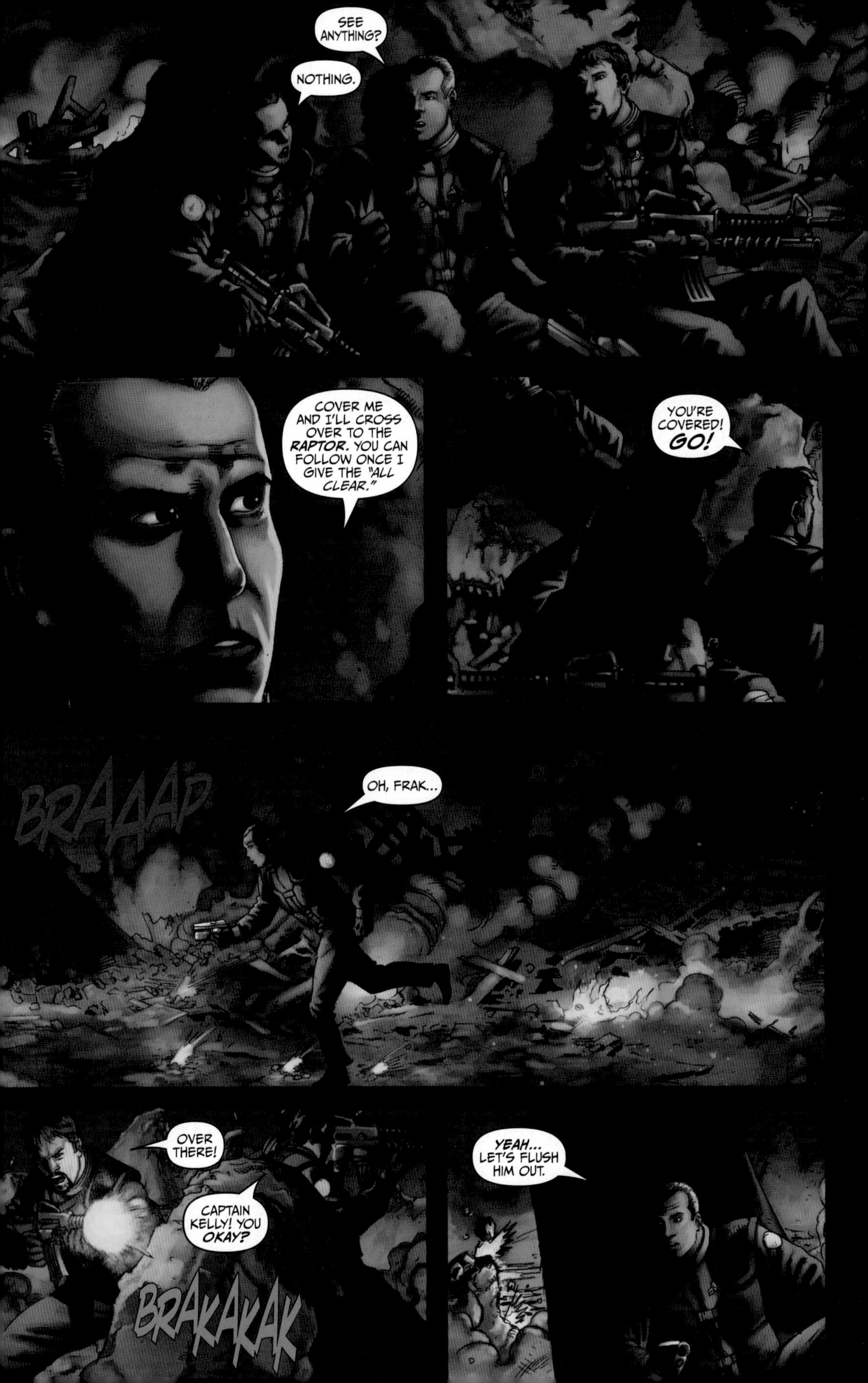
SEE ANYTHING?
NOTHING.
COVER ME AND I'LL CROSS OVER TO THE RAPTOR. YOU CAN FOLLOW ONCE I GIVE THE "ALL CLEAR."
YOU'RE COVERED! GO!
BRAAAP
OH, FRAK...
OVER THERE!
CAPTAIN KELLY! YOU OKAY?
BRAKAKAK
YEAH... LET'S FLUSH HIM OUT.

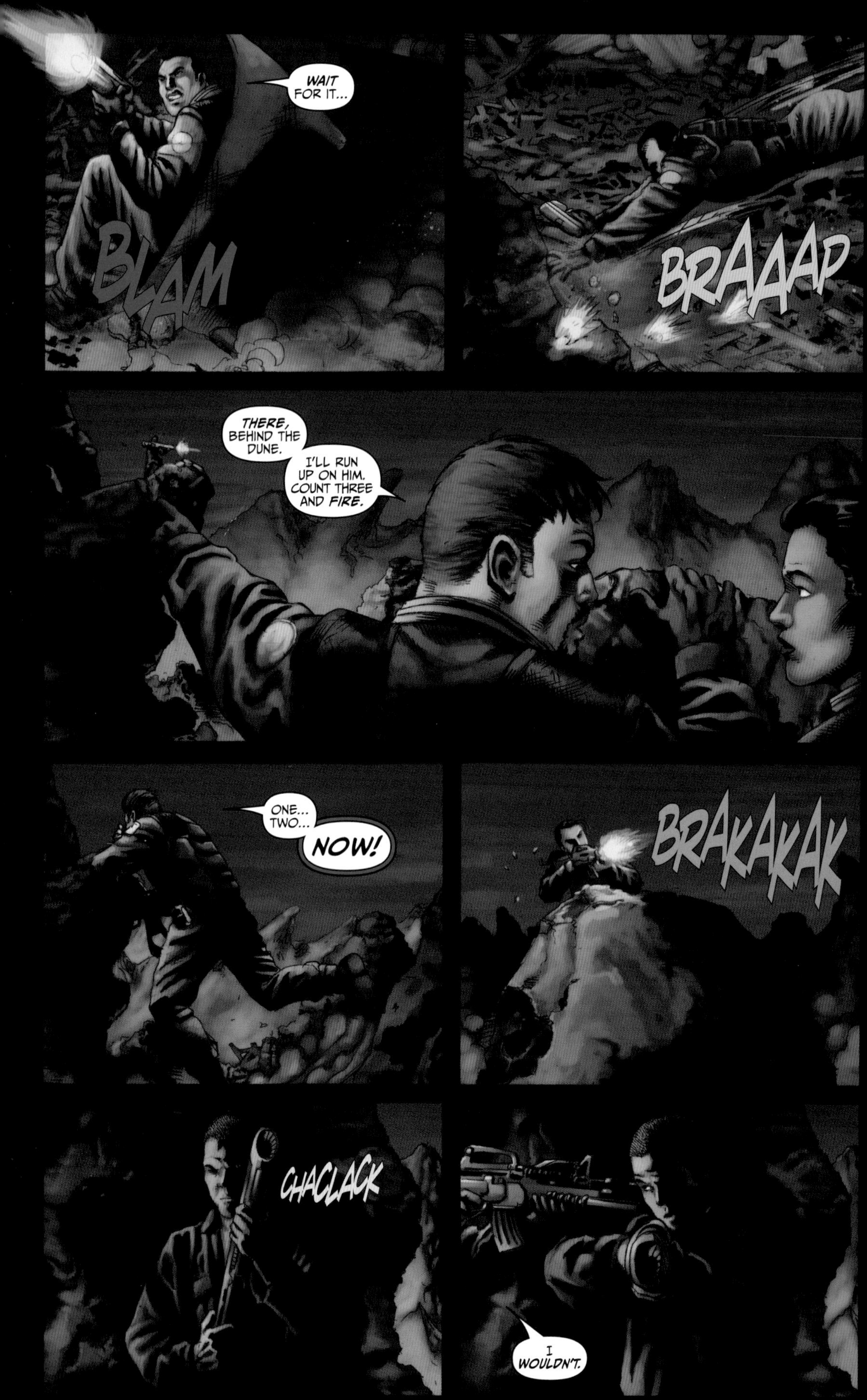
WAIT FOR IT...
BLAM
BRAAAP
THERE, BEHIND THE DUNE.
I'LL RUN UP ON HIM. COUNT THREE AND FIRE.
ONE... TWO...
NOW!
BRAKAKAK
CHACLACK
I WOULDN'T.

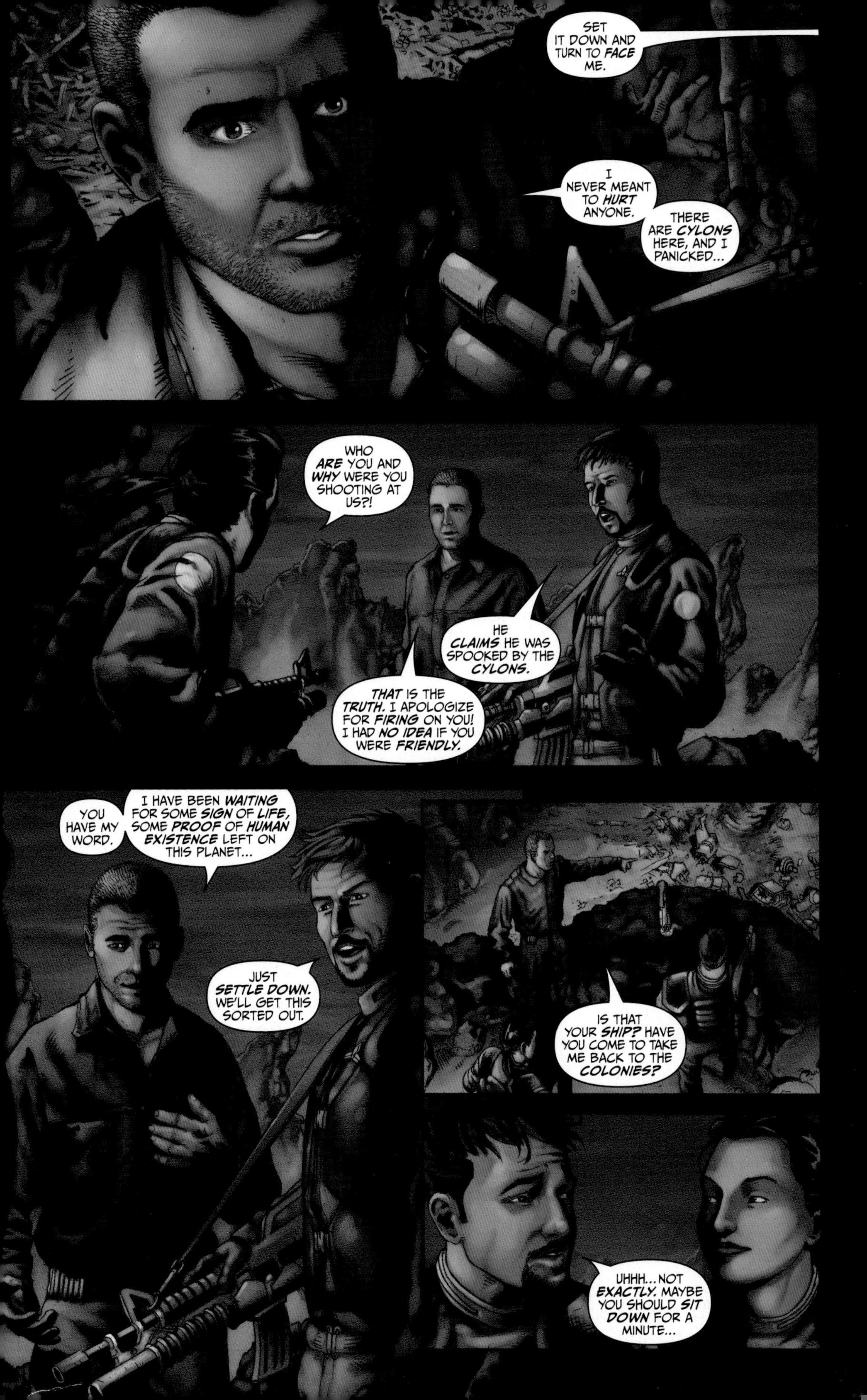
SET IT DOWN AND TURN TO FACE ME.
I NEVER MEANT TO HURT ANYONE.
THERE ARE CYLONS HERE, AND I PANICKED...
WHO ARE YOU AND WHY WERE YOU SHOOTING AT US?!
HE CLAIMS HE WAS SPOOKED BY THE CYLONS.
THAT IS THE TRUTH. I APOLOGIZE FOR FIRING ON YOU! I HAD NO IDEA IF YOU WERE FRIENDLY.
YOU HAVE MY WORD.
I HAVE BEEN WAITING FOR SOME SIGN OF LIFE, SOME PROOF OF HUMAN EXISTENCE LEFT ON THIS PLANET...
JUST SETTLE DOWN. WE'LL GET THIS SORTED OUT.
IS THAT YOUR SHIP? HAVE YOU COME TO TAKE ME BACK TO THE COLONIES?
UHHH...NOT EXACTLY. MAYBE YOU SHOULD SIT DOWN FOR A MINUTE...

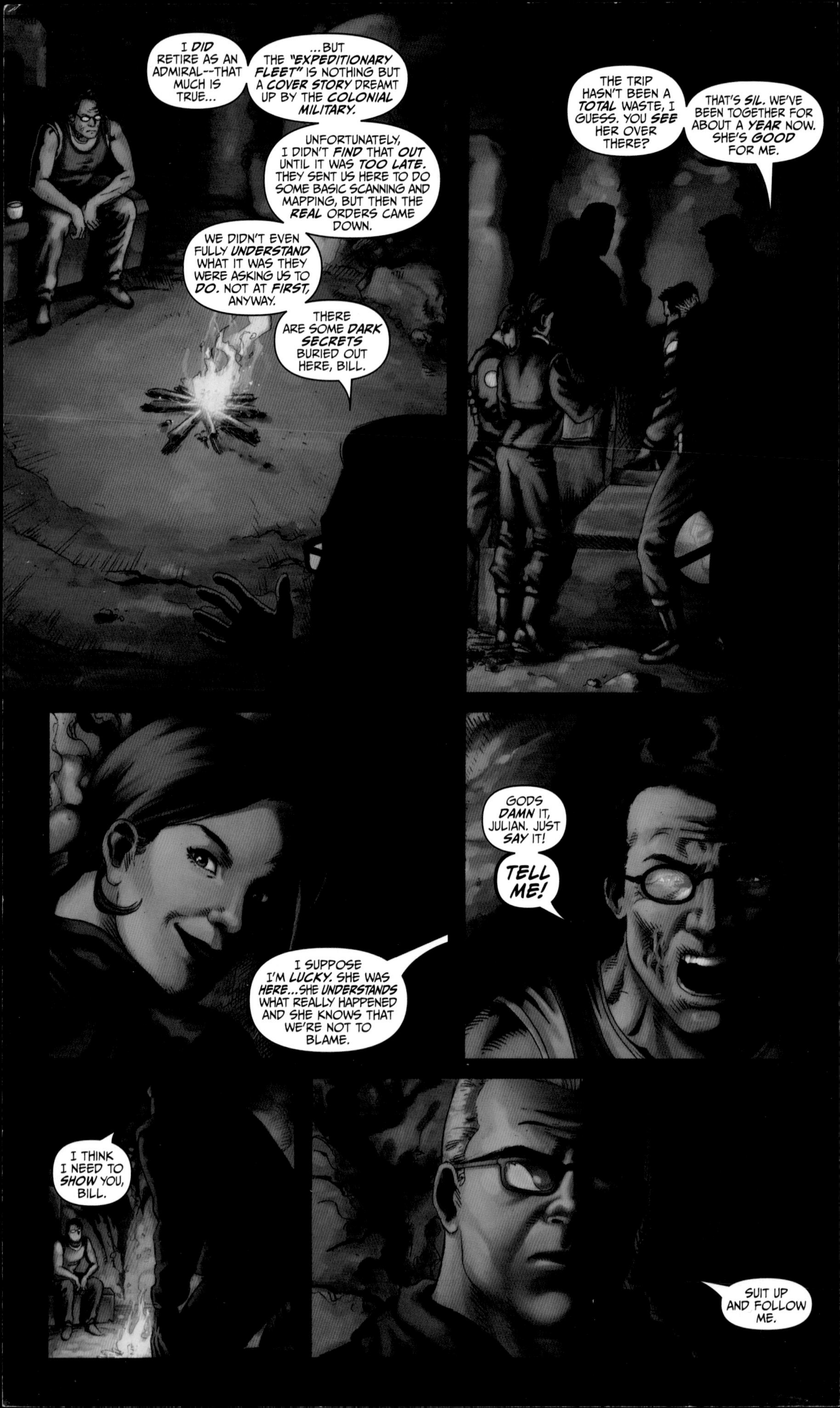
I DID RETIRE AS AN ADMIRAL--THAT MUCH IS TRUE...
...BUT THE "EXPEDITIONARY FLEET" IS NOTHING BUT A COVER STORY DREAMT UP BY THE COLONIAL MILITARY.
UNFORTUNATELY, I DIDN'T FIND THAT OUT UNTIL IT WAS TOO LATE. THEY SENT US HERE TO DO SOME BASIC SCANNING AND MAPPING, BUT THEN THE REAL ORDERS CAME DOWN.
WE DIDN'T EVEN FULLY UNDERSTAND WHAT IT WAS THEY WERE ASKING US TO DO. NOT AT FIRST, ANYWAY.
THERE ARE SOME DARK SECRETS BURIED OUT HERE, BILL.
THE TRIP HASN'T BEEN A TOTAL WASTE, I GUESS. YOU SEE HER OVER THERE?
THAT'S SIL. WE'VE BEEN TOGETHER FOR ABOUT A YEAR NOW. SHE'S GOOD FOR ME.
I SUPPOSE I'M LUCKY. SHE WAS HERE...SHE UNDERSTANDS WHAT REALLY HAPPENED AND SHE KNOWS THAT WE'RE NOT TO BLAME.
GODS DAMN IT, JULIAN. JUST SAY IT!
TELL ME!
I THINK I NEED TO SHOW YOU, BILL.
SUIT UP AND FOLLOW ME.

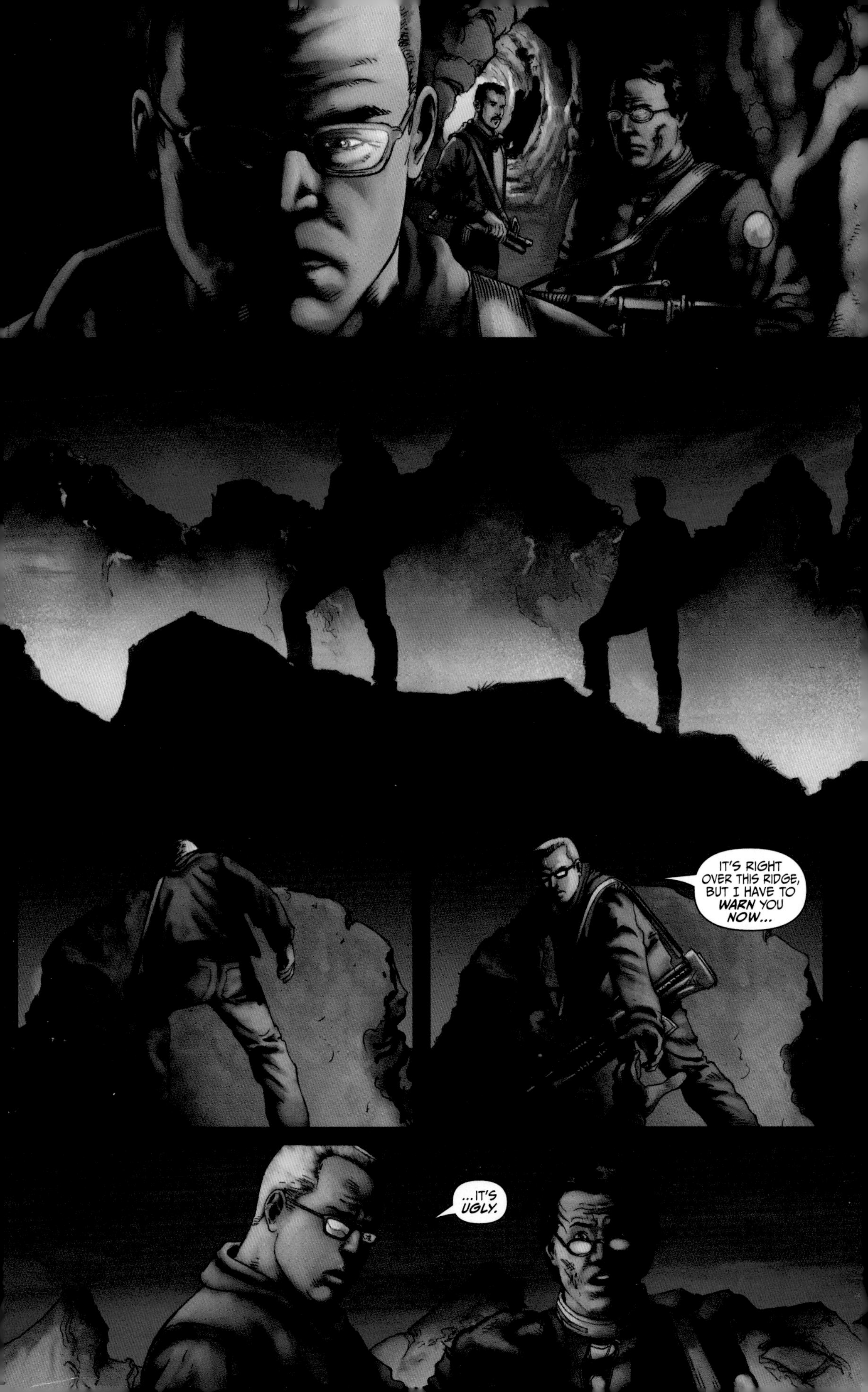
IT'S RIGHT OVER THIS RIDGE, BUT I HAVE TO WARN YOU NOW...
...IT'S UGLY.

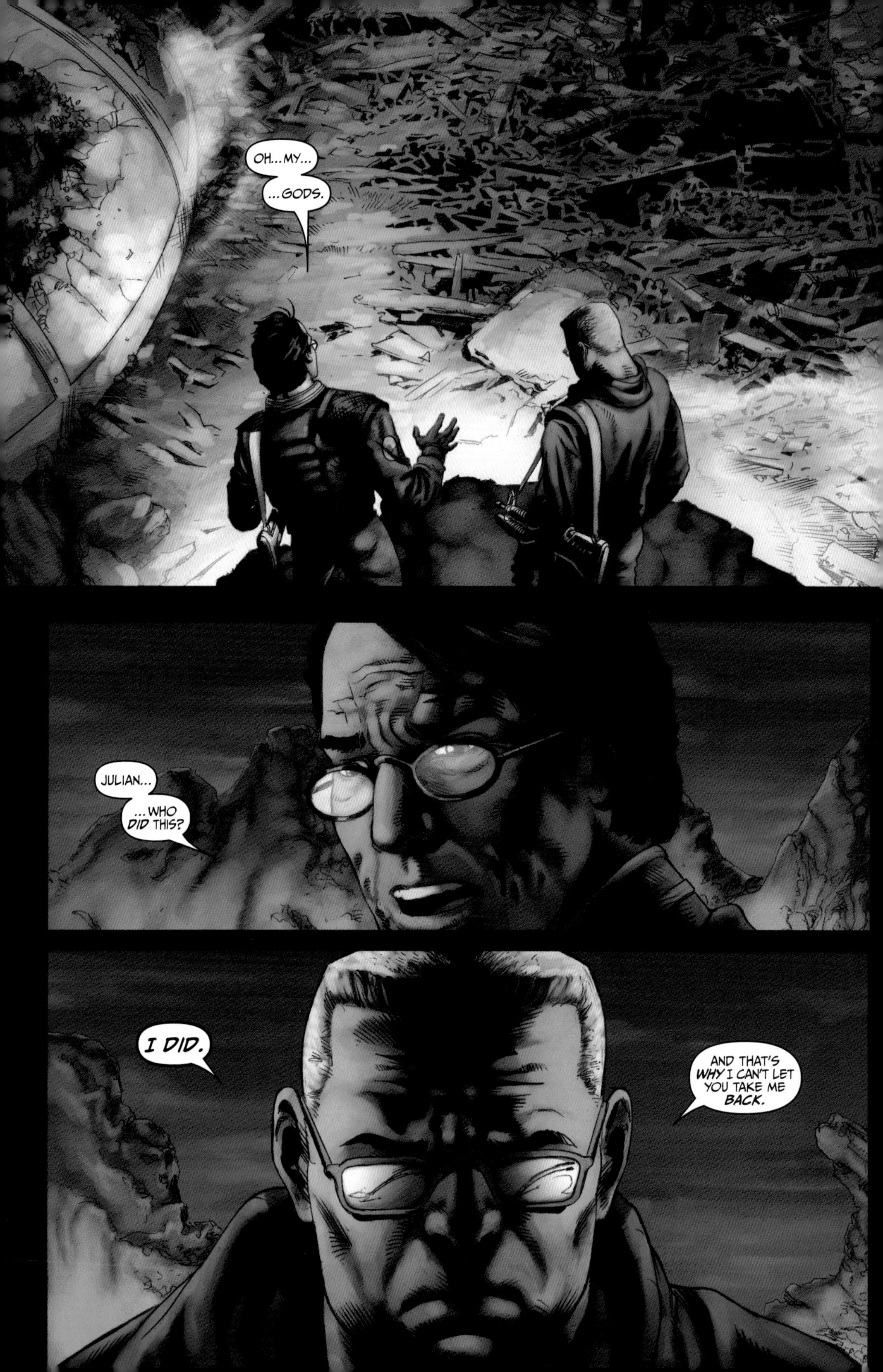
OH... MY...
...GODS.
JULIAN...
...WHO DID THIS?
I DID.
AND THAT'S WHY I CAN'T LET YOU TAKE ME BACK.

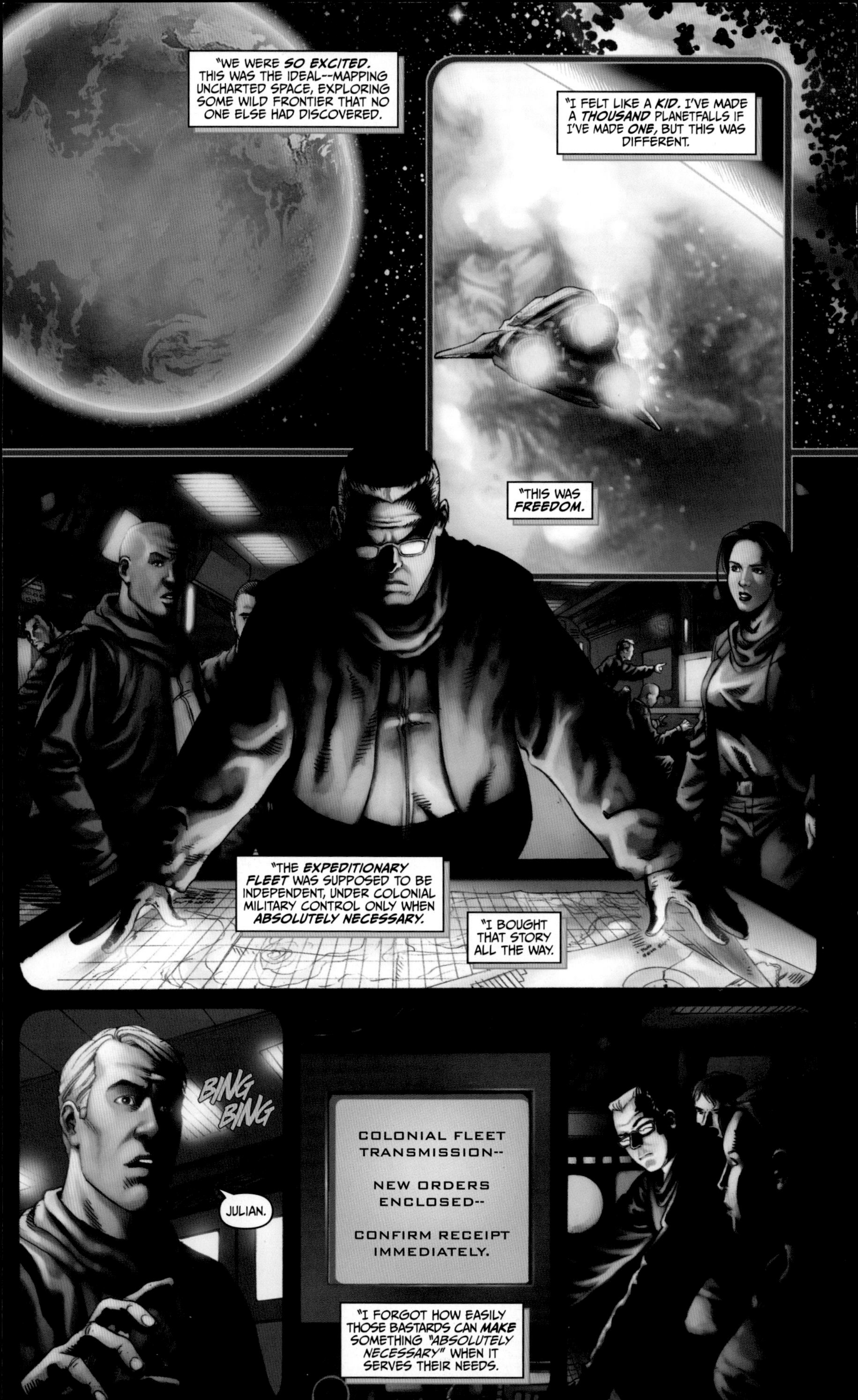
"WE WERE SO EXCITED. THIS WAS THE IDEAL--MAPPING UNCHARTED SPACE, EXPLORING SOME WILD FRONTIER THAT NO ONE ELSE HAD DISCOVERED.
"I FELT LIKE A KID. I'VE MADE A THOUSAND PLANETFALLS IF I'VE MADE ONE, BUT THIS WAS DIFFERENT.
"THIS WAS FREEDOM.
"THE EXPEDITIONARY FLEET WAS SUPPOSED TO BE INDEPENDENT, UNDER COLONIAL MILITARY CONTROL ONLY WHEN ABSOLUTELY NECESSARY.
"I BOUGHT THAT STORY ALL THE WAY.
BING BING
JULIAN.
COLONIAL FLEET TRANSMISSION--
NEW ORDERS ENCLOSED--
CONFIRM RECEIPT IMMEDIATELY.
"I FORGOT HOW EASILY THOSE BASTARDS CAN MAKE SOMETHING "ABSOLUTELY NECESSARY" WHEN IT SERVES THEIR NEEDS.

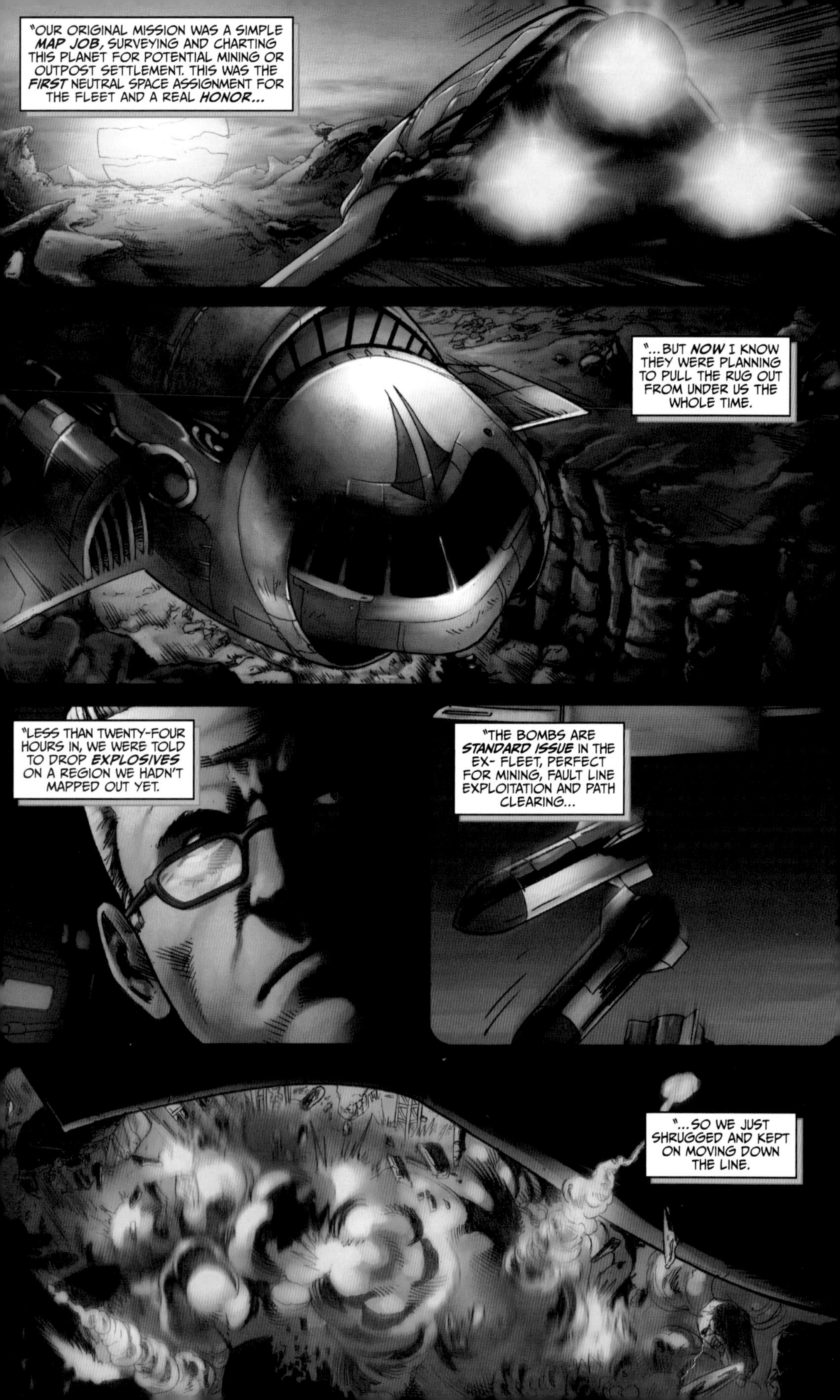
"OUR ORIGINAL MISSION WAS A SIMPLE MAP JOB, SURVEYING AND CHARTING THIS PLANET FOR POTENTIAL MINING OR OUTPOST SETTLEMENT. THIS WAS THE FIRST NEUTRAL SPACE ASSIGNMENT FOR THE FLEET AND A REAL HONOR...
"...BUT NOW I KNOW THEY WERE PLANNING TO PULL THE RUG OUT FROM UNDER US THE WHOLE TIME.
"LESS THAN TWENTY-FOUR HOURS IN, WE WERE TOLD TO DROP EXPLOSIVES ON A REGION WE HADN'T MAPPED OUT YET.
"THE BOMBS ARE STANDARD ISSUE IN THE EX- FLEET, PERFECT FOR MINING, FAULT LINE EXPLOITATION AND PATH CLEARING...
"...SO WE JUST SHRUGGED AND KEPT ON MOVING DOWN THE LINE.

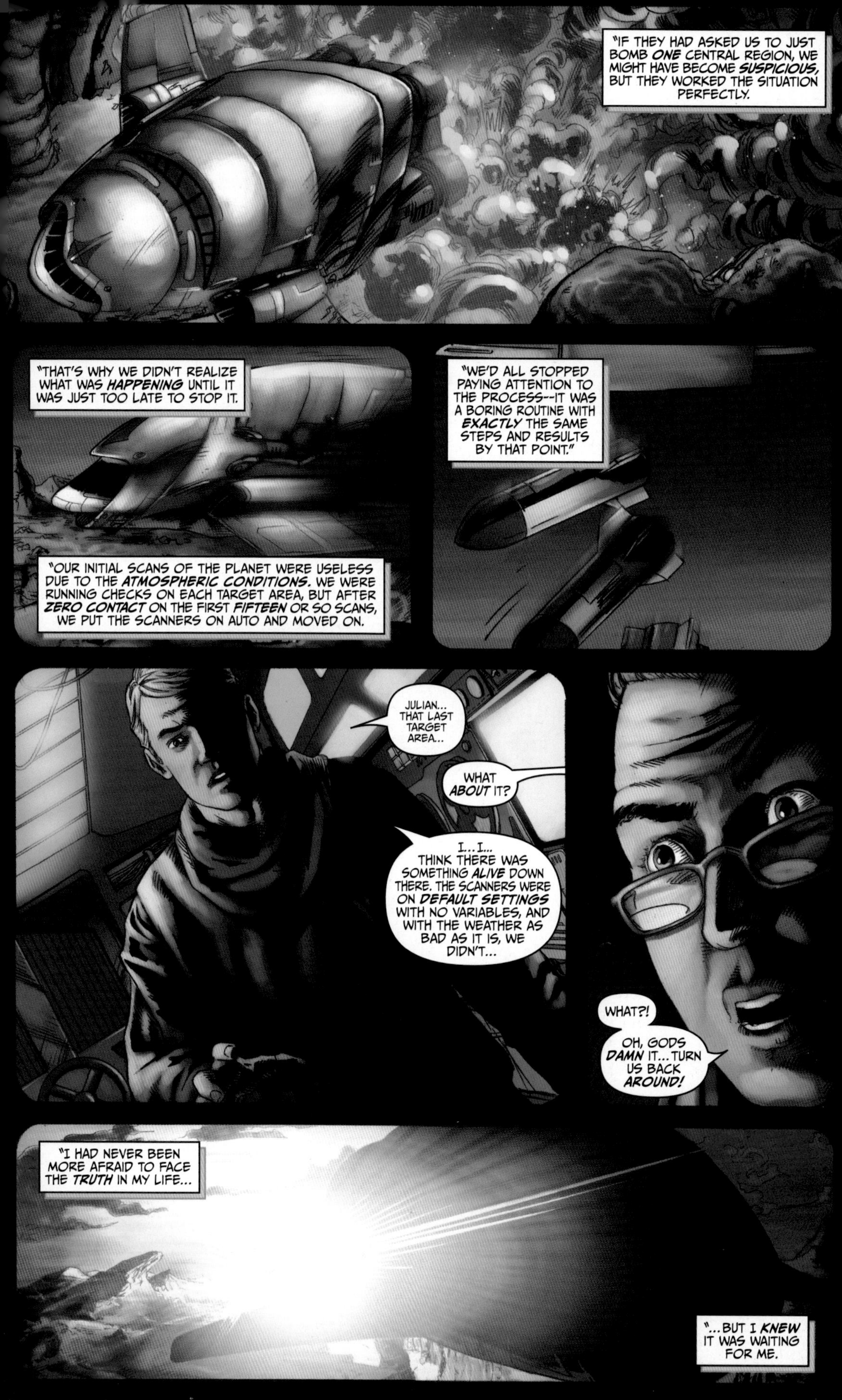
"IF THEY HAD ASKED US TO JUST BOMB ONE CENTRAL REGION, WE MIGHT HAVE BECOME SUSPICIOUS, BUT THEY WORKED THE SITUATION PERFECTLY.
"THAT'S WHY WE DIDN'T REALIZE WHAT WAS HAPPENING UNTIL IT WAS JUST TOO LATE TO STOP IT.
"OUR INITIAL SCANS OF THE PLANET WERE USELESS DUE TO THE ATMOSPHERIC CONDITIONS. WE WERE RUNNING CHECKS ON EACH TARGET AREA, BUT AFTER ZERO CONTACT ON THE FIRST FIFTEEN OR SO SCANS, WE PUT THE SCANNERS ON AUTO AND MOVED ON.
"WE'D ALL STOPPED PAYING ATTENTION TO THE PROCESS--IT WAS A BORING ROUTINE WITH EXACTLY THE SAME STEPS AND RESULTS BY THAT POINT."
JULIAN... THAT LAST TARGET AREA...
WHAT ABOUT IT?
I...I... THINK THERE WAS SOMETHING ALIVE DOWN THERE. THE SCANNERS WERE ON DEFAULT SETTINGS WITH NO VARIABLES, AND WITH THE WEATHER AS BAD AS IT IS, WE DIDN'T...
WHAT?!
OH, GODS DAMN IT...TURN US BACK AROUND!
"I HAD NEVER BEEN MORE AFRAID TO FACE THE TRUTH IN MY LIFE...
"...BUT I KNEW IT WAS WAITING FOR ME.

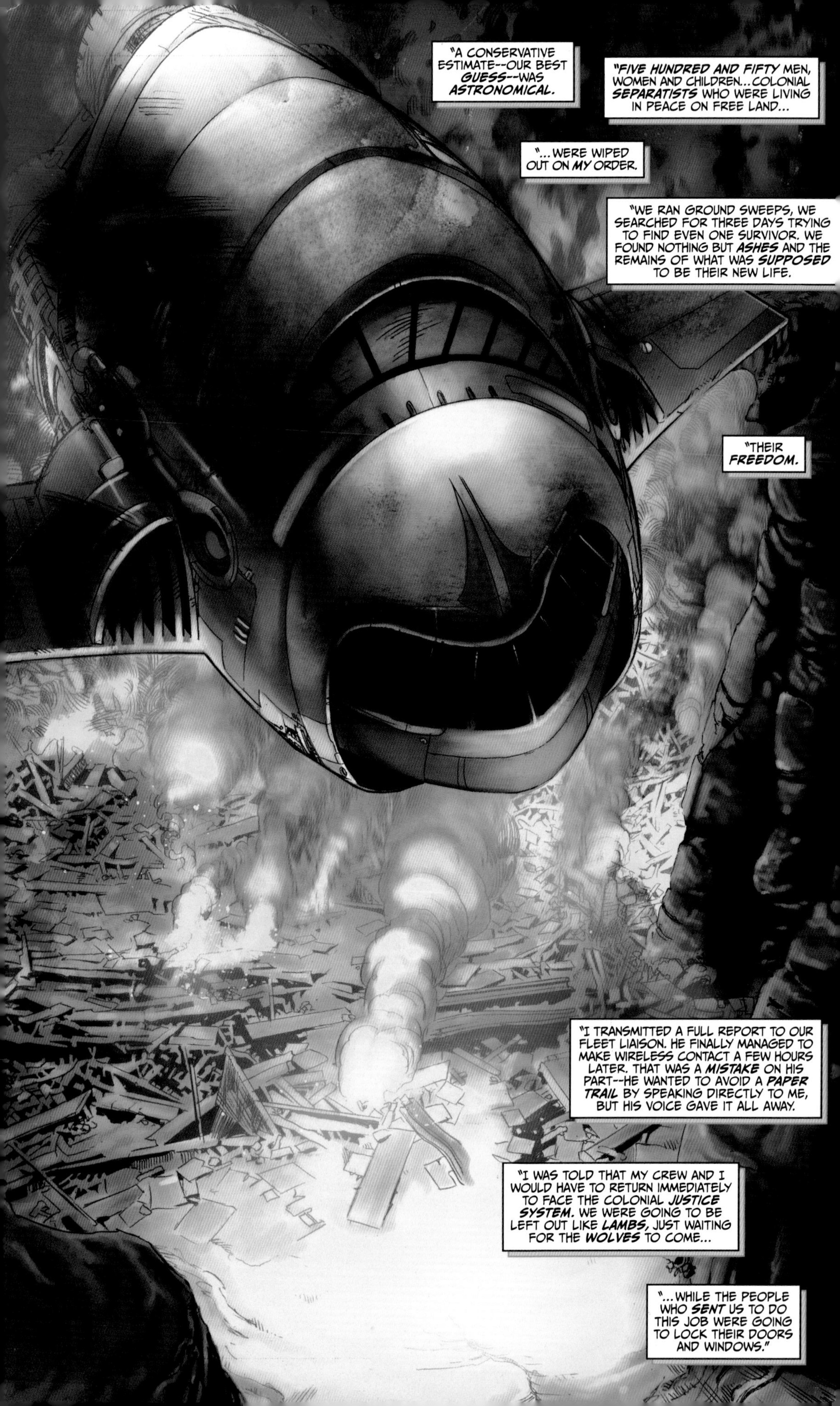
"A CONSERVATIVE ESTIMATE--OUR BEST GUESS--WAS ASTRONOMICAL.
"FIVE HUNDRED AND FIFTY MEN, WOMEN AND CHILDREN...COLONIAL SEPARATISTS WHO WERE LIVING IN PEACE ON FREE LAND...
"...WERE WIPED OUT ON MY ORDER.
"WE RAN GROUND SWEEPS, WE SEARCHED FOR THREE DAYS TRYING TO FIND EVEN ONE SURVIVOR. WE FOUND NOTHING BUT ASHES AND THE REMAINS OF WHAT WAS SUPPOSED TO BE THEIR NEW LIFE.
"THEIR FREEDOM.
"I TRANSMITTED A FULL REPORT TO OUR FLEET LIAISON. HE FINALLY MANAGED TO MAKE WIRELESS CONTACT A FEW HOURS LATER. THAT WAS A MISTAKE ON HIS PART--HE WANTED TO AVOID A PAPER TRAIL BY SPEAKING DIRECTLY TO ME, BUT HIS VOICE GAVE IT ALL AWAY.
"I WAS TOLD THAT MY CREW AND I WOULD HAVE TO RETURN IMMEDIATELY TO FACE THE COLONIAL JUSTICE SYSTEM. WE WERE GOING TO BE LEFT OUT LIKE LAMBS, JUST WAITING FOR THE WOLVES TO COME...
"...WHILE THE PEOPLE WHO SENT US TO DO THIS JOB WERE GOING TO LOCK THEIR DOORS AND WINDOWS."

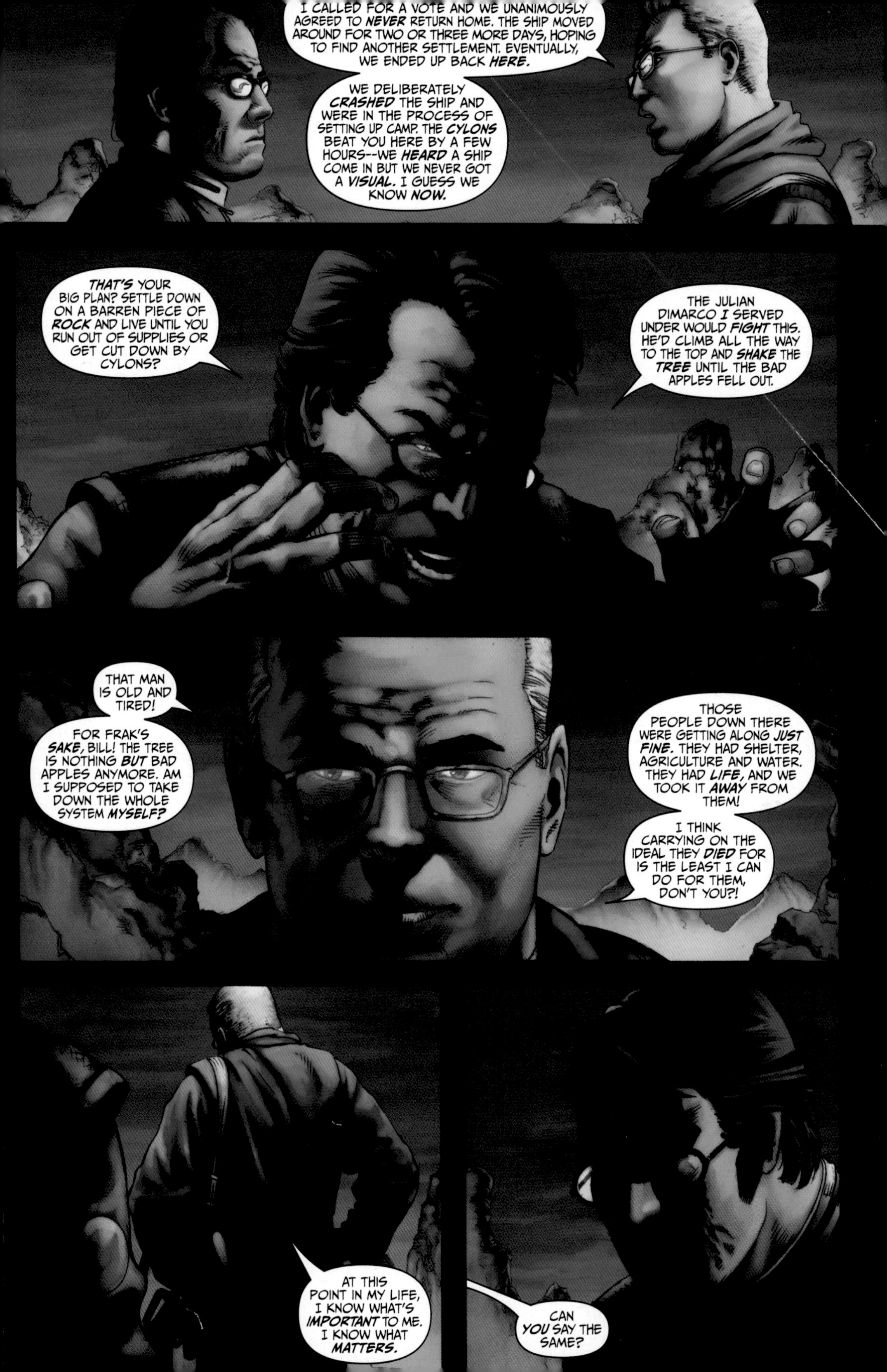
I CALLED FOR A VOTE AND WE UNANIMOUSLY AGREED TO NEVER RETURN HOME. THE SHIP MOVED AROUND FOR TWO OR THREE MORE DAYS, HOPING TO FIND ANOTHER SETTLEMENT. EVENTUALLY, WE ENDED UP BACK HERE.
WE DELIBERATELY CRASHED THE SHIP AND WERE IN THE PROCESS OF SETTING UP CAMP. THE CYLONS BEAT YOU HERE BY A FEW HOURS--WE HEARD A SHIP COME IN BUT WE NEVER GOT A VISUAL. I GUESS WE KNOW NOW.
THAT'S YOUR BIG PLAN? SETTLE DOWN ON A BARREN PIECE OF ROCK AND LIVE UNTIL YOU RUN OUT OF SUPPLIES OR GET CUT DOWN BY CYLONS?
THE JULIAN DIMARCO I SERVED UNDER WOULD FIGHT THIS. HE'D CLIMB ALL THE WAY TO THE TOP AND SHAKE THE TREE UNTIL THE BAD APPLES FELL OUT.
THAT MAN IS OLD AND TIRED!
FOR FRAK'S SAKE, BILL! THE TREE IS NOTHING BUT BAD APPLES ANYMORE. AM I SUPPOSED TO TAKE DOWN THE WHOLE SYSTEM MYSELF?
THOSE PEOPLE DOWN THERE WERE GETTING ALONG JUST FINE. THEY HAD SHELTER, AGRICULTURE AND WATER. THEY HAD LIFE, AND WE TOOK IT AWAY FROM THEM!
I THINK CARRYING ON THE IDEAL THEY DIED FOR IS THE LEAST I CAN DO FOR THEM, DON'T YOU?!
AT THIS POINT IN MY LIFE, I KNOW WHAT'S IMPORTANT TO ME. I KNOW WHAT MATTERS.
CAN YOU SAY THE SAME?

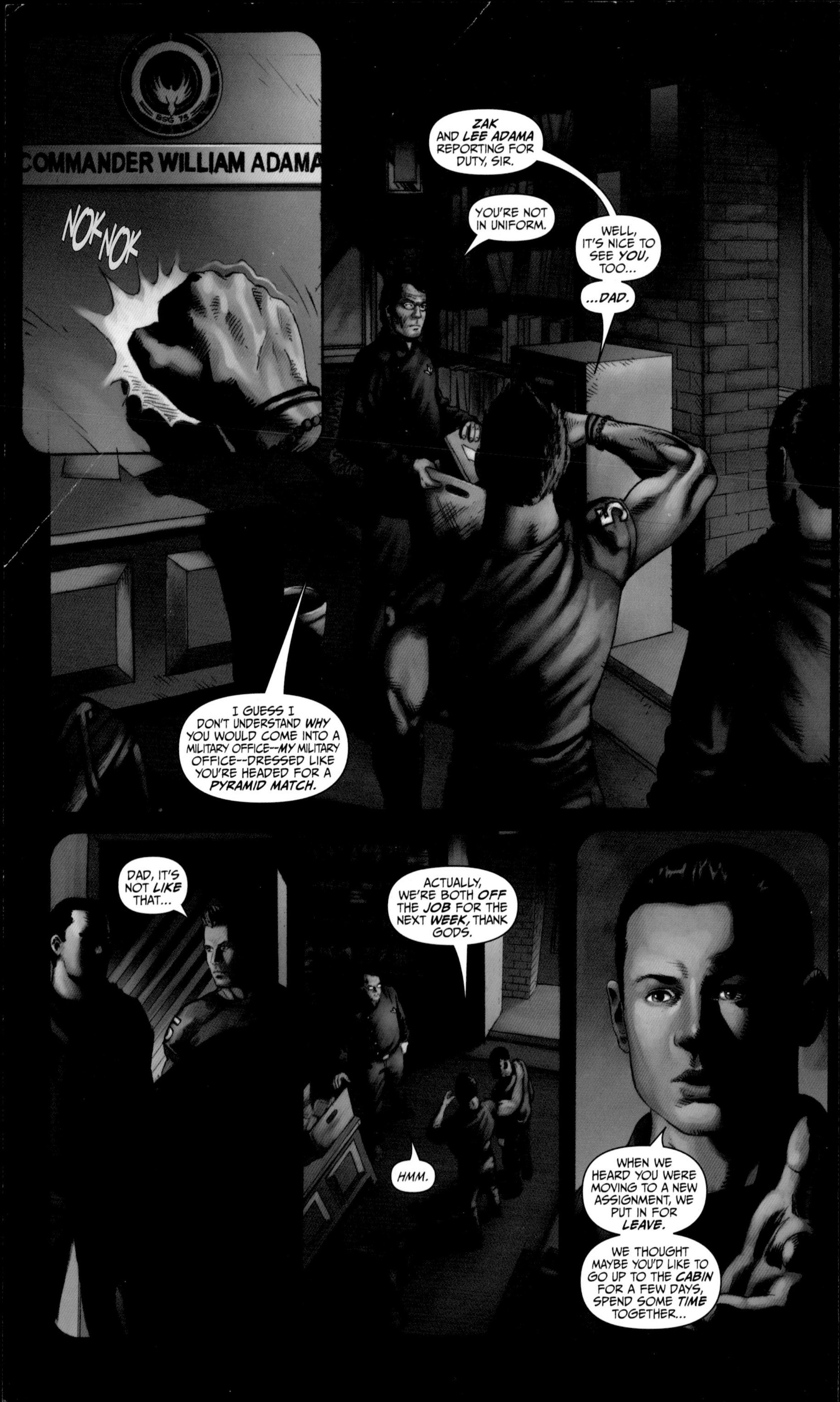
COMMANDER WILLIAM ADAMA
BSG 75
NOK NOK
ZAK AND LEE ADAMA REPORTING FOR DUTY, SIR.
YOU'RE NOT IN UNIFORM.
WELL, IT'S NICE TO SEE YOU, TOO...
...DAD.
I GUESS I DON'T UNDERSTAND WHY YOU WOULD COME INTO A MILITARY OFFICE--MY MILITARY OFFICE--DRESSED LIKE YOU'RE HEADED FOR A PYRAMID MATCH.
DAD, IT'S NOT LIKE THAT...
ACTUALLY, WE'RE BOTH OFF THE JOB FOR THE NEXT WEEK, THANK GODS.
HMM.
WHEN WE HEARD YOU WERE MOVING TO A NEW ASSIGNMENT, WE PUT IN FOR LEAVE.
WE THOUGHT MAYBE YOU'D LIKE TO GO UP TO THE CABIN FOR A FEW DAYS, SPEND SOME TIME TOGETHER...

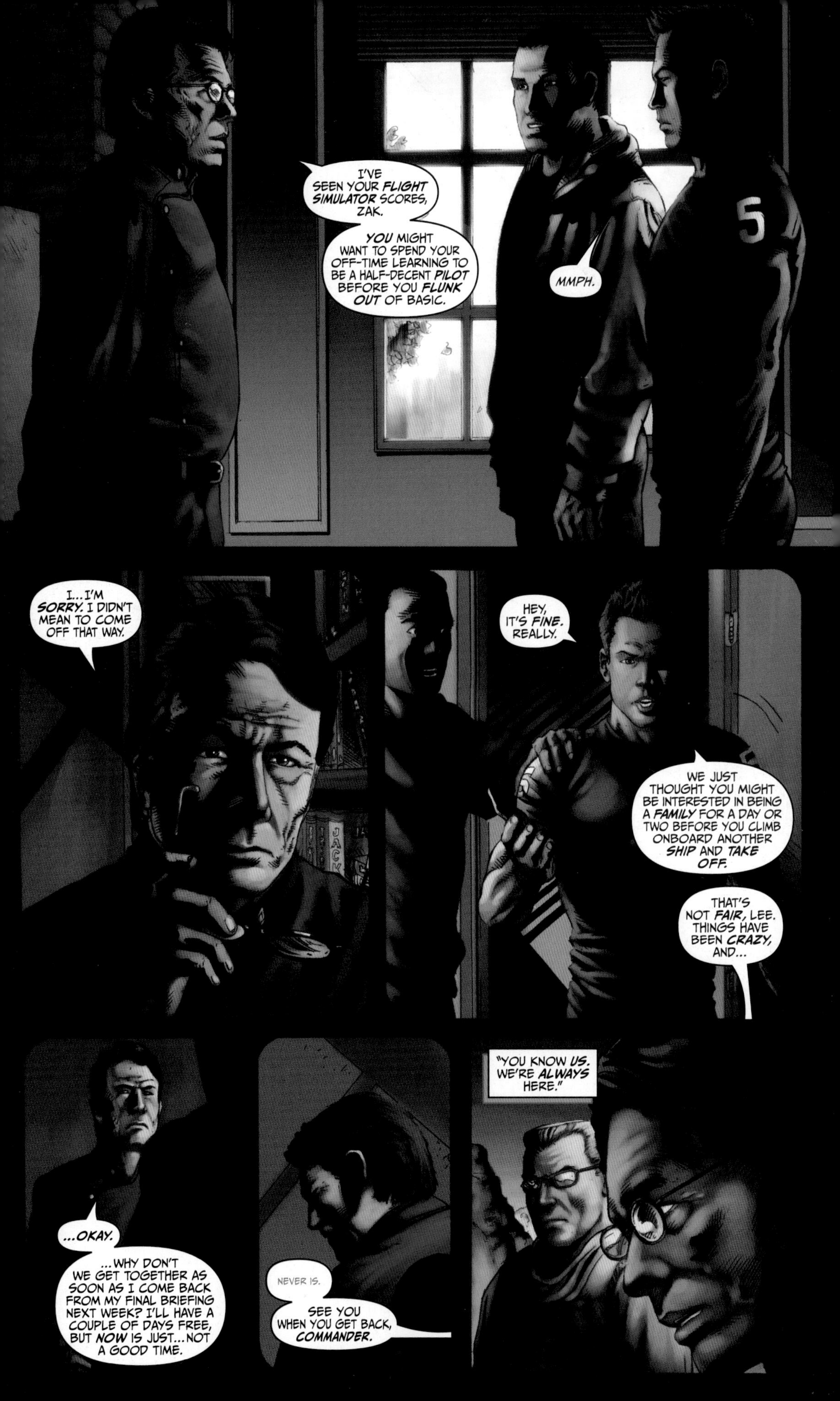
I'VE SEEN YOUR FLIGHT SIMULATOR SCORES, ZAK.
YOU MIGHT WANT TO SPEND YOUR OFF-TIME LEARNING TO BE A HALF-DECENT PILOT BEFORE YOU FLUNK OUT OF BASIC.
MMPH.
I...I'M SORRY. I DIDN'T MEAN TO COME OFF THAT WAY.
HEY, IT'S FINE. REALLY.
WE JUST THOUGHT YOU MIGHT BE INTERESTED IN BEING A FAMILY FOR A DAY OR TWO BEFORE YOU CLIMB ONBOARD ANOTHER SHIP AND TAKE OFF.
THAT'S NOT FAIR, LEE. THINGS HAVE BEEN CRAZY, AND...
...OKAY.
...WHY DON'T WE GET TOGETHER AS SOON AS I COME BACK FROM MY FINAL BRIEFING NEXT WEEK? I'LL HAVE A COUPLE OF DAYS FREE, BUT NOW IS JUST...NOT A GOOD TIME.
NEVER IS.
SEE YOU WHEN YOU GET BACK, COMMANDER.
"YOU KNOW US. WE'RE ALWAYS HERE."

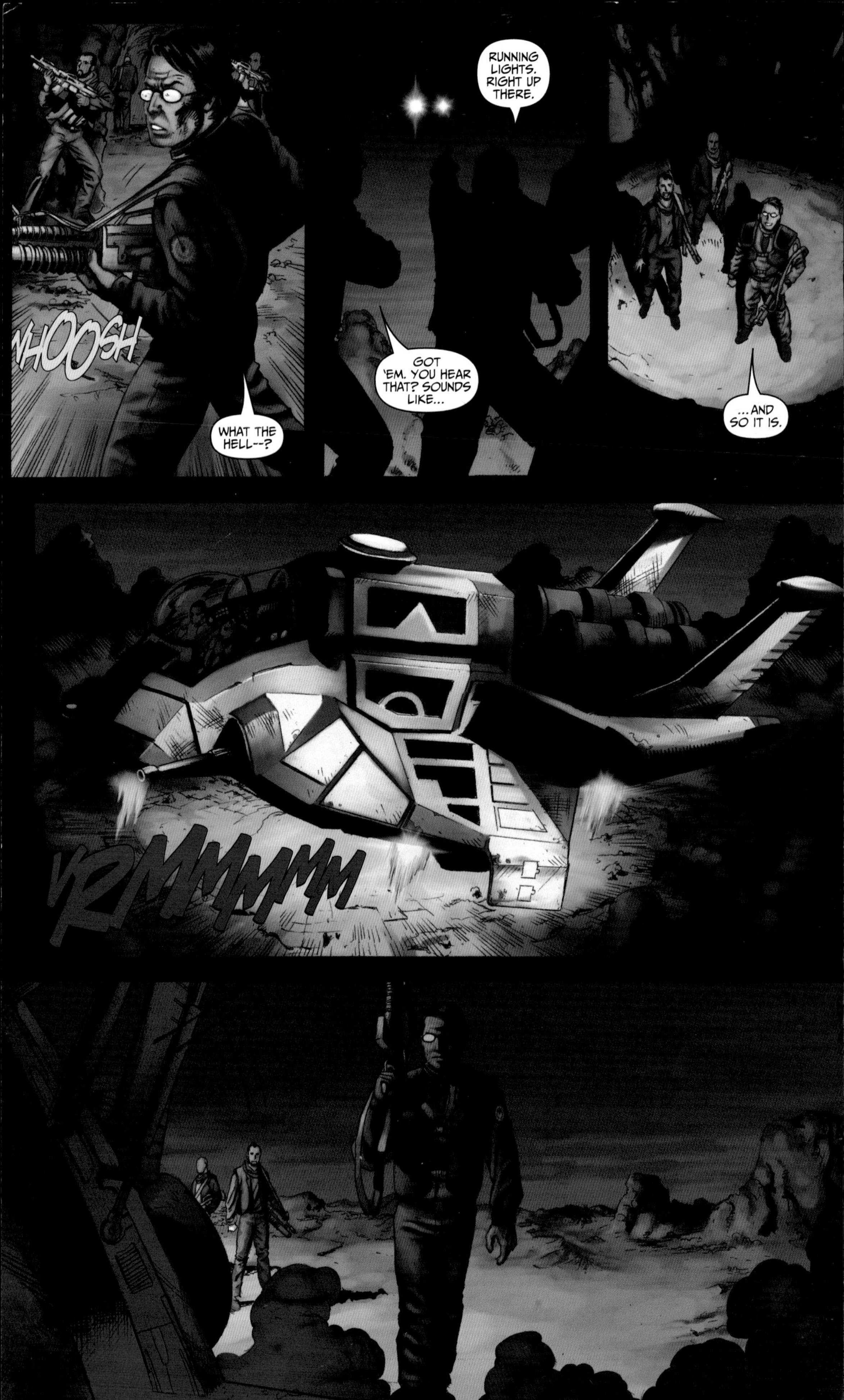
WHOOSH
WHAT THE HELL--?
RUNNING LIGHTS. RIGHT UP THERE.
GOT 'EM. YOU HEAR THAT? SOUNDS LIKE...
...AND SO IT IS.
VRMMMMMM

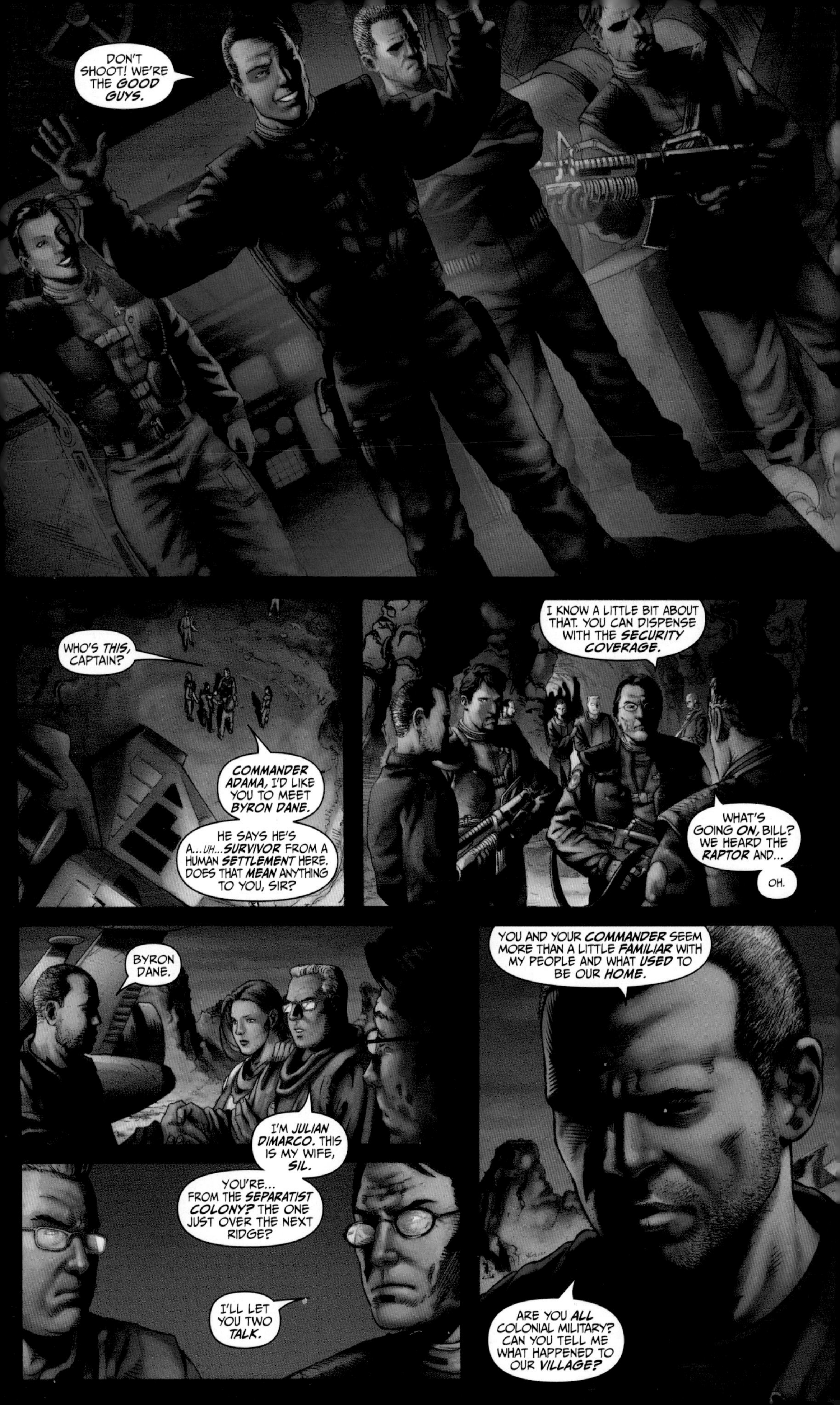
DON'T SHOOT! WE'RE THE GOOD GUYS.
WHO'S THIS, CAPTAIN?
COMMANDER ADAMA, I'D LIKE YOU TO MEET BYRON DANE.
HE SAYS HE'S A...UH...SURVIVOR FROM A HUMAN SETTLEMENT HERE. DOES THAT MEAN ANYTHING TO YOU, SIR?
I KNOW A LITTLE BIT ABOUT THAT. YOU CAN DISPENSE WITH THE SECURITY COVERAGE.
WHAT'S GOING ON, BILL? WE HEARD THE RAPTOR AND...
OH.
BYRON DANE.
I'M JULIAN DIMARCO. THIS IS MY WIFE, SIL.
YOU'RE... FROM THE SEPARATIST COLONY? THE ONE JUST OVER THE NEXT RIDGE?
I'LL LET YOU TWO TALK.
YOU AND YOUR COMMANDER SEEM MORE THAN A LITTLE FAMILIAR WITH MY PEOPLE AND WHAT USED TO BE OUR HOME.
ARE YOU ALL COLONIAL MILITARY? CAN YOU TELL ME WHAT HAPPENED TO OUR VILLAGE?

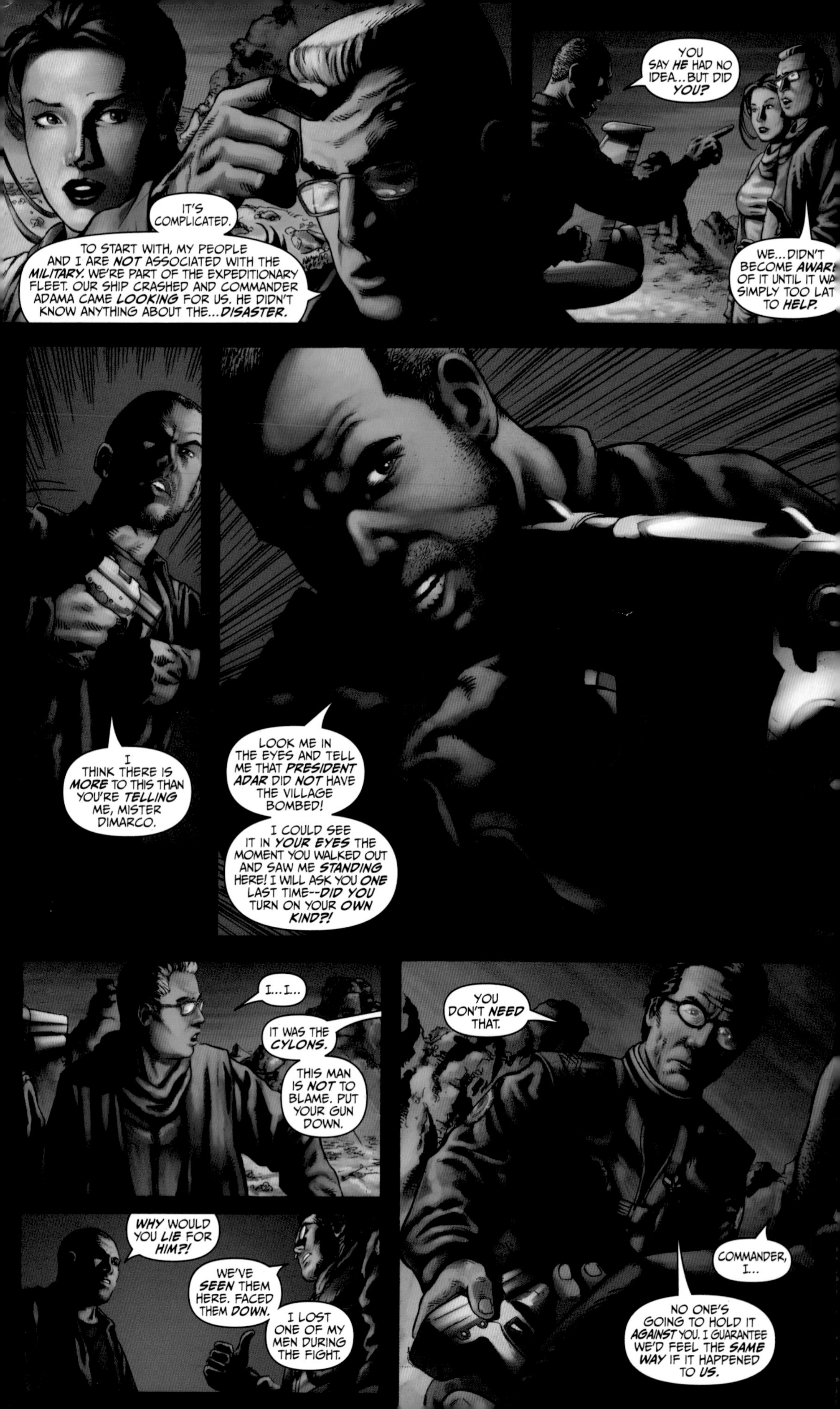

IT'S COMPLICATED.
TO START WITH, MY PEOPLE AND I ARE NOT ASSOCIATED WITH THE MILITARY. WE'RE PART OF THE EXPEDITIONARY FLEET. OUR SHIP CRASHED AND COMMANDER ADAMA CAME LOOKING FOR US. HE DIDN'T KNOW ANYTHING ABOUT THE...DISASTER.
YOU SAY HE HAD NO IDEA...BUT DID YOU?
WE...DIDN'T BECOME AWAR OF IT UNTIL IT WA SIMPLY TOO LAT TO HELP.
I THINK THERE IS MORE TO THIS THAN YOU'RE TELLING ME, MISTER DIMARCO.
LOOK ME IN THE EYES AND TELL ME THAT PRESIDENT ADAR DID NOT HAVE THE VILLAGE BOMBED!
I COULD SEE IT IN YOUR EYES THE MOMENT YOU WALKED OUT AND SAW ME STANDING HERE! I WILL ASK YOU ONE LAST TIME--DID YOU TURN ON YOUR OWN KIND?!
I...I...
IT WAS THE CYLONS.
THIS MAN IS NOT TO BLAME. PUT YOUR GUN DOWN.
WHY WOULD YOU LIE FOR HIM?!
WE'VE SEEN THEM HERE. FACED THEM DOWN.
I LOST ONE OF MY MEN DURING THE FIGHT.
YOU DON'T NEED THAT.
COMMANDER, I...
NO ONE'S GOING TO HOLD IT AGAINST YOU. I GUARANTEE WE'D FEEL THE SAME WAY IF IT HAPPENED TO US.

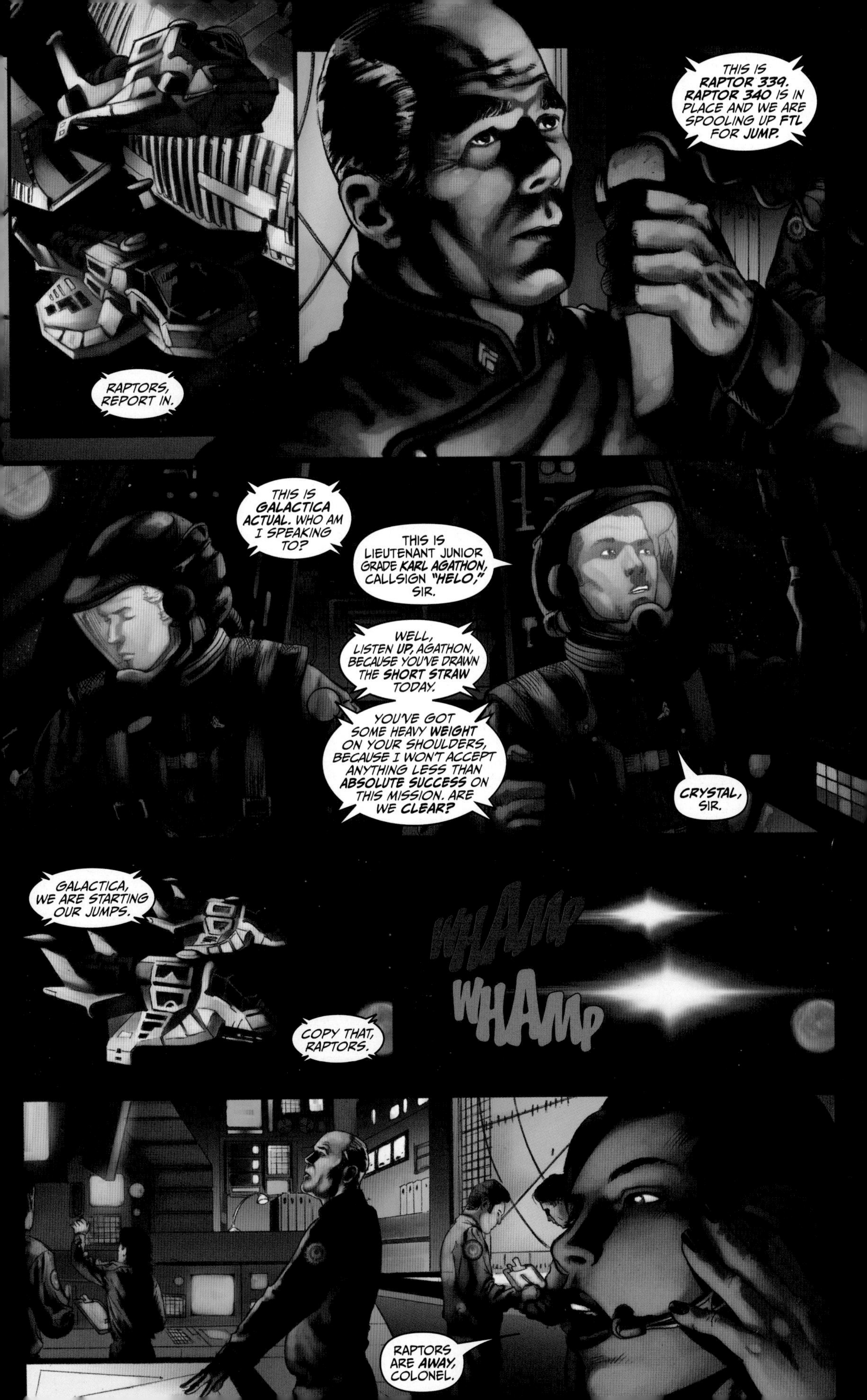
RAPTORS, REPORT IN.
THIS IS RAPTOR 339. RAPTOR 340 IS IN PLACE AND WE ARE SPOOLING UP FTL FOR JUMP.
THIS IS GALACTICA ACTUAL. WHO AM I SPEAKING TO?
THIS IS LIEUTENANT JUNIOR GRADE KARL AGATHON, CALLSIGN "HELO," SIR.
WELL, LISTEN UP, AGATHON, BECAUSE YOU'VE DRAWN THE SHORT STRAW TODAY.
YOU'VE GOT SOME HEAVY WEIGHT ON YOUR SHOULDERS, BECAUSE I WON'T ACCEPT ANYTHING LESS THAN ABSOLUTE SUCCESS ON THIS MISSION. ARE WE CLEAR?
CRYSTAL, SIR.
GALACTICA, WE ARE STARTING OUR JUMPS.
COPY THAT, RAPTORS.
WHAMP
WHAMP
RAPTORS ARE AWAY, COLONEL.

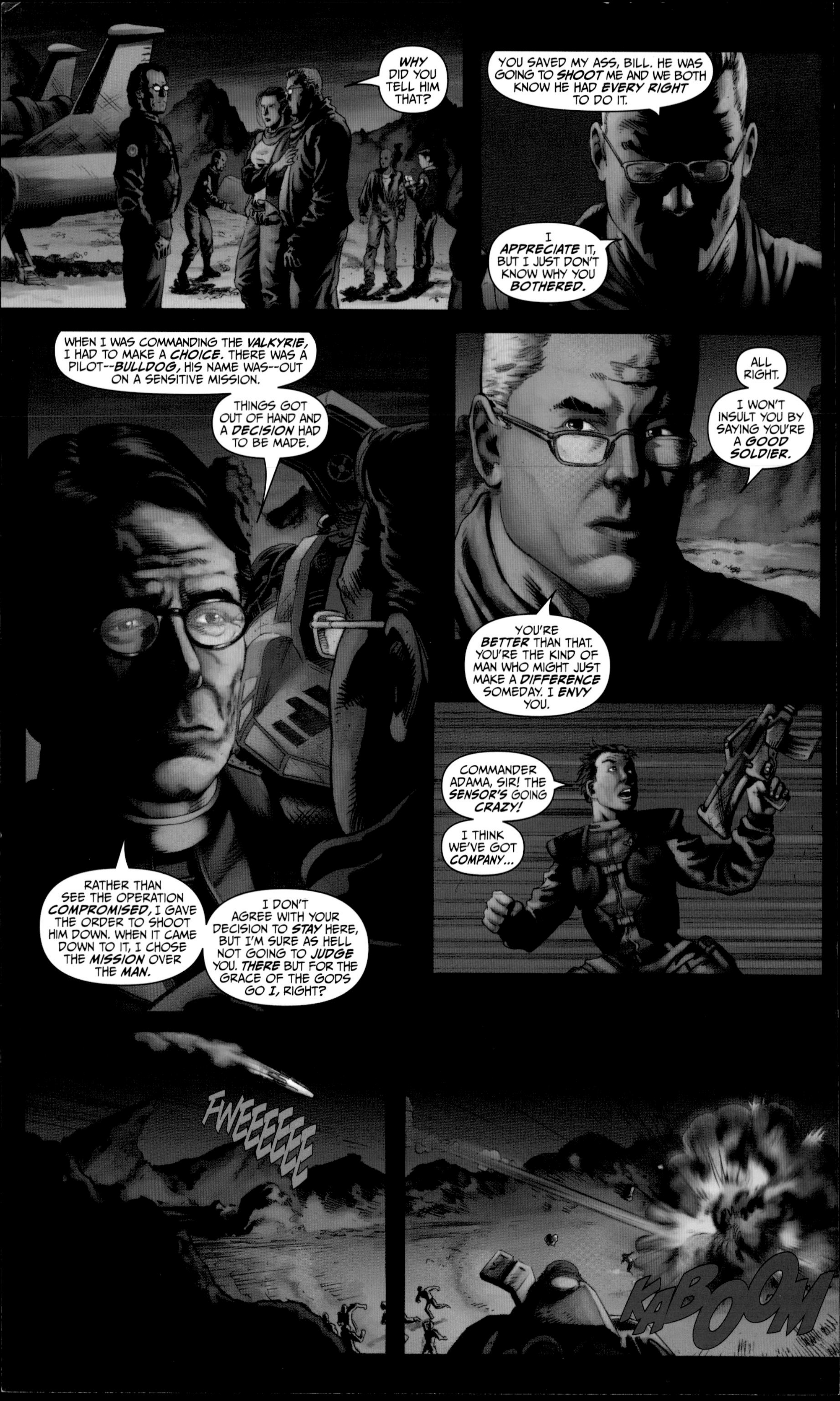
WHY DID YOU TELL HIM THAT?
YOU SAVED MY ASS, BILL. HE WAS GOING TO SHOOT ME AND WE BOTH KNOW HE HAD EVERY RIGHT TO DO IT.
I APPRECIATE IT, BUT I JUST DON'T KNOW WHY YOU BOTHERED.
WHEN I WAS COMMANDING THE VALKYRIE, I HAD TO MAKE A CHOICE. THERE WAS A PILOT--BULLDOG, HIS NAME WAS--OUT ON A SENSITIVE MISSION.
THINGS GOT OUT OF HAND AND A DECISION HAD TO BE MADE.
RATHER THAN SEE THE OPERATION COMPROMISED, I GAVE THE ORDER TO SHOOT HIM DOWN. WHEN IT CAME DOWN TO IT, I CHOSE THE MISSION OVER THE MAN.
I DON'T AGREE WITH YOUR DECISION TO STAY HERE, BUT I'M SURE AS HELL NOT GOING TO JUDGE YOU. THERE BUT FOR THE GRACE OF THE GODS GO I, RIGHT?
ALL RIGHT.
I WON'T INSULT YOU BY SAYING YOU'RE A GOOD SOLDIER.
YOU'RE BETTER THAN THAT. YOU'RE THE KIND OF MAN WHO MIGHT JUST MAKE A DIFFERENCE SOMEDAY. I ENVY YOU.
COMMANDER ADAMA, SIR! THE SENSOR'S GOING CRAZY!
I THINK WE'VE GOT COMPANY...
FWEEEEEEE
KABOOM

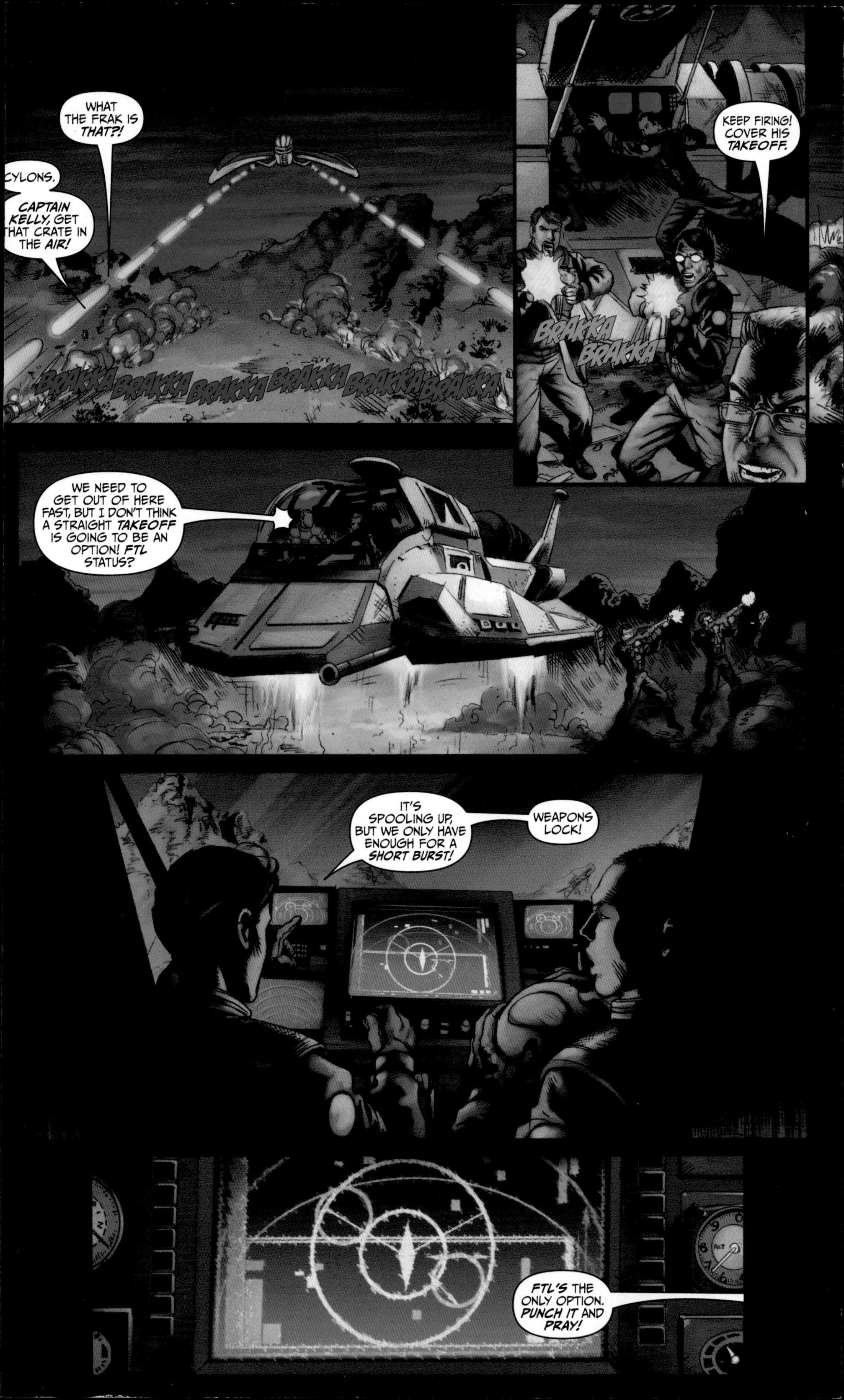
WHAT THE FRAK IS THAT?!
CYLONS.
CAPTAIN KELLY, GET THAT CRATE IN THE AIR!
BRAKKA BRAKKA BRAKKA BRAKKA BRAKKA BRAKKA
KEEP FIRING! COVER HIS TAKEOFF.
BRAKKA BRAKKA
WE NEED TO GET OUT OF HERE FAST, BUT I DON'T THINK A STRAIGHT TAKEOFF IS GOING TO BE AN OPTION! FTL STATUS?
IT'S SPOOLING UP, BUT WE ONLY HAVE ENOUGH FOR A SHORT BURST!
WEAPONS LOCK!
FTL'S THE ONLY OPTION. PUNCH IT AND PRAY!

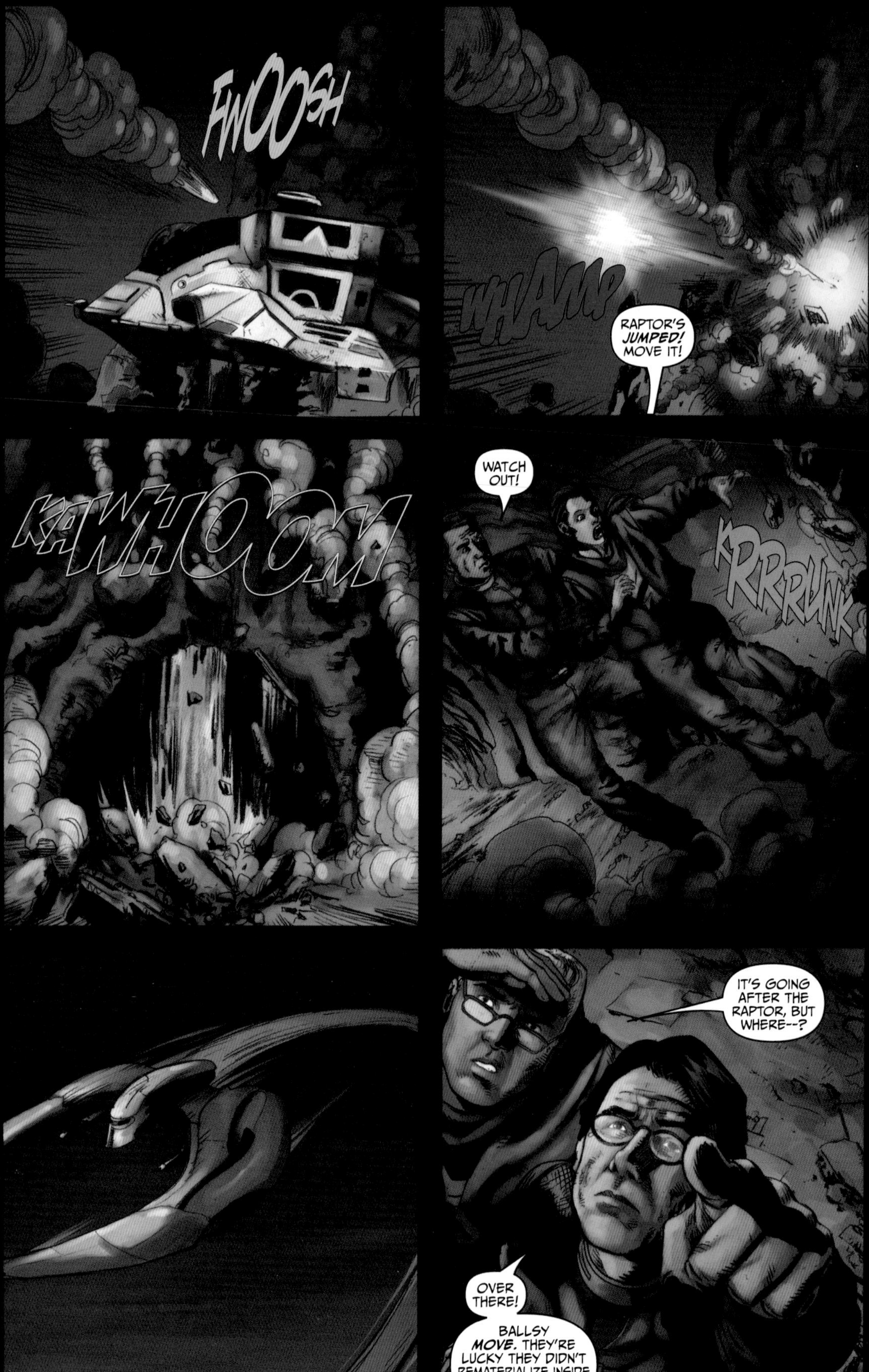
FWOOSH
WHAMP
RAPTOR'S JUMPED! MOVE IT!
KAWHOOOM
WATCH OUT!
KRRRUNK
IT'S GOING AFTER THE RAPTOR, BUT WHERE--?
OVER THERE!
BALLSY MOVE. THEY'RE LUCKY THEY DIDN'T REMATERIALIZE INSIDE ONE OF THOSE MOUNTAINS...

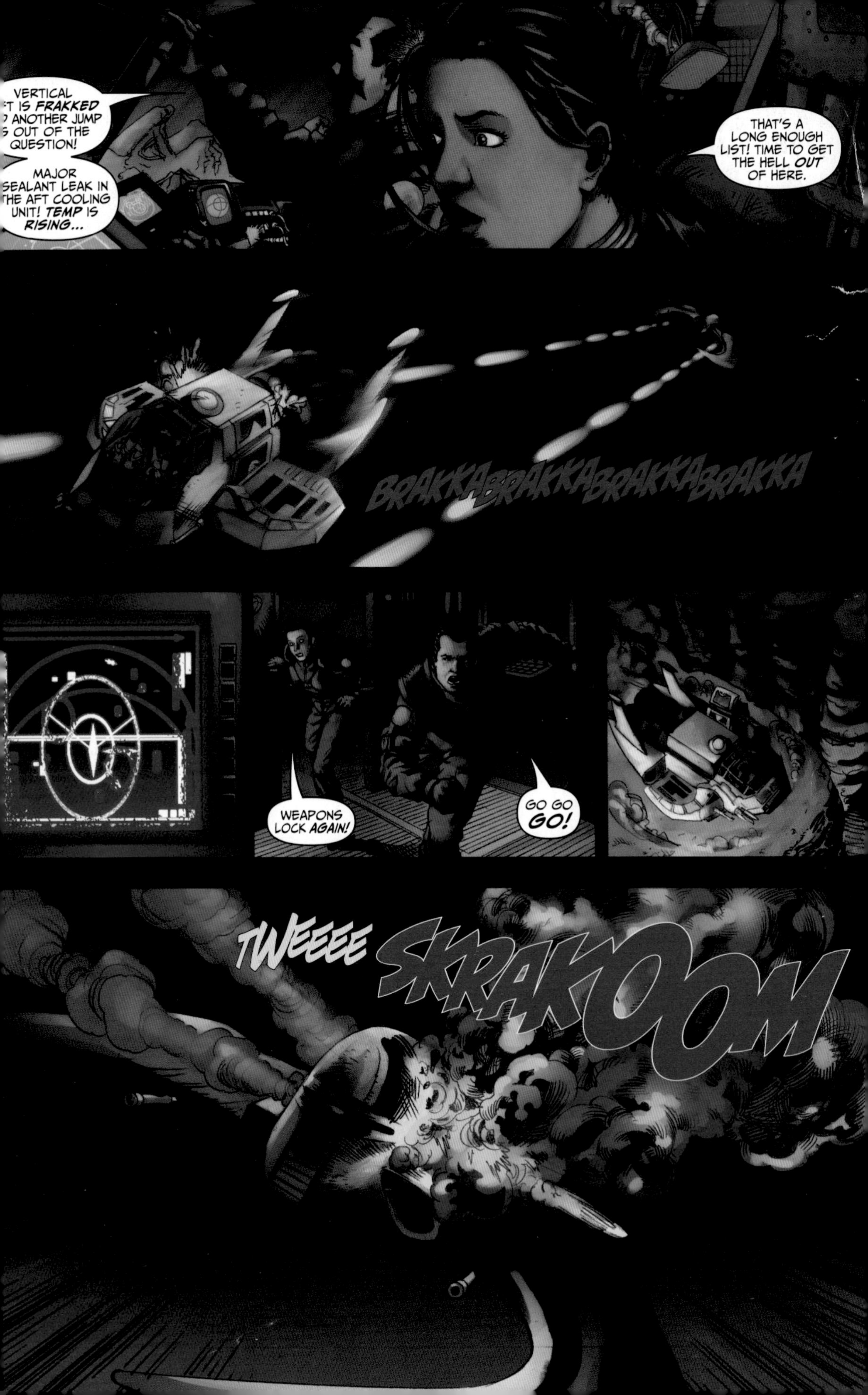
VERTICAL
-T IS FRAKKED
-D ANOTHER JUMP
-S OUT OF THE QUESTION!
MAJOR SEALANT LEAK IN THE AFT COOLING UNIT! TEMP IS RISING...
THAT'S A LONG ENOUGH LIST! TIME TO GET THE HELL OUT OF HERE.
BRAKKABRAKKABRAKKABRAKKA
WEAPONS LOCK AGAIN!
GO GO GO!
TWEEEE
SKRAKOOOM

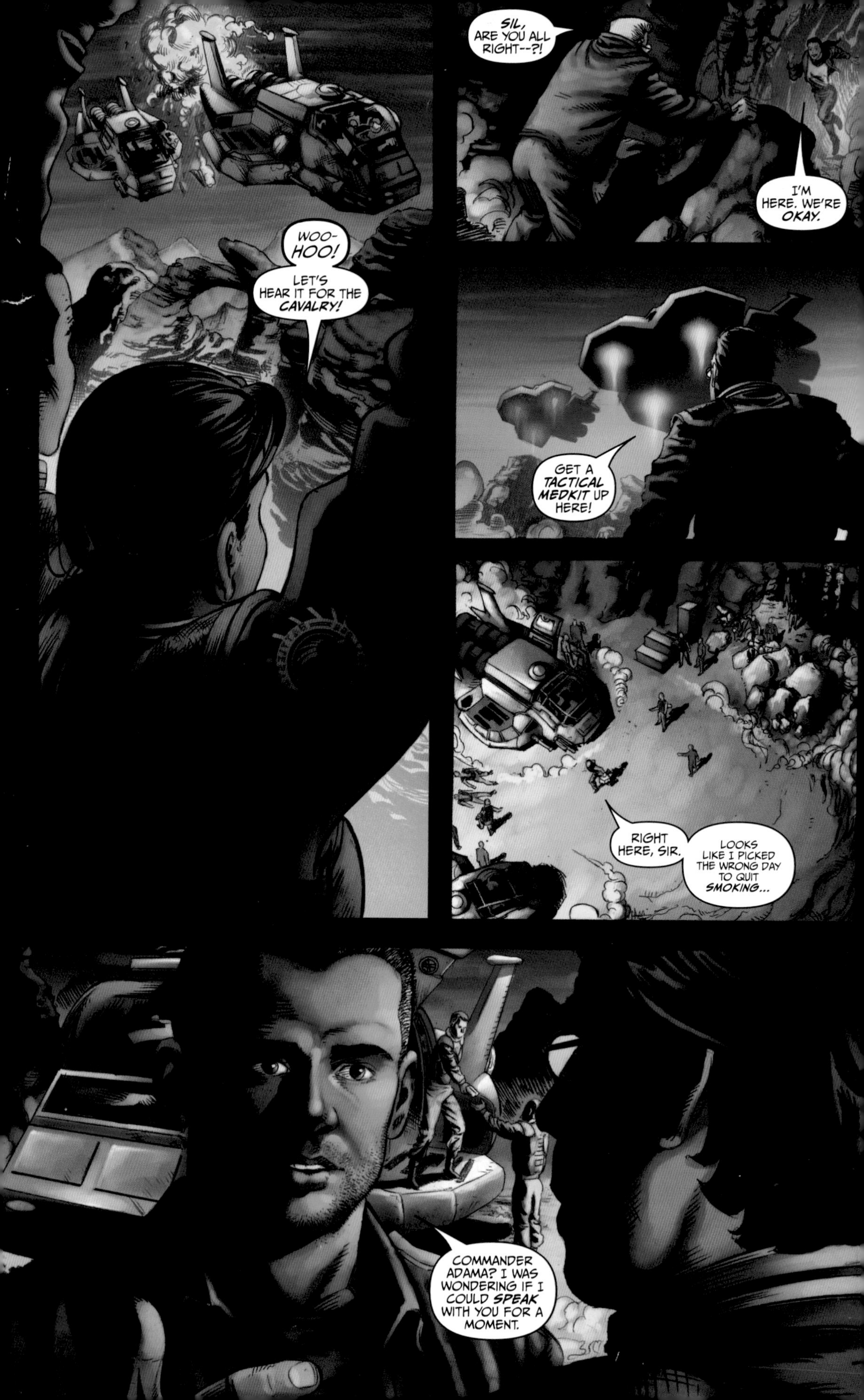
WOO-HOO!
LET'S HEAR IT FOR THE CAVALRY!
SIL, ARE YOU ALL RIGHT--?!
I'M HERE. WE'RE OKAY.
GET A TACTICAL MEDKIT UP HERE!
RIGHT HERE, SIR.
LOOKS LIKE I PICKED THE WRONG DAY TO QUIT SMOKING...
COMMANDER ADAMA? I WAS WONDERING IF I COULD SPEAK WITH YOU FOR A MOMENT.

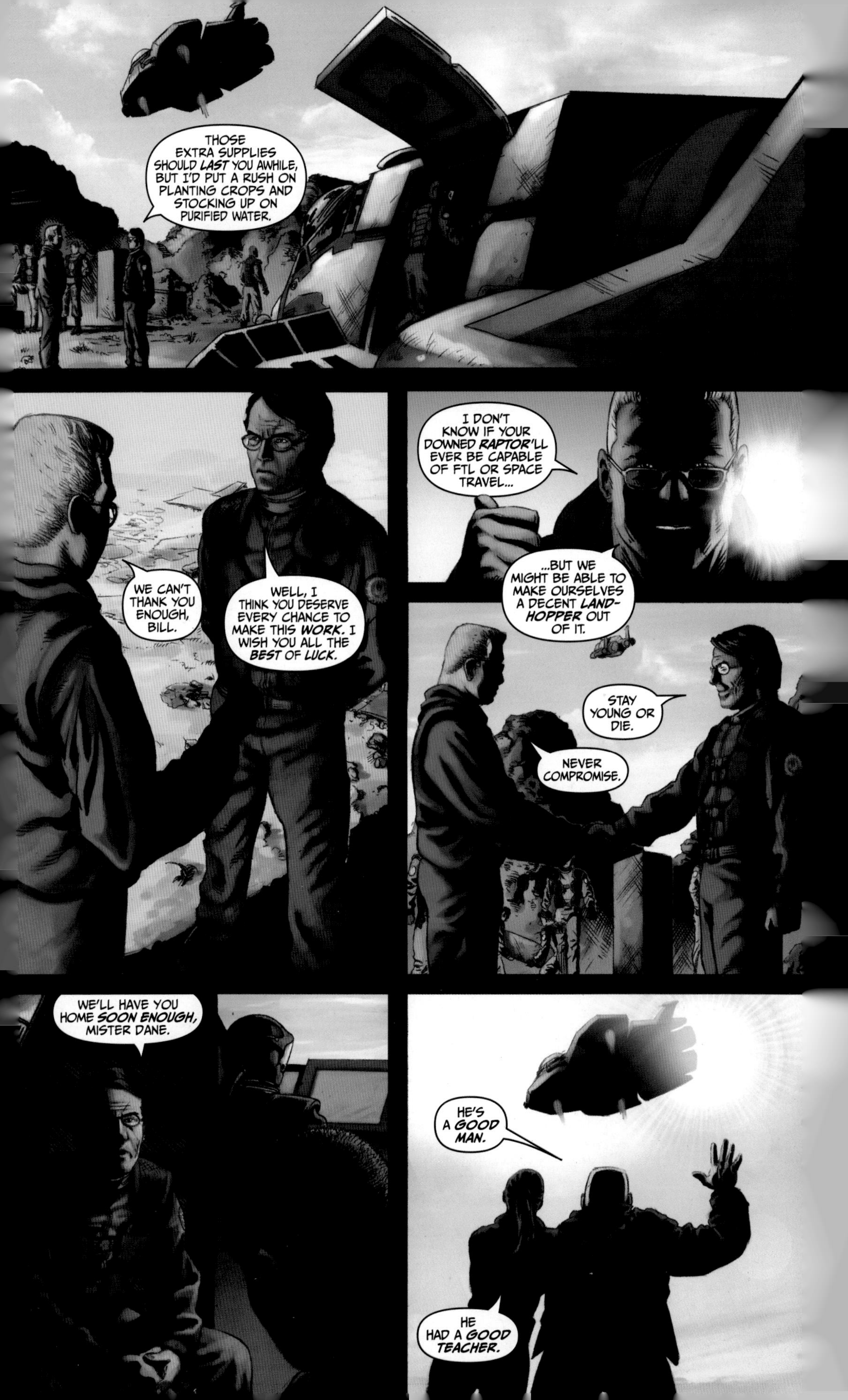
THOSE EXTRA SUPPLIES SHOULD LAST YOU AWHILE, BUT I'D PUT A RUSH ON PLANTING CROPS AND STOCKING UP ON PURIFIED WATER.
WE CAN'T THANK YOU ENOUGH, BILL.
WELL, I THINK YOU DESERVE EVERY CHANCE TO MAKE THIS WORK. I WISH YOU ALL THE BEST OF LUCK.
I DON'T KNOW IF YOUR DOWNED RAPTOR'LL EVER BE CAPABLE OF FTL OR SPACE TRAVEL...
...BUT WE MIGHT BE ABLE TO MAKE OURSELVES A DECENT LAND-HOPPER OUT OF IT.
STAY YOUNG OR DIE.
NEVER COMPROMISE.
WE'LL HAVE YOU HOME SOON ENOUGH, MISTER DANE.
HE'S A GOOD MAN.
HE HAD A GOOD TEACHER.

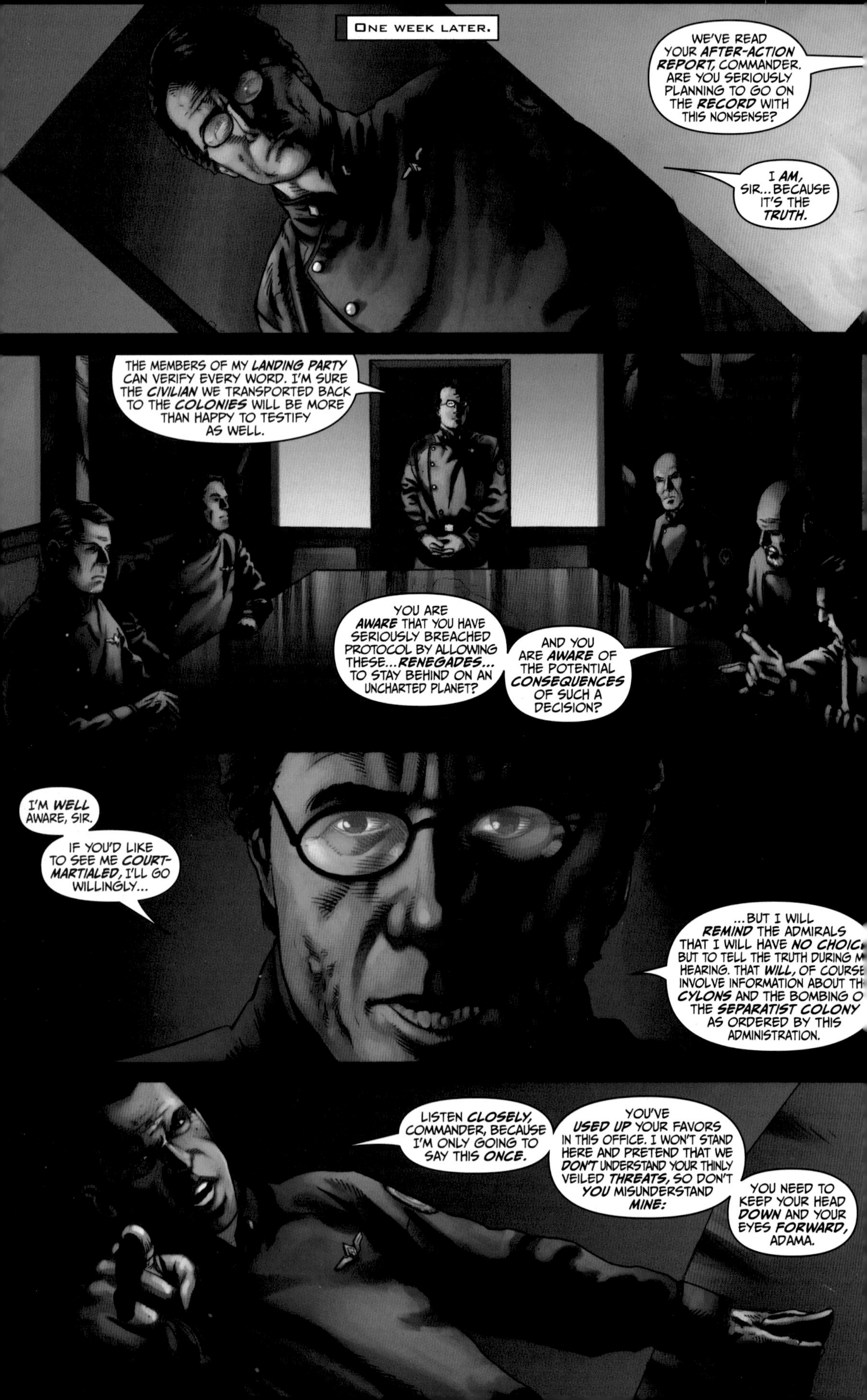
ONE WEEK LATER.
WE'VE READ YOUR AFTER-ACTION REPORT, COMMANDER. ARE YOU SERIOUSLY PLANNING TO GO ON THE RECORD WITH THIS NONSENSE?
I AM, SIR...BECAUSE IT'S THE TRUTH.
THE MEMBERS OF MY LANDING PARTY CAN VERIFY EVERY WORD. I'M SURE THE CIVILIAN WE TRANSPORTED BACK TO THE COLONIES WILL BE MORE THAN HAPPY TO TESTIFY AS WELL.
YOU ARE AWARE THAT YOU HAVE SERIOUSLY BREACHED PROTOCOL BY ALLOWING THESE...RENEGADES... TO STAY BEHIND ON AN UNCHARTED PLANET?
AND YOU ARE AWARE OF THE POTENTIAL CONSEQUENCES OF SUCH A DECISION?
I'M WELL AWARE, SIR.
IF YOU'D LIKE TO SEE ME COURT-MARTIALED, I'LL GO WILLINGLY...
...BUT I WILL REMIND THE ADMIRALS THAT I WILL HAVE NO CHOIC BUT TO TELL THE TRUTH DURING M HEARING. THAT WILL, OF COURSE INVOLVE INFORMATION ABOUT TH CYLONS AND THE BOMBING O THE SEPARATIST COLONY AS ORDERED BY THIS ADMINISTRATION.
LISTEN CLOSELY, COMMANDER, BECAUSE I'M ONLY GOING TO SAY THIS ONCE.
YOU'VE USED UP YOUR FAVORS IN THIS OFFICE. I WON'T STAND HERE AND PRETEND THAT WE DON'T UNDERSTAND YOUR THINLY VEILED THREATS, SO DON'T YOU MISUNDERSTAND MINE:
YOU NEED TO KEEP YOUR HEAD DOWN AND YOUR EYES FORWARD, ADAMA.

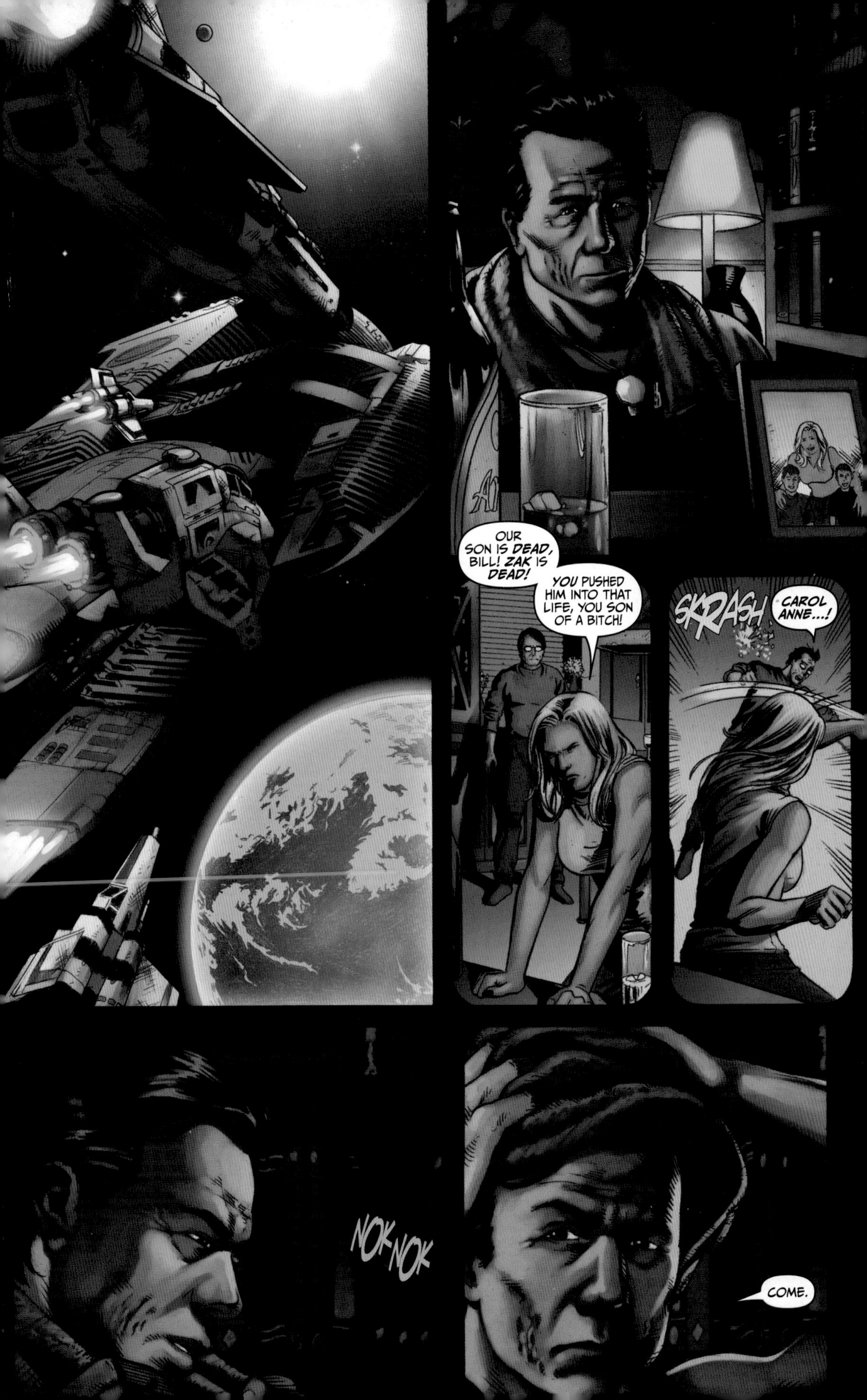
OUR SON IS DEAD, BILL! ZAK IS DEAD!
YOU PUSHED HIM INTO THAT LIFE, YOU SON OF A BITCH!
SKRASH
CAROL ANNE...!
NOK-NOK
COME.

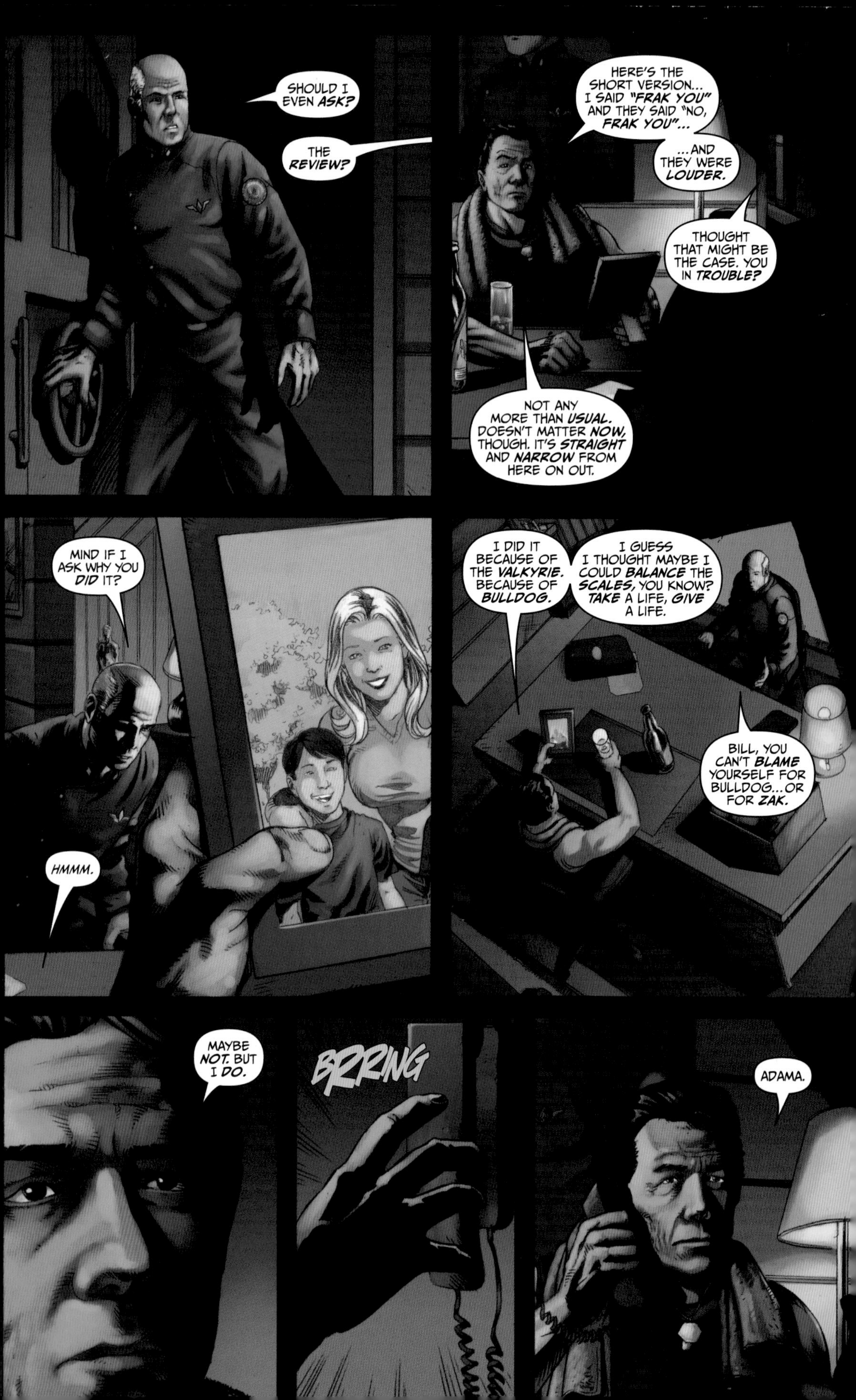

SHOULD I EVEN ASK?
THE REVIEW?
HERE'S THE SHORT VERSION... I SAID "FRAK YOU" AND THEY SAID "NO, FRAK YOU"...
...AND THEY WERE LOUDER.
THOUGHT THAT MIGHT BE THE CASE. YOU IN TROUBLE?
NOT ANY MORE THAN USUAL. DOESN'T MATTER NOW, THOUGH. IT'S STRAIGHT AND NARROW FROM HERE ON OUT.
MIND IF I ASK WHY YOU DID IT?
HMMM.
I DID IT BECAUSE OF THE VALKYRIE. BECAUSE OF BULLDOG.
I GUESS I THOUGHT MAYBE I COULD BALANCE THE SCALES, YOU KNOW? TAKE A LIFE, GIVE A LIFE.
BILL, YOU CAN'T BLAME YOURSELF FOR BULLDOG...OR FOR ZAK.
MAYBE NOT. BUT I DO.
BRRING
ADAMA.

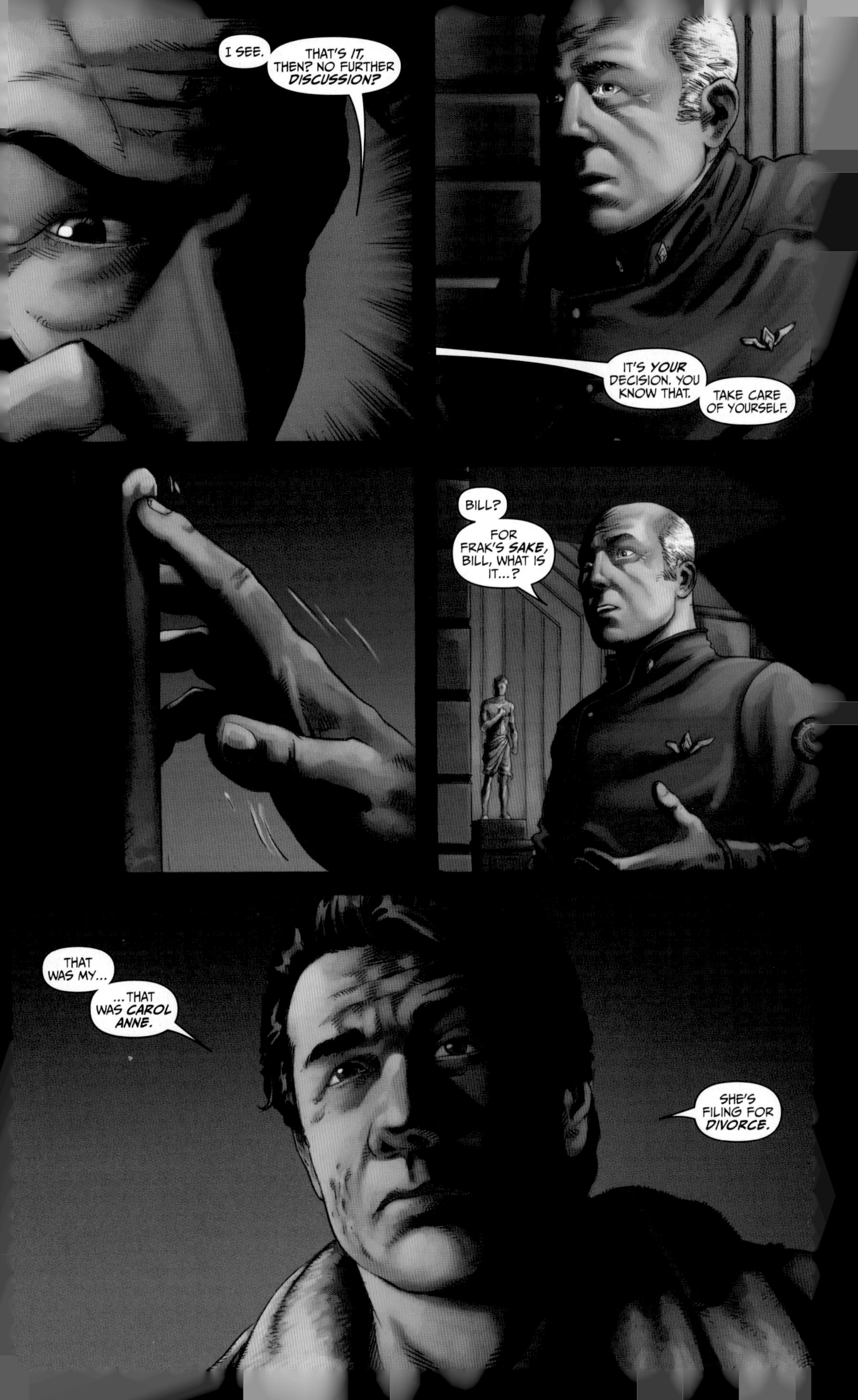
I SEE.
THAT'S *IT*, THEN? NO FURTHER ***DISCUSSION?***
IT'S ***YOUR*** DECISION. YOU KNOW THAT.
TAKE CARE OF YOURSELF.
BILL?
FOR FRAK'S ***SAKE***, BILL, WHAT IS IT...?
THAT WAS MY...
...THAT WAS ***CAROL ANNE.***
SHE'S FILING FOR ***DIVORCE.***

RAPTOR'S *CLEAR*. PREP FOR OFFLOAD.

CHIEF TYROL! WE NEED YOU FOR SIGN-OFF!

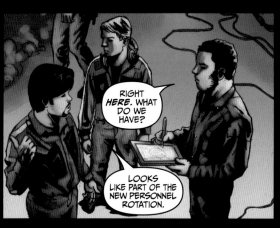

RIGHT *HERE*. WHAT DO WE HAVE?

LOOKS LIKE PART OF THE NEW PERSONNEL ROTATION.

NAME?

LIEUTENANT *FELIX GAETA*, TACTICAL.

OH, GOOD. COMMANDER'S *EXPECTING* YOU.

LLEWELLYN AND *DAVIS?* REPORT TO ENGINEERING.

OKAY, THAT JUST LEAVES *ONE MORE* NAME ON THE LIST...

WELCOME TO THE BATTLESTAR GALACTICA, *LIEUTENANT THRACE.*

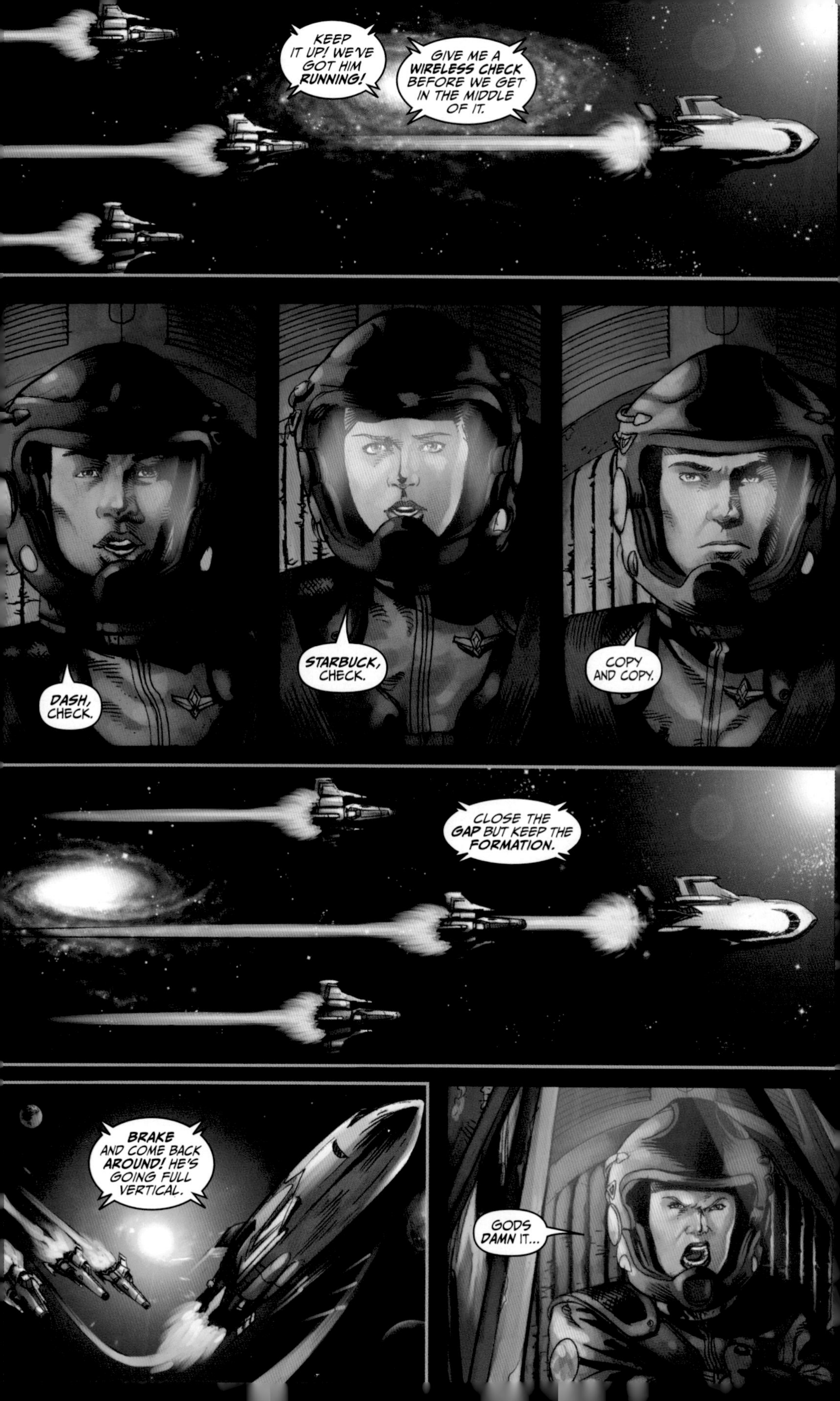
KEEP IT UP! WE'VE GOT HIM RUNNING!
GIVE ME A WIRELESS CHECK BEFORE WE GET IN THE MIDDLE OF IT.
DASH, CHECK.
STARBUCK, CHECK.
COPY AND COPY.
CLOSE THE GAP BUT KEEP THE FORMATION.
BRAKE AND COME BACK AROUND! HE'S GOING FULL VERTICAL.
GODS DAMN IT...

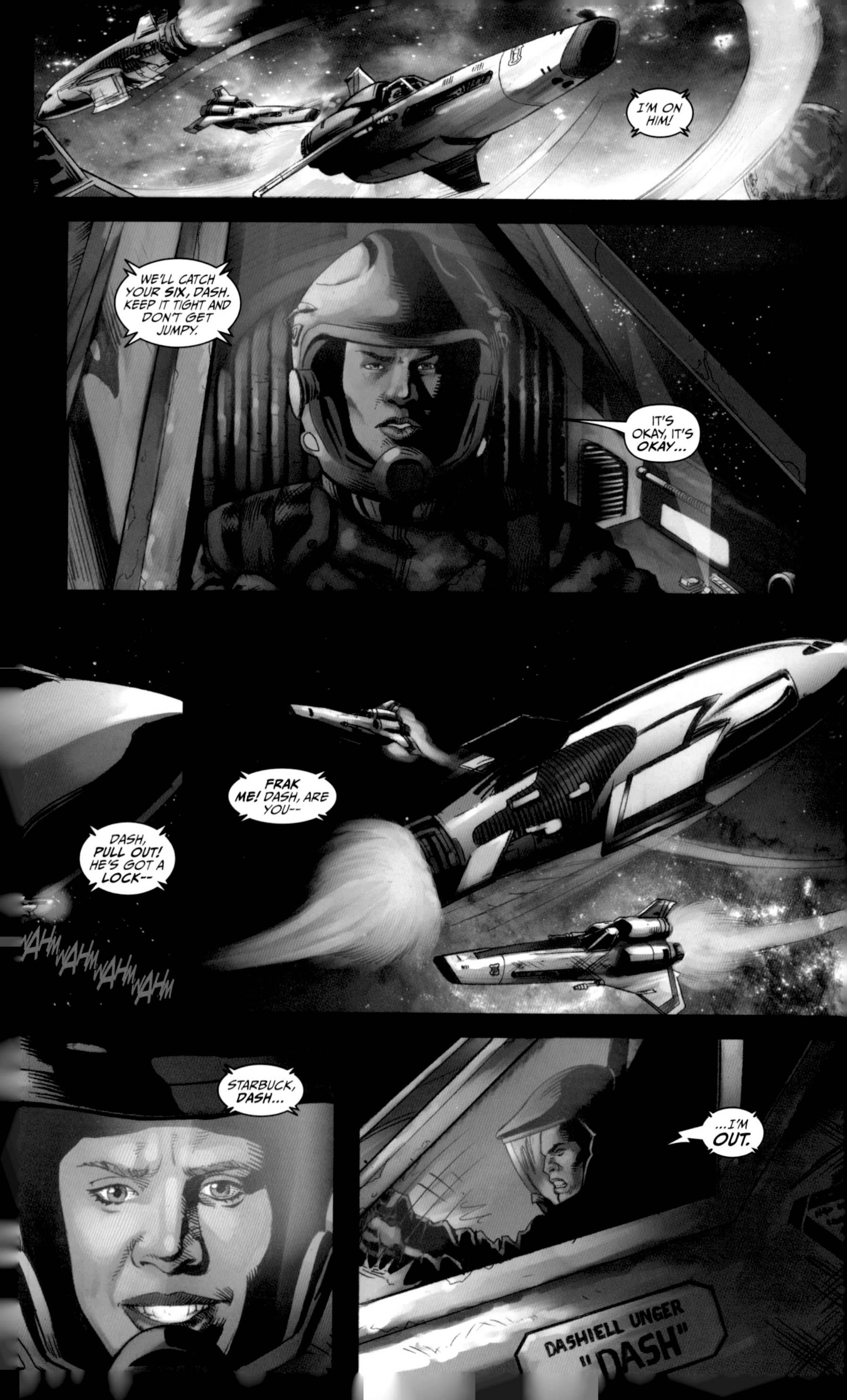
I'M ON HIM!
WE'LL CATCH YOUR SIX, DASH. KEEP IT TIGHT AND DON'T GET JUMPY.
IT'S OKAY, IT'S OKAY...
FRAK ME! DASH, ARE YOU--
DASH, PULL OUT! HE'S GOT A LOCK--
WAHM WAHM WAHM WAHM
STARBUCK, DASH...
...I'M OUT.
DASHIELL UNGER "DASH"

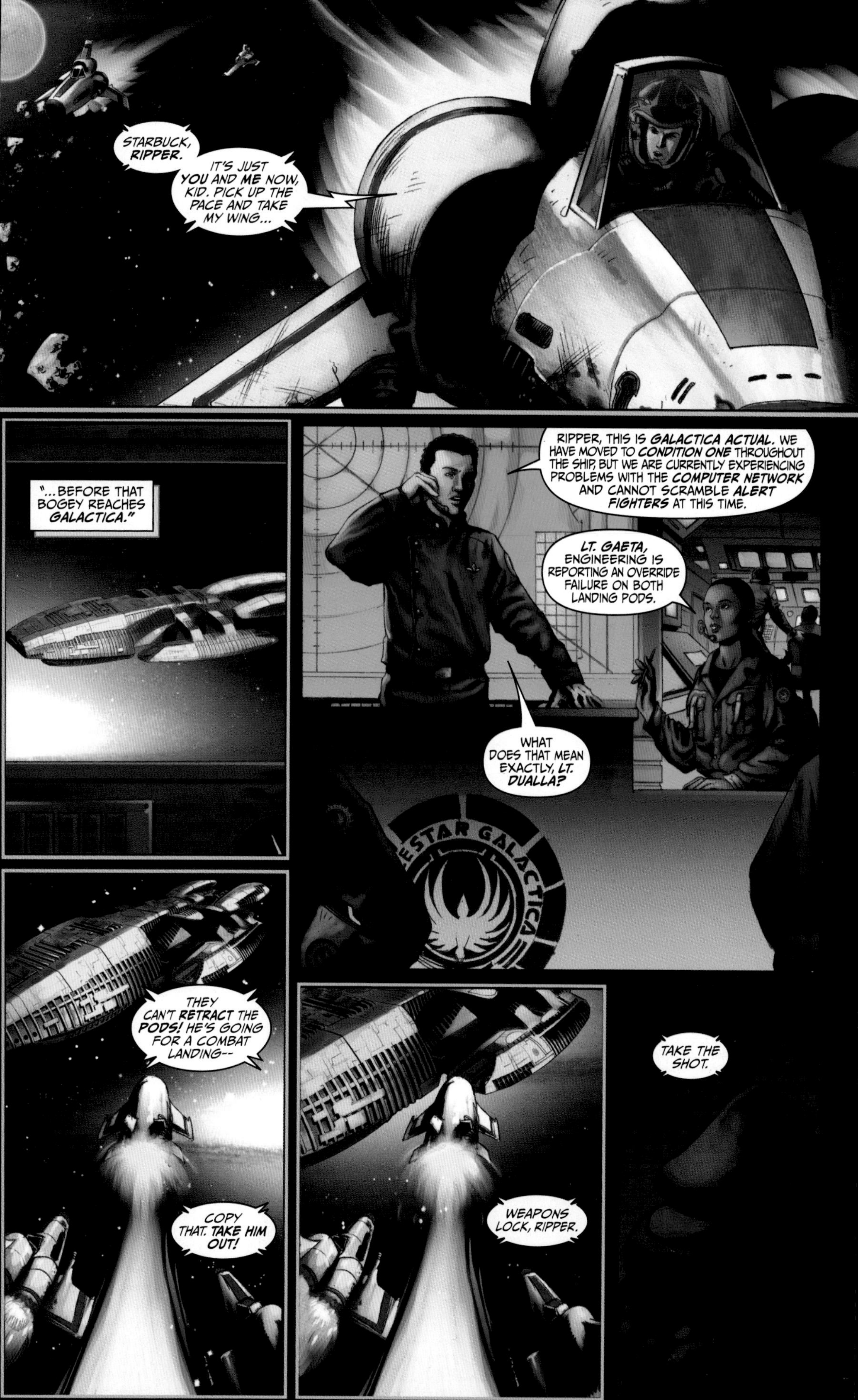
STARBUCK, RIPPER.
IT'S JUST YOU AND ME NOW, KID. PICK UP THE PACE AND TAKE MY WING...
"...BEFORE THAT BOGEY REACHES GALACTICA."
RIPPER, THIS IS GALACTICA ACTUAL. WE HAVE MOVED TO CONDITION ONE THROUGHOUT THE SHIP, BUT WE ARE CURRENTLY EXPERIENCING PROBLEMS WITH THE COMPUTER NETWORK AND CANNOT SCRAMBLE ALERT FIGHTERS AT THIS TIME.
LT. GAETA, ENGINEERING IS REPORTING AN OVERRIDE FAILURE ON BOTH LANDING PODS.
WHAT DOES THAT MEAN EXACTLY, LT. DUALLA?
THEY CAN'T RETRACT THE PODS! HE'S GOING FOR A COMBAT LANDING--
COPY THAT. TAKE HIM OUT!
WEAPONS LOCK, RIPPER.
TAKE THE SHOT.

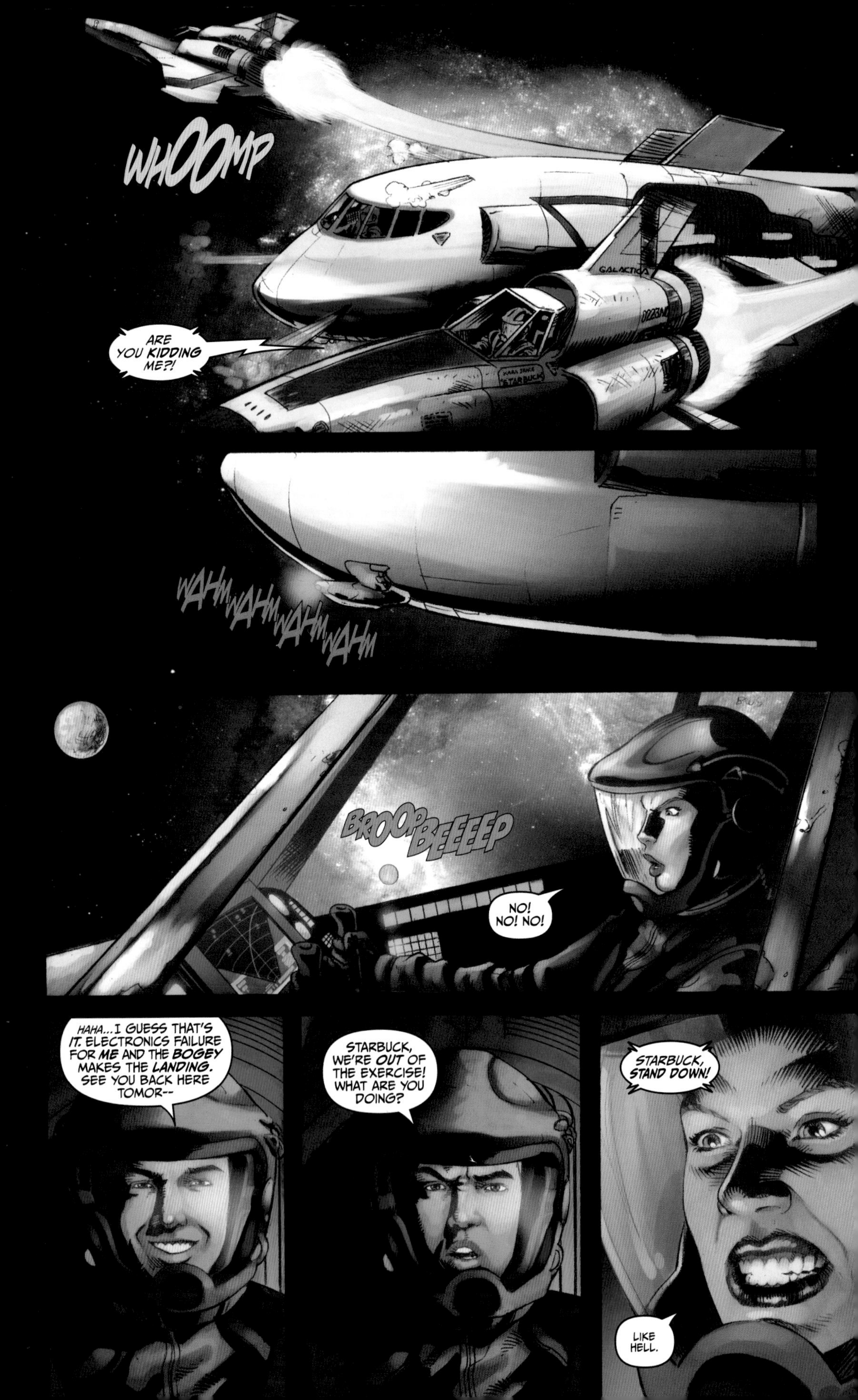

WHOOMP
ARE YOU KIDDING ME?!
WAHM WAHM WAHM WAHM
BROOP BEEEEP
NO! NO! NO!
HAHA... I GUESS THAT'S IT. ELECTRONICS FAILURE FOR ME AND THE BOGEY MAKES THE LANDING. SEE YOU BACK HERE TOMOR--
STARBUCK, WE'RE OUT OF THE EXERCISE! WHAT ARE YOU DOING?
STARBUCK, STAND DOWN!
LIKE HELL.

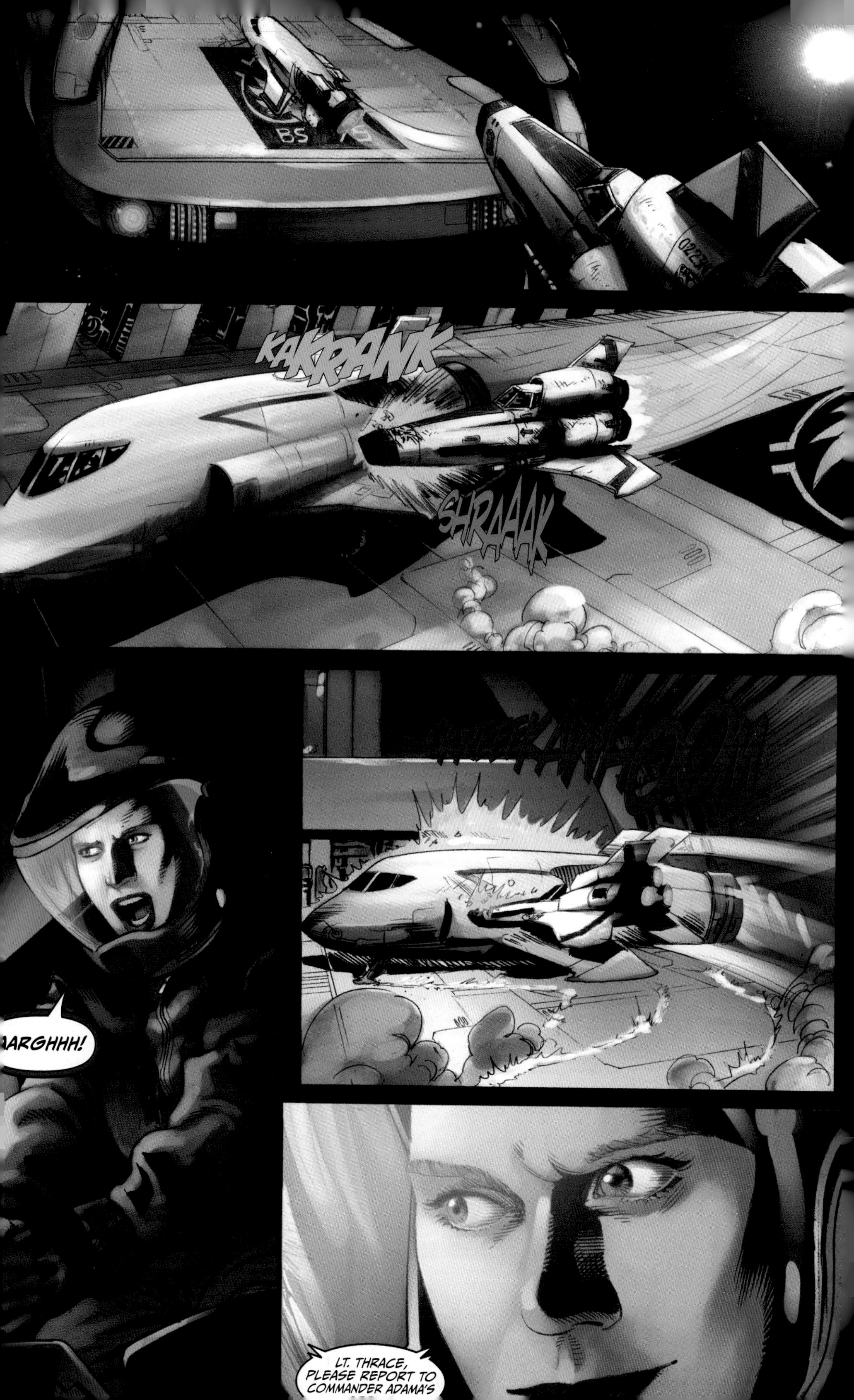
KAKRANK
SHRAAAK
ARGHHH!
LT. THRACE, PLEASE REPORT TO COMMANDER ADAMA'S

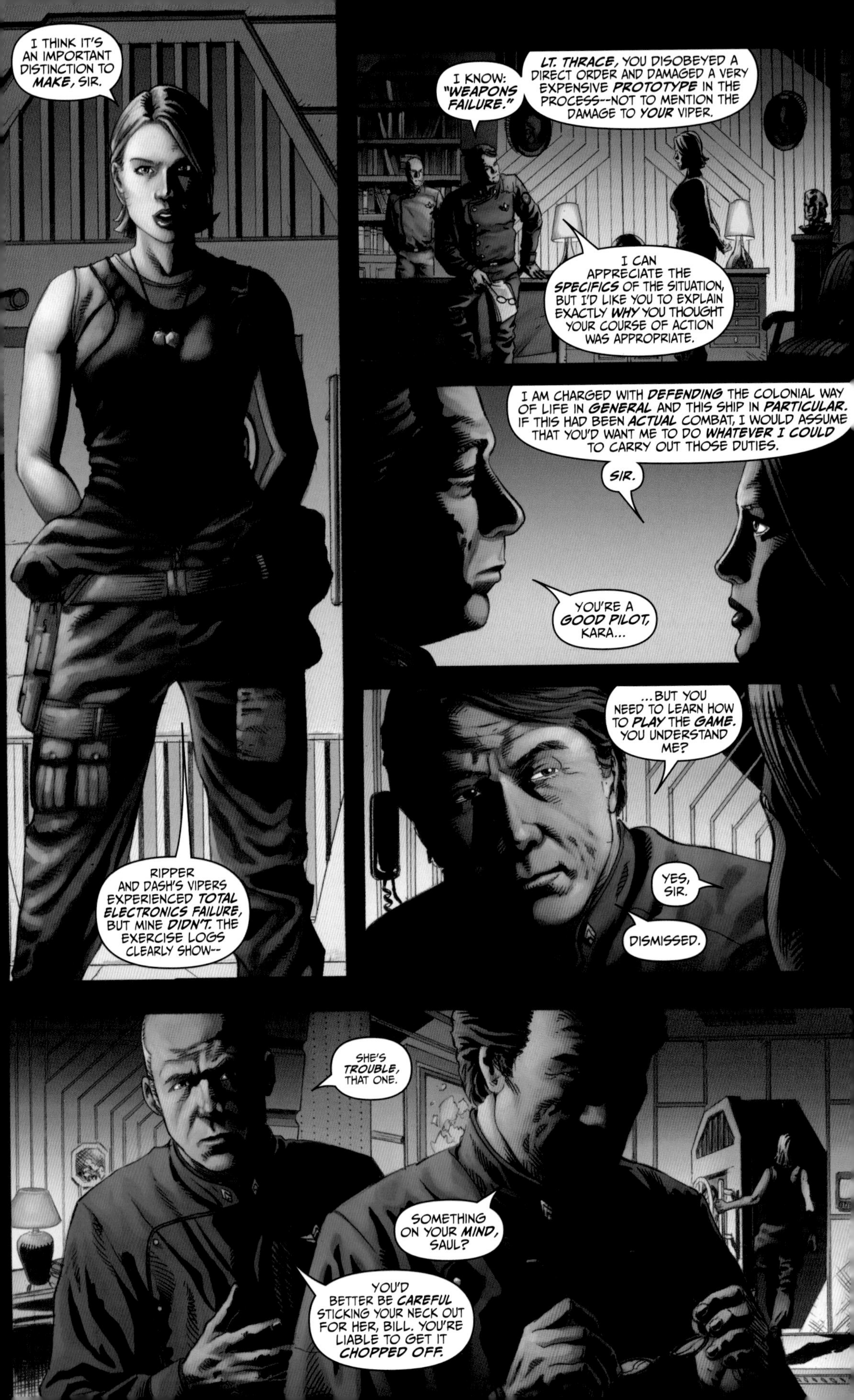

I THINK IT'S AN IMPORTANT DISTINCTION TO MAKE, SIR.
RIPPER AND DASH'S VIPERS EXPERIENCED TOTAL ELECTRONICS FAILURE, BUT MINE DIDN'T. THE EXERCISE LOGS CLEARLY SHOW--
I KNOW: "WEAPONS FAILURE."
LT. THRACE, YOU DISOBEYED A DIRECT ORDER AND DAMAGED A VERY EXPENSIVE PROTOTYPE IN THE PROCESS--NOT TO MENTION THE DAMAGE TO YOUR VIPER.
I CAN APPRECIATE THE SPECIFICS OF THE SITUATION, BUT I'D LIKE YOU TO EXPLAIN EXACTLY WHY YOU THOUGHT YOUR COURSE OF ACTION WAS APPROPRIATE.
I AM CHARGED WITH DEFENDING THE COLONIAL WAY OF LIFE IN GENERAL AND THIS SHIP IN PARTICULAR. IF THIS HAD BEEN ACTUAL COMBAT, I WOULD ASSUME THAT YOU'D WANT ME TO DO WHATEVER I COULD TO CARRY OUT THOSE DUTIES.
SIR.
YOU'RE A GOOD PILOT, KARA...
...BUT YOU NEED TO LEARN HOW TO PLAY THE GAME. YOU UNDERSTAND ME?
YES, SIR.
DISMISSED.
SHE'S TROUBLE, THAT ONE.
SOMETHING ON YOUR MIND, SAUL?
YOU'D BETTER BE CAREFUL STICKING YOUR NECK OUT FOR HER, BILL. YOU'RE LIABLE TO GET IT CHOPPED OFF.

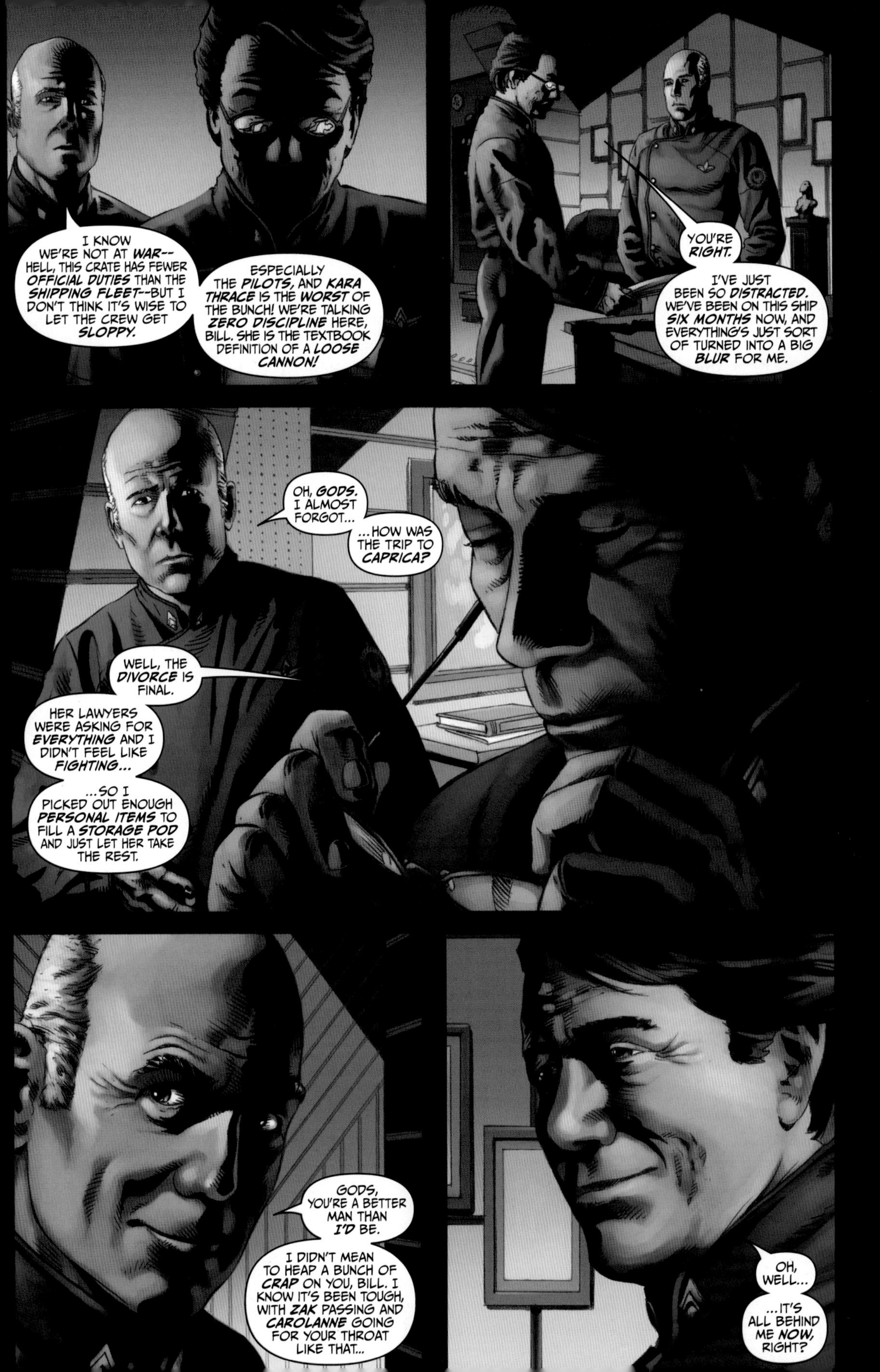
I KNOW WE'RE NOT AT WAR-- HELL, THIS CRATE HAS FEWER OFFICIAL DUTIES THAN THE SHIPPING FLEET--BUT I DON'T THINK IT'S WISE TO LET THE CREW GET SLOPPY.
ESPECIALLY THE PILOTS, AND KARA THRACE IS THE WORST OF THE BUNCH! WE'RE TALKING ZERO DISCIPLINE HERE, BILL. SHE IS THE TEXTBOOK DEFINITION OF A LOOSE CANNON!
YOU'RE RIGHT.
I'VE JUST BEEN SO DISTRACTED. WE'VE BEEN ON THIS SHIP SIX MONTHS NOW, AND EVERYTHING'S JUST SORT OF TURNED INTO A BIG BLUR FOR ME.
OH, GODS. I ALMOST FORGOT... ...HOW WAS THE TRIP TO CAPRICA?
WELL, THE DIVORCE IS FINAL.
HER LAWYERS WERE ASKING FOR EVERYTHING AND I DIDN'T FEEL LIKE FIGHTING...
...SO I PICKED OUT ENOUGH PERSONAL ITEMS TO FILL A STORAGE POD AND JUST LET HER TAKE THE REST.
GODS, YOU'RE A BETTER MAN THAN I'D BE.
I DIDN'T MEAN TO HEAP A BUNCH OF CRAP ON YOU, BILL. I KNOW IT'S BEEN TOUGH, WITH ZAK PASSING AND CAROLANNE GOING FOR YOUR THROAT LIKE THAT...
OH, WELL...
...IT'S ALL BEHIND ME NOW, RIGHT?

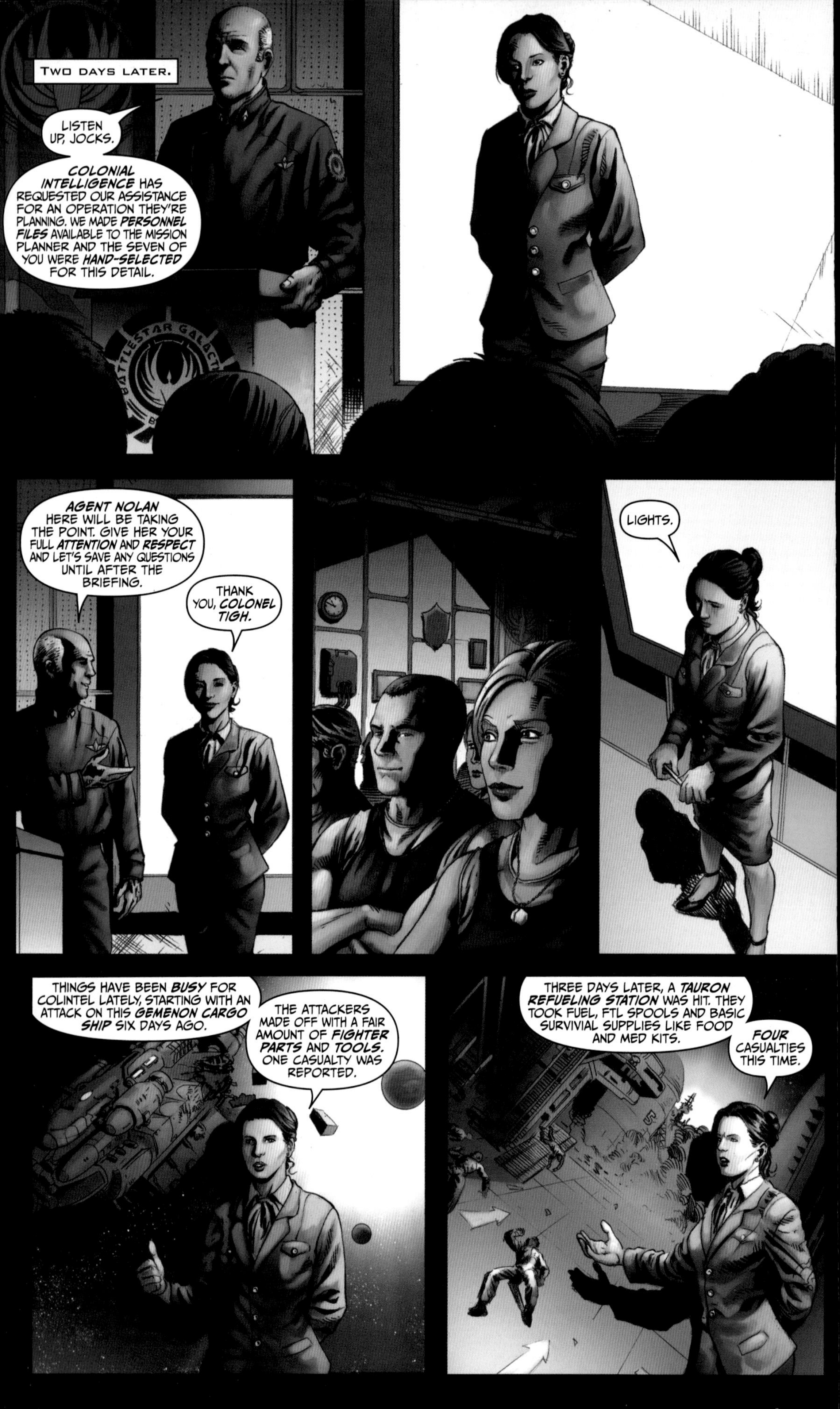
TWO DAYS LATER.
LISTEN UP, JOCKS.
COLONIAL INTELLIGENCE HAS REQUESTED OUR ASSISTANCE FOR AN OPERATION THEY'RE PLANNING. WE MADE PERSONNEL FILES AVAILABLE TO THE MISSION PLANNER AND THE SEVEN OF YOU WERE HAND-SELECTED FOR THIS DETAIL.
AGENT NOLAN HERE WILL BE TAKING THE POINT. GIVE HER YOUR FULL ATTENTION AND RESPECT AND LET'S SAVE ANY QUESTIONS UNTIL AFTER THE BRIEFING.
THANK YOU, COLONEL TIGH.
LIGHTS.
THINGS HAVE BEEN BUSY FOR COLINTEL LATELY, STARTING WITH AN ATTACK ON THIS GEMENON CARGO SHIP SIX DAYS AGO.
THE ATTACKERS MADE OFF WITH A FAIR AMOUNT OF FIGHTER PARTS AND TOOLS. ONE CASUALTY WAS REPORTED.
THREE DAYS LATER, A TAURON REFUELING STATION WAS HIT. THEY TOOK FUEL, FTL SPOOLS AND BASIC SURVIVIAL SUPPLIES LIKE FOOD AND MED KITS.
FOUR CASUALTIES THIS TIME.

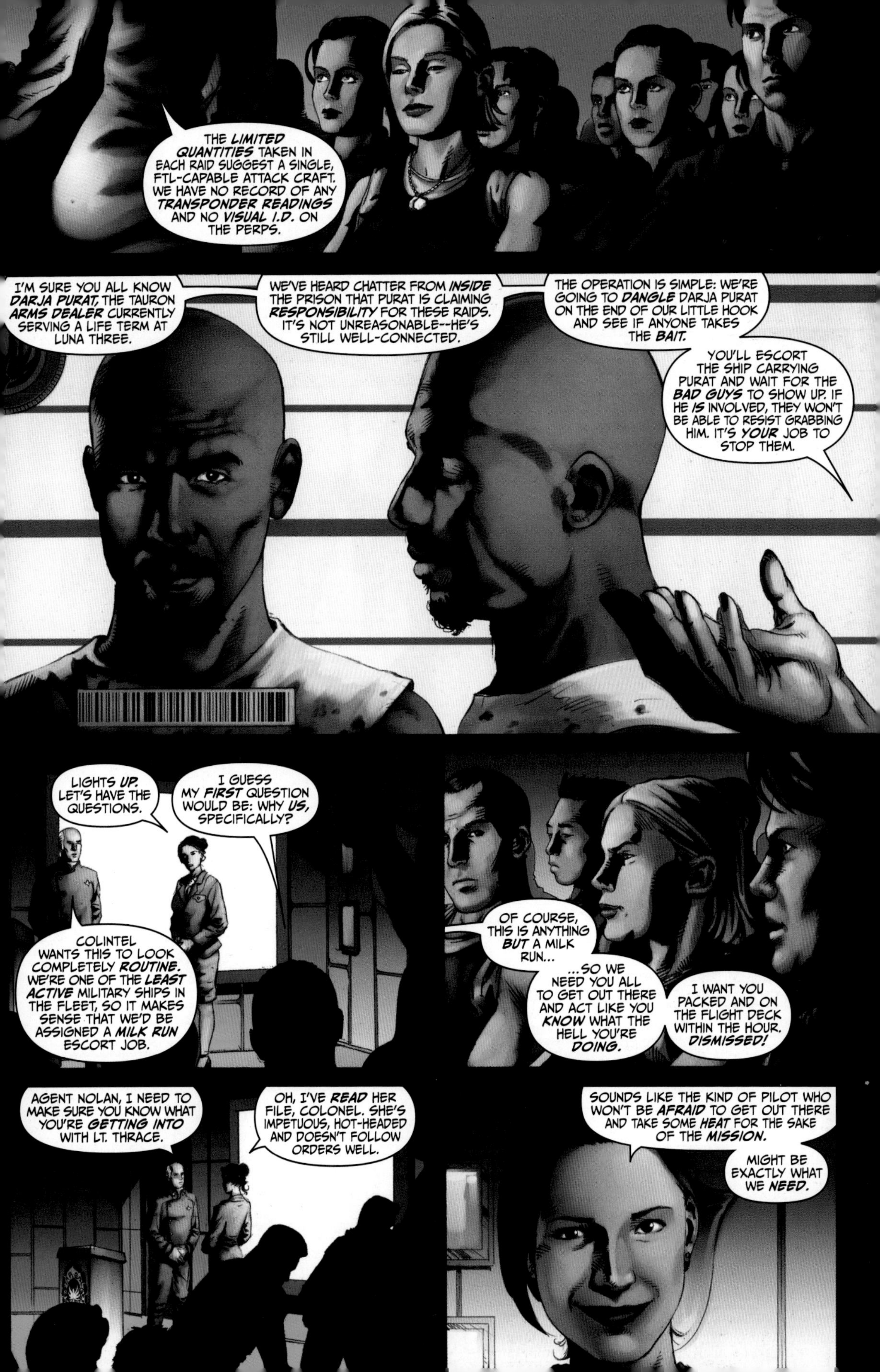
THE LIMITED QUANTITIES TAKEN IN EACH RAID SUGGEST A SINGLE, FTL-CAPABLE ATTACK CRAFT. WE HAVE NO RECORD OF ANY TRANSPONDER READINGS AND NO VISUAL I.D. ON THE PERPS.
I'M SURE YOU ALL KNOW DARJA PURAT, THE TAURON ARMS DEALER CURRENTLY SERVING A LIFE TERM AT LUNA THREE.
WE'VE HEARD CHATTER FROM INSIDE THE PRISON THAT PURAT IS CLAIMING RESPONSIBILITY FOR THESE RAIDS. IT'S NOT UNREASONABLE--HE'S STILL WELL-CONNECTED.
THE OPERATION IS SIMPLE: WE'RE GOING TO DANGLE DARJA PURAT ON THE END OF OUR LITTLE HOOK AND SEE IF ANYONE TAKES THE BAIT.
YOU'LL ESCORT THE SHIP CARRYING PURAT AND WAIT FOR THE BAD GUYS TO SHOW UP. IF HE IS INVOLVED, THEY WON'T BE ABLE TO RESIST GRABBING HIM. IT'S YOUR JOB TO STOP THEM.
LIGHTS UP. LET'S HAVE THE QUESTIONS.
I GUESS MY FIRST QUESTION WOULD BE: WHY US, SPECIFICALLY?
COLINTEL WANTS THIS TO LOOK COMPLETELY ROUTINE. WE'RE ONE OF THE LEAST ACTIVE MILITARY SHIPS IN THE FLEET, SO IT MAKES SENSE THAT WE'D BE ASSIGNED A MILK RUN ESCORT JOB.
OF COURSE, THIS IS ANYTHING BUT A MILK RUN...
...SO WE NEED YOU ALL TO GET OUT THERE AND ACT LIKE YOU KNOW WHAT THE HELL YOU'RE DOING.
I WANT YOU PACKED AND ON THE FLIGHT DECK WITHIN THE HOUR. DISMISSED!
AGENT NOLAN, I NEED TO MAKE SURE YOU KNOW WHAT YOU'RE GETTING INTO WITH LT. THRACE.
OH, I'VE READ HER FILE, COLONEL. SHE'S IMPETUOUS, HOT-HEADED AND DOESN'T FOLLOW ORDERS WELL.
SOUNDS LIKE THE KIND OF PILOT WHO WON'T BE AFRAID TO GET OUT THERE AND TAKE SOME HEAT FOR THE SAKE OF THE MISSION.
MIGHT BE EXACTLY WHAT WE NEED.

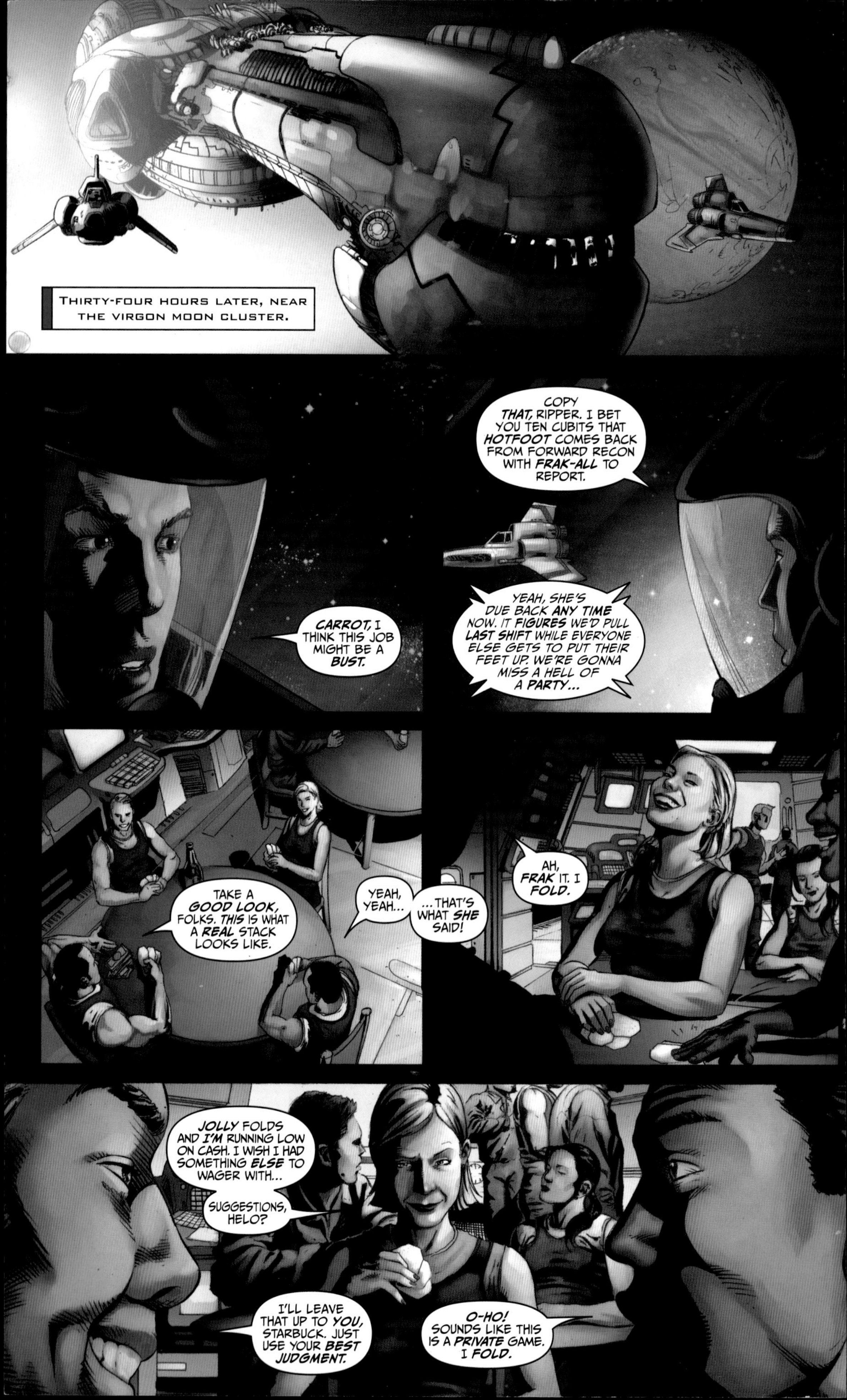
THIRTY-FOUR HOURS LATER, NEAR THE VIRGON MOON CLUSTER.
CARROT, I THINK THIS JOB MIGHT BE A BUST.
COPY THAT, RIPPER. I BET YOU TEN CUBITS THAT HOTFOOT COMES BACK FROM FORWARD RECON WITH FRAK-ALL TO REPORT.
YEAH, SHE'S DUE BACK ANY TIME NOW. IT FIGURES WE'D PULL LAST SHIFT WHILE EVERYONE ELSE GETS TO PUT THEIR FEET UP. WE'RE GONNA MISS A HELL OF A PARTY...
TAKE A GOOD LOOK, FOLKS. THIS IS WHAT A REAL STACK LOOKS LIKE.
YEAH, YEAH...
...THAT'S WHAT SHE SAID!
AH, FRAK IT. I FOLD.
JOLLY FOLDS AND I'M RUNNING LOW ON CASH. I WISH I HAD SOMETHING ELSE TO WAGER WITH...
SUGGESTIONS, HELO?
I'LL LEAVE THAT UP TO YOU, STARBUCK. JUST USE YOUR BEST JUDGMENT.
O-HO! SOUNDS LIKE THIS IS A PRIVATE GAME. I FOLD.

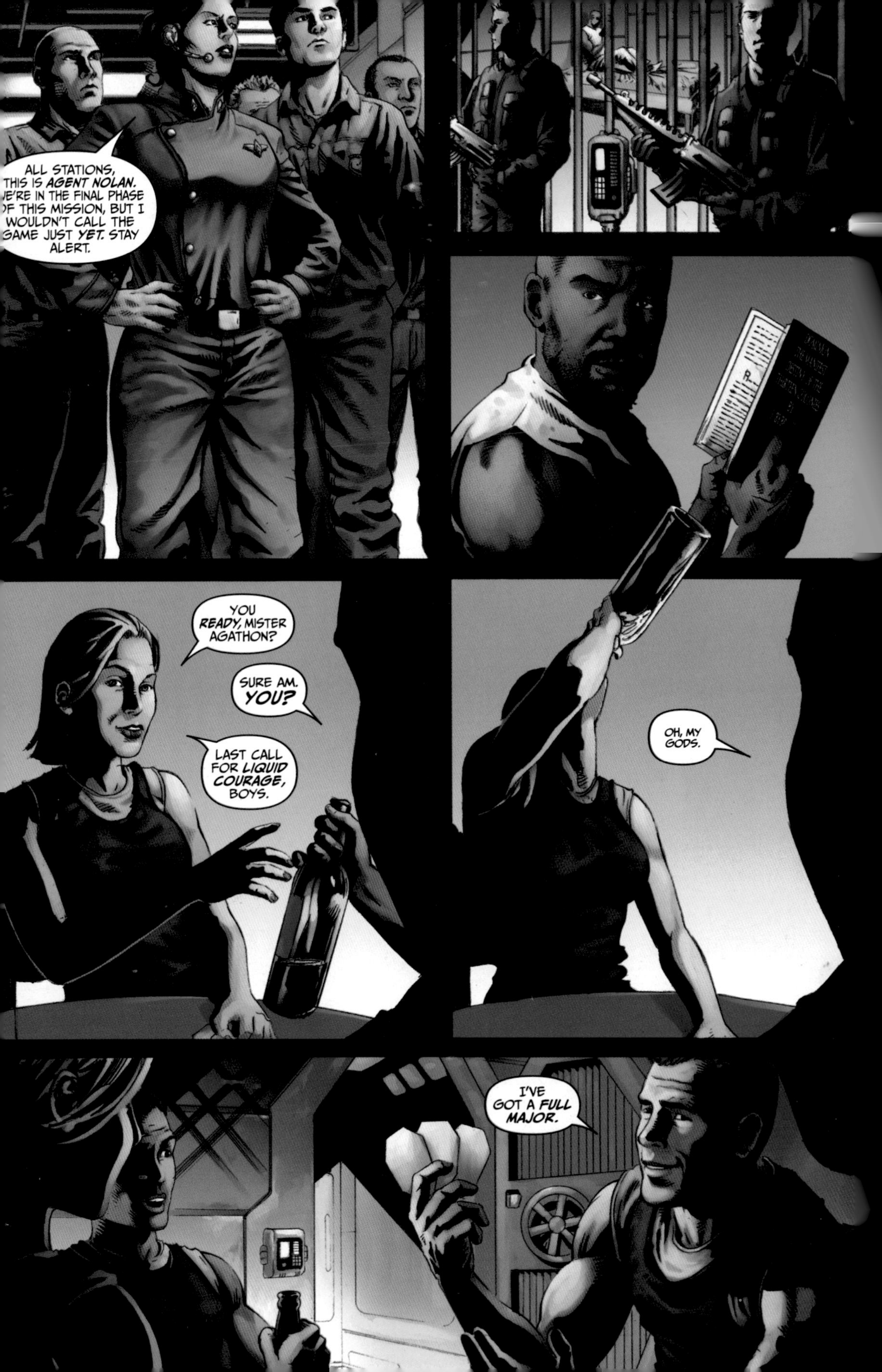
ALL STATIONS, THIS IS AGENT NOLAN. WE'RE IN THE FINAL PHASE OF THIS MISSION, BUT I WOULDN'T CALL THE GAME JUST YET. STAY ALERT.
YOU READY, MISTER AGATHON?
SURE AM. YOU?
LAST CALL FOR LIQUID COURAGE, BOYS.
OH, MY GODS.
I'VE GOT A FULL MAJOR.

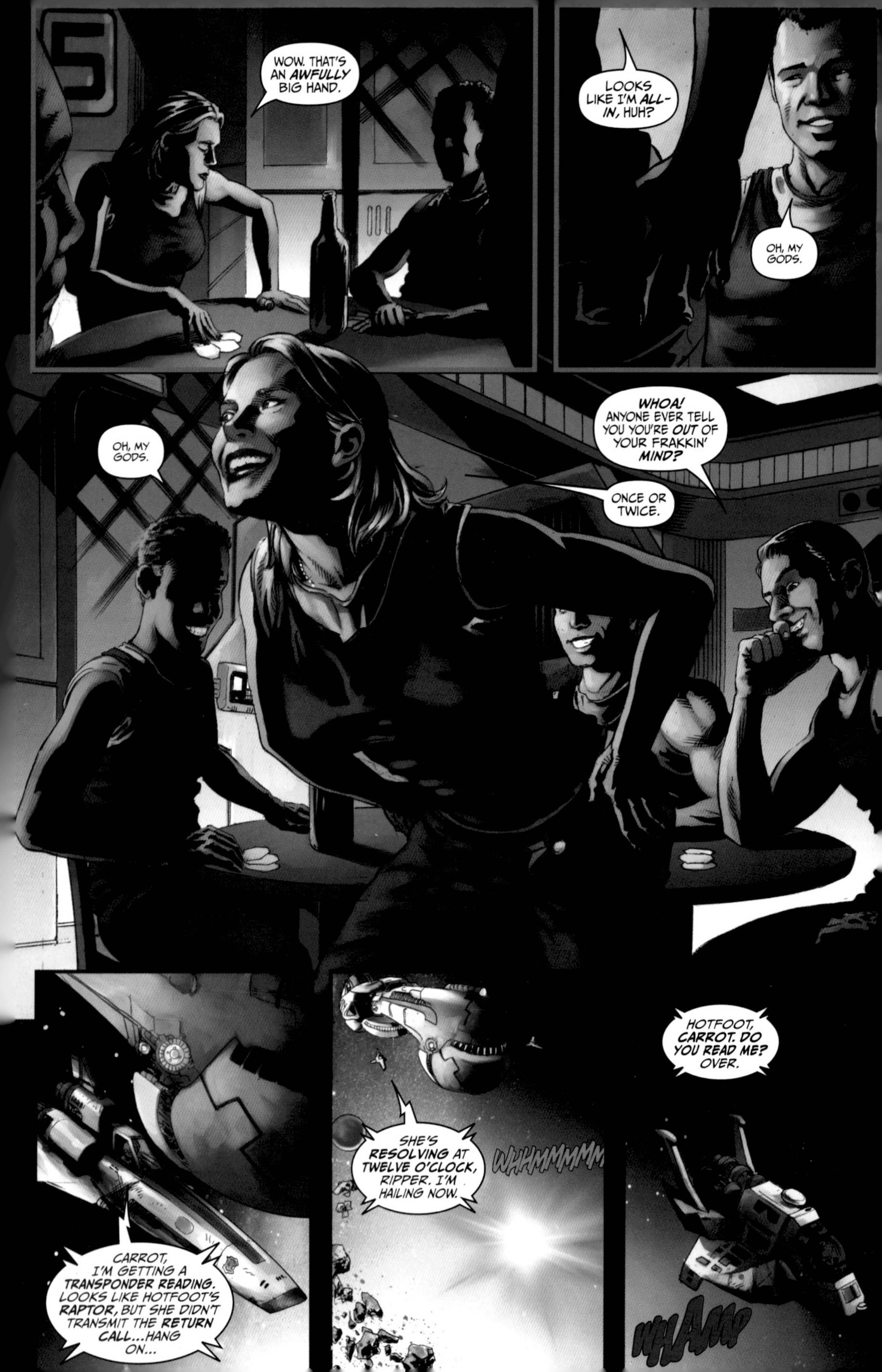

WOW. THAT'S AN AWFULLY BIG HAND.
LOOKS LIKE I'M ALL-IN, HUH?
OH, MY GODS.
OH, MY GODS.
WHOA! ANYONE EVER TELL YOU YOU'RE OUT OF YOUR FRAKKIN' MIND?
ONCE OR TWICE.
CARROT, I'M GETTING A TRANSPONDER READING. LOOKS LIKE HOTFOOT'S RAPTOR, BUT SHE DIDN'T TRANSMIT THE RETURN CALL...HANG ON...
SHE'S RESOLVING AT TWELVE O'CLOCK, RIPPER. I'M HAILING NOW.
WHHMMMMMM
HOTFOOT, CARROT. DO YOU READ ME? OVER.
WHAMP

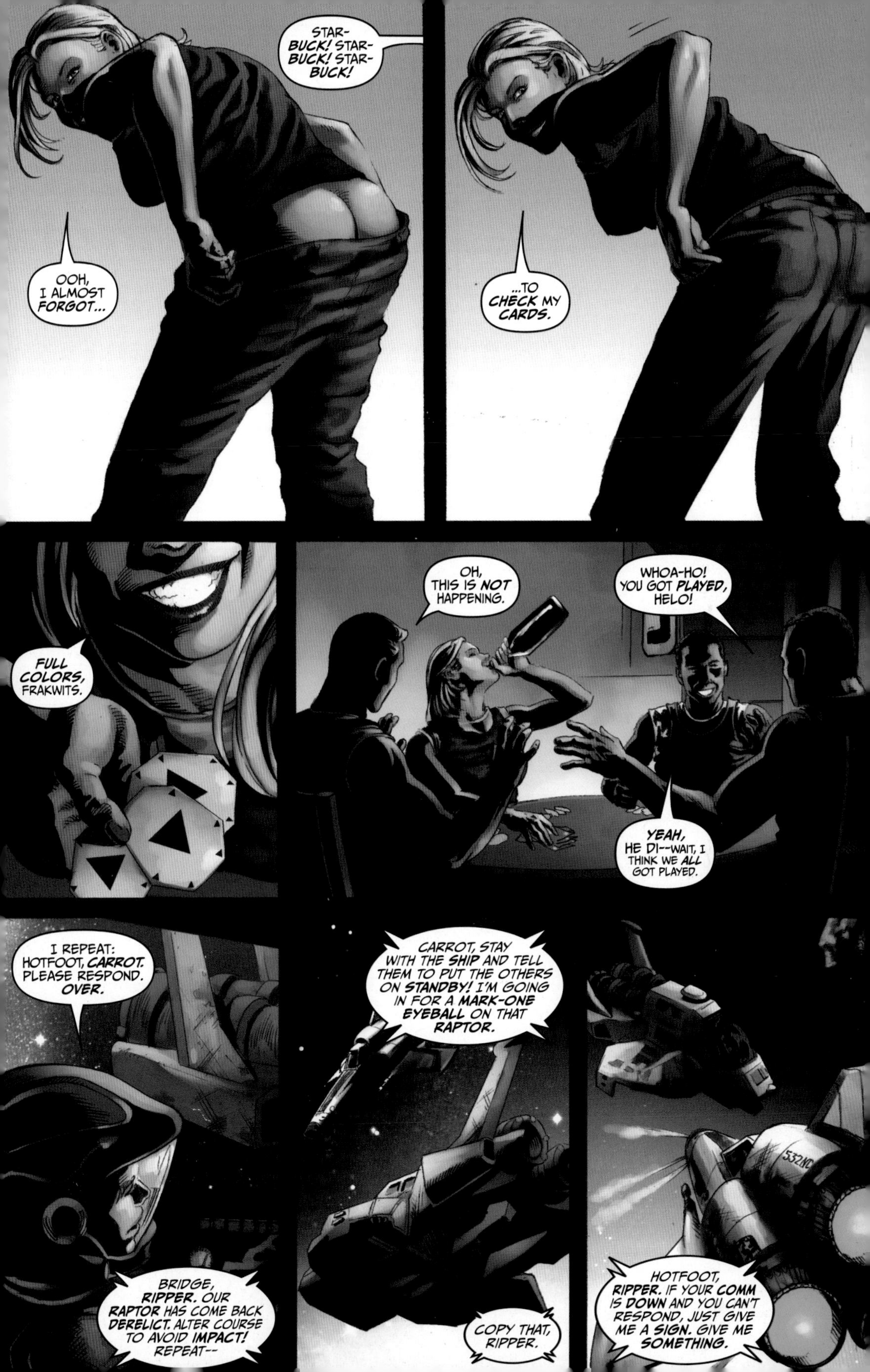
STAR-BUCK! STAR-BUCK! STAR-BUCK!
OOH, I ALMOST FORGOT...
...TO CHECK MY CARDS.
FULL COLORS, FRAKWITS.
OH, THIS IS NOT HAPPENING.
WHOA-HO! YOU GOT PLAYED, HELO!
YEAH, HE DI--WAIT, I THINK WE ALL GOT PLAYED.
I REPEAT: HOTFOOT, CARROT. PLEASE RESPOND. OVER.
BRIDGE, RIPPER. OUR RAPTOR HAS COME BACK DERELICT. ALTER COURSE TO AVOID IMPACT! REPEAT--
CARROT, STAY WITH THE SHIP AND TELL THEM TO PUT THE OTHERS ON STANDBY! I'M GOING IN FOR A MARK-ONE EYEBALL ON THAT RAPTOR.
COPY THAT, RIPPER.
532NC
HOTFOOT, RIPPER. IF YOUR COMM IS DOWN AND YOU CAN'T RESPOND, JUST GIVE ME A SIGN. GIVE ME SOMETHING.

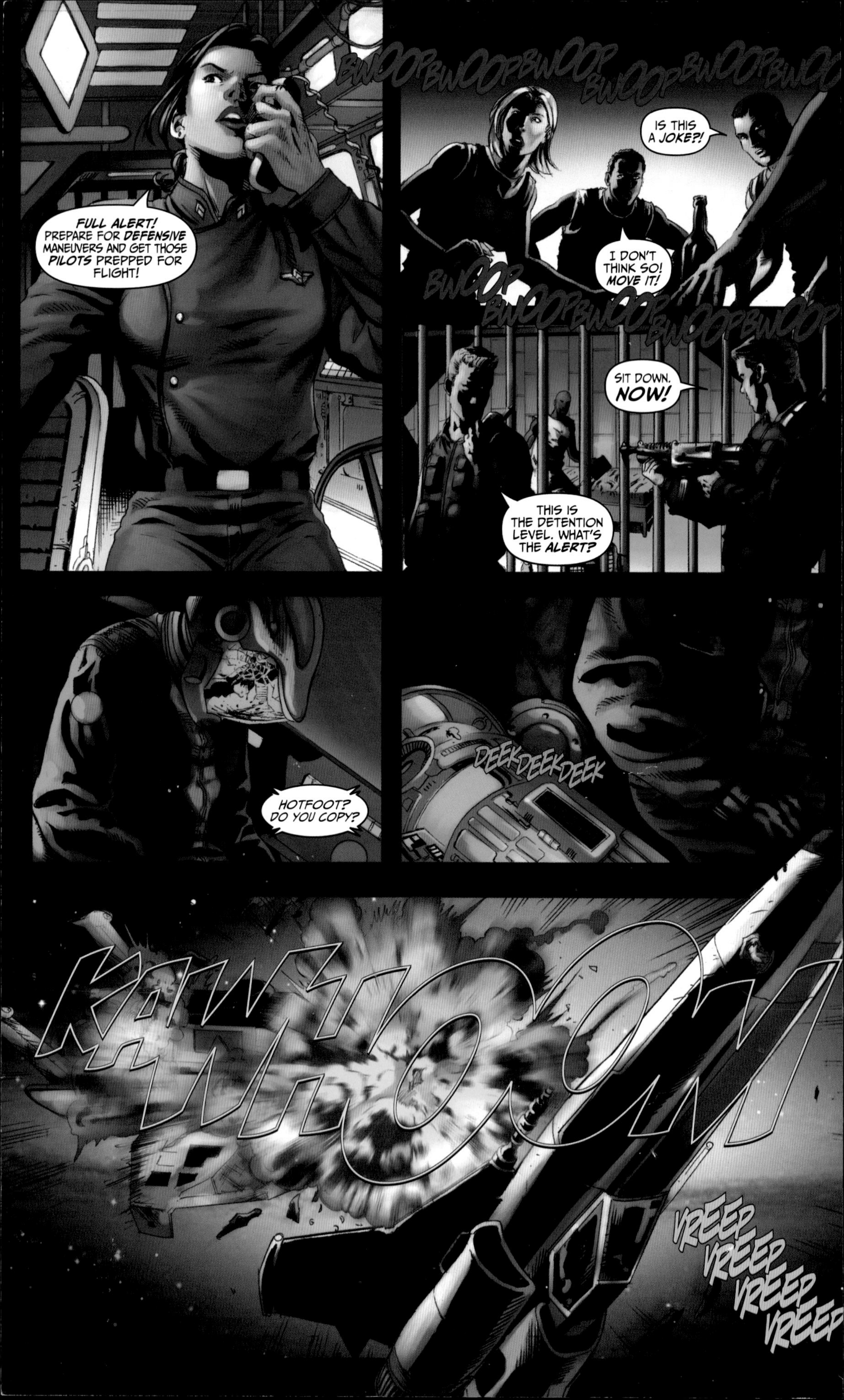
FULL ALERT! PREPARE FOR DEFENSIVE MANEUVERS AND GET THOSE PILOTS PREPPED FOR FLIGHT!
BWOOPBWOOPBWOOP
BWOOPBWOOPBWOO
IS THIS A JOKE?!
I DON'T THINK SO! MOVE IT!
BWOOP
BWOOPBWOOP
BWOOPBWOOP
SIT DOWN. NOW!
THIS IS THE DETENTION LEVEL. WHAT'S THE ALERT?
HOTFOOT? DO YOU COPY?
DEEKDEEKDEEK
KAWHOOM
VREEP
VREEP
VREEP
VREEP

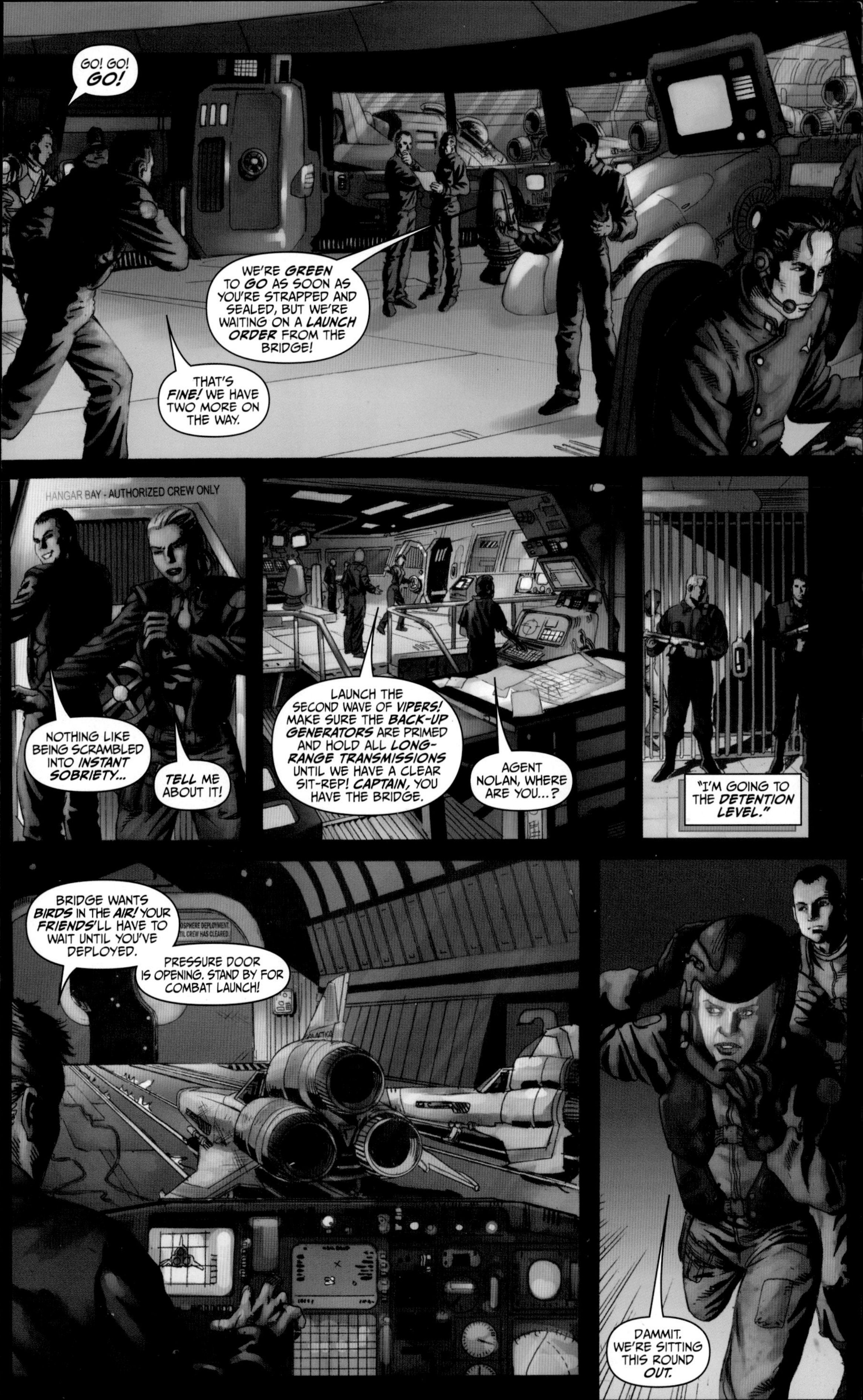
GO! GO! GO!
WE'RE GREEN TO GO AS SOON AS YOU'RE STRAPPED AND SEALED, BUT WE'RE WAITING ON A LAUNCH ORDER FROM THE BRIDGE!
THAT'S FINE! WE HAVE TWO MORE ON THE WAY.
HANGAR BAY - AUTHORIZED CREW ONLY
NOTHING LIKE BEING SCRAMBLED INTO INSTANT SOBRIETY...
TELL ME ABOUT IT!
LAUNCH THE SECOND WAVE OF VIPERS! MAKE SURE THE BACK-UP GENERATORS ARE PRIMED AND HOLD ALL LONG-RANGE TRANSMISSIONS UNTIL WE HAVE A CLEAR SIT-REP! CAPTAIN, YOU HAVE THE BRIDGE.
AGENT NOLAN, WHERE ARE YOU...?
"I'M GOING TO THE DETENTION LEVEL."
BRIDGE WANTS BIRDS IN THE AIR! YOUR FRIENDS'LL HAVE TO WAIT UNTIL YOU'VE DEPLOYED.
PRESSURE DOOR IS OPENING. STAND BY FOR COMBAT LAUNCH!
DAMMIT. WE'RE SITTING THIS ROUND OUT.

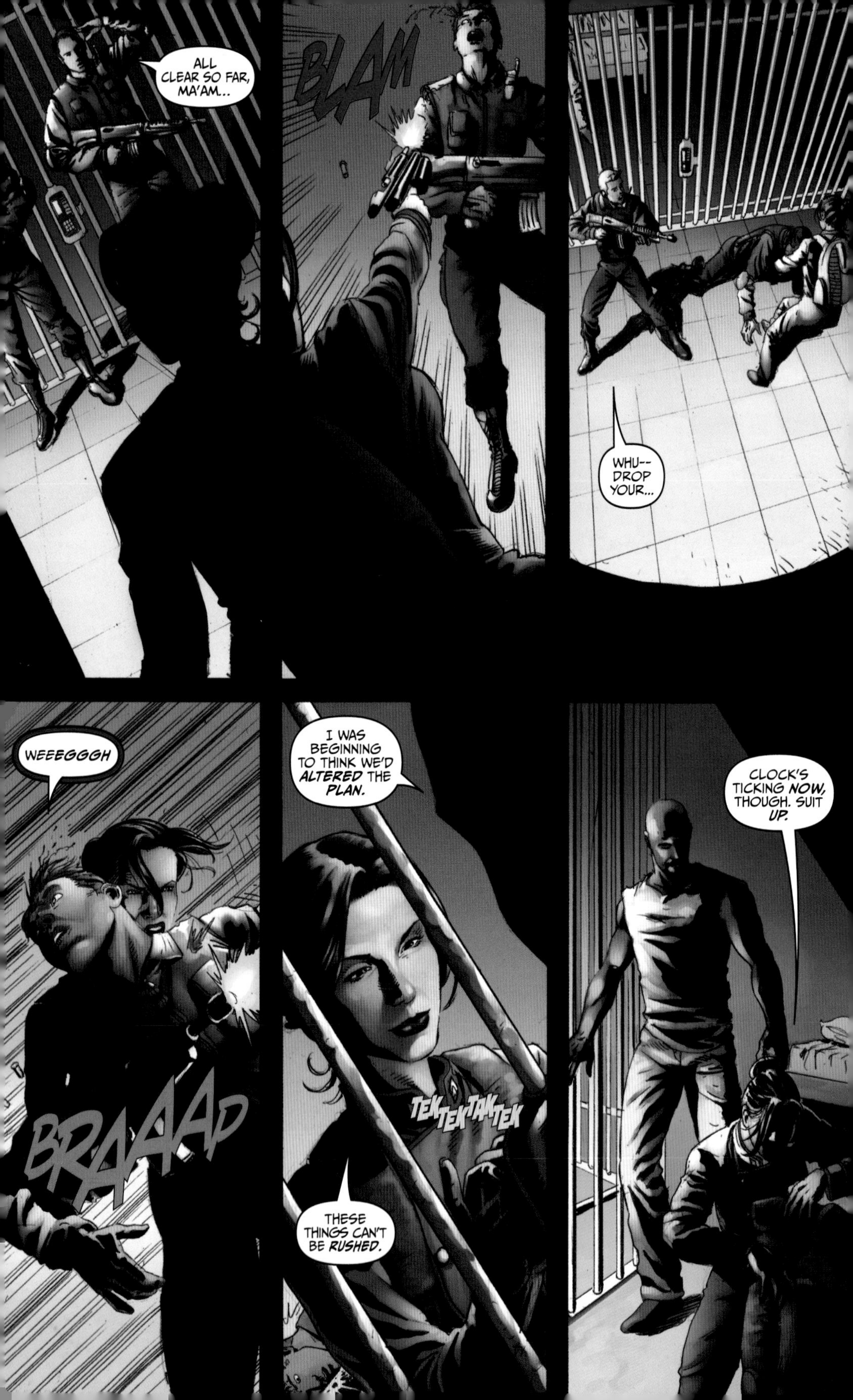
ALL CLEAR SO FAR, MA'AM...
BLAM
WHU-- DROP YOUR...
WEEEGGGH
BRAAAP
I WAS BEGINNING TO THINK WE'D *ALTERED* THE *PLAN.*
TEKTEKTAKTEK
THESE THINGS CAN'T BE *RUSHED*.
CLOCK'S TICKING *NOW,* THOUGH. SUIT *UP.*

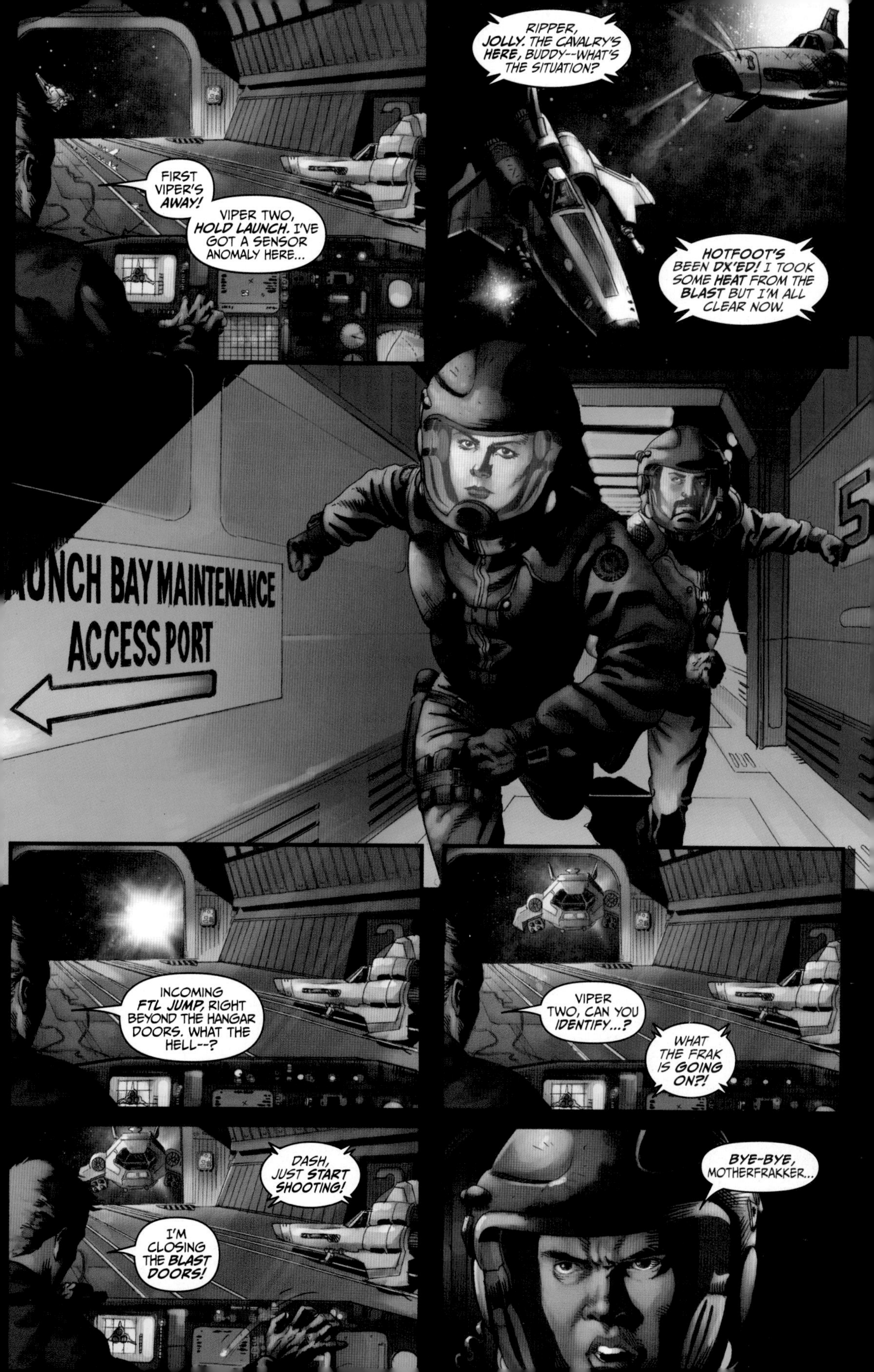

FIRST VIPER'S AWAY!
VIPER TWO, HOLD LAUNCH. I'VE GOT A SENSOR ANOMALY HERE...
RIPPER, JOLLY. THE CAVALRY'S HERE, BUDDY--WHAT'S THE SITUATION?
HOTFOOT'S BEEN DX'ED! I TOOK SOME HEAT FROM THE BLAST BUT I'M ALL CLEAR NOW.
UNCH BAY MAINTENANCE ACCESS PORT
5
INCOMING FTL JUMP, RIGHT BEYOND THE HANGAR DOORS. WHAT THE HELL--?
VIPER TWO, CAN YOU IDENTIFY...?
WHAT THE FRAK IS GOING ON?!
DASH, JUST START SHOOTING!
I'M CLOSING THE BLAST DOORS!
BYE-BYE, MOTHERFRAKKER...

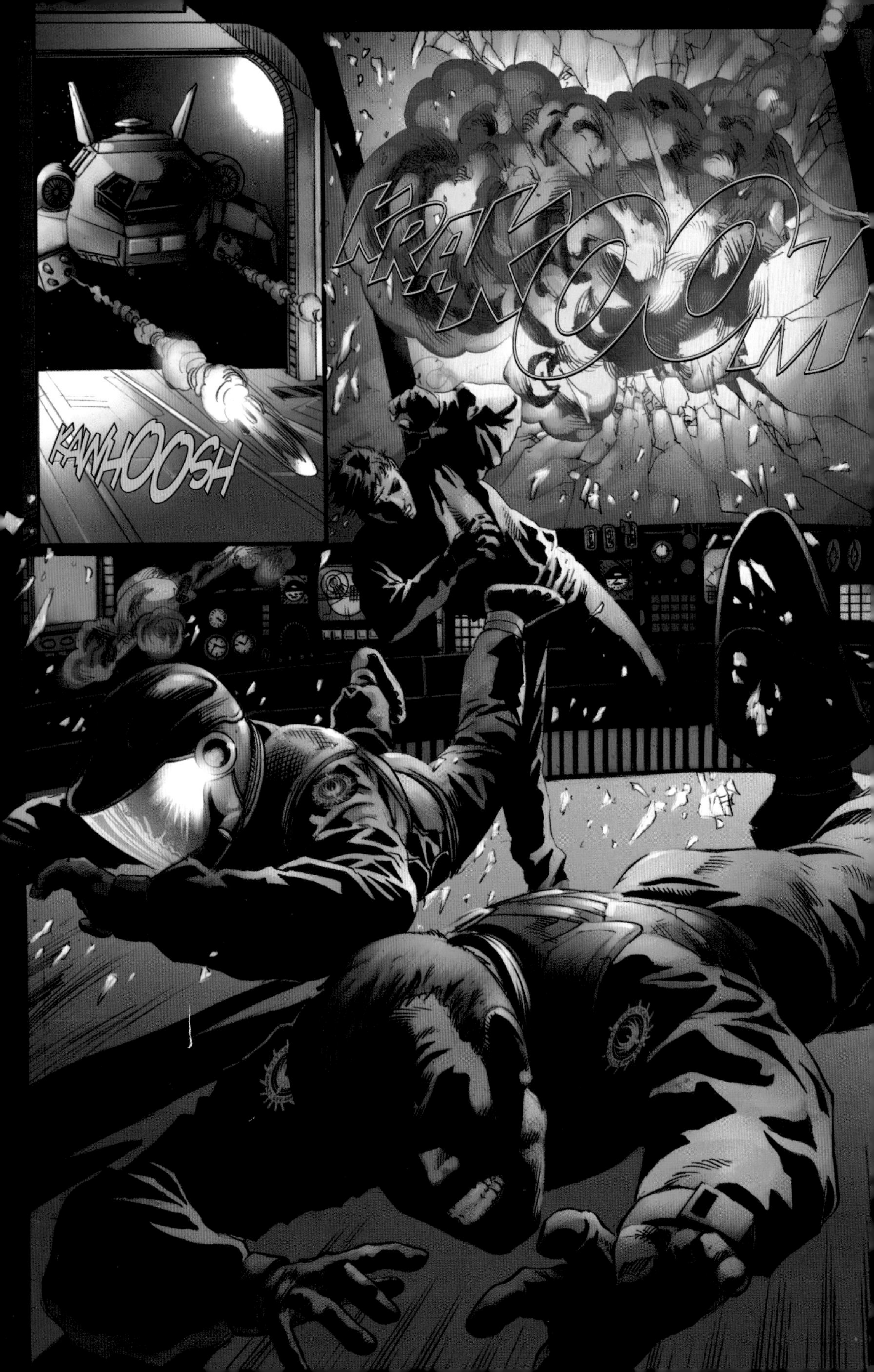
KAWHOOSH
KRAKOOOM

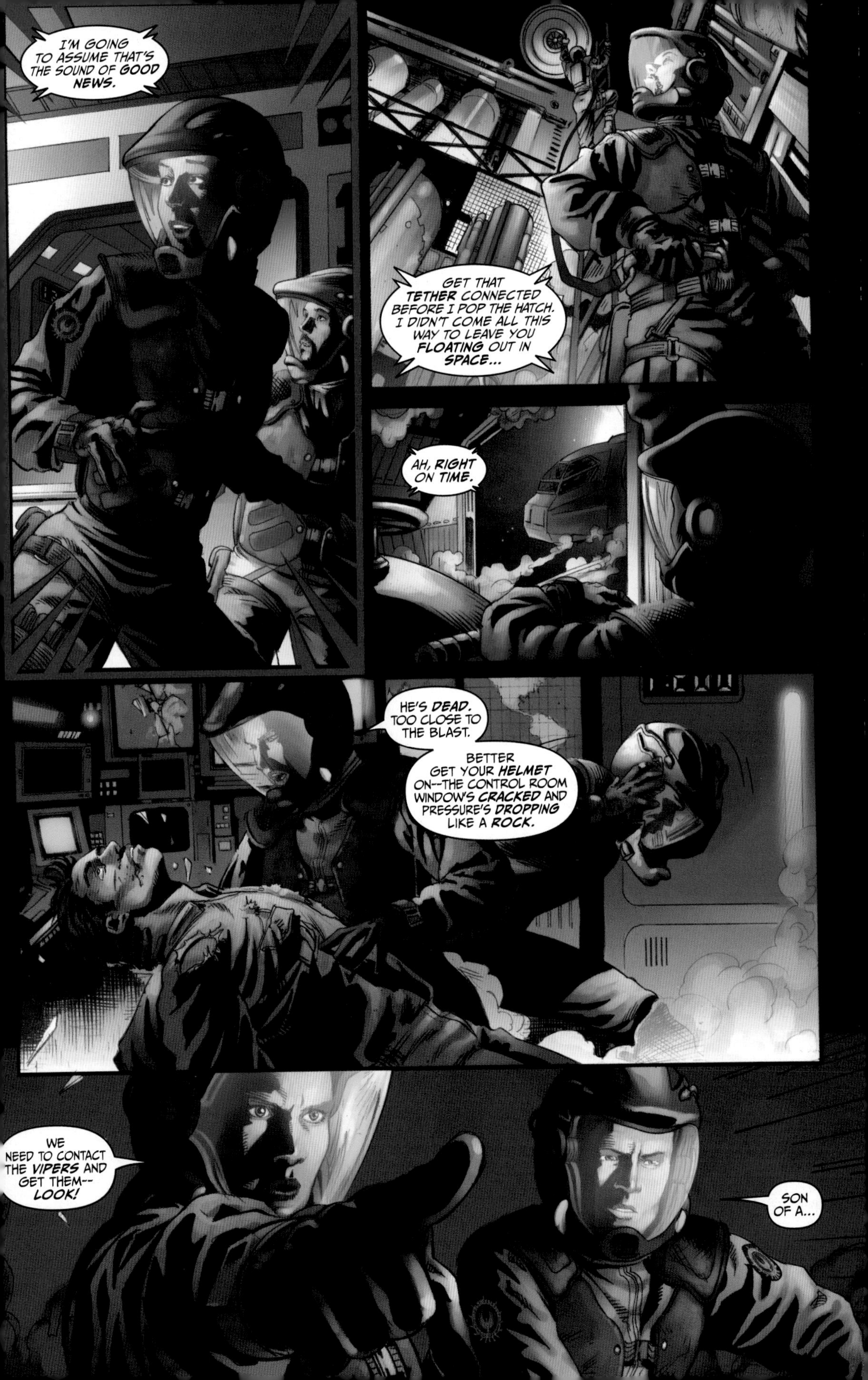
I'M GOING TO ASSUME THAT'S THE SOUND OF GOOD NEWS.
GET THAT TETHER CONNECTED BEFORE I POP THE HATCH. I DIDN'T COME ALL THIS WAY TO LEAVE YOU FLOATING OUT IN SPACE...
AH, RIGHT ON TIME.
HE'S DEAD. TOO CLOSE TO THE BLAST.
BETTER GET YOUR HELMET ON--THE CONTROL ROOM WINDOW'S CRACKED AND PRESSURE'S DROPPING LIKE A ROCK.
WE NEED TO CONTACT THE VIPERS AND GET THEM-- LOOK!
SON OF A...

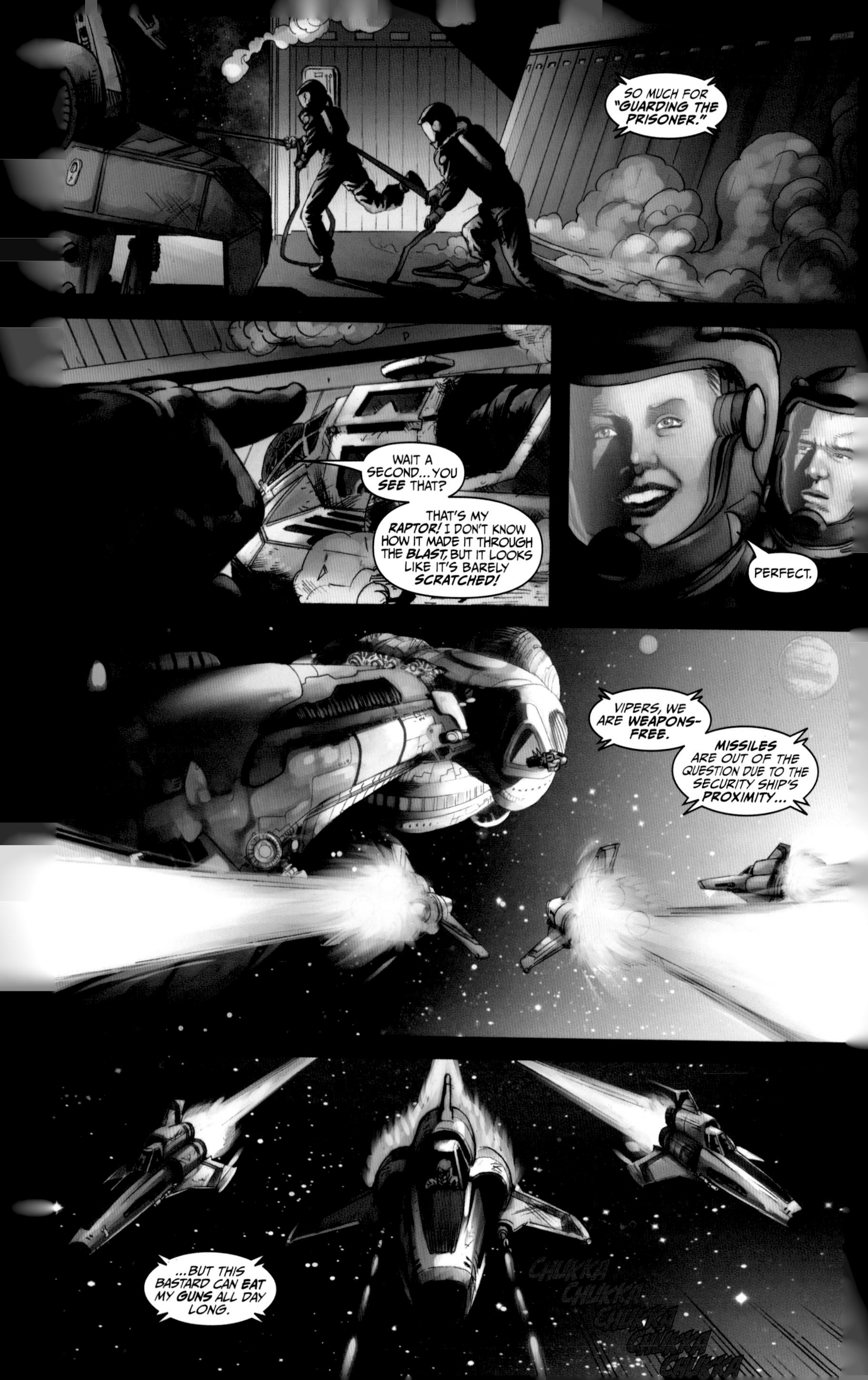
SO MUCH FOR "GUARDING THE PRISONER."
WAIT A SECOND... YOU SEE THAT?
THAT'S MY RAPTOR! I DON'T KNOW HOW IT MADE IT THROUGH THE BLAST, BUT IT LOOKS LIKE IT'S BARELY SCRATCHED!
PERFECT.
VIPERS, WE ARE WEAPONS-FREE.
MISSILES ARE OUT OF THE QUESTION DUE TO THE SECURITY SHIP'S PROXIMITY...
...BUT THIS BASTARD CAN EAT MY GUNS ALL DAY LONG.
CHUKKA CHUKKA CHUKKA CHUKKA CHUKKA

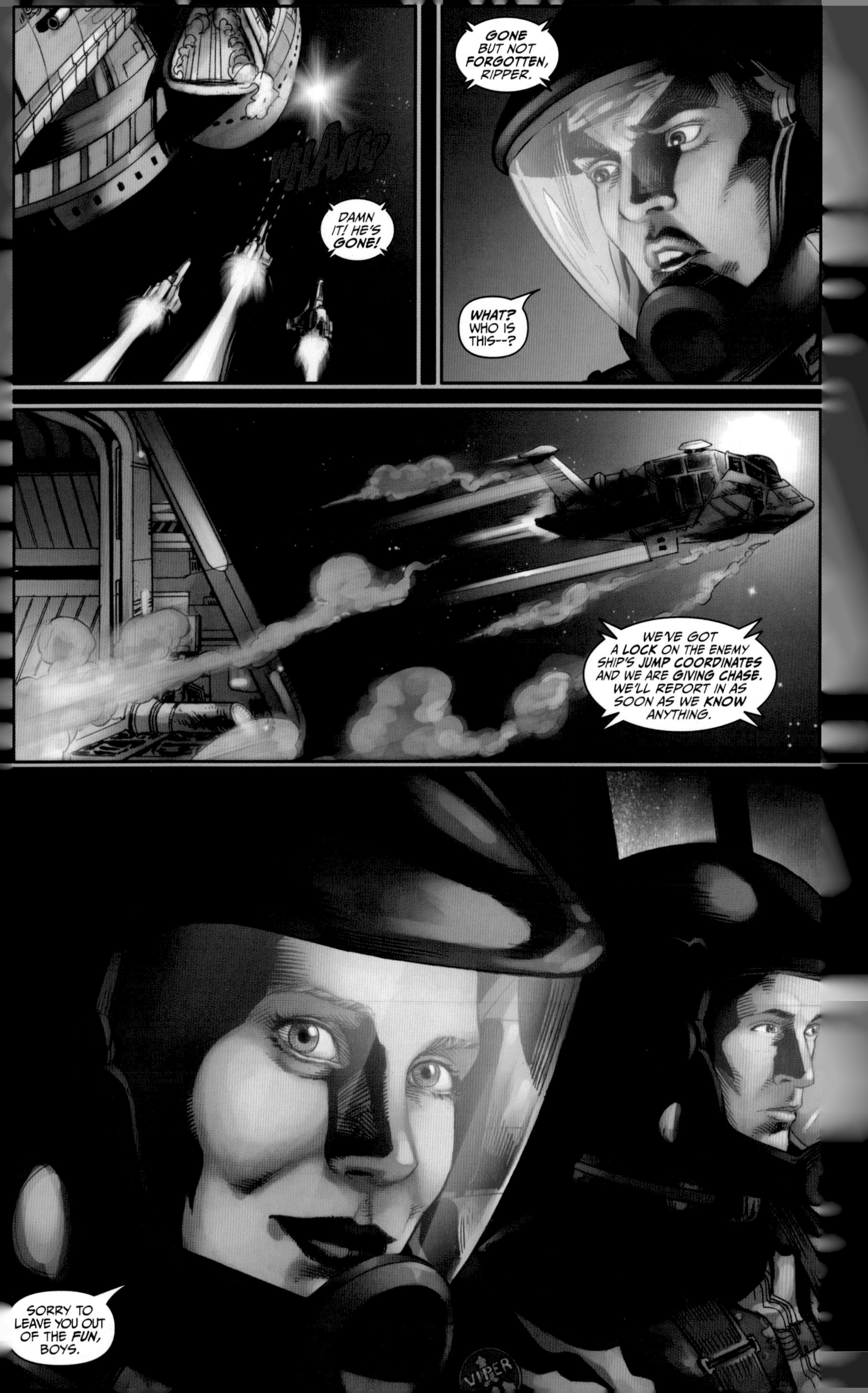
WHAM!
DAMN IT! HE'S GONE!
GONE BUT NOT FORGOTTEN, RIPPER.
WHAT? WHO IS THIS--?
WE'VE GOT A LOCK ON THE ENEMY SHIP'S JUMP COORDINATES AND WE ARE GIVING CHASE. WE'LL REPORT IN AS SOON AS WE KNOW ANYTHING.
SORRY TO LEAVE YOU OUT OF THE FUN, BOYS.
VIPER

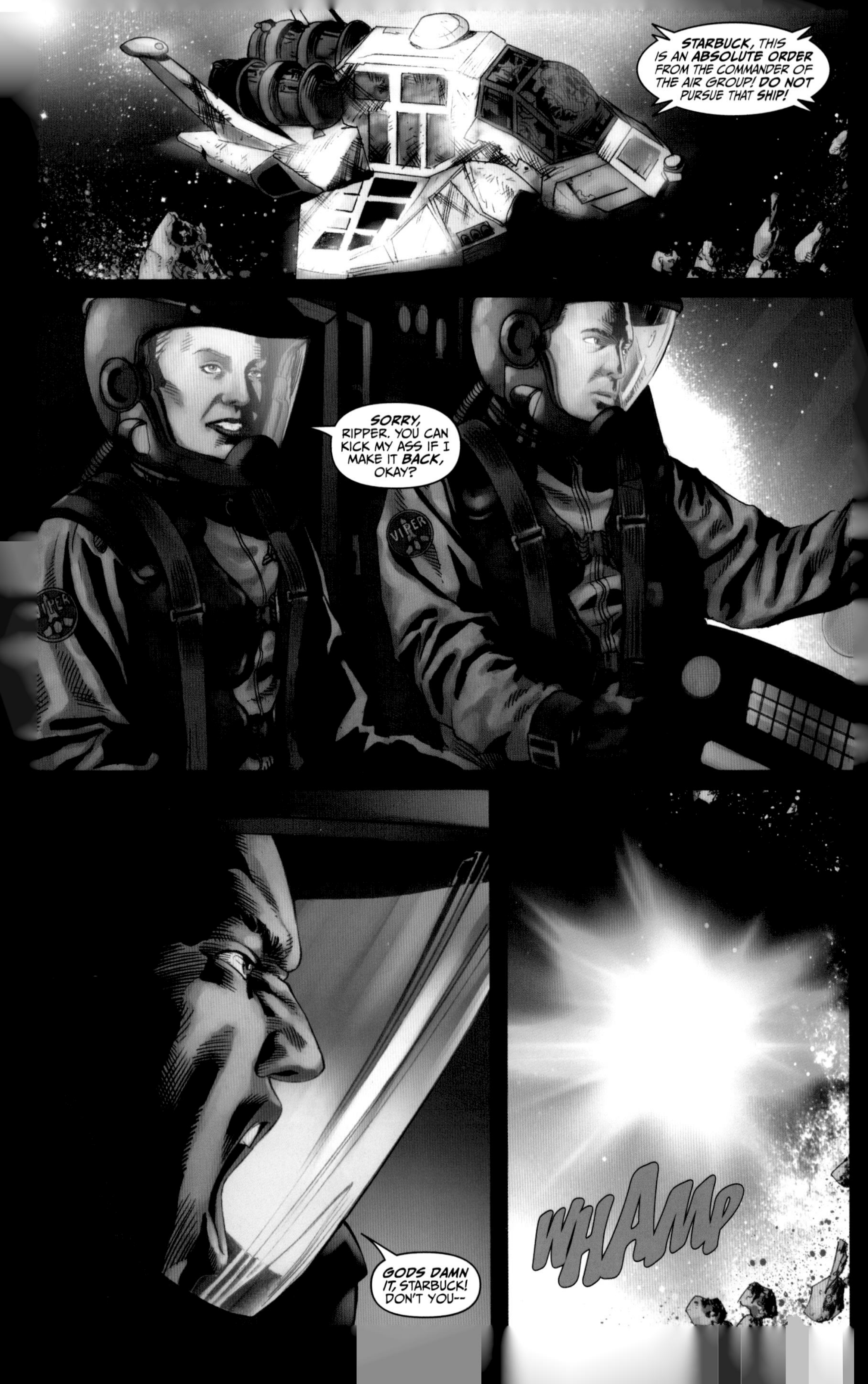
STARBUCK, THIS IS AN ABSOLUTE ORDER FROM THE COMMANDER OF THE AIR GROUP! DO NOT PURSUE THAT SHIP!
SORRY, RIPPER. YOU CAN KICK MY ASS IF I MAKE IT BACK, OKAY?
VIPER
VIPER
GODS DAMN IT, STARBUCK! DON'T YOU--
WHAM

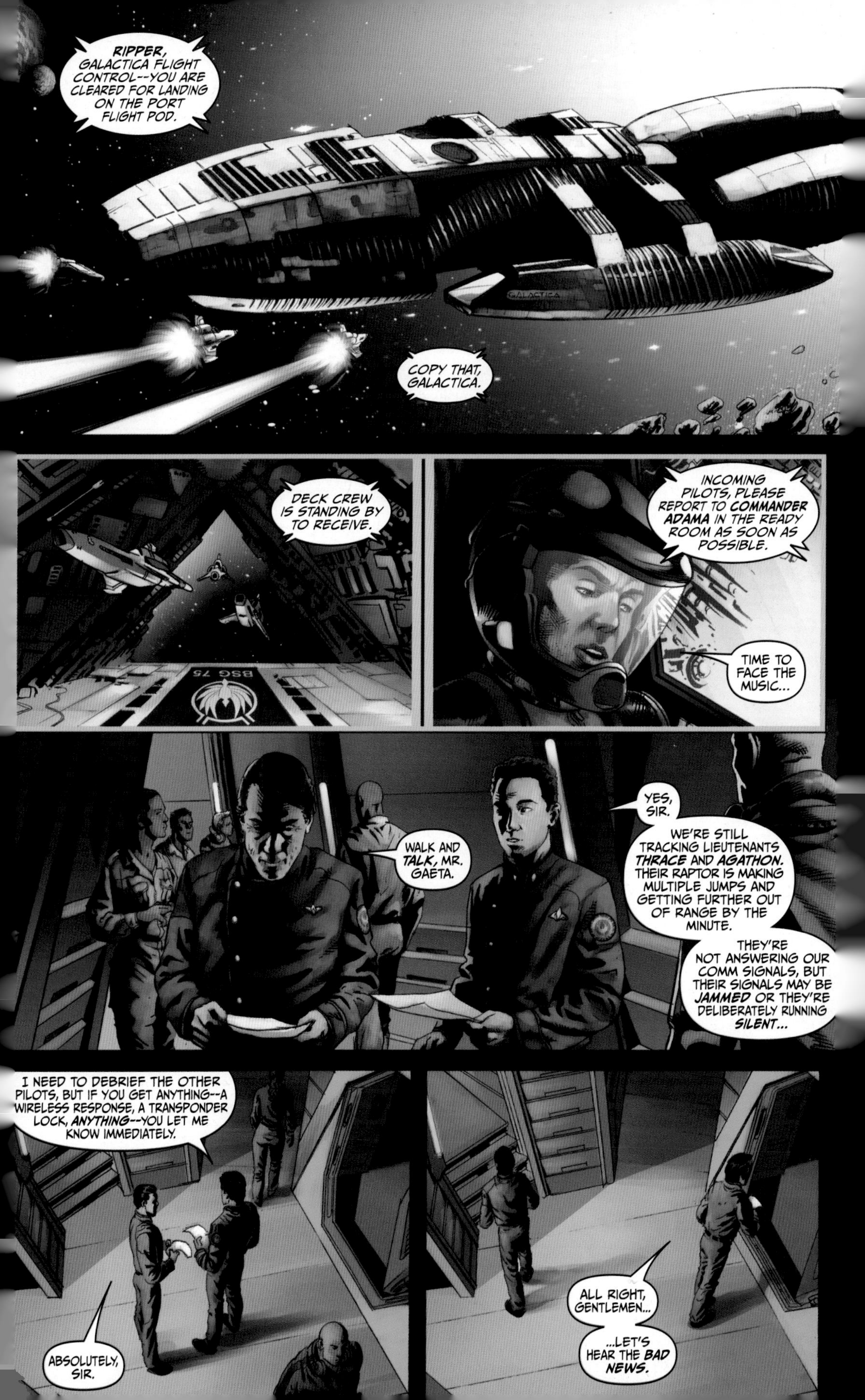
RIPPER, GALACTICA FLIGHT CONTROL--YOU ARE CLEARED FOR LANDING ON THE PORT FLIGHT POD.
GALACTICA
COPY THAT, GALACTICA.
DECK CREW IS STANDING BY TO RECEIVE.
BSG 75
INCOMING PILOTS, PLEASE REPORT TO COMMANDER ADAMA IN THE READY ROOM AS SOON AS POSSIBLE.
TIME TO FACE THE MUSIC...
WALK AND TALK, MR. GAETA.
YES, SIR.
WE'RE STILL TRACKING LIEUTENANTS THRACE AND AGATHON. THEIR RAPTOR IS MAKING MULTIPLE JUMPS AND GETTING FURTHER OUT OF RANGE BY THE MINUTE.
THEY'RE NOT ANSWERING OUR COMM SIGNALS, BUT THEIR SIGNALS MAY BE JAMMED OR THEY'RE DELIBERATELY RUNNING SILENT...
I NEED TO DEBRIEF THE OTHER PILOTS, BUT IF YOU GET ANYTHING--A WIRELESS RESPONSE, A TRANSPONDER LOCK, ANYTHING--YOU LET ME KNOW IMMEDIATELY.
ABSOLUTELY, SIR.
ALL RIGHT, GENTLEMEN...
...LET'S HEAR THE BAD NEWS.

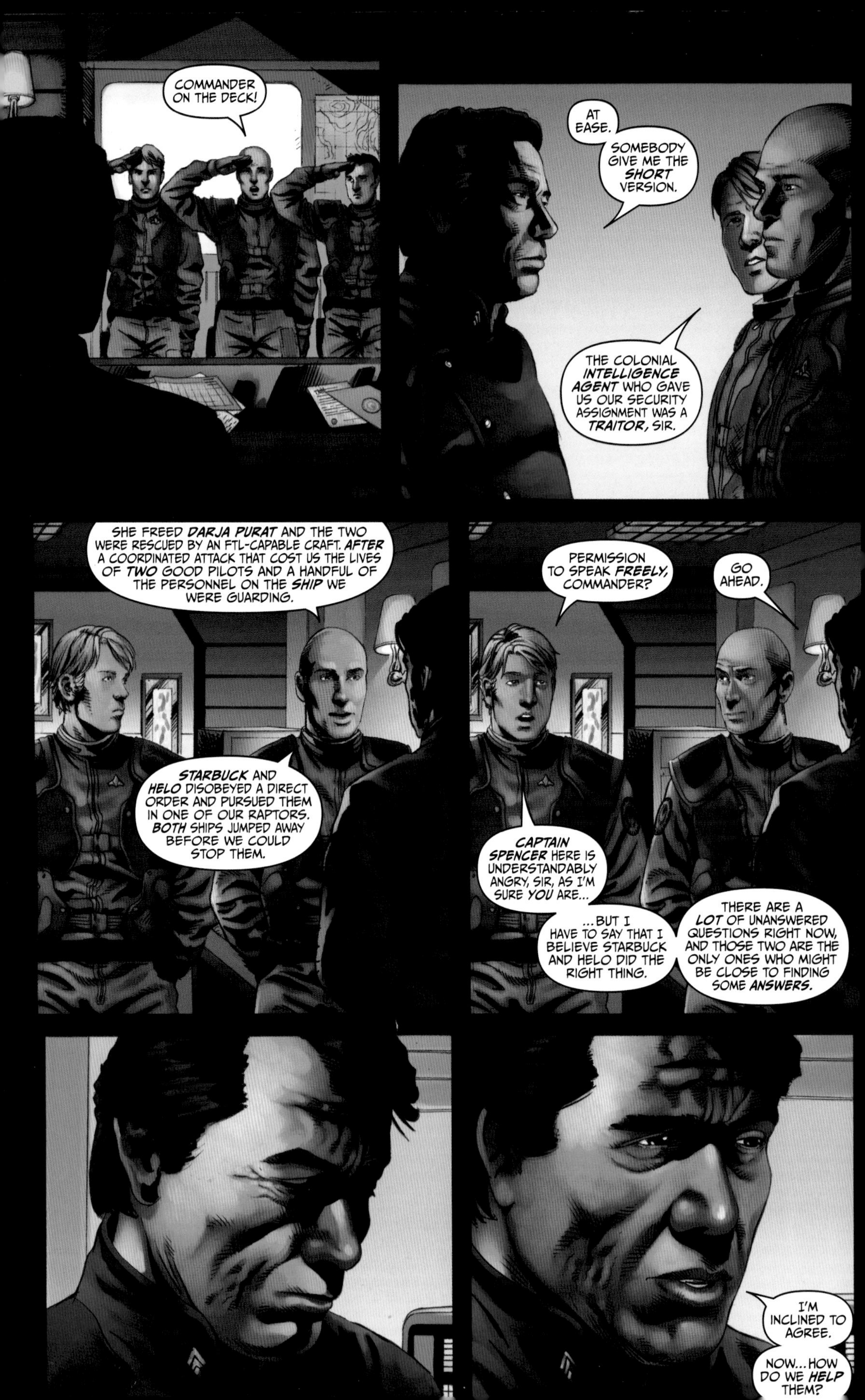

COMMANDER ON THE DECK!
AT EASE.
SOMEBODY GIVE ME THE SHORT VERSION.
THE COLONIAL INTELLIGENCE AGENT WHO GAVE US OUR SECURITY ASSIGNMENT WAS A TRAITOR, SIR.
SHE FREED DARJA PURAT AND THE TWO WERE RESCUED BY AN FTL-CAPABLE CRAFT. AFTER A COORDINATED ATTACK THAT COST US THE LIVES OF TWO GOOD PILOTS AND A HANDFUL OF THE PERSONNEL ON THE SHIP WE WERE GUARDING.
STARBUCK AND HELO DISOBEYED A DIRECT ORDER AND PURSUED THEM IN ONE OF OUR RAPTORS. BOTH SHIPS JUMPED AWAY BEFORE WE COULD STOP THEM.
PERMISSION TO SPEAK FREELY, COMMANDER?
GO AHEAD.
CAPTAIN SPENCER HERE IS UNDERSTANDABLY ANGRY, SIR, AS I'M SURE YOU ARE...
...BUT I HAVE TO SAY THAT I BELIEVE STARBUCK AND HELO DID THE RIGHT THING.
THERE ARE A LOT OF UNANSWERED QUESTIONS RIGHT NOW, AND THOSE TWO ARE THE ONLY ONES WHO MIGHT BE CLOSE TO FINDING SOME ANSWERS.
I'M INCLINED TO AGREE.
NOW... HOW DO WE HELP THEM?

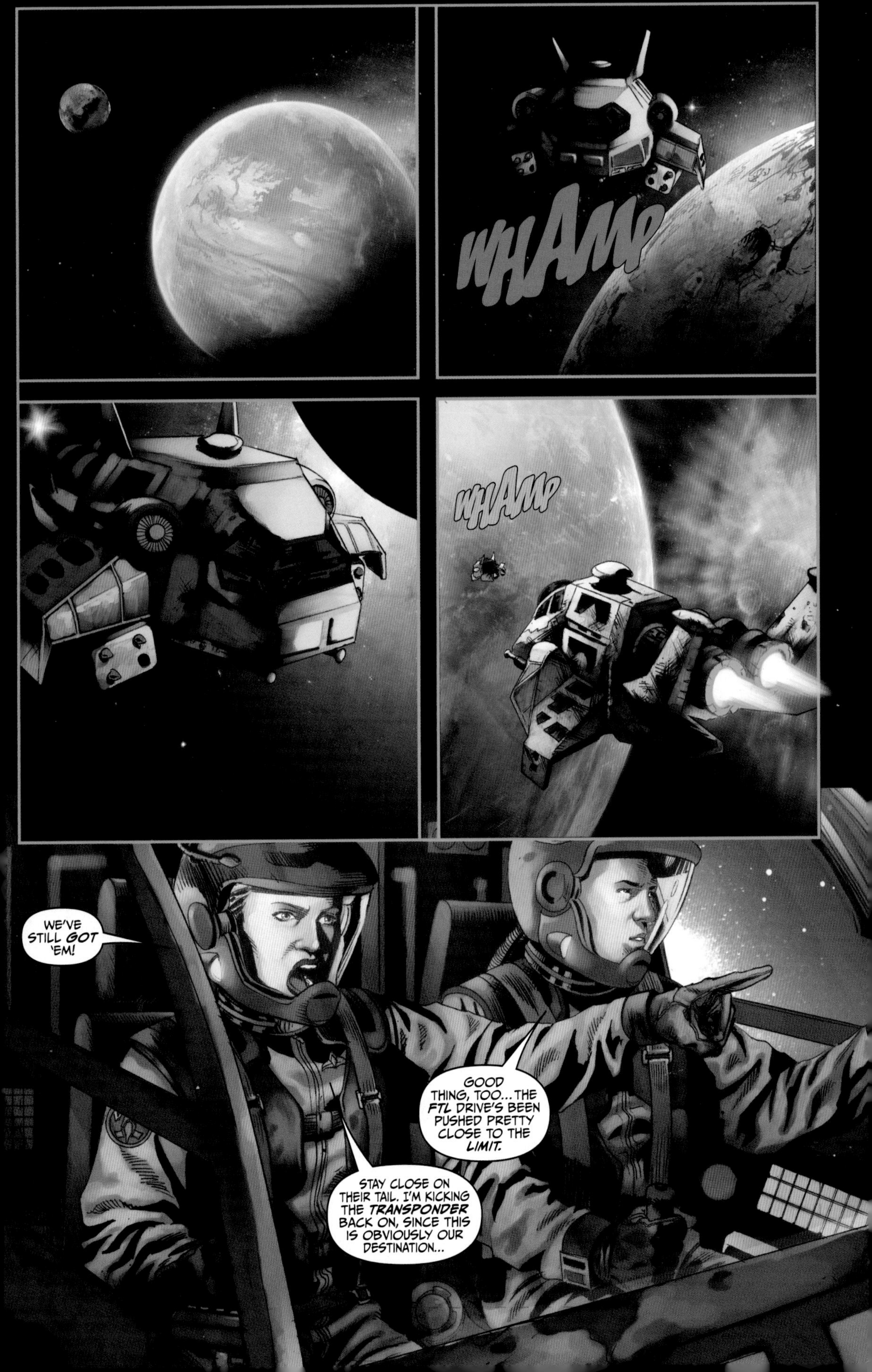
WHAMP
WHAMP
WE'VE STILL GOT 'EM!
GOOD THING, TOO... THE FTL DRIVE'S BEEN PUSHED PRETTY CLOSE TO THE LIMIT.
STAY CLOSE ON THEIR TAIL. I'M KICKING THE TRANSPONDER BACK ON, SINCE THIS IS OBVIOUSLY OUR DESTINATION...

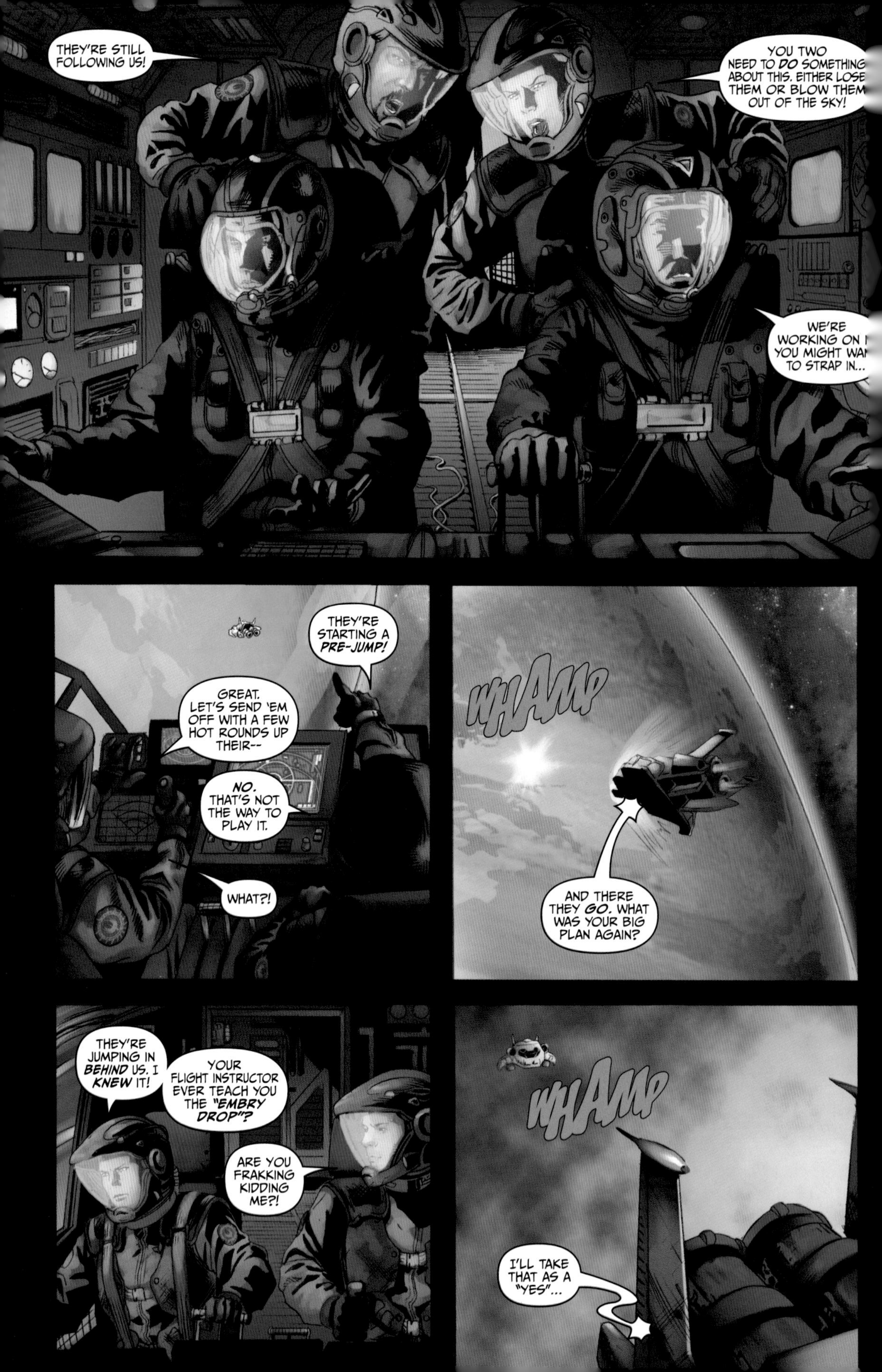
THEY'RE STILL FOLLOWING US!
YOU TWO NEED TO DO SOMETHING ABOUT THIS. EITHER LOSE THEM OR BLOW THEM OUT OF THE SKY!
WE'RE WORKING ON IT. YOU MIGHT WANT TO STRAP IN...
THEY'RE STARTING A PRE-JUMP!
GREAT. LET'S SEND 'EM OFF WITH A FEW HOT ROUNDS UP THEIR--
NO. THAT'S NOT THE WAY TO PLAY IT.
WHAT?!
WHAM
AND THERE THEY GO. WHAT WAS YOUR BIG PLAN AGAIN?
THEY'RE JUMPING IN BEHIND US. I KNEW IT!
YOUR FLIGHT INSTRUCTOR EVER TEACH YOU THE "EMBRY DROP"?
ARE YOU FRAKKING KIDDING ME?!
WHAM
I'LL TAKE THAT AS A "YES"...

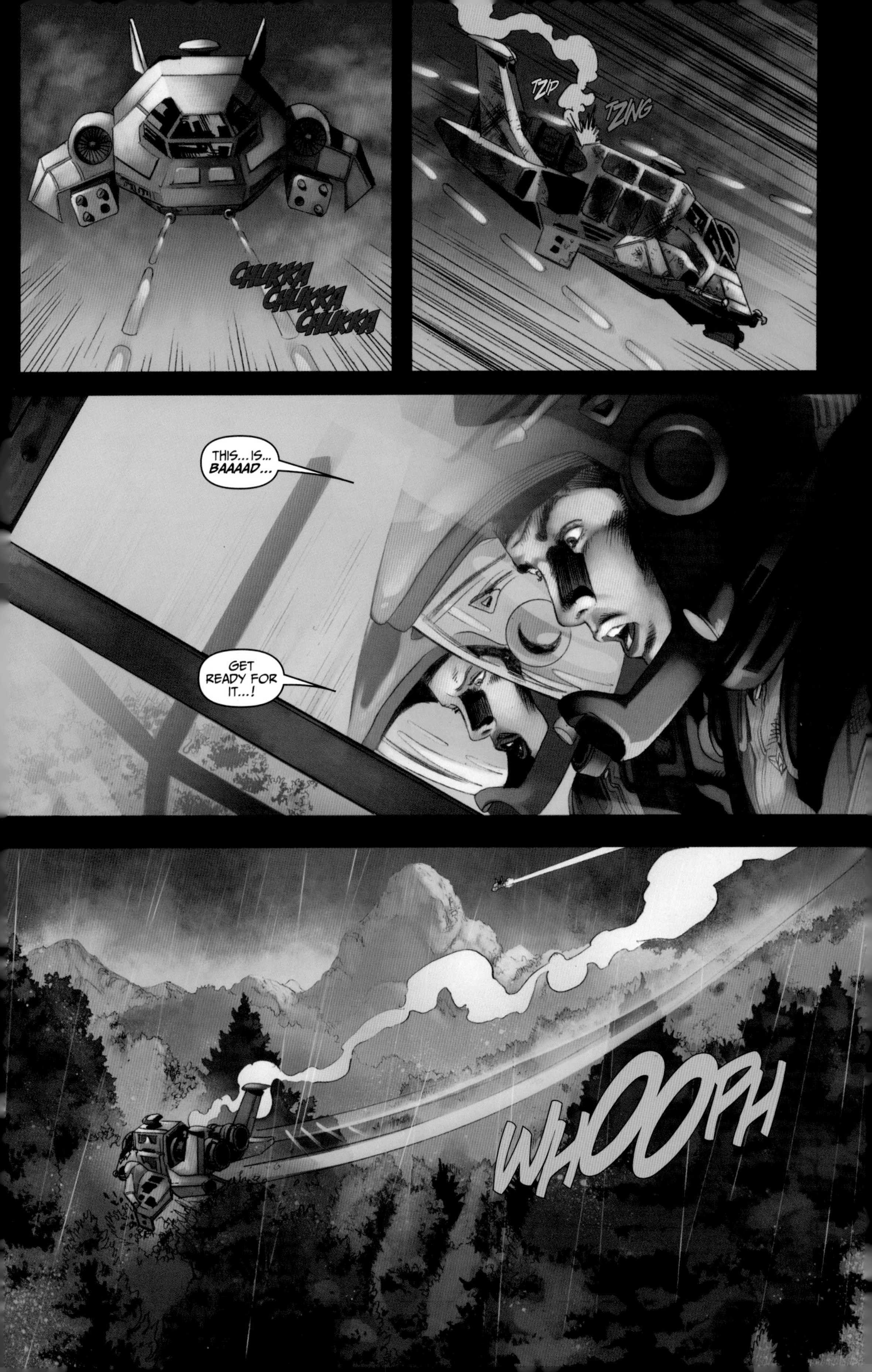
CHUKKA CHUKKA CHUKKA
TZIP
TZING
THIS...IS... BAAAAD...
GET READY FOR IT...!
WHOOPH

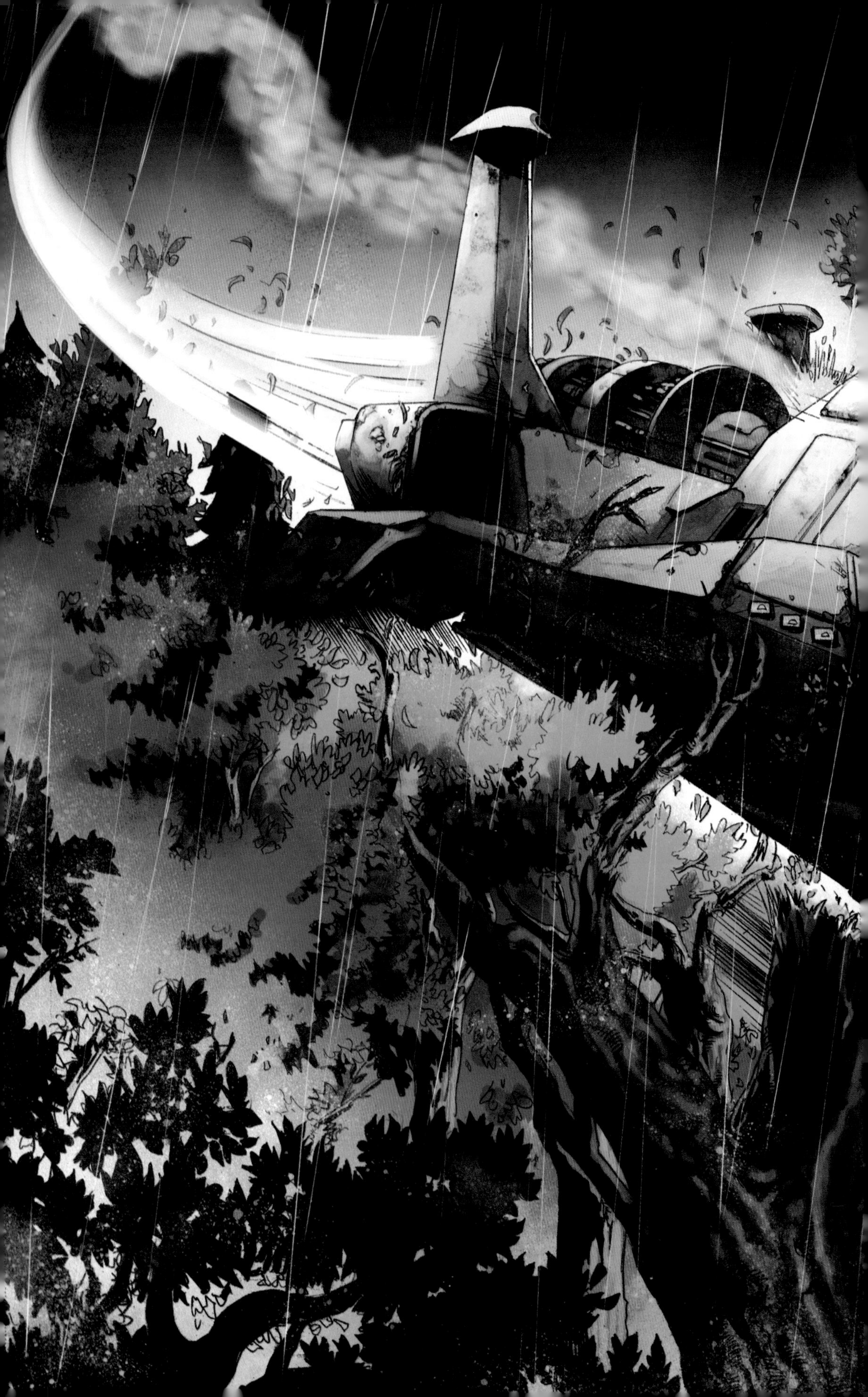

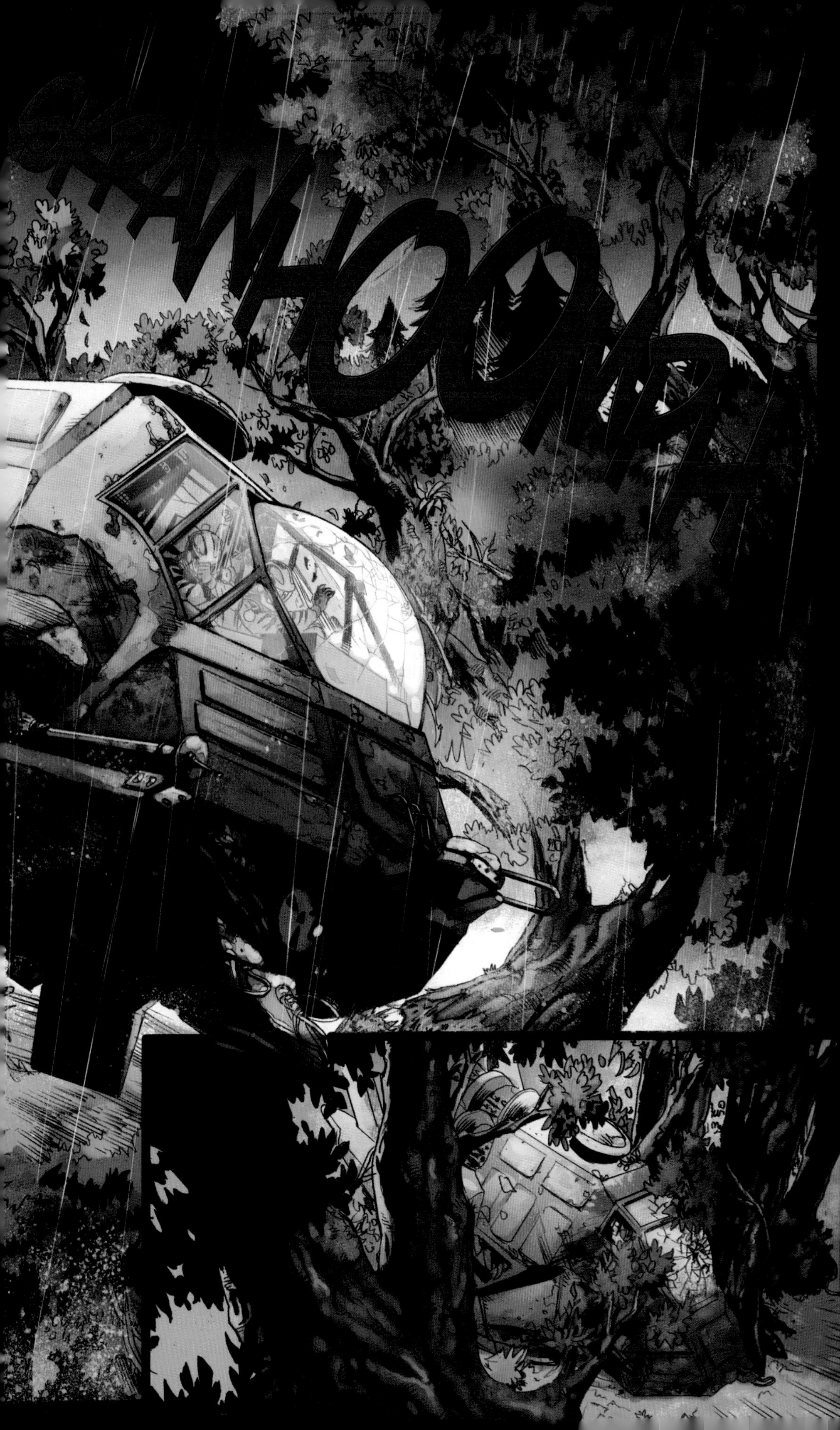
SKRAWHOOM!!

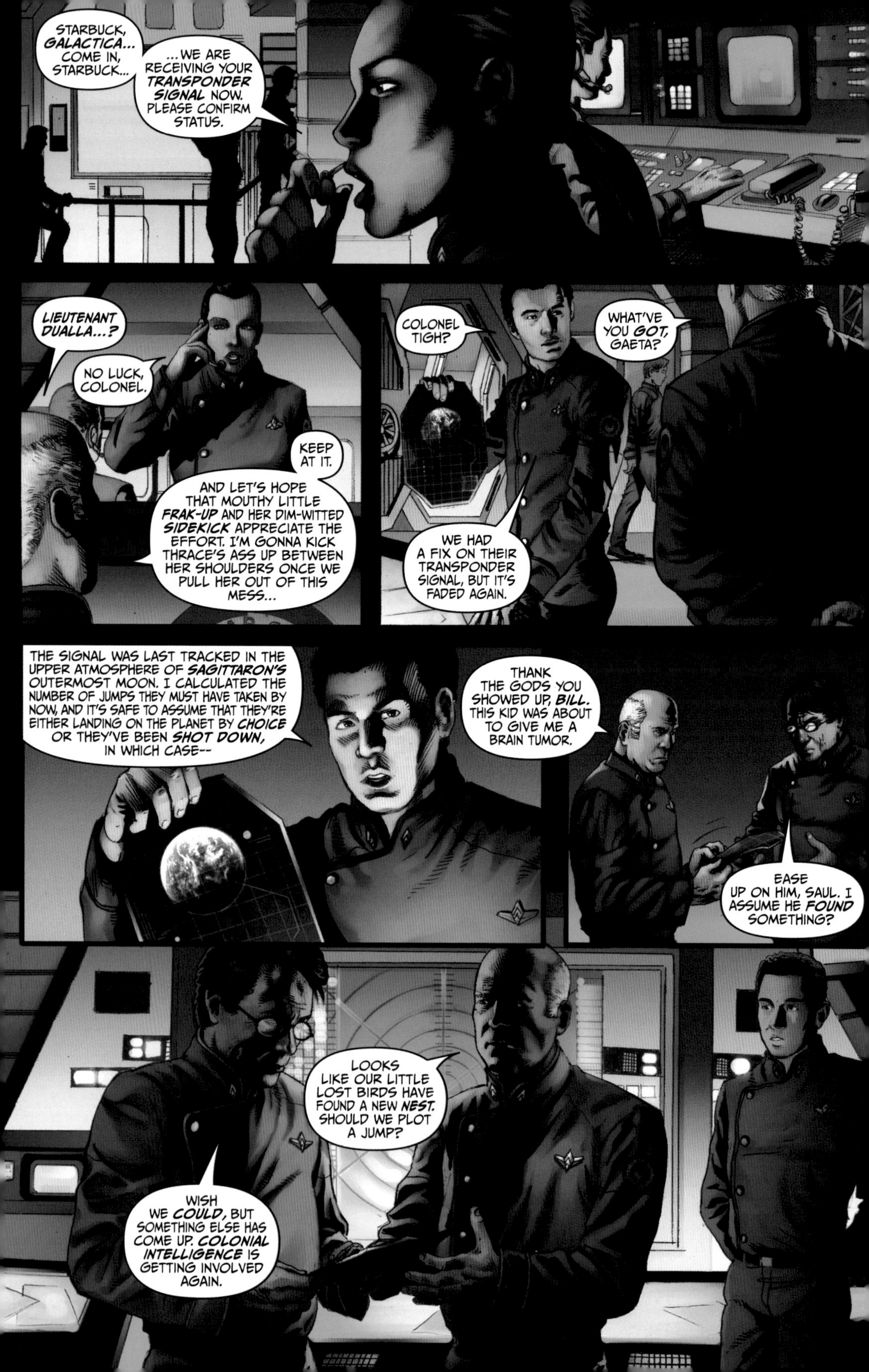
STARBUCK, GALACTICA... COME IN, STARBUCK...
...WE ARE RECEIVING YOUR TRANSPONDER SIGNAL NOW. PLEASE CONFIRM STATUS.
LIEUTENANT DUALLA...?
NO LUCK, COLONEL.
KEEP AT IT.
AND LET'S HOPE THAT MOUTHY LITTLE FRAK-UP AND HER DIM-WITTED SIDEKICK APPRECIATE THE EFFORT. I'M GONNA KICK THRACE'S ASS UP BETWEEN HER SHOULDERS ONCE WE PULL HER OUT OF THIS MESS...
COLONEL TIGH?
WHAT'VE YOU GOT, GAETA?
WE HAD A FIX ON THEIR TRANSPONDER SIGNAL, BUT IT'S FADED AGAIN.
THE SIGNAL WAS LAST TRACKED IN THE UPPER ATMOSPHERE OF SAGITTARON'S OUTERMOST MOON. I CALCULATED THE NUMBER OF JUMPS THEY MUST HAVE TAKEN BY NOW, AND IT'S SAFE TO ASSUME THAT THEY'RE EITHER LANDING ON THE PLANET BY CHOICE OR THEY'VE BEEN SHOT DOWN, IN WHICH CASE--
THANK THE GODS YOU SHOWED UP, BILL. THIS KID WAS ABOUT TO GIVE ME A BRAIN TUMOR.
EASE UP ON HIM, SAUL. I ASSUME HE FOUND SOMETHING?
LOOKS LIKE OUR LITTLE LOST BIRDS HAVE FOUND A NEW NEST. SHOULD WE PLOT A JUMP?
WISH WE COULD, BUT SOMETHING ELSE HAS COME UP. COLONIAL INTELLIGENCE IS GETTING INVOLVED AGAIN.

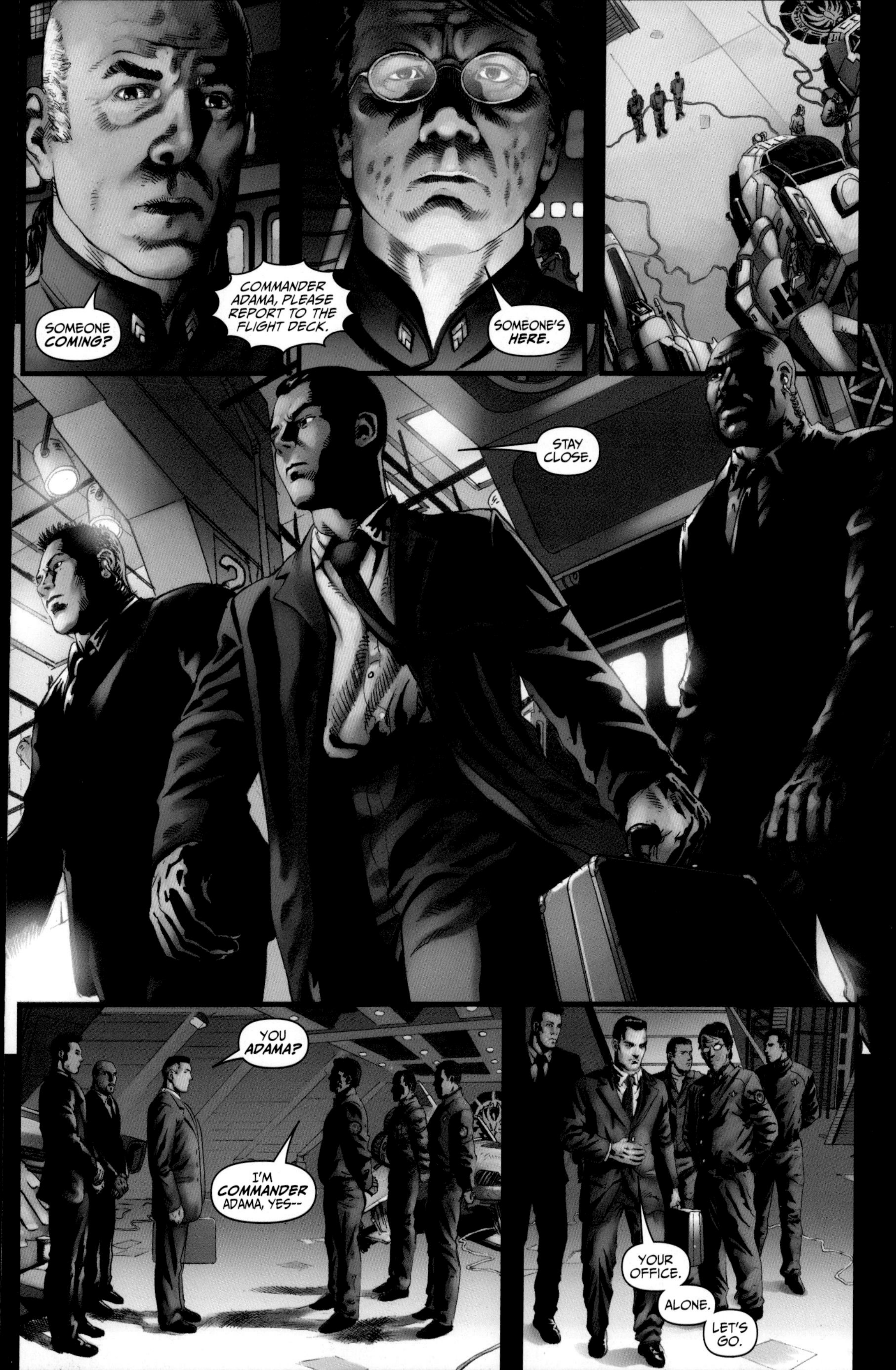
SOMEONE COMING?
COMMANDER ADAMA, PLEASE REPORT TO THE FLIGHT DECK.
SOMEONE'S HERE.
STAY CLOSE.
YOU ADAMA?
I'M COMMANDER ADAMA, YES--
YOUR OFFICE.
ALONE.
LET'S GO.

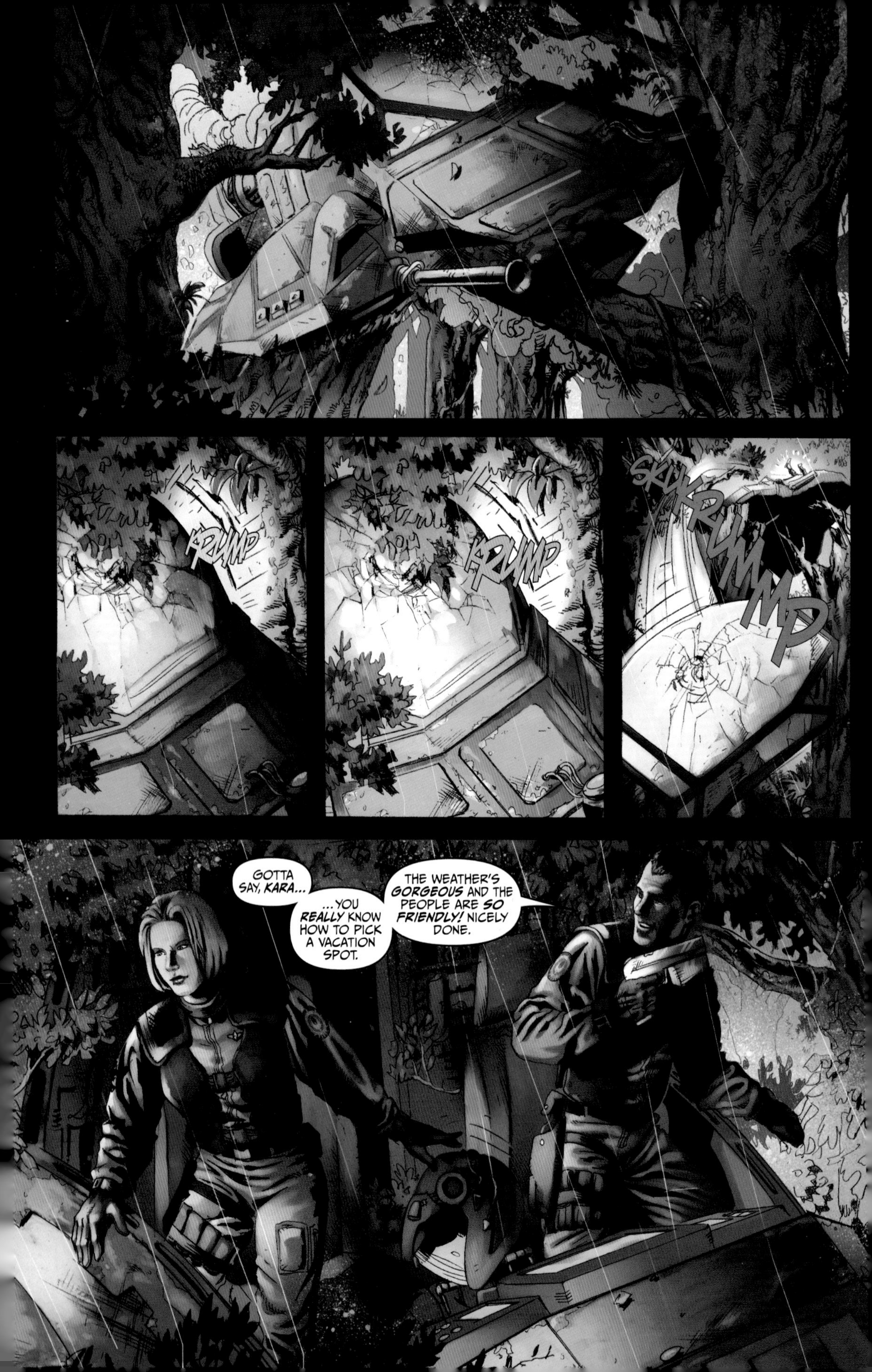
KRUMP
KRUMP
SKUKRUMMMP
GOTTA SAY, KARA...
...YOU REALLY KNOW HOW TO PICK A VACATION SPOT.
THE WEATHER'S GORGEOUS AND THE PEOPLE ARE SO FRIENDLY! NICELY DONE.

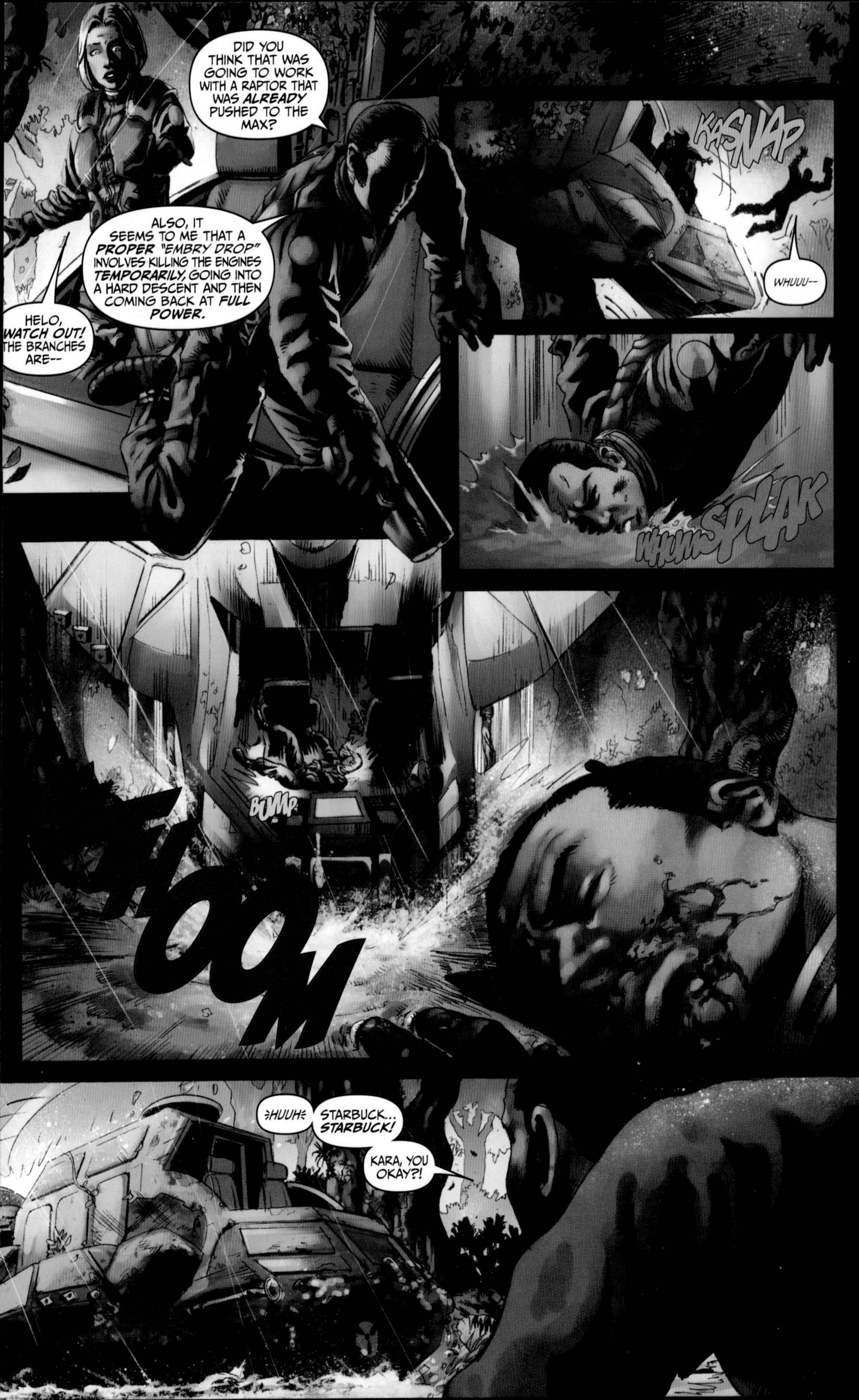
DID YOU THINK THAT WAS GOING TO WORK WITH A RAPTOR THAT WAS ALREADY PUSHED TO THE MAX?
ALSO, IT SEEMS TO ME THAT A PROPER "EMBRY DROP" INVOLVES KILLING THE ENGINES TEMPORARILY, GOING INTO A HARD DESCENT AND THEN COMING BACK AT FULL POWER.
HELO, WATCH OUT! THE BRANCHES ARE--
KASNAP
WHUUU--
WHUM SPLAK
BUMP
FOOOM
HUUH STARBUCK... STARBUCK!
KARA, YOU OKAY?!

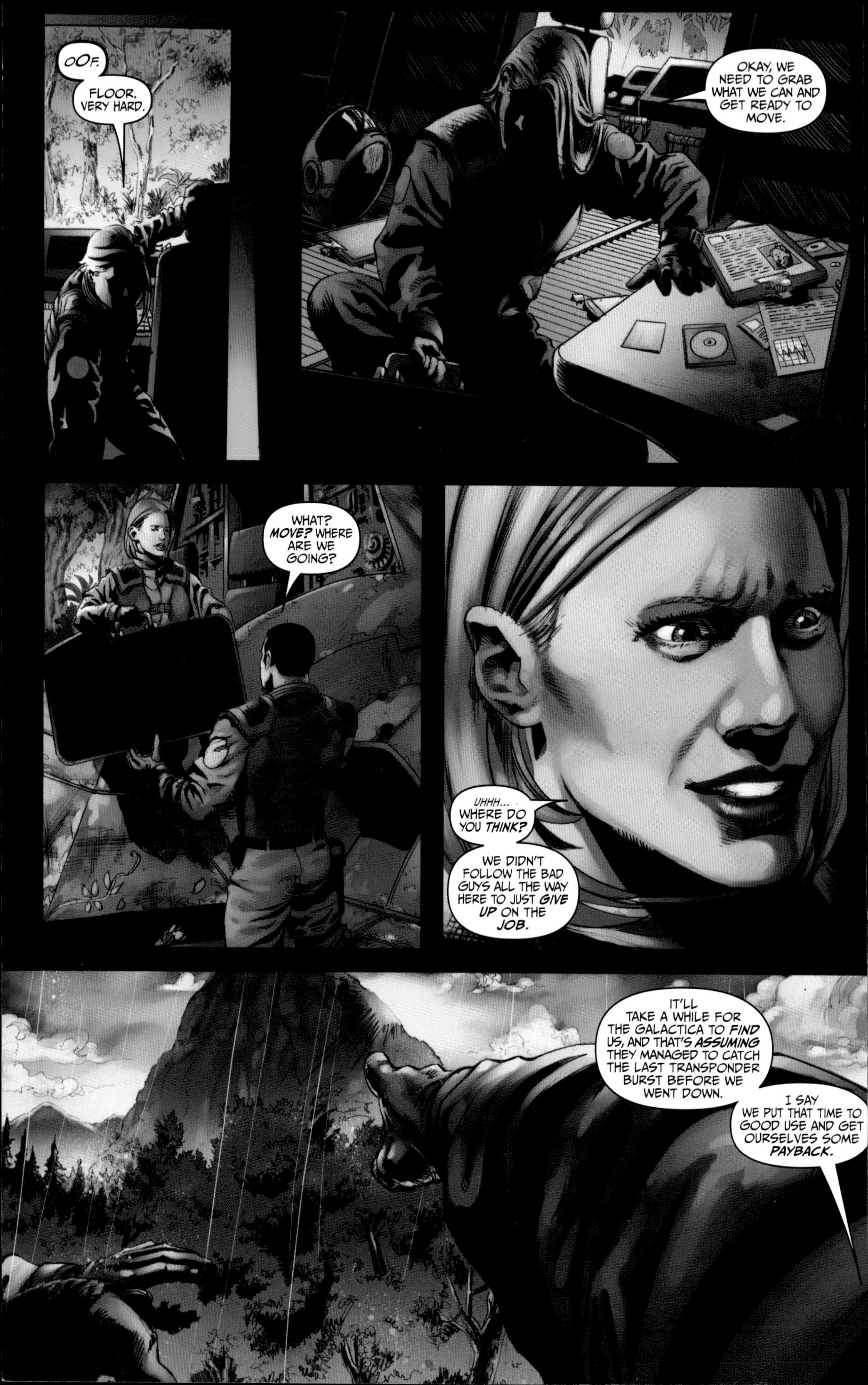
OOF.
FLOOR. VERY HARD.
OKAY, WE NEED TO GRAB WHAT WE CAN AND GET READY TO MOVE.
WHAT? MOVE? WHERE ARE WE GOING?
UHHH... WHERE DO YOU THINK?
WE DIDN'T FOLLOW THE BAD GUYS ALL THE WAY HERE TO JUST GIVE UP ON THE JOB.
IT'LL TAKE A WHILE FOR THE GALACTICA TO FIND US, AND THAT'S ASSUMING THEY MANAGED TO CATCH THE LAST TRANSPONDER BURST BEFORE WE WENT DOWN.
I SAY WE PUT THAT TIME TO GOOD USE AND GET OURSELVES SOME PAYBACK.

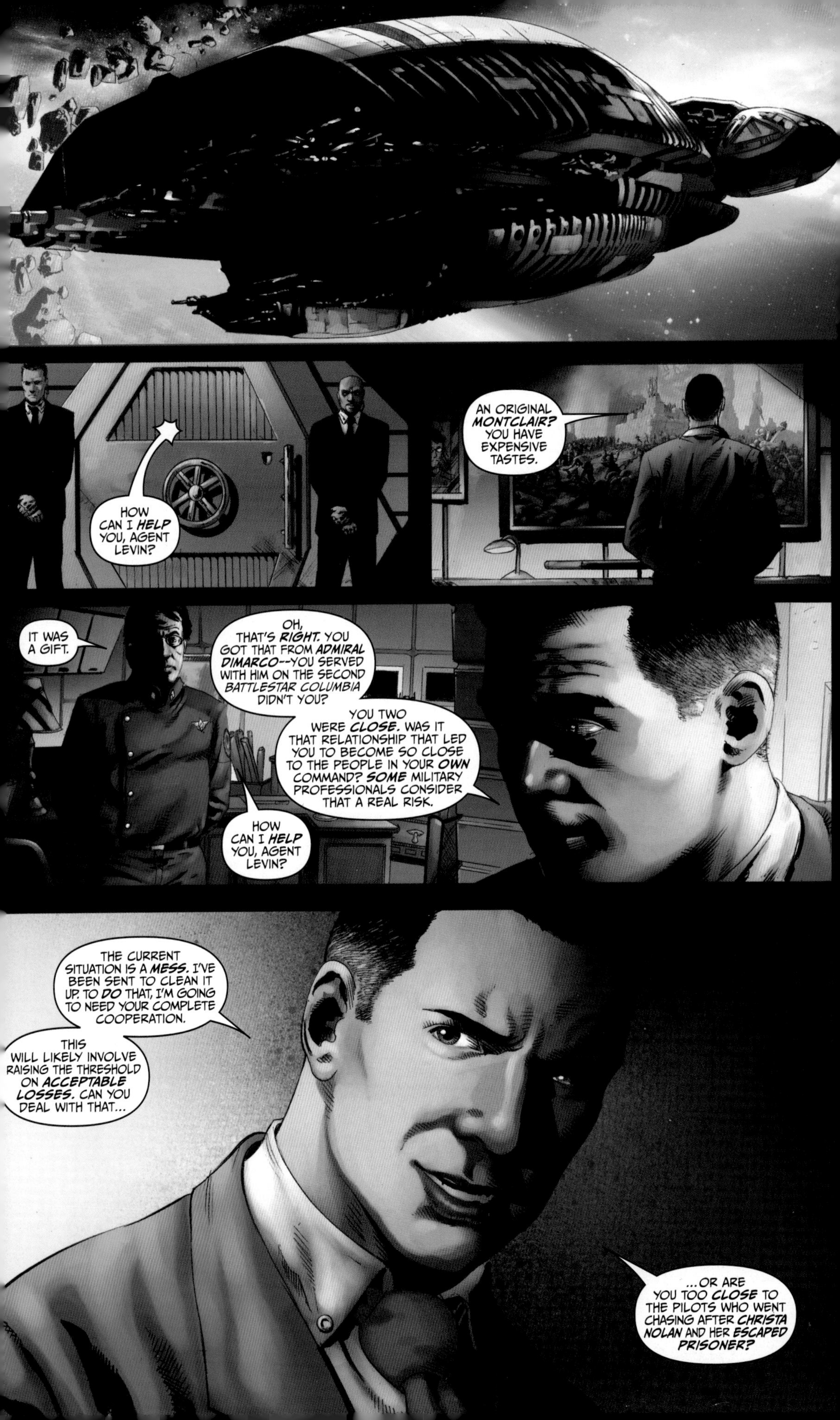
HOW CAN I HELP YOU, AGENT LEVIN?
AN ORIGINAL MONTCLAIR? YOU HAVE EXPENSIVE TASTES.
IT WAS A GIFT.
OH, THAT'S RIGHT. YOU GOT THAT FROM ADMIRAL DIMARCO--YOU SERVED WITH HIM ON THE SECOND BATTLESTAR COLUMBIA DIDN'T YOU?
YOU TWO WERE CLOSE. WAS IT THAT RELATIONSHIP THAT LED YOU TO BECOME SO CLOSE TO THE PEOPLE IN YOUR OWN COMMAND? SOME MILITARY PROFESSIONALS CONSIDER THAT A REAL RISK.
HOW CAN I HELP YOU, AGENT LEVIN?
THE CURRENT SITUATION IS A MESS. I'VE BEEN SENT TO CLEAN IT UP. TO DO THAT, I'M GOING TO NEED YOUR COMPLETE COOPERATION.
THIS WILL LIKELY INVOLVE RAISING THE THRESHOLD ON ACCEPTABLE LOSSES. CAN YOU DEAL WITH THAT...
...OR ARE YOU TOO CLOSE TO THE PILOTS WHO WENT CHASING AFTER CHRISTA NOLAN AND HER ESCAPED PRISONER?

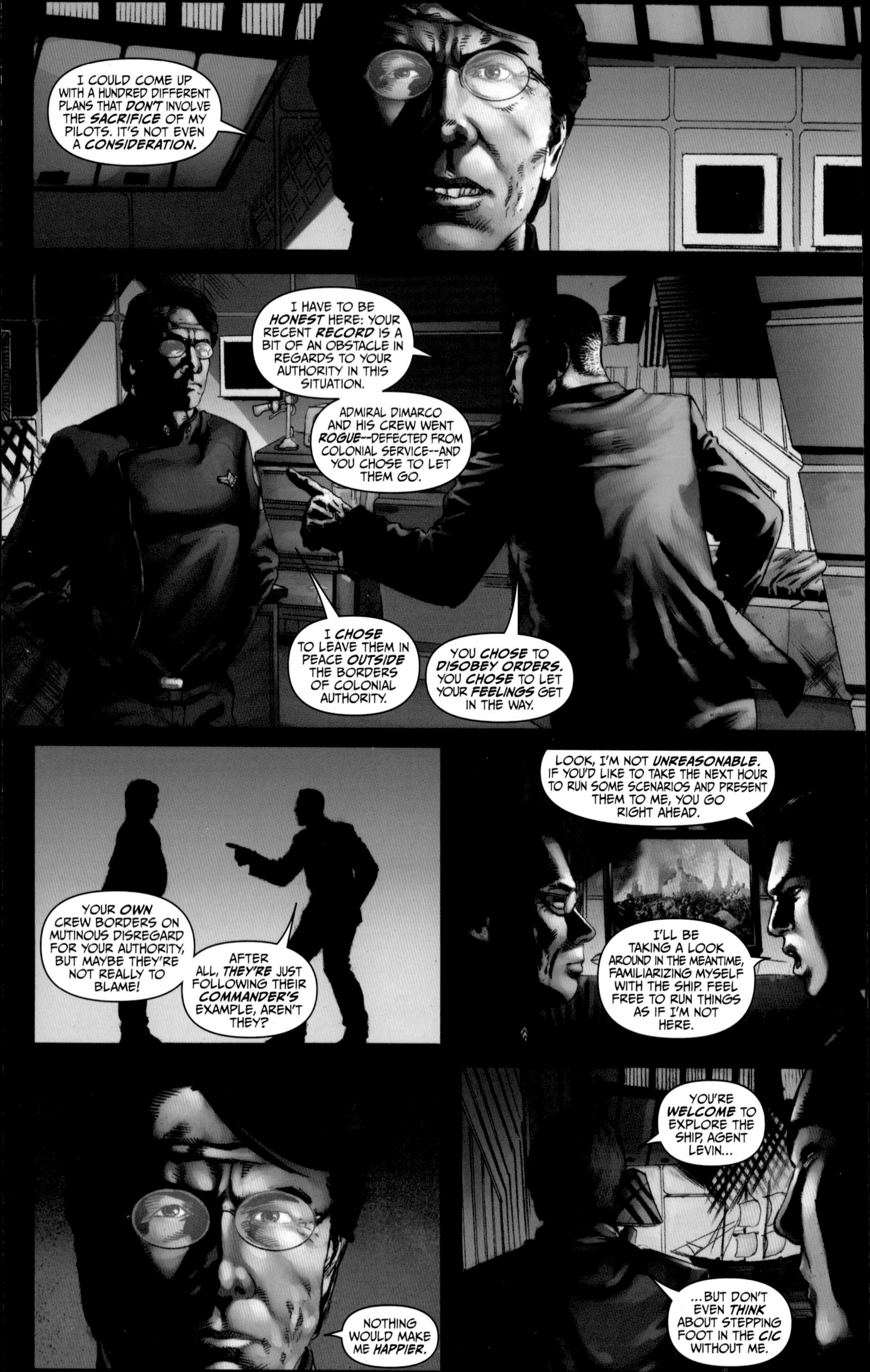
I COULD COME UP WITH A HUNDRED DIFFERENT PLANS THAT DON'T INVOLVE THE SACRIFICE OF MY PILOTS. IT'S NOT EVEN A CONSIDERATION.
I HAVE TO BE HONEST HERE: YOUR RECENT RECORD IS A BIT OF AN OBSTACLE IN REGARDS TO YOUR AUTHORITY IN THIS SITUATION.
ADMIRAL DIMARCO AND HIS CREW WENT ROGUE--DEFECTED FROM COLONIAL SERVICE--AND YOU CHOSE TO LET THEM GO.
I CHOSE TO LEAVE THEM IN PEACE OUTSIDE THE BORDERS OF COLONIAL AUTHORITY.
YOU CHOSE TO DISOBEY ORDERS. YOU CHOSE TO LET YOUR FEELINGS GET IN THE WAY.
YOUR OWN CREW BORDERS ON MUTINOUS DISREGARD FOR YOUR AUTHORITY, BUT MAYBE THEY'RE NOT REALLY TO BLAME!
AFTER ALL, THEY'RE JUST FOLLOWING THEIR COMMANDER'S EXAMPLE, AREN'T THEY?
LOOK, I'M NOT UNREASONABLE. IF YOU'D LIKE TO TAKE THE NEXT HOUR TO RUN SOME SCENARIOS AND PRESENT THEM TO ME, YOU GO RIGHT AHEAD.
I'LL BE TAKING A LOOK AROUND IN THE MEANTIME, FAMILIARIZING MYSELF WITH THE SHIP. FEEL FREE TO RUN THINGS AS IF I'M NOT HERE.
NOTHING WOULD MAKE ME HAPPIER.
YOU'RE WELCOME TO EXPLORE THE SHIP, AGENT LEVIN...
...BUT DON'T EVEN THINK ABOUT STEPPING FOOT IN THE CIC WITHOUT ME.

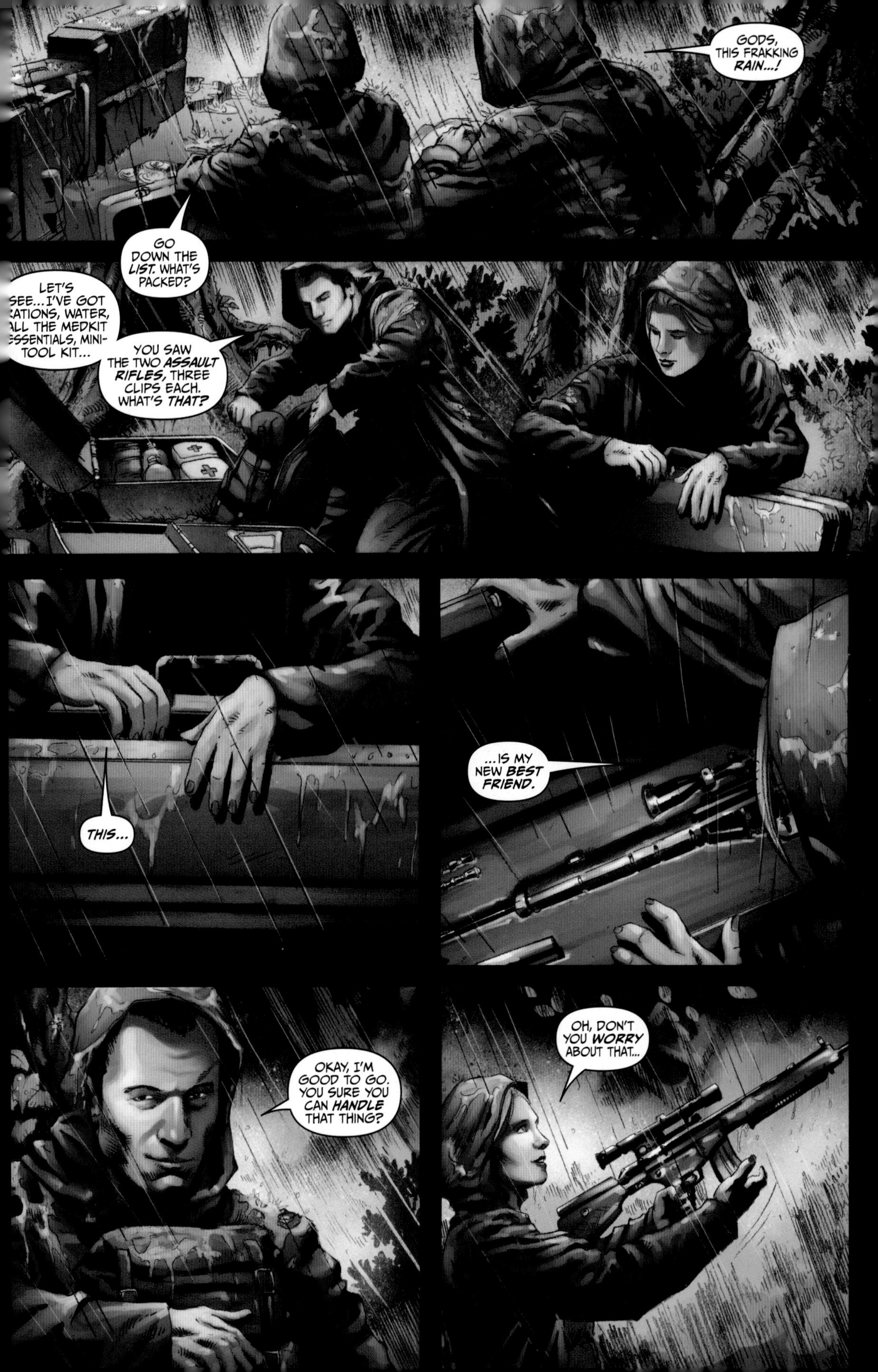
GODS, THIS FRAKKING RAIN...!
GO DOWN THE LIST. WHAT'S PACKED?
LET'S SEE... I'VE GOT RATIONS, WATER, ALL THE MEDKIT ESSENTIALS, MINI-TOOL KIT...
YOU SAW THE TWO ASSAULT RIFLES, THREE CLIPS EACH. WHAT'S THAT?
THIS...
...IS MY NEW BEST FRIEND.
OKAY, I'M GOOD TO GO. YOU SURE YOU CAN HANDLE THAT THING?
OH, DON'T YOU WORRY ABOUT THAT...

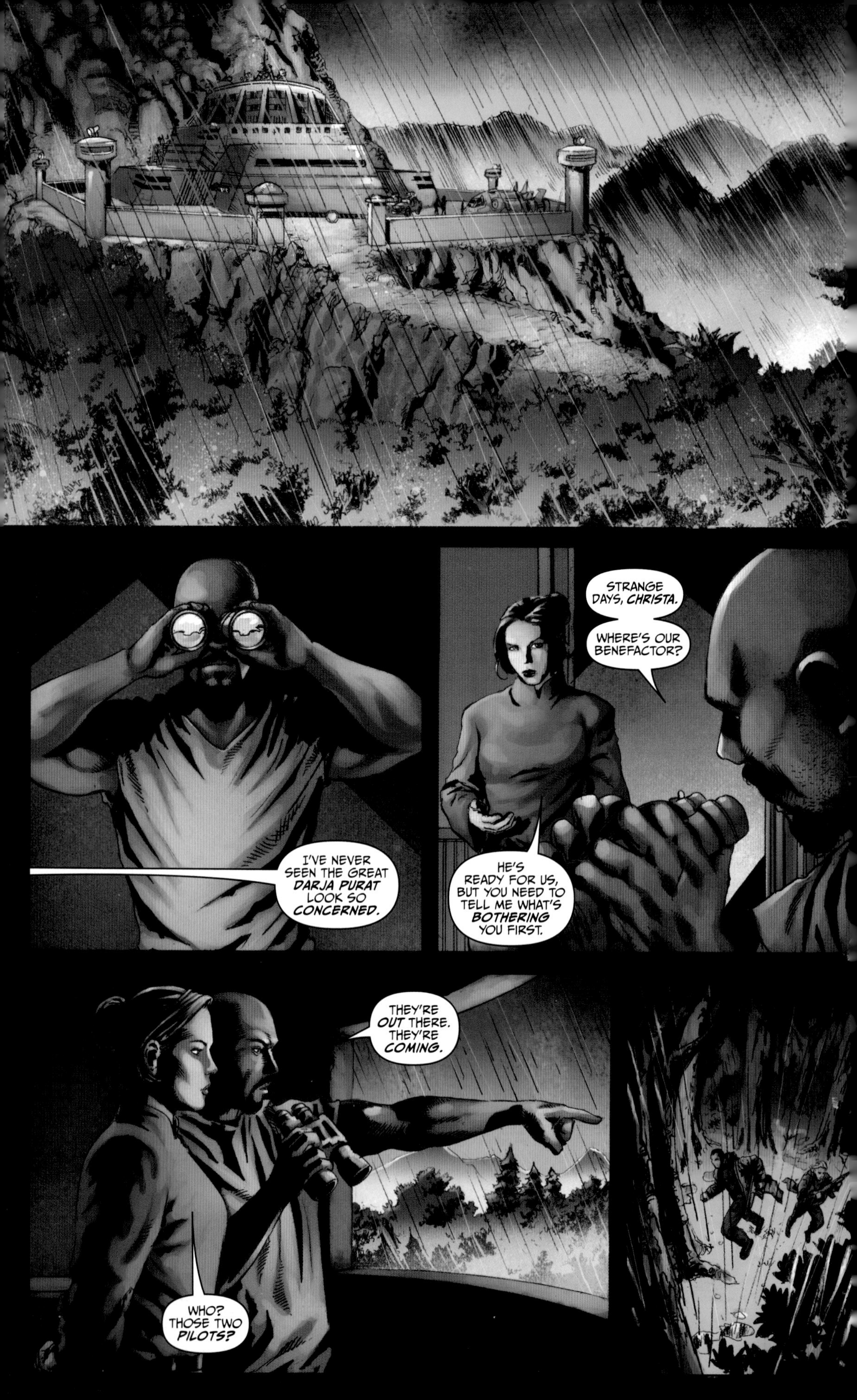

I'VE NEVER SEEN THE GREAT DARJA PURAT LOOK SO CONCERNED.
STRANGE DAYS, CHRISTA.
WHERE'S OUR BENEFACTOR?
HE'S READY FOR US, BUT YOU NEED TO TELL ME WHAT'S BOTHERING YOU FIRST.
THEY'RE OUT THERE. THEY'RE COMING.
WHO? THOSE TWO PILOTS?

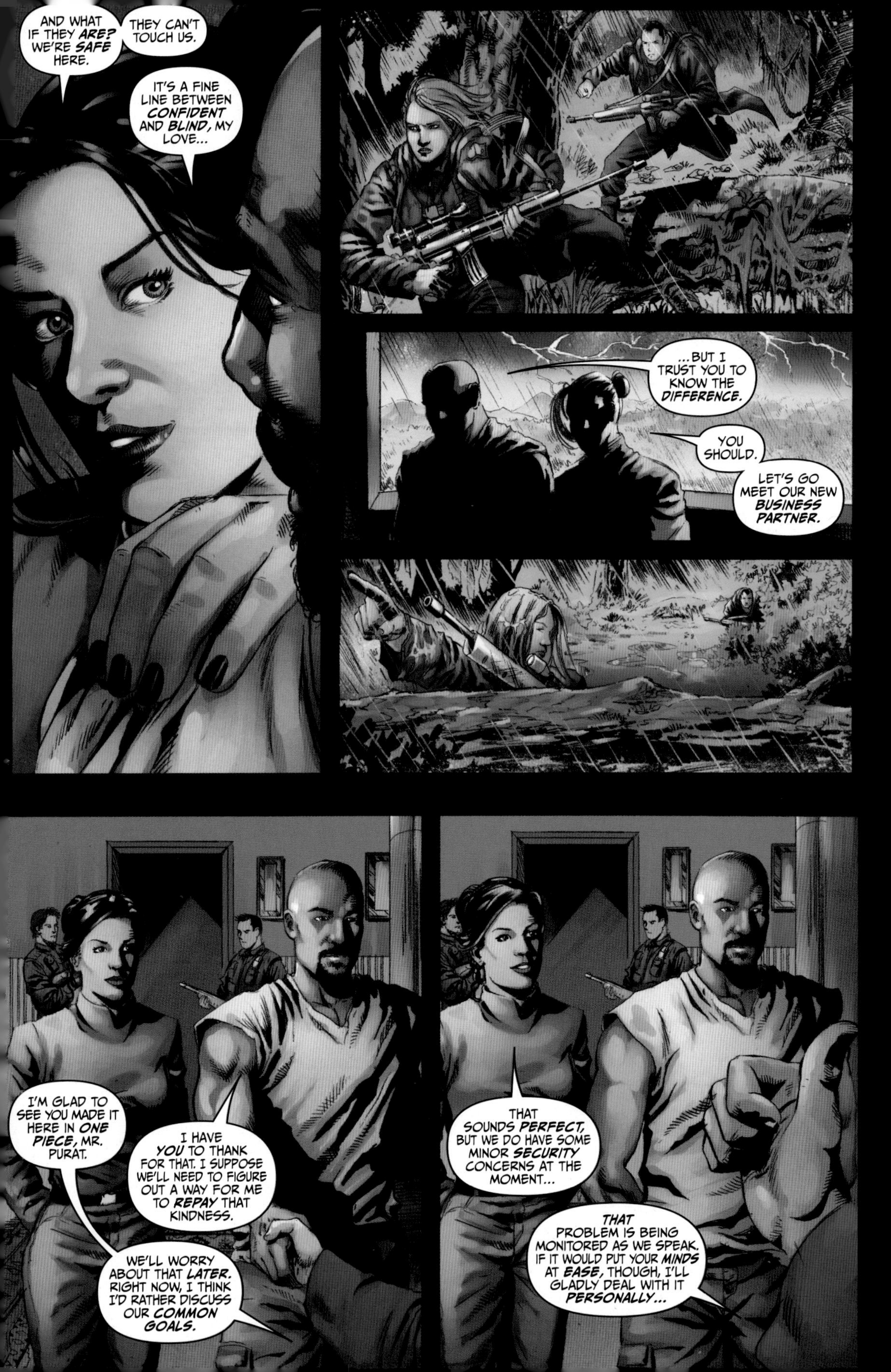
AND WHAT IF THEY ARE? WE'RE SAFE HERE.
THEY CAN'T TOUCH US.
IT'S A FINE LINE BETWEEN CONFIDENT AND BLIND, MY LOVE...
...BUT I TRUST YOU TO KNOW THE DIFFERENCE.
YOU SHOULD.
LET'S GO MEET OUR NEW BUSINESS PARTNER.
I'M GLAD TO SEE YOU MADE IT HERE IN ONE PIECE, MR. PURAT.
I HAVE YOU TO THANK FOR THAT. I SUPPOSE WE'LL NEED TO FIGURE OUT A WAY FOR ME TO REPAY THAT KINDNESS.
WE'LL WORRY ABOUT THAT LATER. RIGHT NOW, I THINK I'D RATHER DISCUSS OUR COMMON GOALS.
THAT SOUNDS PERFECT, BUT WE DO HAVE SOME MINOR SECURITY CONCERNS AT THE MOMENT...
THAT PROBLEM IS BEING MONITORED AS WE SPEAK. IF IT WOULD PUT YOUR MINDS AT EASE, THOUGH, I'LL GLADLY DEAL WITH IT PERSONALLY...

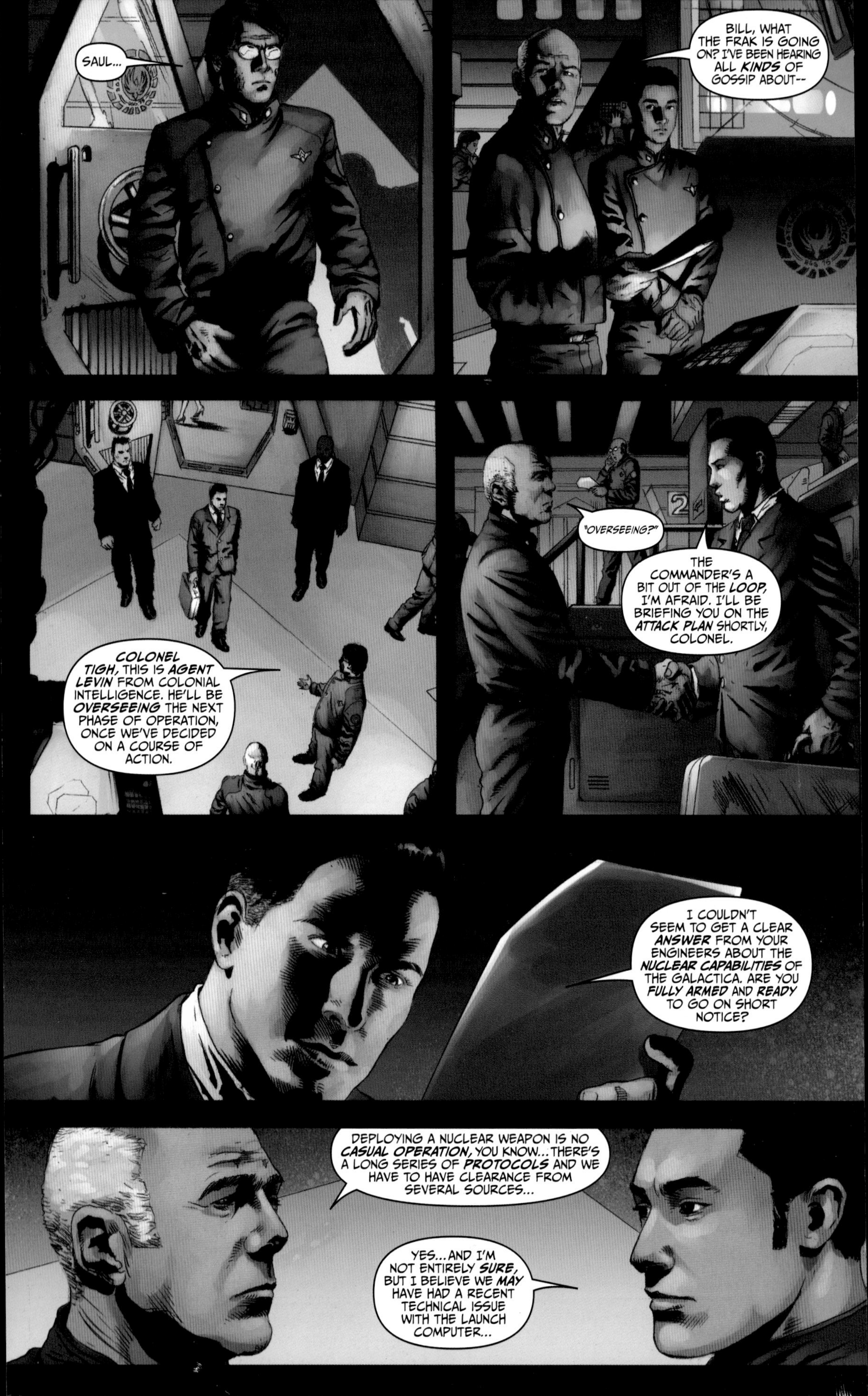
SAUL...
BILL, WHAT THE FRAK IS GOING ON? I'VE BEEN HEARING ALL KINDS OF GOSSIP ABOUT--
COLONEL TIGH, THIS IS AGENT LEVIN FROM COLONIAL INTELLIGENCE. HE'LL BE OVERSEEING THE NEXT PHASE OF OPERATION, ONCE WE'VE DECIDED ON A COURSE OF ACTION.
"OVERSEEING?"
THE COMMANDER'S A BIT OUT OF THE LOOP, I'M AFRAID. I'LL BE BRIEFING YOU ON THE ATTACK PLAN SHORTLY, COLONEL.
I COULDN'T SEEM TO GET A CLEAR ANSWER FROM YOUR ENGINEERS ABOUT THE NUCLEAR CAPABILITIES OF THE GALACTICA. ARE YOU FULLY ARMED AND READY TO GO ON SHORT NOTICE?
DEPLOYING A NUCLEAR WEAPON IS NO CASUAL OPERATION, YOU KNOW... THERE'S A LONG SERIES OF PROTOCOLS AND WE HAVE TO HAVE CLEARANCE FROM SEVERAL SOURCES...
YES... AND I'M NOT ENTIRELY SURE, BUT I BELIEVE WE MAY HAVE HAD A RECENT TECHNICAL ISSUE WITH THE LAUNCH COMPUTER...

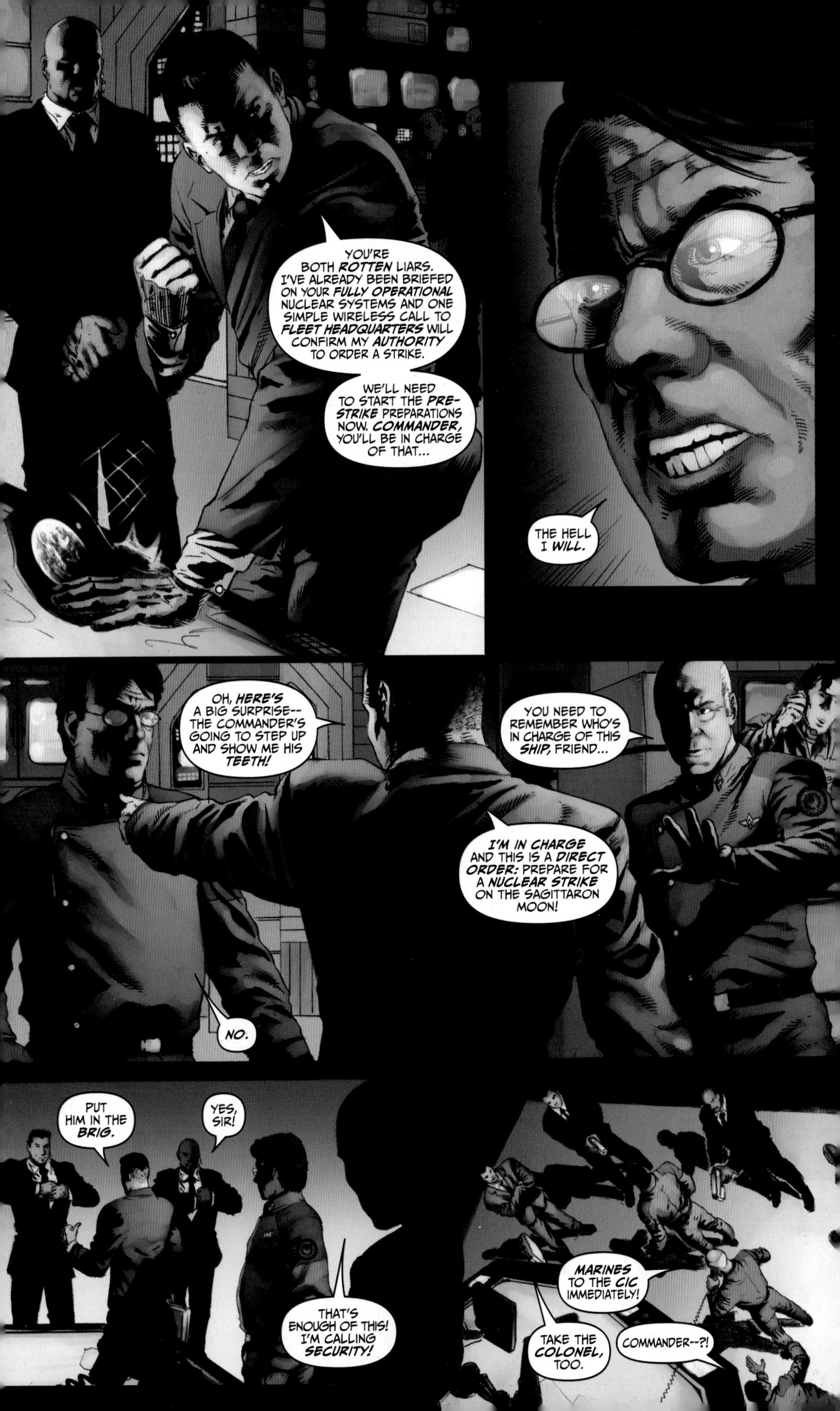
YOU'RE BOTH ROTTEN LIARS. I'VE ALREADY BEEN BRIEFED ON YOUR FULLY OPERATIONAL NUCLEAR SYSTEMS AND ONE SIMPLE WIRELESS CALL TO FLEET HEADQUARTERS WILL CONFIRM MY AUTHORITY TO ORDER A STRIKE.
WE'LL NEED TO START THE PRE-STRIKE PREPARATIONS NOW. COMMANDER, YOU'LL BE IN CHARGE OF THAT...
THE HELL I WILL.
OH, HERE'S A BIG SURPRISE-- THE COMMANDER'S GOING TO STEP UP AND SHOW ME HIS TEETH!
NO.
YOU NEED TO REMEMBER WHO'S IN CHARGE OF THIS SHIP, FRIEND...
I'M IN CHARGE AND THIS IS A DIRECT ORDER: PREPARE FOR A NUCLEAR STRIKE ON THE SAGITTARON MOON!
PUT HIM IN THE BRIG.
YES, SIR!
THAT'S ENOUGH OF THIS! I'M CALLING SECURITY!
MARINES TO THE CIC IMMEDIATELY!
TAKE THE COLONEL, TOO.
COMMANDER--?!

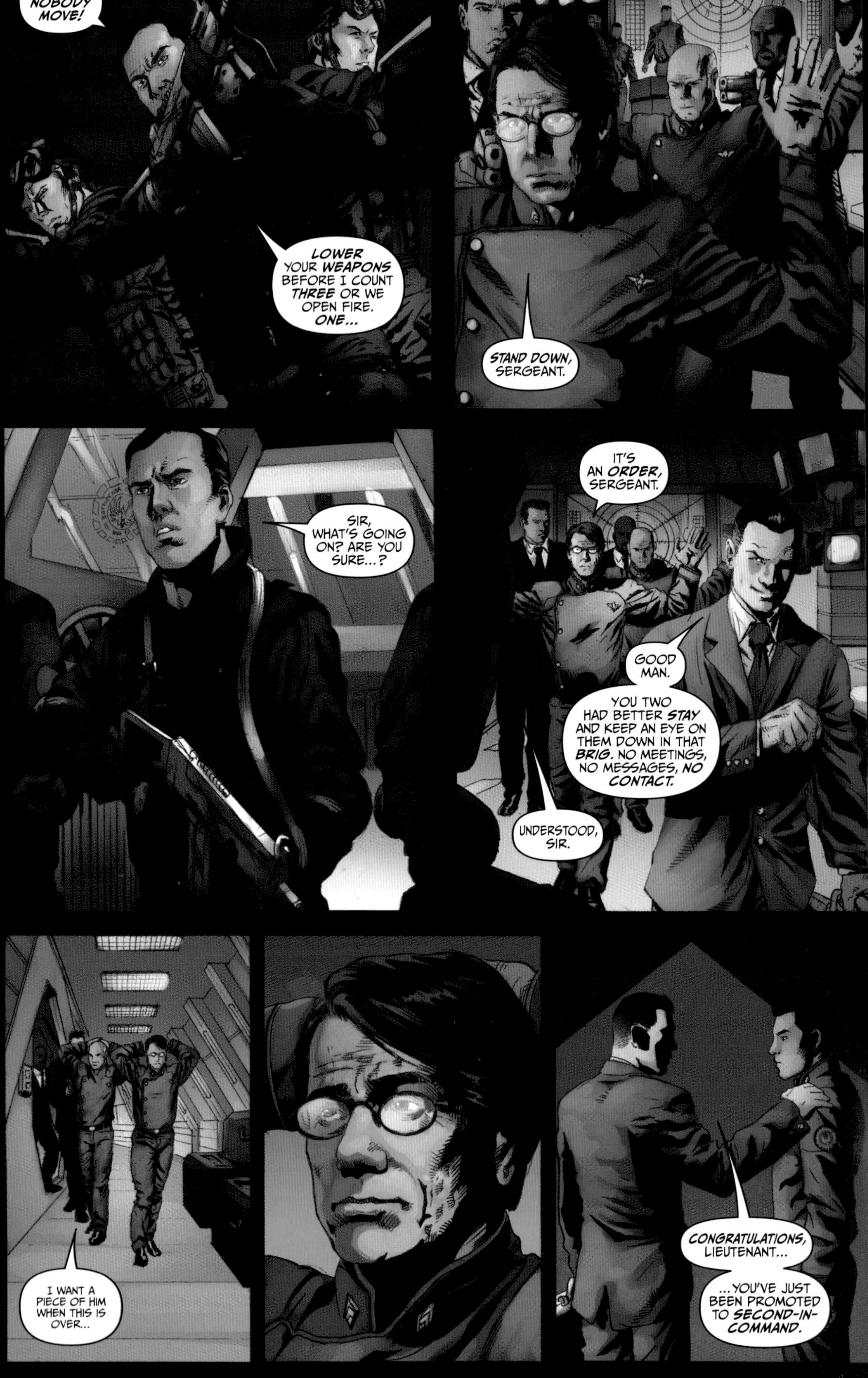
SECURITY! NOBODY MOVE!
LOWER YOUR WEAPONS BEFORE I COUNT THREE OR WE OPEN FIRE. ONE...
STAND DOWN, SERGEANT.
SIR, WHAT'S GOING ON? ARE YOU SURE...?
IT'S AN ORDER, SERGEANT.
GOOD MAN.
YOU TWO HAD BETTER STAY AND KEEP AN EYE ON THEM DOWN IN THAT BRIG. NO MEETINGS, NO MESSAGES, NO CONTACT.
UNDERSTOOD, SIR.
I WANT A PIECE OF HIM WHEN THIS IS OVER...
CONGRATULATIONS, LIEUTENANT...
...YOU'VE JUST BEEN PROMOTED TO SECOND-IN-COMMAND.

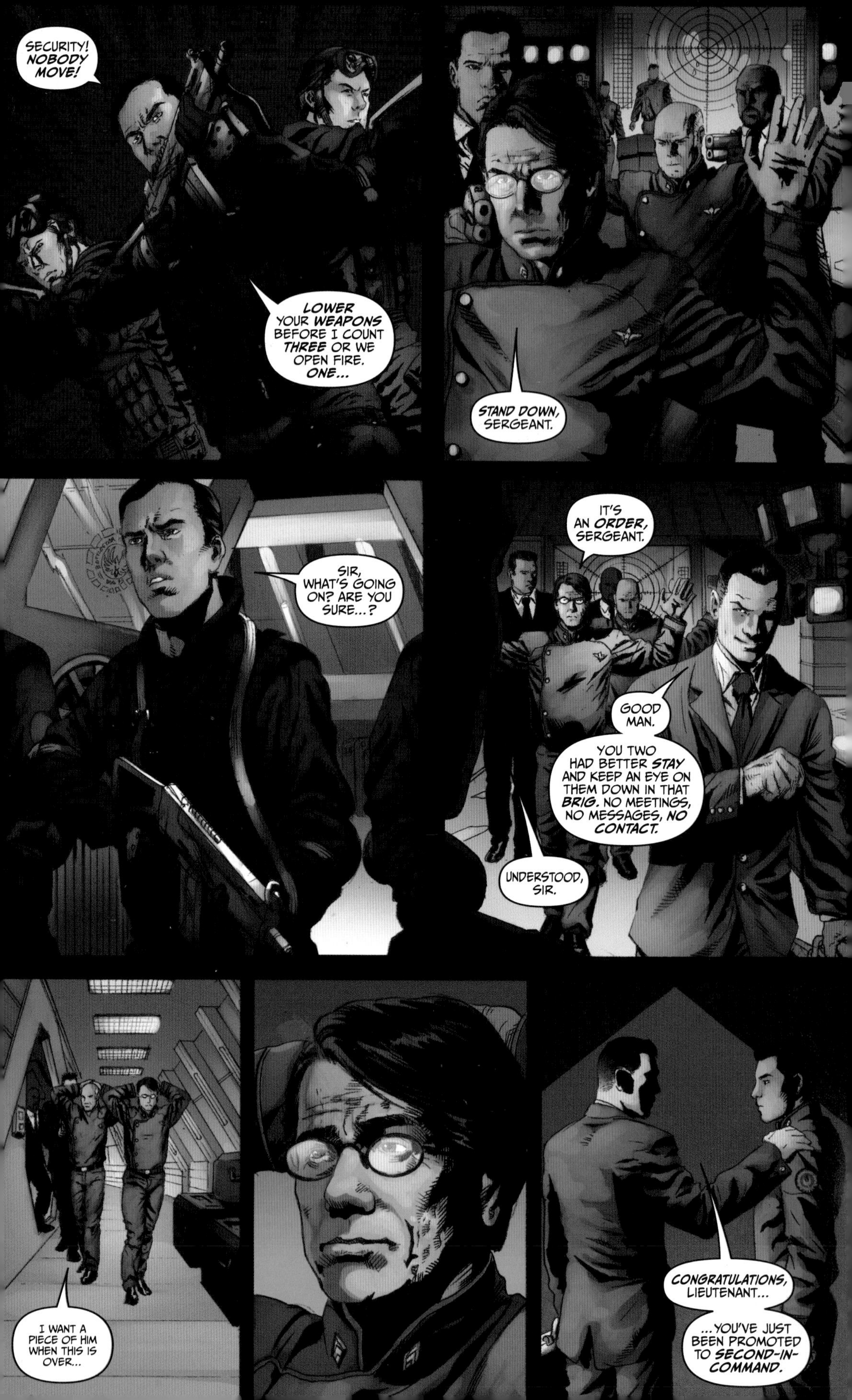
SECURITY! NOBODY MOVE!
LOWER YOUR WEAPONS BEFORE I COUNT THREE OR WE OPEN FIRE. ONE...
STAND DOWN, SERGEANT.
SIR, WHAT'S GOING ON? ARE YOU SURE...?
IT'S AN ORDER, SERGEANT.
GOOD MAN.
YOU TWO HAD BETTER STAY AND KEEP AN EYE ON THEM DOWN IN THAT BRIG. NO MEETINGS, NO MESSAGES, NO CONTACT.
UNDERSTOOD, SIR.
I WANT A PIECE OF HIM WHEN THIS IS OVER...
CONGRATULATIONS, LIEUTENANT...
...YOU'VE JUST BEEN PROMOTED TO SECOND-IN-COMMAND.

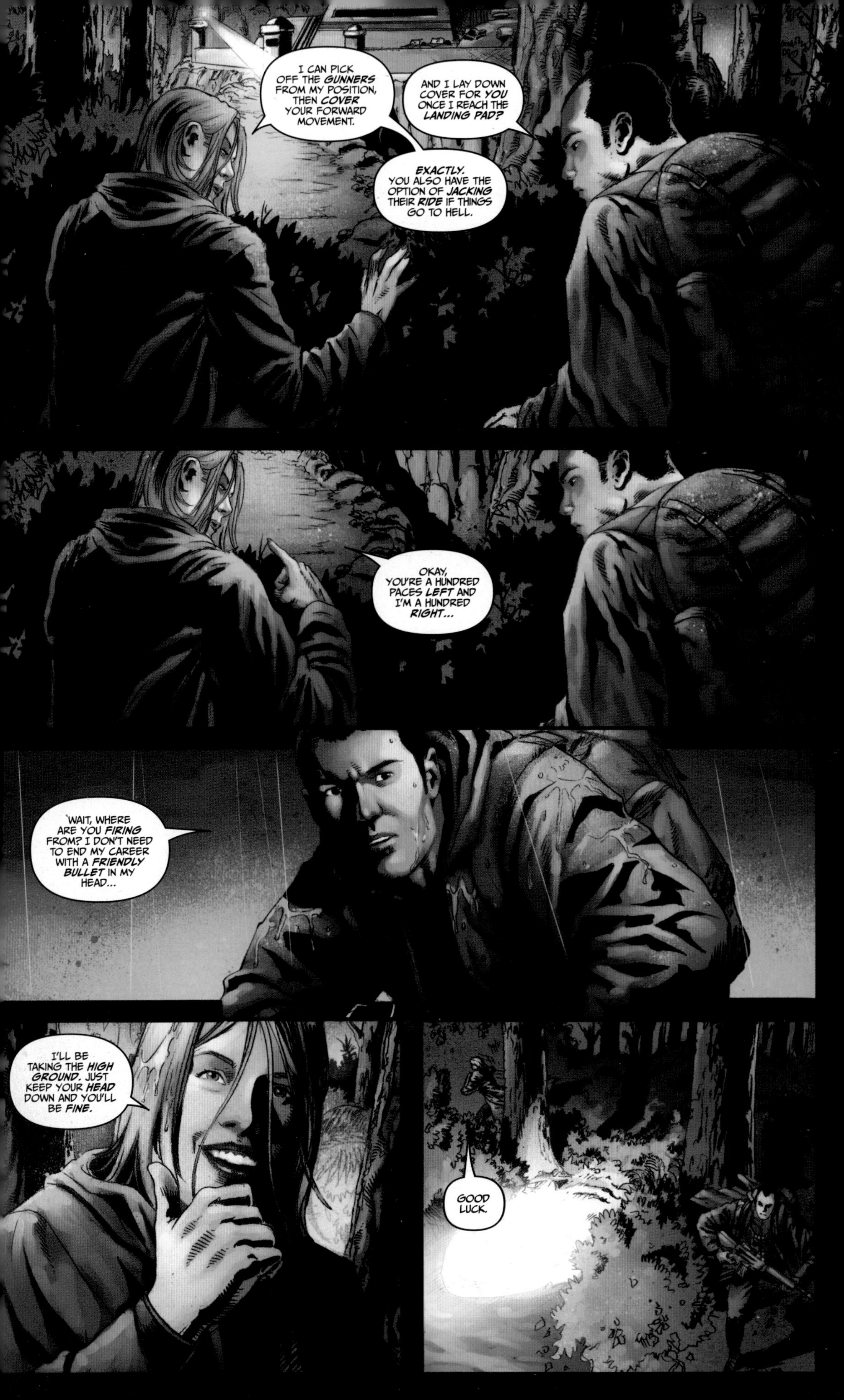

I CAN PICK OFF THE GUNNERS FROM MY POSITION, THEN COVER YOUR FORWARD MOVEMENT.
AND I LAY DOWN COVER FOR YOU ONCE I REACH THE LANDING PAD?
EXACTLY. YOU ALSO HAVE THE OPTION OF JACKING THEIR RIDE IF THINGS GO TO HELL.
OKAY, YOU'RE A HUNDRED PACES LEFT AND I'M A HUNDRED RIGHT...
WAIT, WHERE ARE YOU FIRING FROM? I DON'T NEED TO END MY CAREER WITH A FRIENDLY BULLET IN MY HEAD...
I'LL BE TAKING THE HIGH GROUND. JUST KEEP YOUR HEAD DOWN AND YOU'LL BE FINE.
GOOD LUCK.

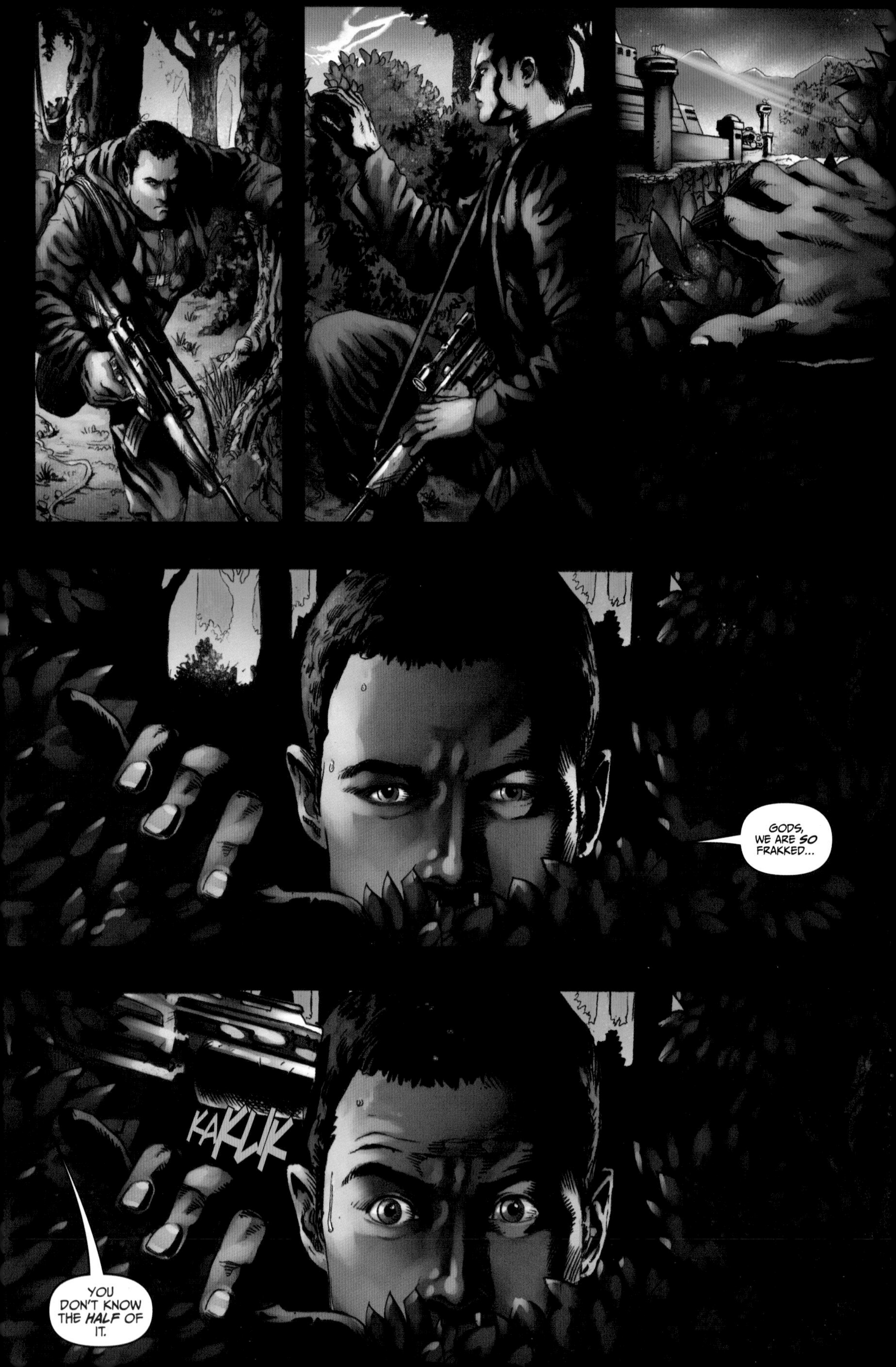
GODS, WE ARE SO FRAKKED...
KAKLIK
YOU DON'T KNOW THE HALF OF IT.

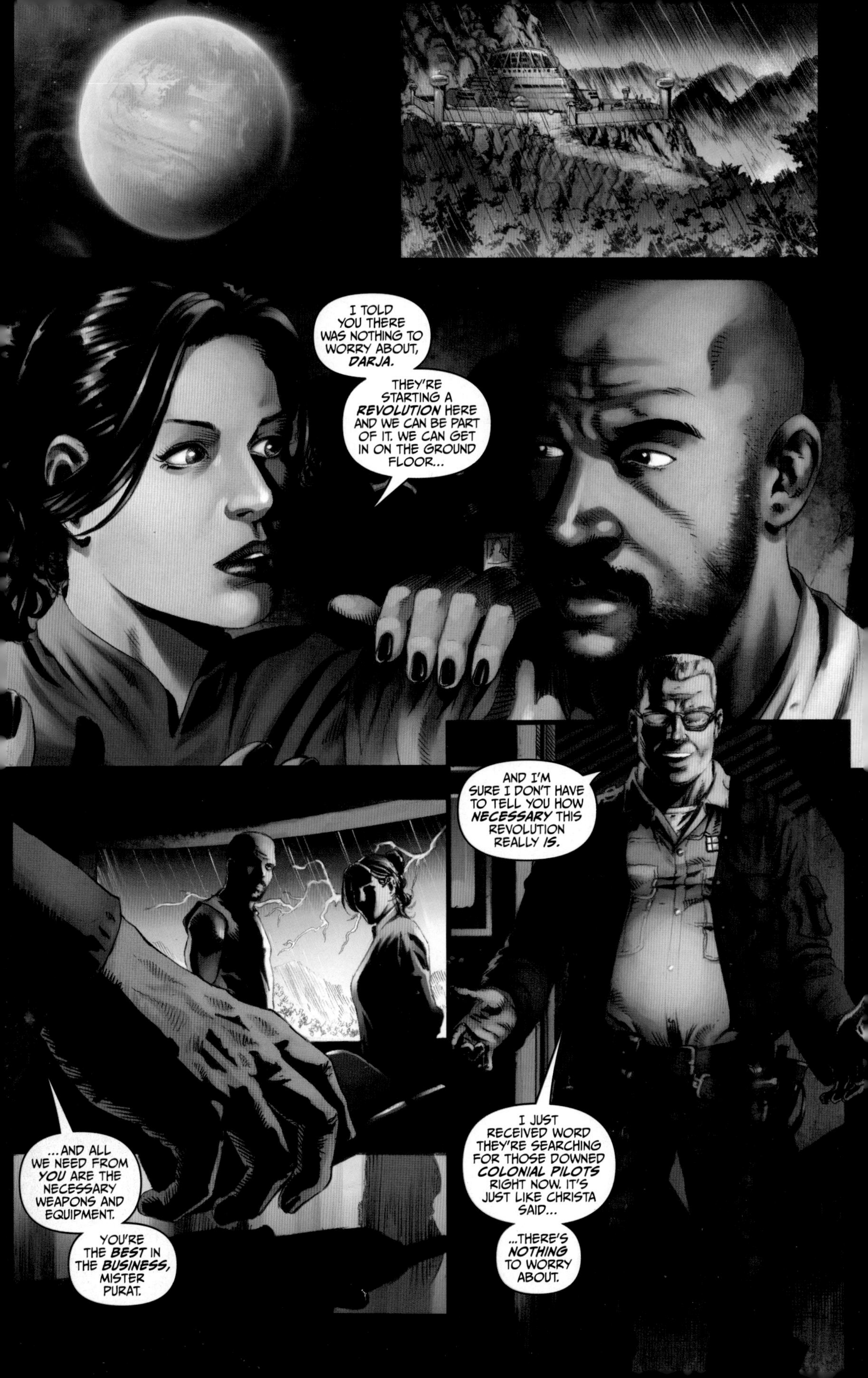
I TOLD YOU THERE WAS NOTHING TO WORRY ABOUT, DARJA.
THEY'RE STARTING A REVOLUTION HERE AND WE CAN BE PART OF IT. WE CAN GET IN ON THE GROUND FLOOR...
AND I'M SURE I DON'T HAVE TO TELL YOU HOW NECESSARY THIS REVOLUTION REALLY IS.
...AND ALL WE NEED FROM YOU ARE THE NECESSARY WEAPONS AND EQUIPMENT.
YOU'RE THE BEST IN THE BUSINESS, MISTER PURAT.
I JUST RECEIVED WORD THEY'RE SEARCHING FOR THOSE DOWNED COLONIAL PILOTS RIGHT NOW. IT'S JUST LIKE CHRISTA SAID...
...THERE'S NOTHING TO WORRY ABOUT.

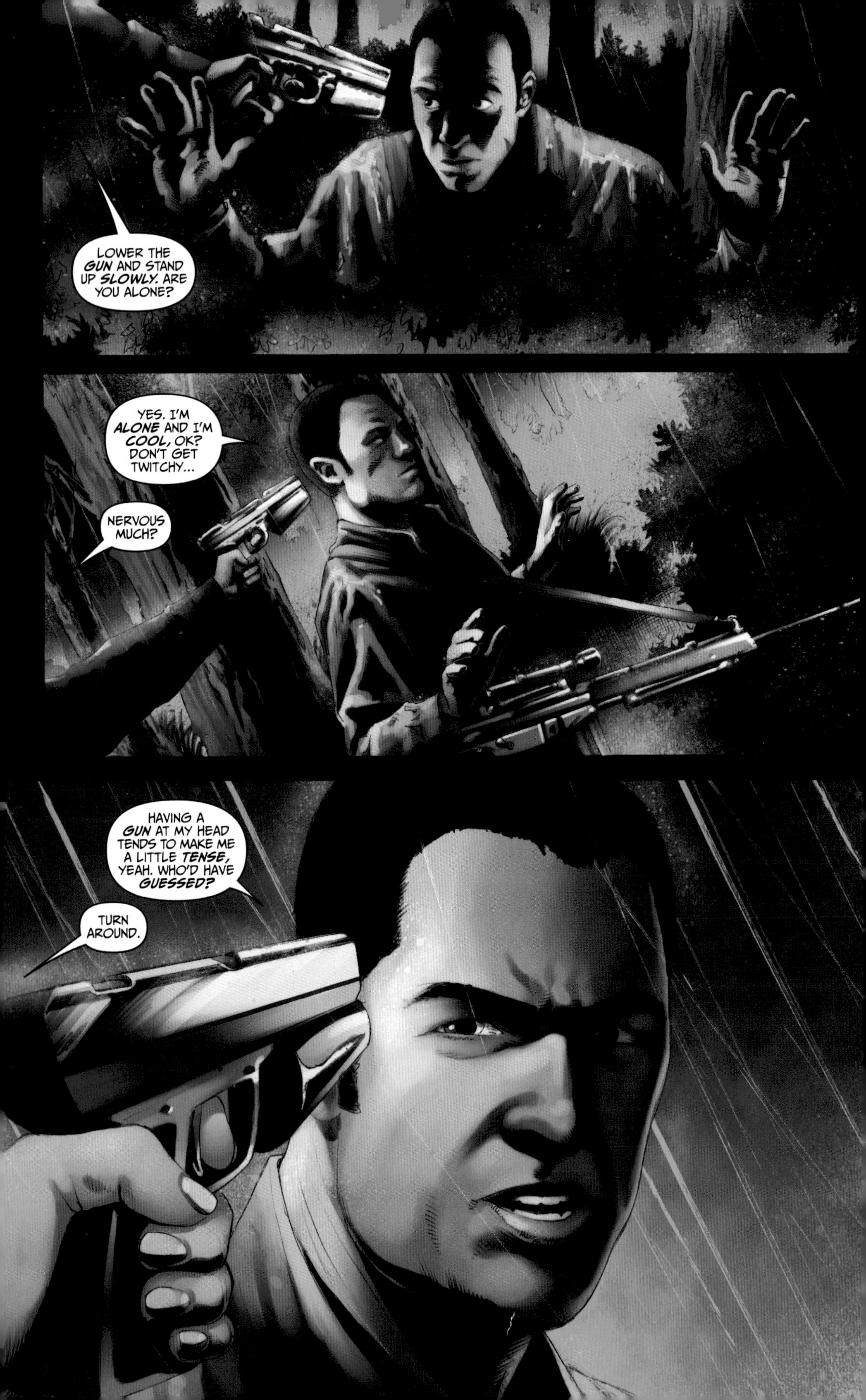
LOWER THE GUN AND STAND UP SLOWLY. ARE YOU ALONE?
YES. I'M ALONE AND I'M COOL, OK? DON'T GET TWITCHY...
NERVOUS MUCH?
HAVING A GUN AT MY HEAD TENDS TO MAKE ME A LITTLE TENSE, YEAH. WHO'D HAVE GUESSED?
TURN AROUND.

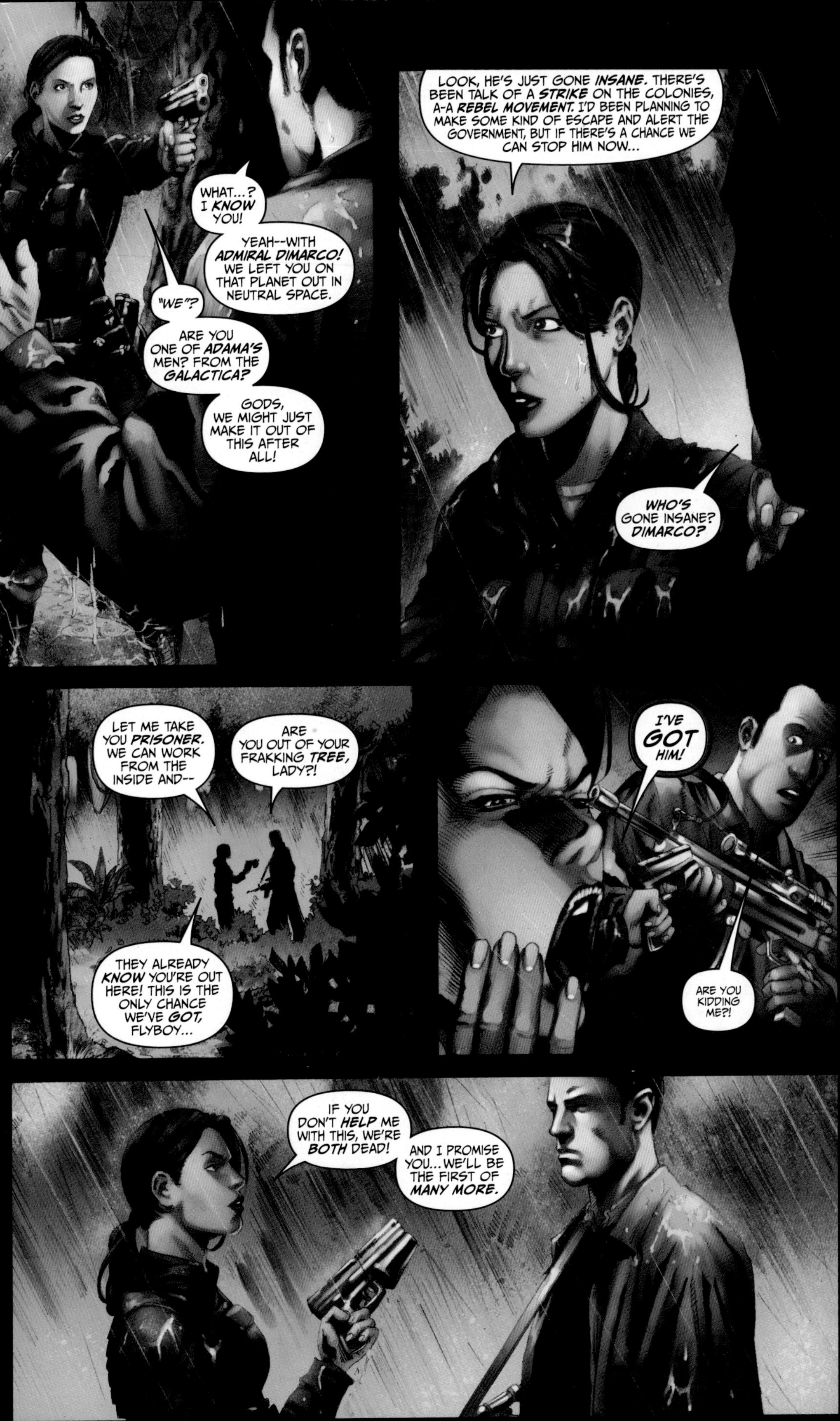
WHAT...? I *KNOW* YOU!
YEAH--WITH *ADMIRAL DIMARCO!* WE LEFT YOU ON THAT PLANET OUT IN NEUTRAL SPACE.
"*WE*"?
ARE YOU ONE OF *ADAMA'S* MEN? FROM THE *GALACTICA?*
GODS, WE MIGHT JUST MAKE IT OUT OF THIS AFTER ALL!
LOOK, HE'S JUST GONE *INSANE.* THERE'S BEEN TALK OF A *STRIKE* ON THE COLONIES, A-A *REBEL MOVEMENT.* I'D BEEN PLANNING TO MAKE SOME KIND OF ESCAPE AND ALERT THE GOVERNMENT, BUT IF THERE'S A CHANCE WE CAN STOP HIM NOW...
WHO'S GONE INSANE? *DIMARCO?*
LET ME TAKE YOU *PRISONER.* WE CAN WORK FROM THE INSIDE AND--
ARE YOU OUT OF YOUR FRAKKING *TREE,* LADY?!
THEY ALREADY *KNOW* YOU'RE OUT HERE! THIS IS THE ONLY CHANCE WE'VE *GOT,* FLYBOY...
I'VE GOT HIM!
ARE YOU KIDDING ME?!
IF YOU DON'T *HELP* ME WITH THIS, WE'RE *BOTH* DEAD!
AND I PROMISE YOU...WE'LL BE THE FIRST OF *MANY MORE.*

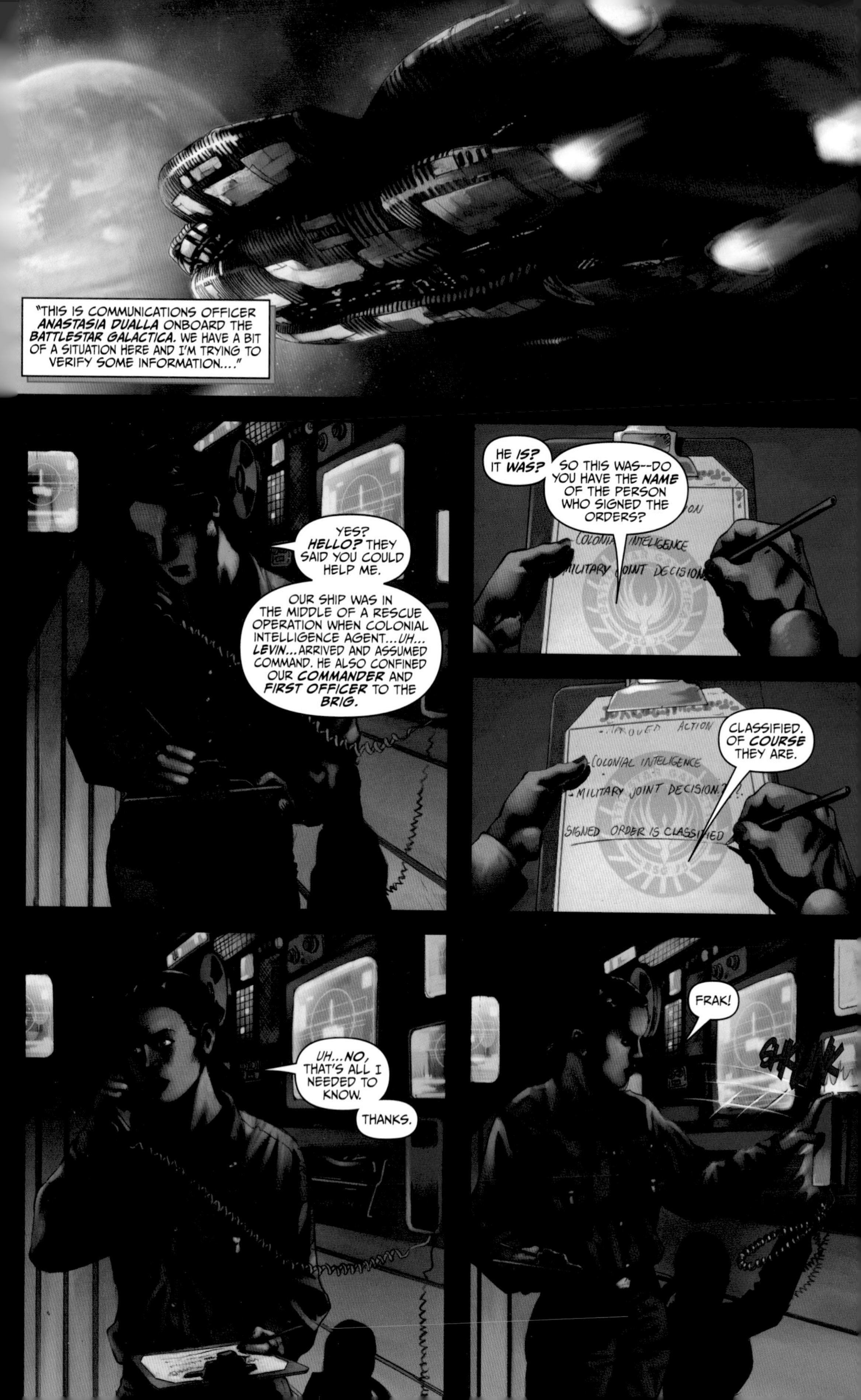
"THIS IS COMMUNICATIONS OFFICER ANASTASIA DUALLA ONBOARD THE BATTLESTAR GALACTICA. WE HAVE A BIT OF A SITUATION HERE AND I'M TRYING TO VERIFY SOME INFORMATION..."
YES? HELLO? THEY SAID YOU COULD HELP ME.
OUR SHIP WAS IN THE MIDDLE OF A RESCUE OPERATION WHEN COLONIAL INTELLIGENCE AGENT...UH... LEVIN...ARRIVED AND ASSUMED COMMAND. HE ALSO CONFINED OUR COMMANDER AND FIRST OFFICER TO THE BRIG.
HE IS? IT WAS?
SO THIS WAS--DO YOU HAVE THE NAME OF THE PERSON WHO SIGNED THE ORDERS?
COLONIAL INTELIGENCE
MILITARY JOINT DECISION
CLASSIFIED. OF COURSE THEY ARE.
COLONIAL INTELIGENCE
MILITARY JOINT DECISION
SIGNED ORDER IS CLASSIFIED
UH...NO, THAT'S ALL I NEEDED TO KNOW.
THANKS.
FRAK!

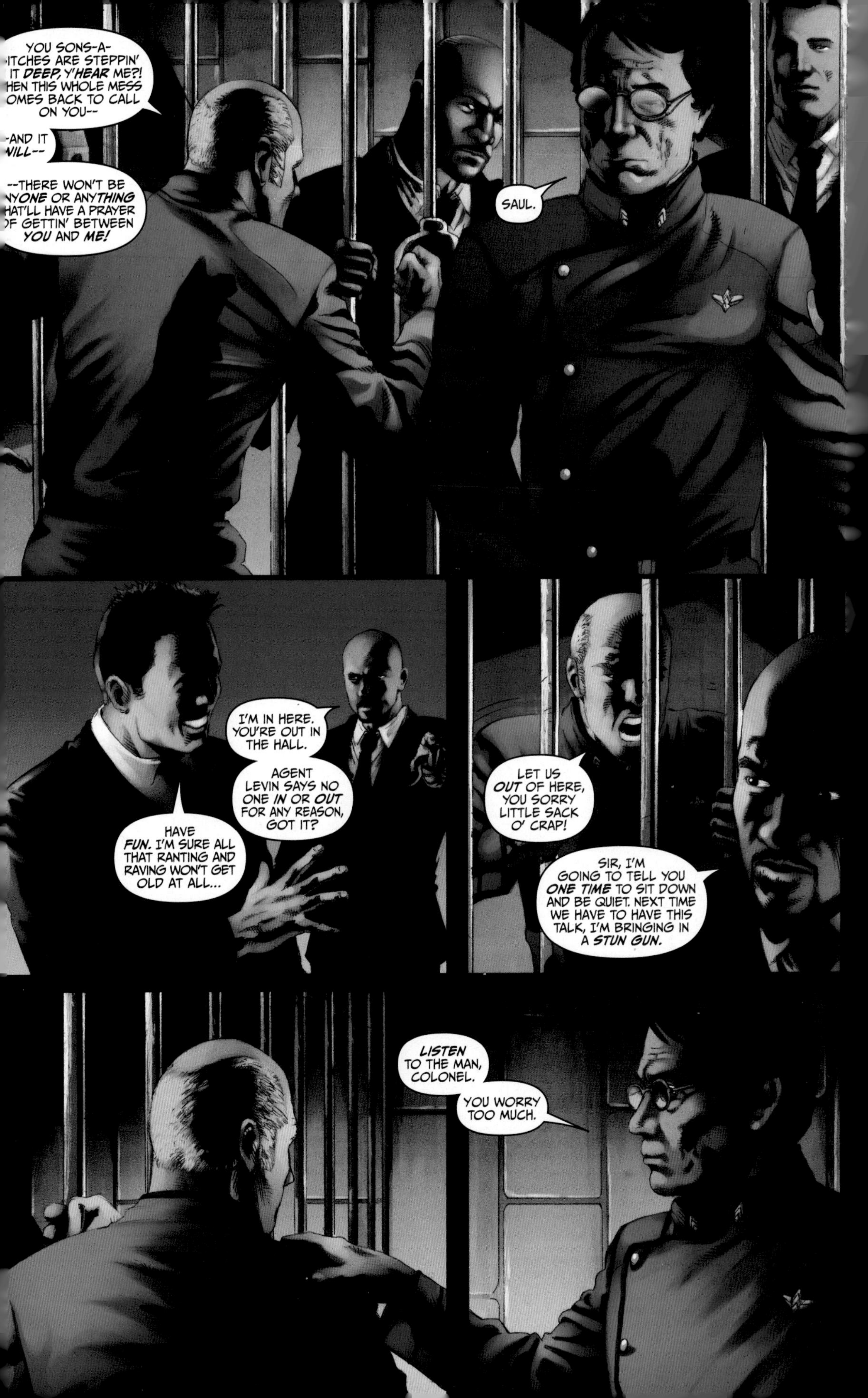

YOU SONS-A-
ITCHES ARE STEPPIN' IT DEEP, Y'HEAR ME?!
HEN THIS WHOLE MESS OMES BACK TO CALL ON YOU--
-AND IT VILL--
--THERE WON'T BE NYONE OR ANYTHING HAT'LL HAVE A PRAYER OF GETTIN' BETWEEN YOU AND ME!
SAUL.
I'M IN HERE. YOU'RE OUT IN THE HALL.
AGENT LEVIN SAYS NO ONE IN OR OUT FOR ANY REASON, GOT IT?
HAVE FUN. I'M SURE ALL THAT RANTING AND RAVING WON'T GET OLD AT ALL...
LET US OUT OF HERE, YOU SORRY LITTLE SACK O' CRAP!
SIR, I'M GOING TO TELL YOU ONE TIME TO SIT DOWN AND BE QUIET. NEXT TIME WE HAVE TO HAVE THIS TALK, I'M BRINGING IN A STUN GUN.
LISTEN TO THE MAN, COLONEL.
YOU WORRY TOO MUCH.

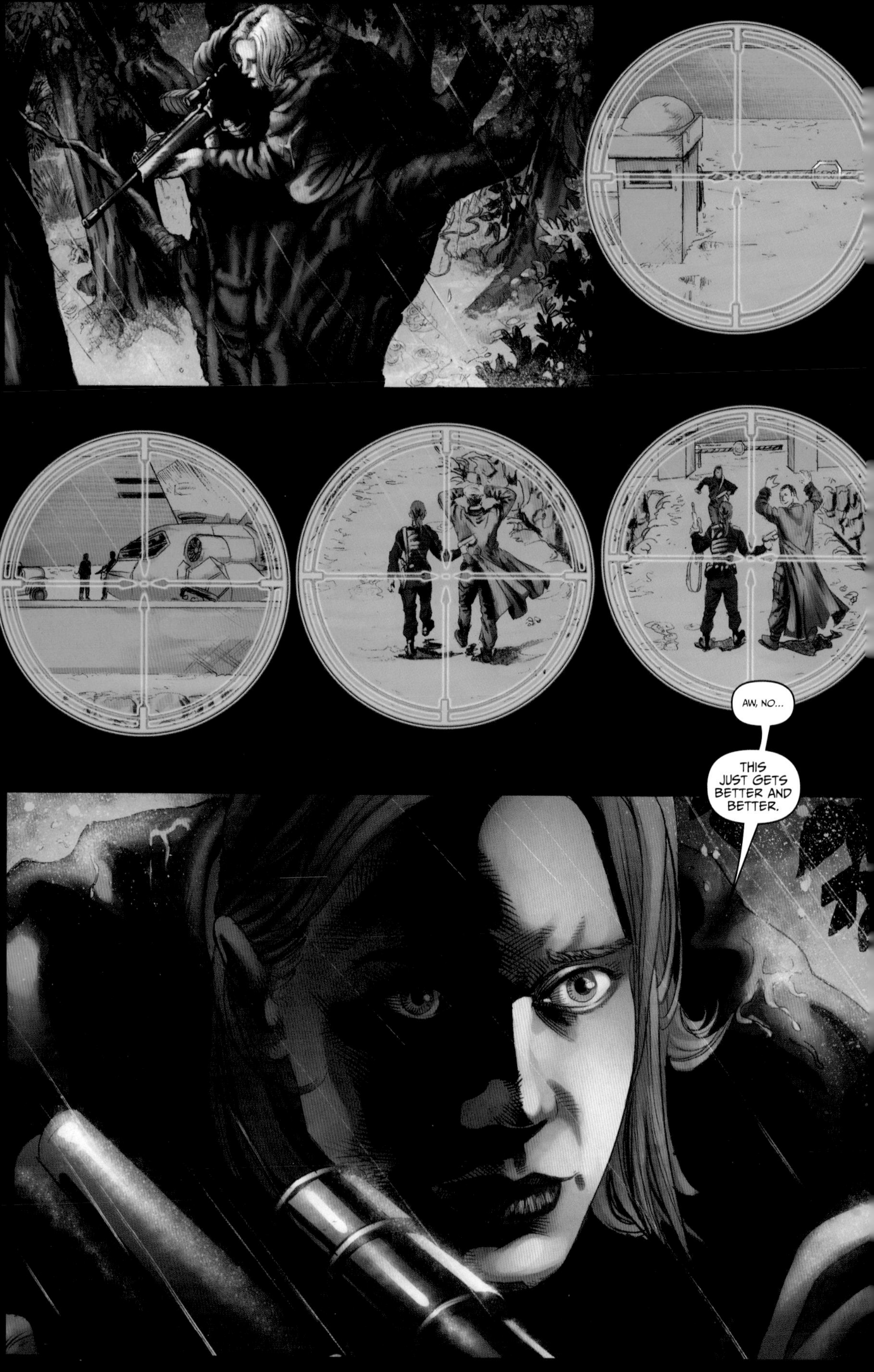
AW, NO...
THIS JUST GETS BETTER AND BETTER.

I'M THE *COMMANDING OFFICER* OF THIS SHIP AS OF FIFTEEN MINUTES AGO. DIDN'T YOU HEAR THE *ANNOUNCEMENT?*

ENGINEERING, THIS IS *AGENT LEVIN.*

WHAT DO YOU *MEAN* "WHO"?

NO? WELL, OPEN YOUR *EARS,* CAPTAIN, BECAUSE I'VE GOT A LIST OF REPORTS THAT I WANT ON MY DESK WITHIN THE *HOUR.*

ANYTHING?

HE'S OFFICIAL. CAN YOU BELIEVE THAT?

HOW DID THIS *HAPPEN?*

THAT'S THE MYSTERY, *GAETA.* THE ORDERS ARE SEALED AND THE SIGNATURES ARE CLASSIFIED.

HERE. TAKE THIS WITH YOU TO THE MEETING.

WHAT IS IT?

DUTY ROSTER. YOU *KNOW*...BECAUSE IT'S *YOUR JOB* TO *POST IT.*

RIIIIGHT.

WHERE ARE YOU GOING, SOLDIER?

I...AH...I HAVE DUTIES TO PERFORM OUTSIDE OF THE *CIC.*

THAT'S INTERESTING. LET'S SEE.

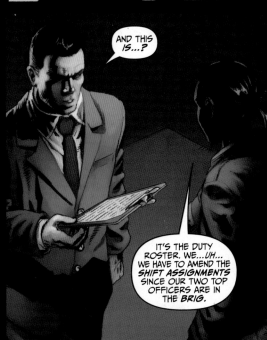

AND THIS IS...?

IT'S THE DUTY ROSTER. WE...*UH*...WE HAVE TO AMEND THE *SHIFT ASSIGNMENTS* SINCE OUR TWO TOP OFFICERS ARE IN THE *BRIG.*

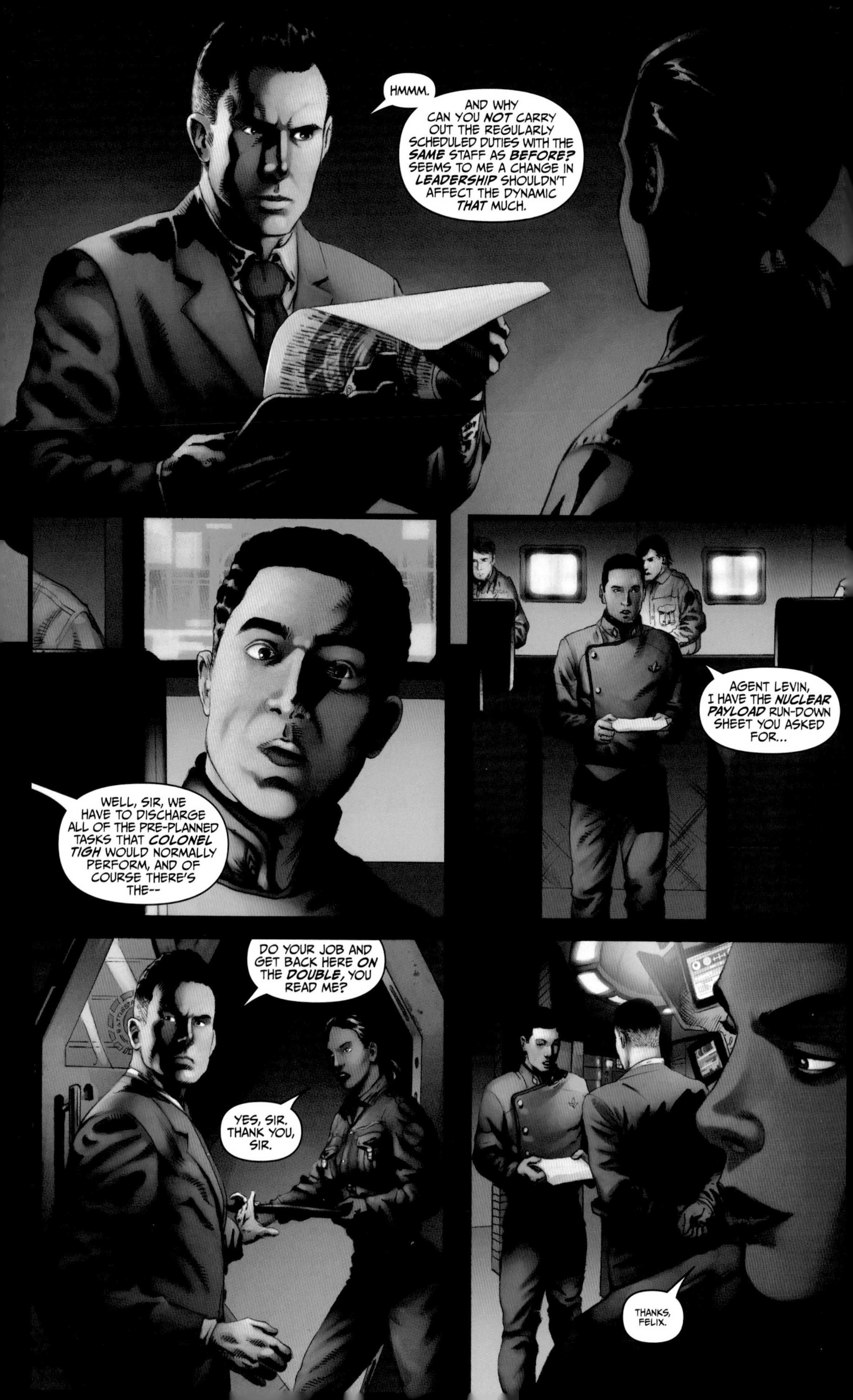
HMMM.
AND WHY CAN YOU NOT CARRY OUT THE REGULARLY SCHEDULED DUTIES WITH THE SAME STAFF AS BEFORE? SEEMS TO ME A CHANGE IN LEADERSHIP SHOULDN'T AFFECT THE DYNAMIC THAT MUCH.
WELL, SIR, WE HAVE TO DISCHARGE ALL OF THE PRE-PLANNED TASKS THAT COLONEL TIGH WOULD NORMALLY PERFORM, AND OF COURSE THERE'S THE--
AGENT LEVIN, I HAVE THE NUCLEAR PAYLOAD RUN-DOWN SHEET YOU ASKED FOR...
DO YOUR JOB AND GET BACK HERE ON THE DOUBLE, YOU READ ME?
YES, SIR. THANK YOU, SIR.
THANKS, FELIX.

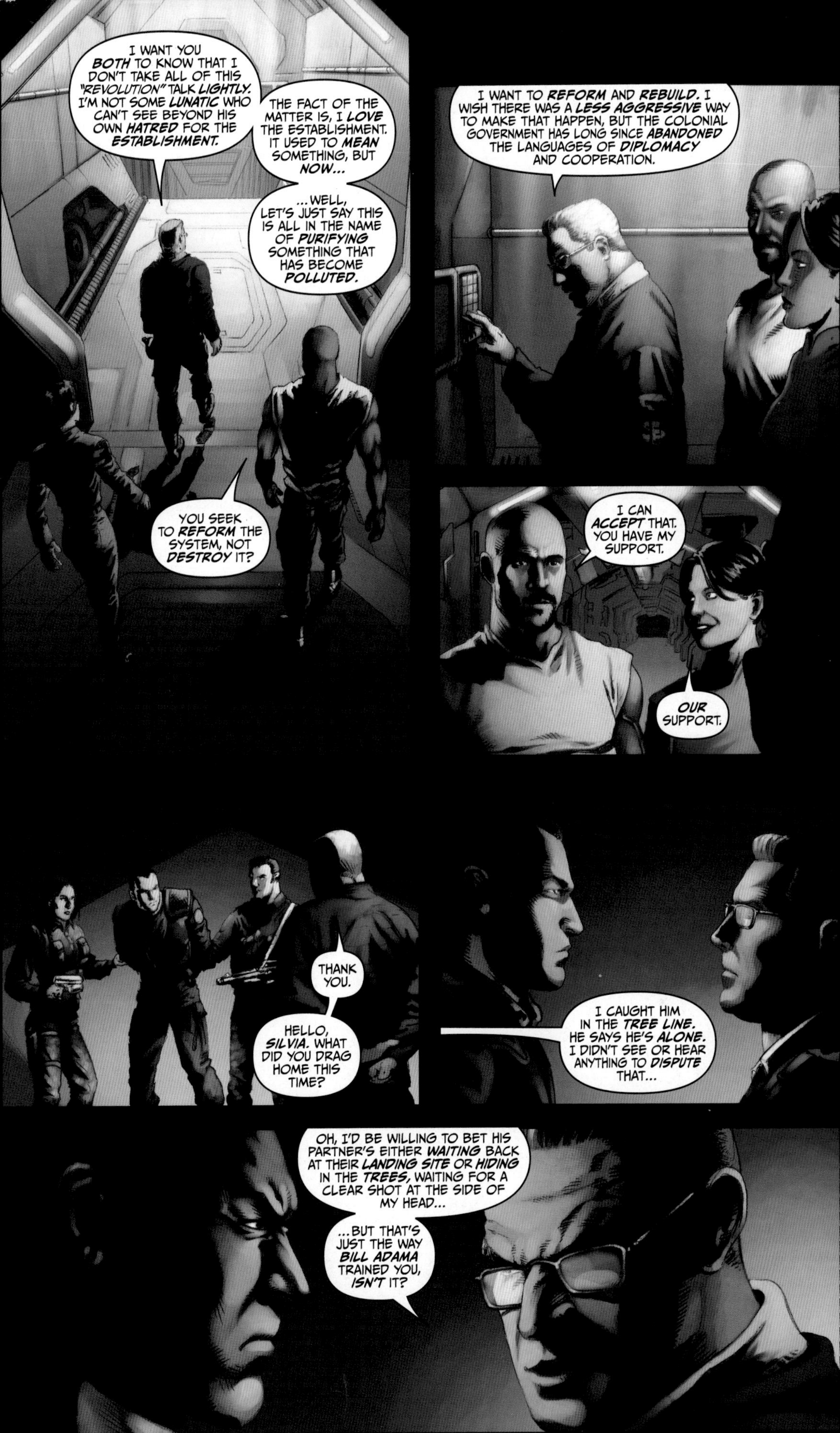
I WANT YOU BOTH TO KNOW THAT I DON'T TAKE ALL OF THIS "REVOLUTION" TALK LIGHTLY. I'M NOT SOME LUNATIC WHO CAN'T SEE BEYOND HIS OWN HATRED FOR THE ESTABLISHMENT.
THE FACT OF THE MATTER IS, I LOVE THE ESTABLISHMENT. IT USED TO MEAN SOMETHING, BUT NOW...
...WELL, LET'S JUST SAY THIS IS ALL IN THE NAME OF PURIFYING SOMETHING THAT HAS BECOME POLLUTED.
YOU SEEK TO REFORM THE SYSTEM, NOT DESTROY IT?
I WANT TO REFORM AND REBUILD. I WISH THERE WAS A LESS AGGRESSIVE WAY TO MAKE THAT HAPPEN, BUT THE COLONIAL GOVERNMENT HAS LONG SINCE ABANDONED THE LANGUAGES OF DIPLOMACY AND COOPERATION.
I CAN ACCEPT THAT. YOU HAVE MY SUPPORT.
OUR SUPPORT.
THANK YOU.
HELLO, SILVIA. WHAT DID YOU DRAG HOME THIS TIME?
I CAUGHT HIM IN THE TREE LINE. HE SAYS HE'S ALONE. I DIDN'T SEE OR HEAR ANYTHING TO DISPUTE THAT...
OH, I'D BE WILLING TO BET HIS PARTNER'S EITHER WAITING BACK AT THEIR LANDING SITE OR HIDING IN THE TREES, WAITING FOR A CLEAR SHOT AT THE SIDE OF MY HEAD...
...BUT THAT'S JUST THE WAY BILL ADAMA TRAINED YOU, ISN'T IT?

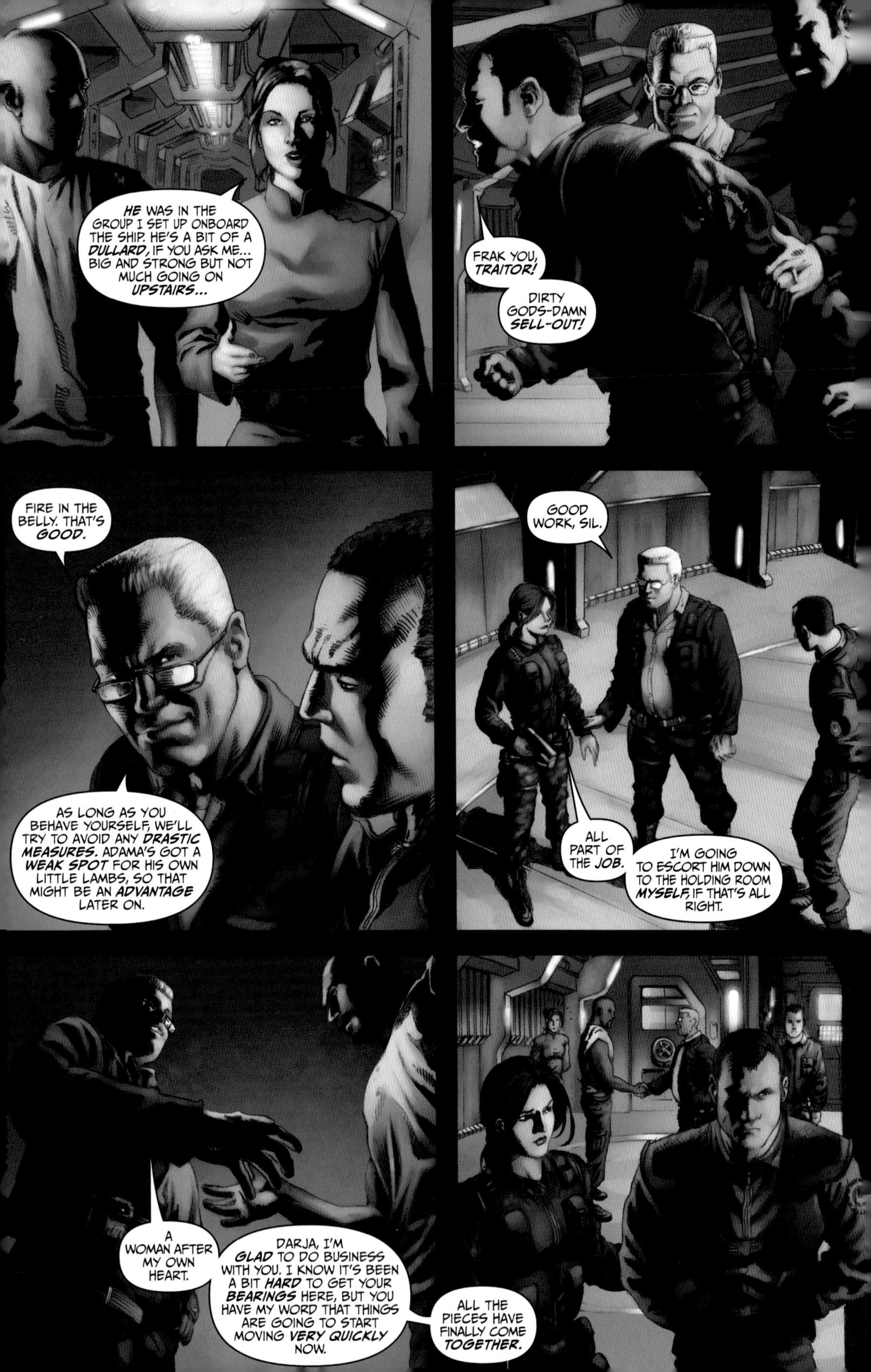
HE WAS IN THE GROUP I SET UP ONBOARD THE SHIP. HE'S A BIT OF A DULLARD, IF YOU ASK ME... BIG AND STRONG BUT NOT MUCH GOING ON UPSTAIRS...
FRAK YOU, TRAITOR!
DIRTY GODS-DAMN SELL-OUT!
FIRE IN THE BELLY. THAT'S GOOD.
AS LONG AS YOU BEHAVE YOURSELF, WE'LL TRY TO AVOID ANY DRASTIC MEASURES. ADAMA'S GOT A WEAK SPOT FOR HIS OWN LITTLE LAMBS, SO THAT MIGHT BE AN ADVANTAGE LATER ON.
GOOD WORK, SIL.
ALL PART OF THE JOB.
I'M GOING TO ESCORT HIM DOWN TO THE HOLDING ROOM MYSELF, IF THAT'S ALL RIGHT.
A WOMAN AFTER MY OWN HEART.
DARJA, I'M GLAD TO DO BUSINESS WITH YOU. I KNOW IT'S BEEN A BIT HARD TO GET YOUR BEARINGS HERE, BUT YOU HAVE MY WORD THAT THINGS ARE GOING TO START MOVING VERY QUICKLY NOW.
ALL THE PIECES HAVE FINALLY COME TOGETHER.

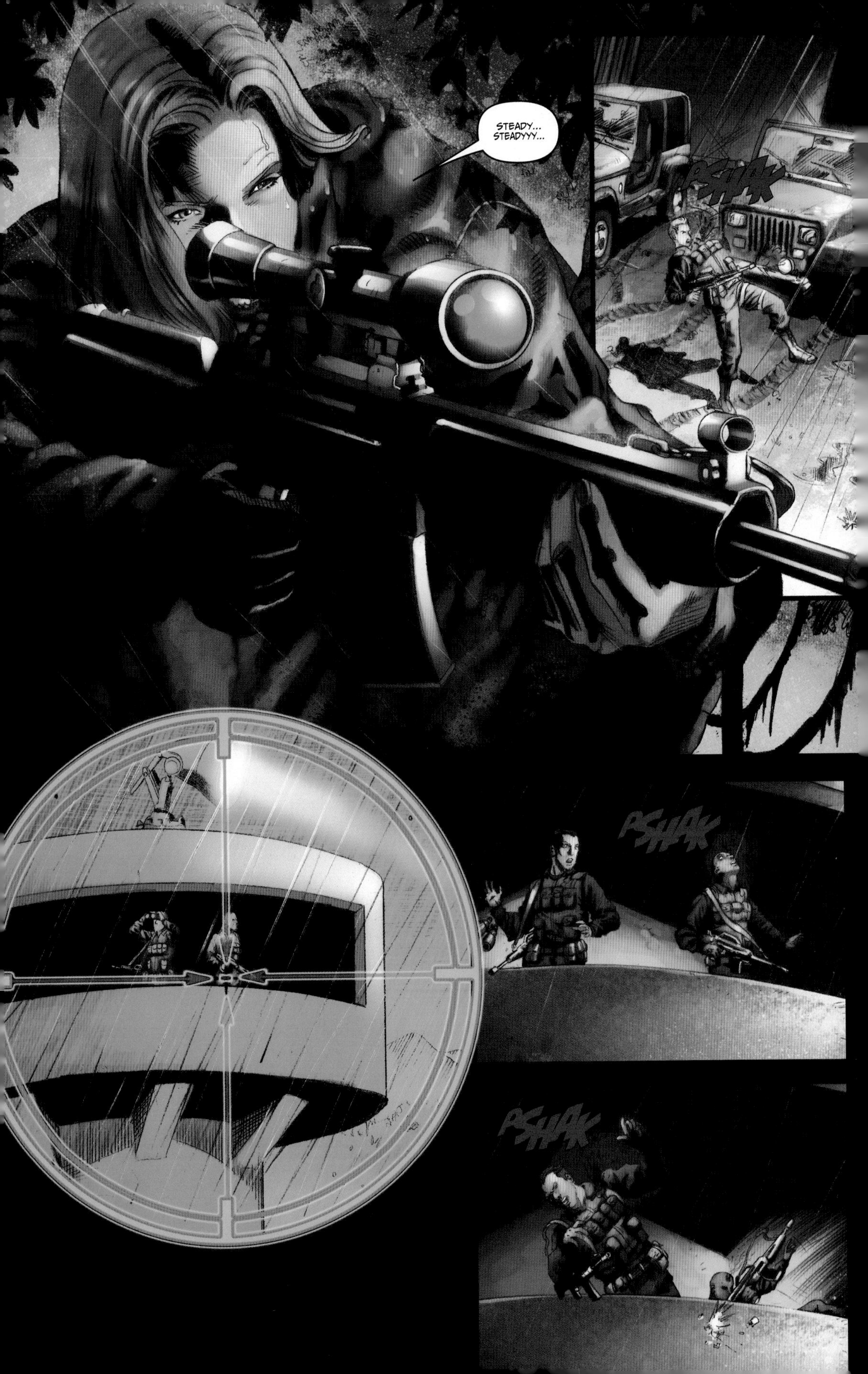
STEADY... STEADYYY...
PSHAK
PSHAK
PSHAK

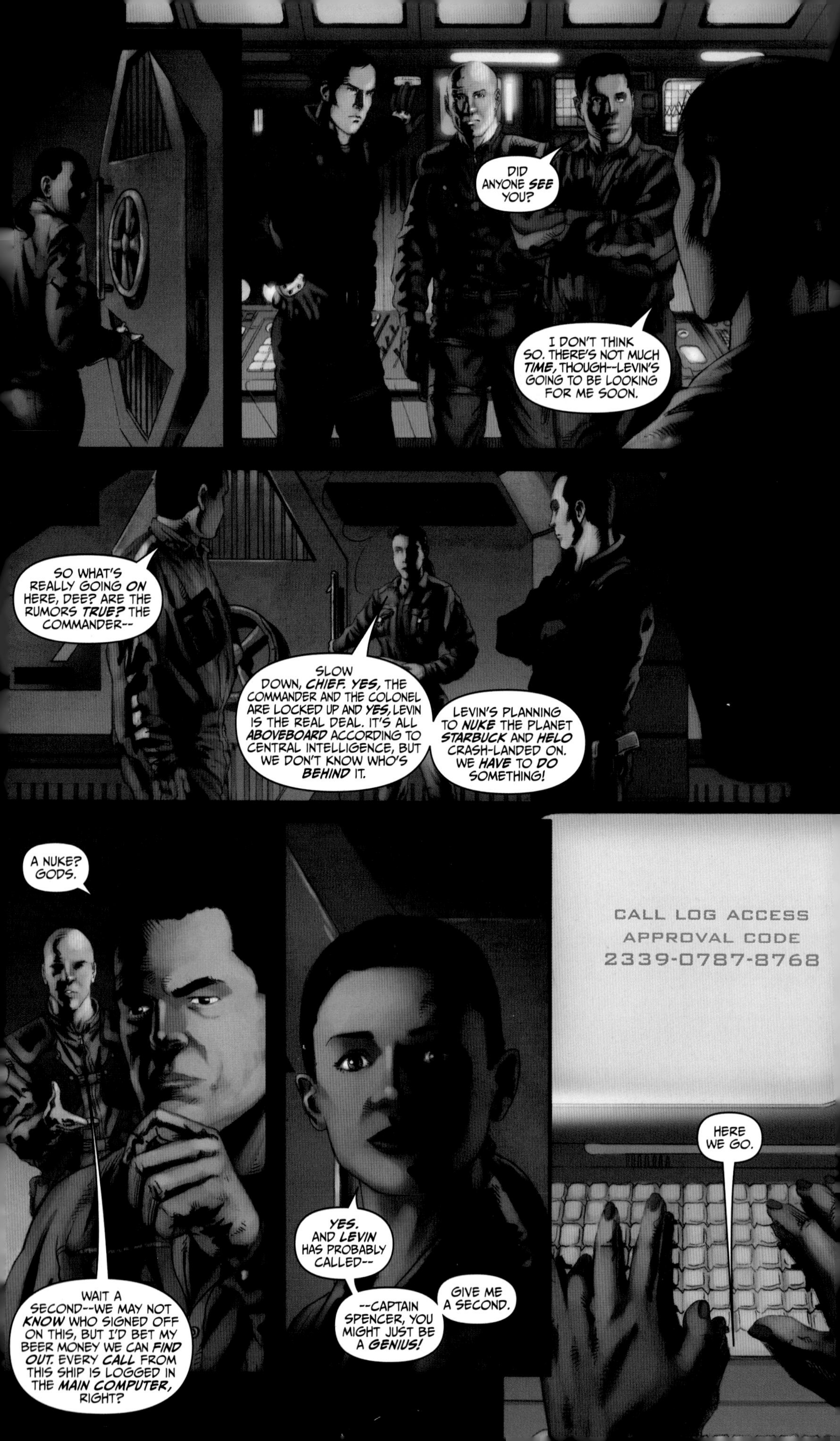
DID ANYONE **SEE** YOU?
I DON'T THINK SO. THERE'S NOT MUCH **TIME,** THOUGH--LEVIN'S GOING TO BE LOOKING FOR ME SOON.
SO WHAT'S REALLY GOING **ON** HERE, DEE? ARE THE RUMORS **TRUE?** THE COMMANDER--
SLOW DOWN, **CHIEF. YES,** THE COMMANDER AND THE COLONEL ARE LOCKED UP AND **YES,** LEVIN IS THE REAL DEAL. IT'S ALL **ABOVEBOARD** ACCORDING TO CENTRAL INTELLIGENCE, BUT WE DON'T KNOW WHO'S **BEHIND** IT.
LEVIN'S PLANNING TO **NUKE** THE PLANET **STARBUCK** AND **HELO** CRASH-LANDED ON. WE **HAVE** TO **DO** SOMETHING!
A NUKE? GODS.
WAIT A SECOND--WE MAY NOT **KNOW** WHO SIGNED OFF ON THIS, BUT I'D BET MY BEER MONEY WE CAN **FIND OUT.** EVERY **CALL** FROM THIS SHIP IS LOGGED IN THE **MAIN COMPUTER,** RIGHT?
YES. AND **LEVIN** HAS PROBABLY CALLED--
--CAPTAIN SPENCER, YOU MIGHT JUST BE A **GENIUS!**
GIVE ME A SECOND.
CALL LOG ACCESS
APPROVAL CODE
2339-0787-8768
HERE WE GO.

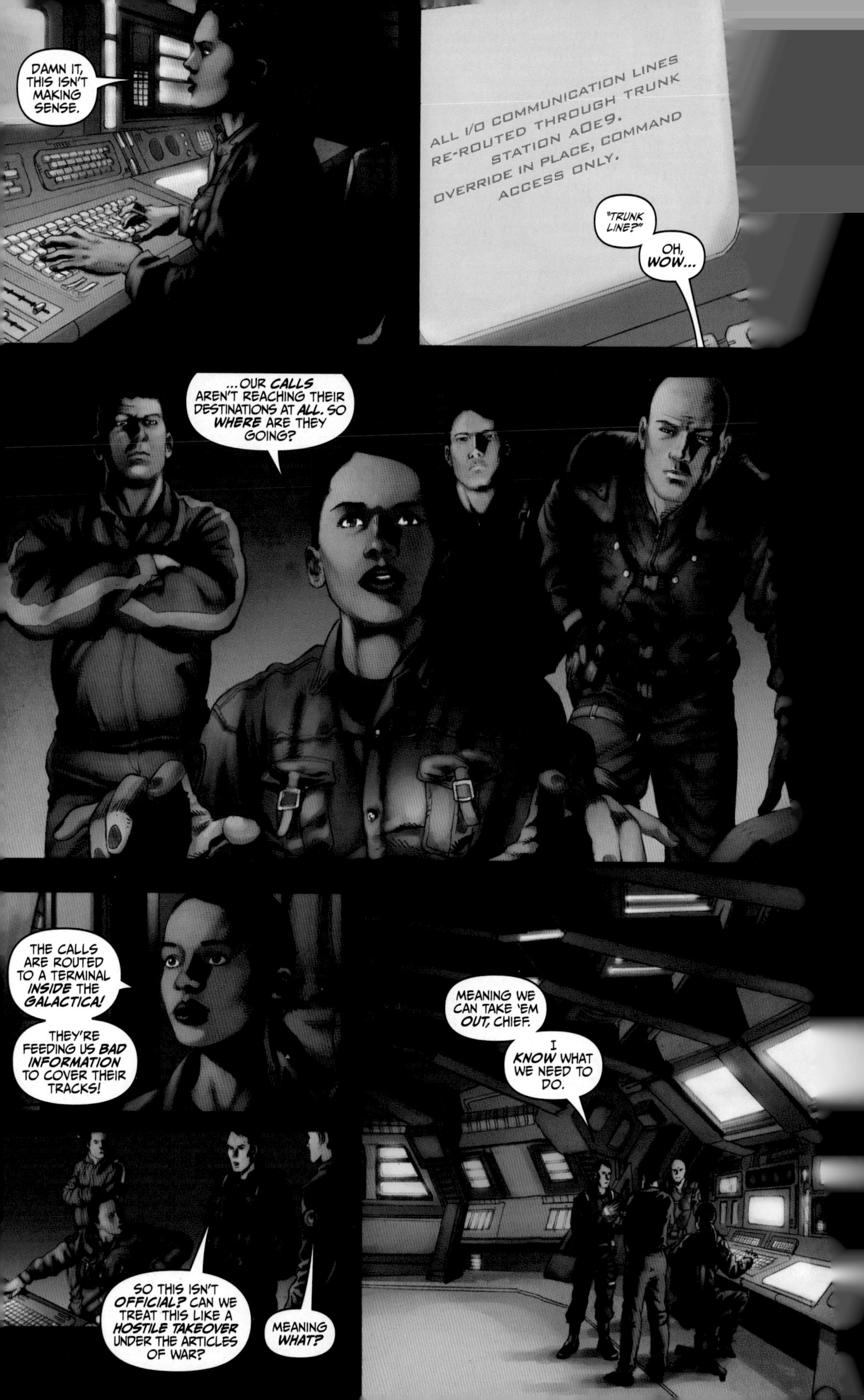
DAMN IT, THIS ISN'T MAKING SENSE.
ALL I/O COMMUNICATION LINES RE-ROUTED THROUGH TRUNK STATION A0E9. OVERRIDE IN PLACE, COMMAND ACCESS ONLY.
"TRUNK LINE?"
OH, WOW...
...OUR CALLS AREN'T REACHING THEIR DESTINATIONS AT ALL. SO WHERE ARE THEY GOING?
THE CALLS ARE ROUTED TO A TERMINAL INSIDE THE GALACTICA!
THEY'RE FEEDING US BAD INFORMATION TO COVER THEIR TRACKS!
SO THIS ISN'T OFFICIAL? CAN WE TREAT THIS LIKE A HOSTILE TAKEOVER UNDER THE ARTICLES OF WAR?
MEANING WHAT?
MEANING WE CAN TAKE 'EM OUT, CHIEF.
I KNOW WHAT WE NEED TO DO.

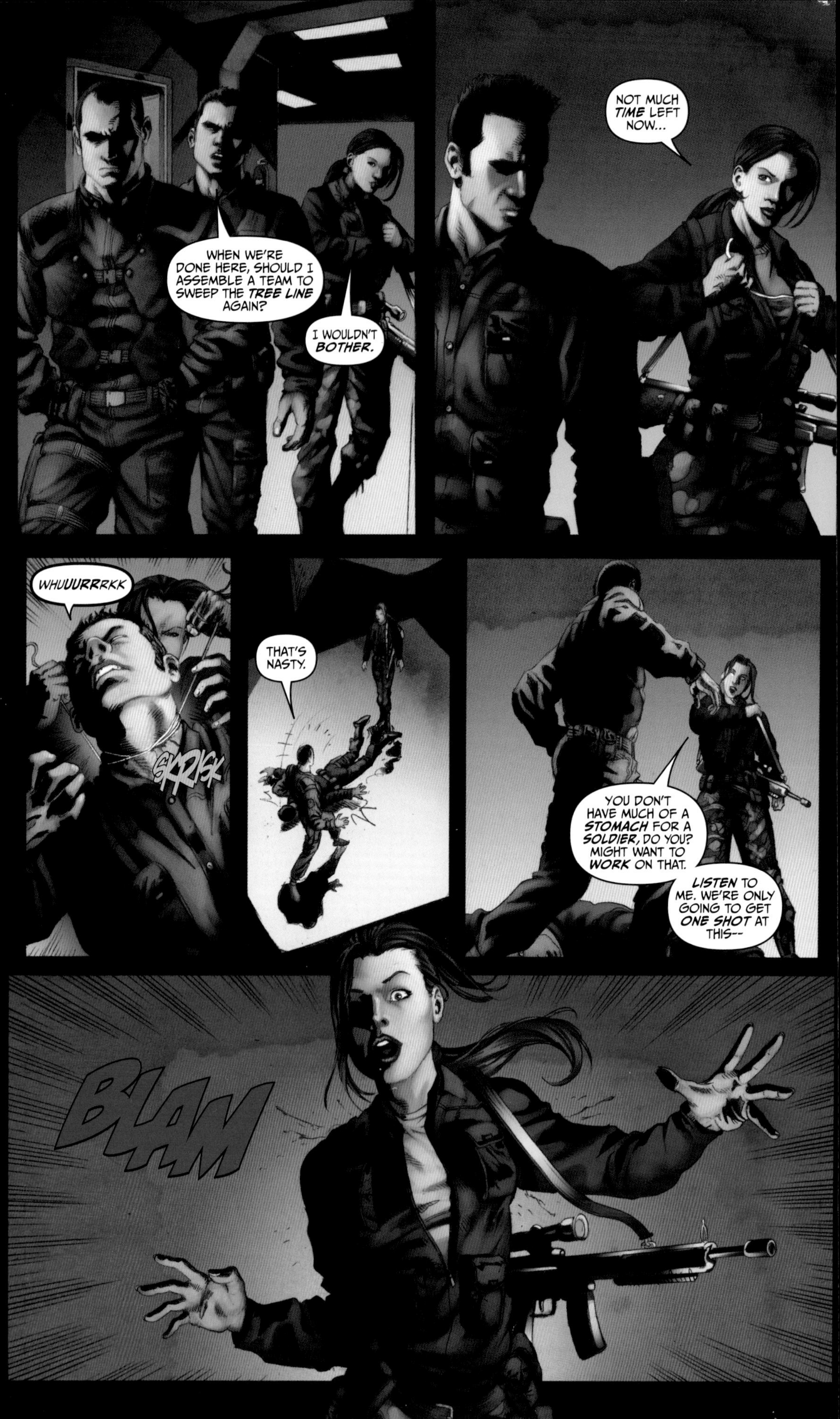

WHEN WE'RE DONE HERE, SHOULD I ASSEMBLE A TEAM TO SWEEP THE TREE LINE AGAIN?
I WOULDN'T BOTHER.
NOT MUCH TIME LEFT NOW...
WHUUURRRKK
SKRISK
THAT'S NASTY.
YOU DON'T HAVE MUCH OF A STOMACH FOR A SOLDIER, DO YOU? MIGHT WANT TO WORK ON THAT.
LISTEN TO ME. WE'RE ONLY GOING TO GET ONE SHOT AT THIS--
BLAM

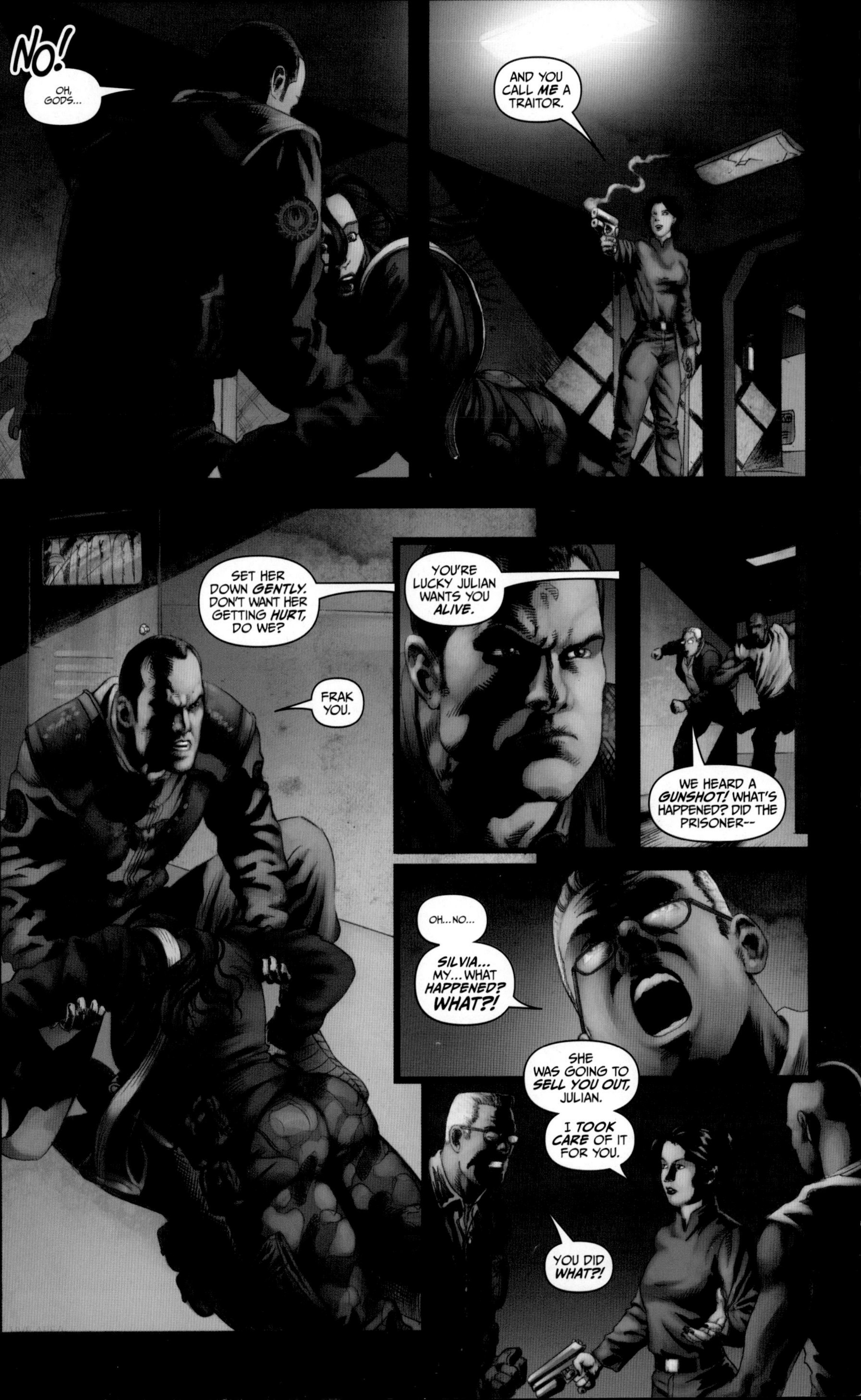
NO!
OH, GODS...
AND YOU CALL *ME* A TRAITOR.
SET HER DOWN *GENTLY.* DON'T WANT HER GETTING *HURT,* DO WE?
FRAK YOU.
YOU'RE LUCKY JULIAN WANTS YOU *ALIVE.*
WE HEARD A *GUNSHOT!* WHAT'S HAPPENED? DID THE PRISONER--
OH...NO...
SILVIA... MY...WHAT *HAPPENED? WHAT?!*
SHE WAS GOING TO *SELL YOU OUT,* JULIAN.
I *TOOK CARE* OF IT FOR YOU.
YOU DID *WHAT?!*

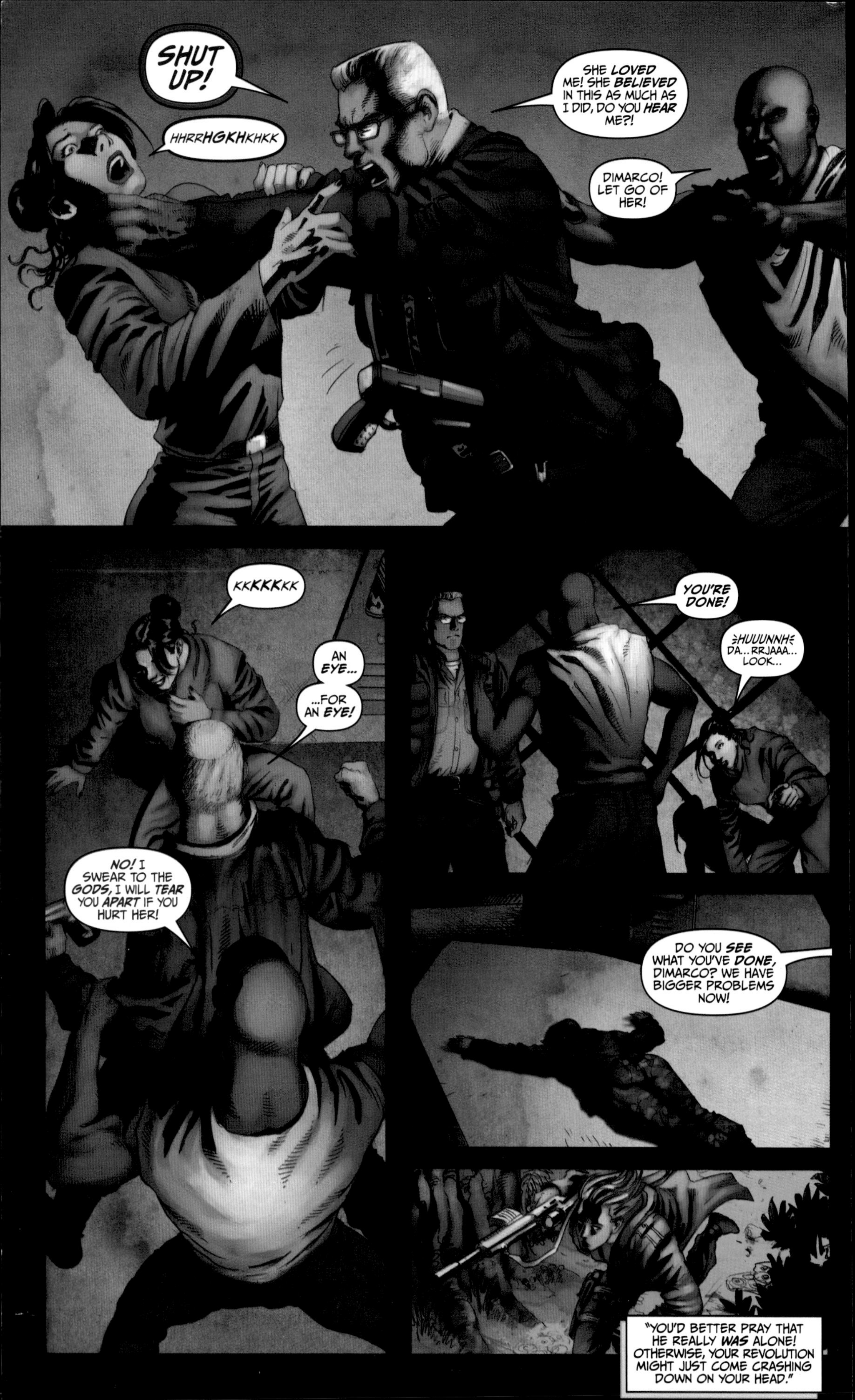
SHUT UP!
HHRRHGKHKHKK
SHE LOVED ME! SHE BELIEVED IN THIS AS MUCH AS I DID, DO YOU HEAR ME?!
DIMARCO! LET GO OF HER!
KKKKKKK
AN EYE...
...FOR AN EYE!
NO! I SWEAR TO THE GODS, I WILL TEAR YOU APART IF YOU HURT HER!
YOU'RE DONE!
HUUUNNH DA...RRJAAA... LOOK...
DO YOU SEE WHAT YOU'VE DONE, DIMARCO? WE HAVE BIGGER PROBLEMS NOW!
"YOU'D BETTER PRAY THAT HE REALLY WAS ALONE! OTHERWISE, YOUR REVOLUTION MIGHT JUST COME CRASHING DOWN ON YOUR HEAD."

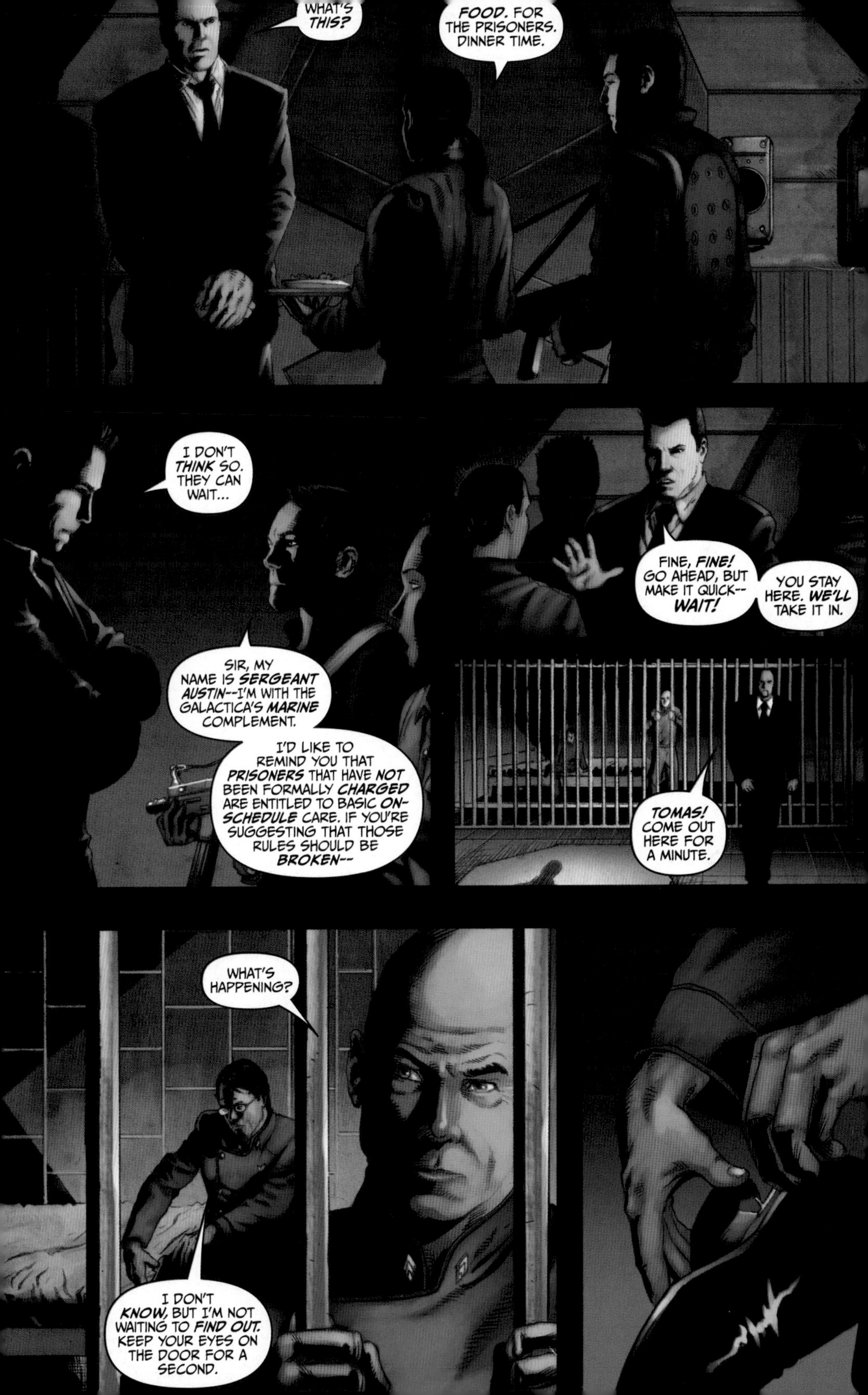

WHAT'S THIS?
FOOD. FOR THE PRISONERS. DINNER TIME.
I DON'T THINK SO. THEY CAN WAIT...
SIR, MY NAME IS SERGEANT AUSTIN--I'M WITH THE GALACTICA'S MARINE COMPLEMENT.
I'D LIKE TO REMIND YOU THAT PRISONERS THAT HAVE NOT BEEN FORMALLY CHARGED ARE ENTITLED TO BASIC ON-SCHEDULE CARE. IF YOU'RE SUGGESTING THAT THOSE RULES SHOULD BE BROKEN--
FINE, FINE! GO AHEAD, BUT MAKE IT QUICK-- WAIT!
YOU STAY HERE. WE'LL TAKE IT IN.
TOMAS! COME OUT HERE FOR A MINUTE.
WHAT'S HAPPENING?
I DON'T KNOW, BUT I'M NOT WAITING TO FIND OUT. KEEP YOUR EYES ON THE DOOR FOR A SECOND.

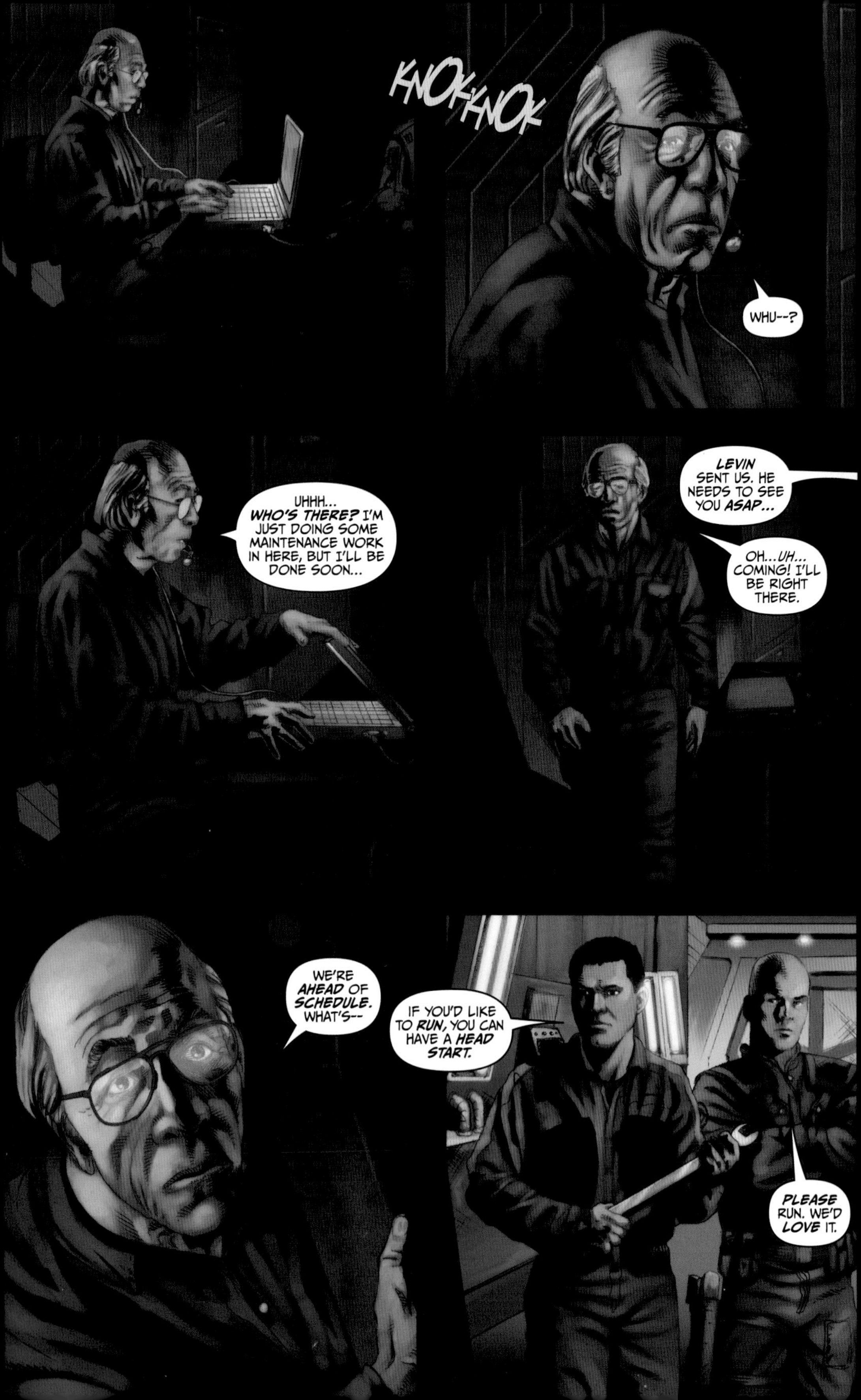
KNOK KNOK
WHU--?
UHHH... WHO'S THERE? I'M JUST DOING SOME MAINTENANCE WORK IN HERE, BUT I'LL BE DONE SOON...
LEVIN SENT US. HE NEEDS TO SEE YOU ASAP...
OH...UH... COMING! I'LL BE RIGHT THERE.
WE'RE AHEAD OF SCHEDULE. WHAT'S--
IF YOU'D LIKE TO RUN, YOU CAN HAVE A HEAD START.
PLEASE RUN. WE'D LOVE IT.

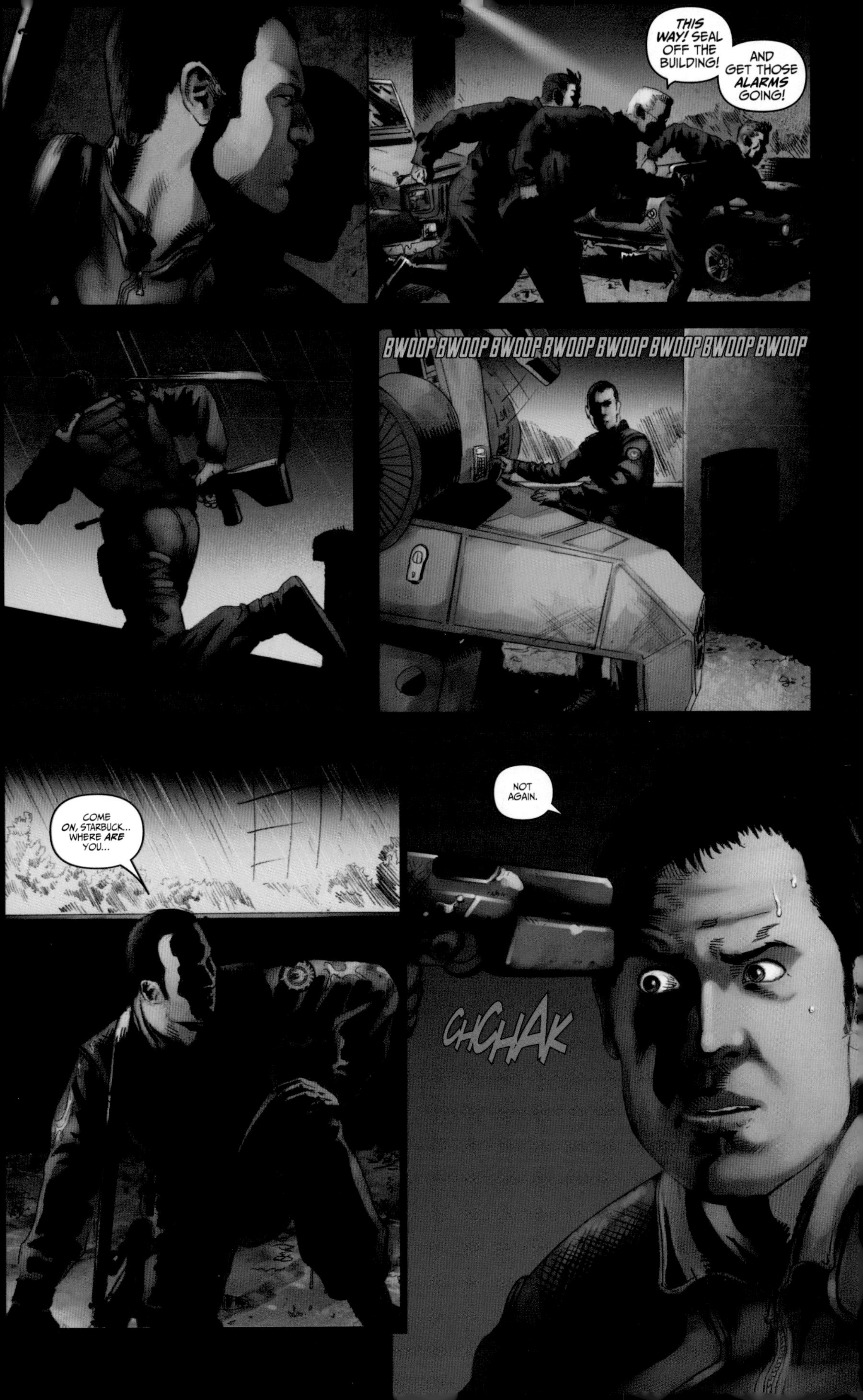
THIS WAY! SEAL OFF THE BUILDING!
AND GET THOSE ALARMS GOING!
BWOOP BWOOP BWOOP BWOOP BWOOP BWOOP BWOOP BWOOP
COME ON, STARBUCK... WHERE ARE YOU...
NOT AGAIN.
CHCHAK

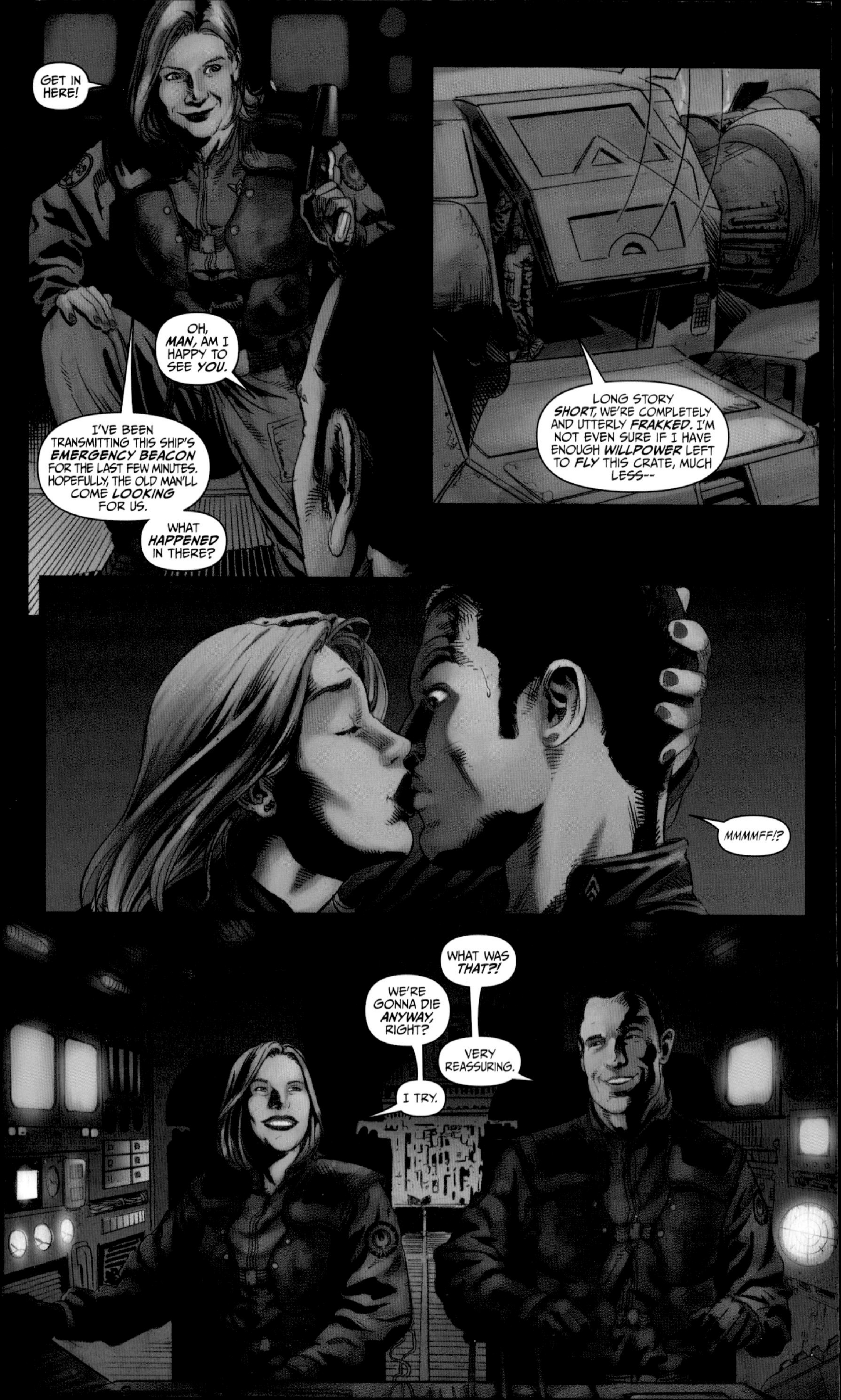
GET IN HERE!
OH, MAN, AM I HAPPY TO SEE YOU.
I'VE BEEN TRANSMITTING THIS SHIP'S EMERGENCY BEACON FOR THE LAST FEW MINUTES. HOPEFULLY, THE OLD MAN'LL COME LOOKING FOR US.
WHAT HAPPENED IN THERE?
LONG STORY SHORT, WE'RE COMPLETELY AND UTTERLY FRAKKED. I'M NOT EVEN SURE IF I HAVE ENOUGH WILLPOWER LEFT TO FLY THIS CRATE, MUCH LESS--
MMMMFF!?
WHAT WAS THAT?!
WE'RE GONNA DIE ANYWAY, RIGHT?
VERY REASSURING.
I TRY.

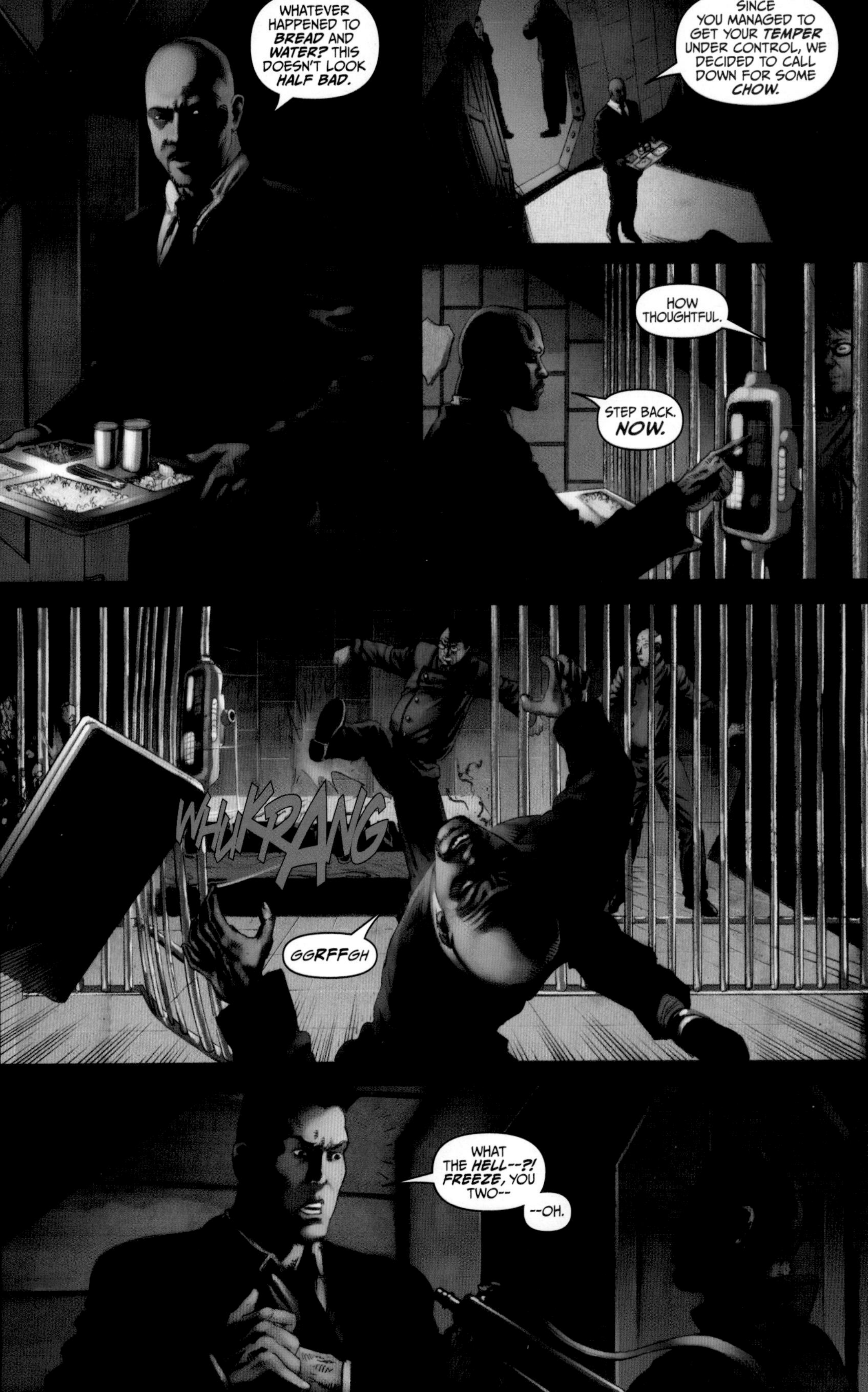
WHATEVER HAPPENED TO BREAD AND WATER? THIS DOESN'T LOOK HALF BAD.
SINCE YOU MANAGED TO GET YOUR TEMPER UNDER CONTROL, WE DECIDED TO CALL DOWN FOR SOME CHOW.
HOW THOUGHTFUL.
STEP BACK. NOW.
WHUKRANG
GGRFFGH
WHAT THE HELL--?! FREEZE, YOU TWO--
--OH.

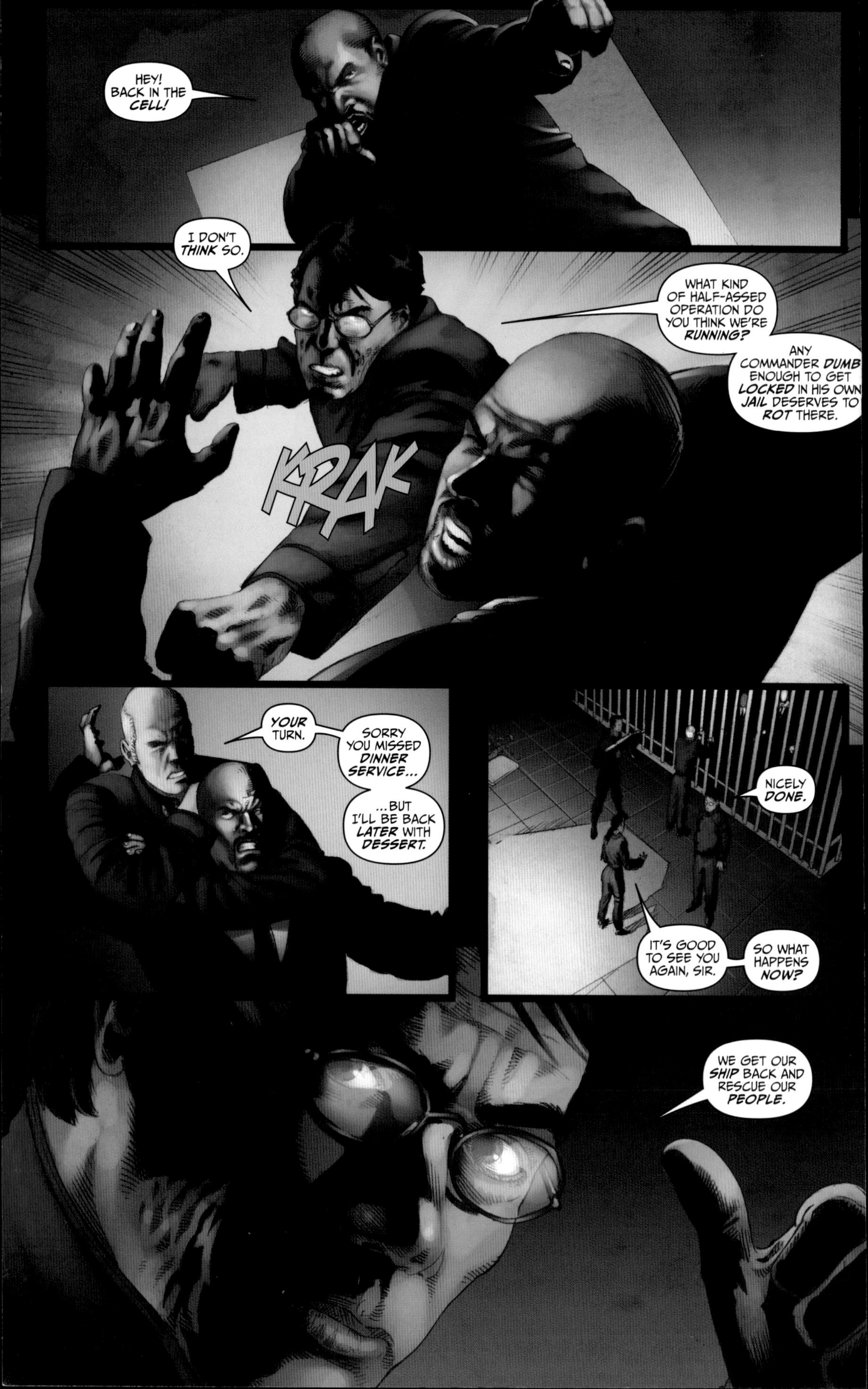

HEY! BACK IN THE *CELL!*
I DON'T *THINK* SO.
WHAT KIND OF HALF-ASSED OPERATION DO YOU THINK WE'RE *RUNNING?*
ANY COMMANDER *DUMB* ENOUGH TO GET *LOCKED* IN HIS OWN *JAIL* DESERVES TO *ROT* THERE.
KRAK
YOUR TURN.
SORRY YOU MISSED *DINNER SERVICE...*
...BUT I'LL BE BACK *LATER* WITH *DESSERT.*
NICELY *DONE.*
IT'S GOOD TO SEE YOU AGAIN, SIR.
SO WHAT HAPPENS *NOW?*
WE GET OUR *SHIP* BACK AND RESCUE OUR *PEOPLE.*

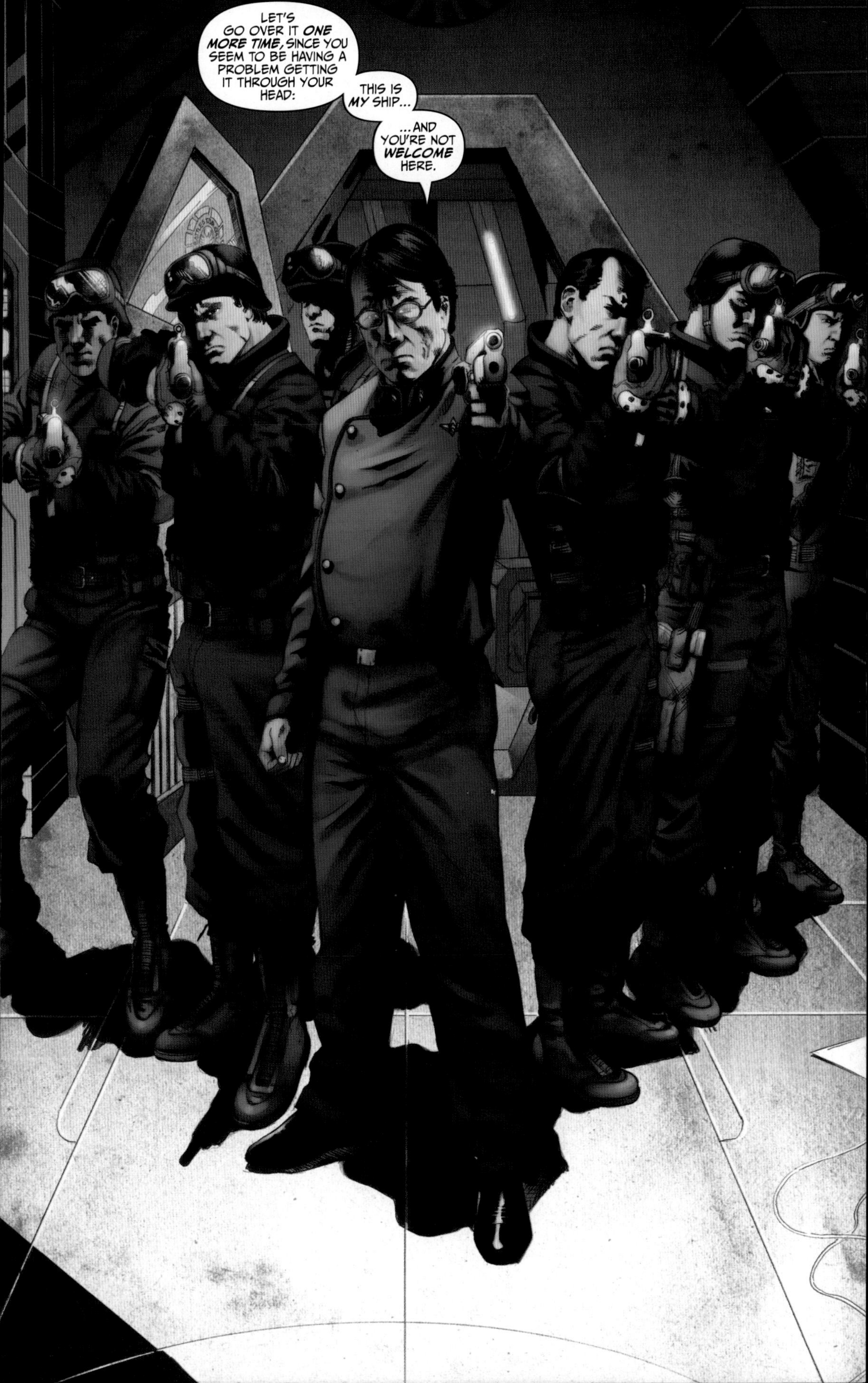
LET'S GO OVER IT ONE MORE TIME, SINCE YOU SEEM TO BE HAVING A PROBLEM GETTING IT THROUGH YOUR HEAD:
THIS IS MY SHIP...
...AND YOU'RE NOT WELCOME HERE.

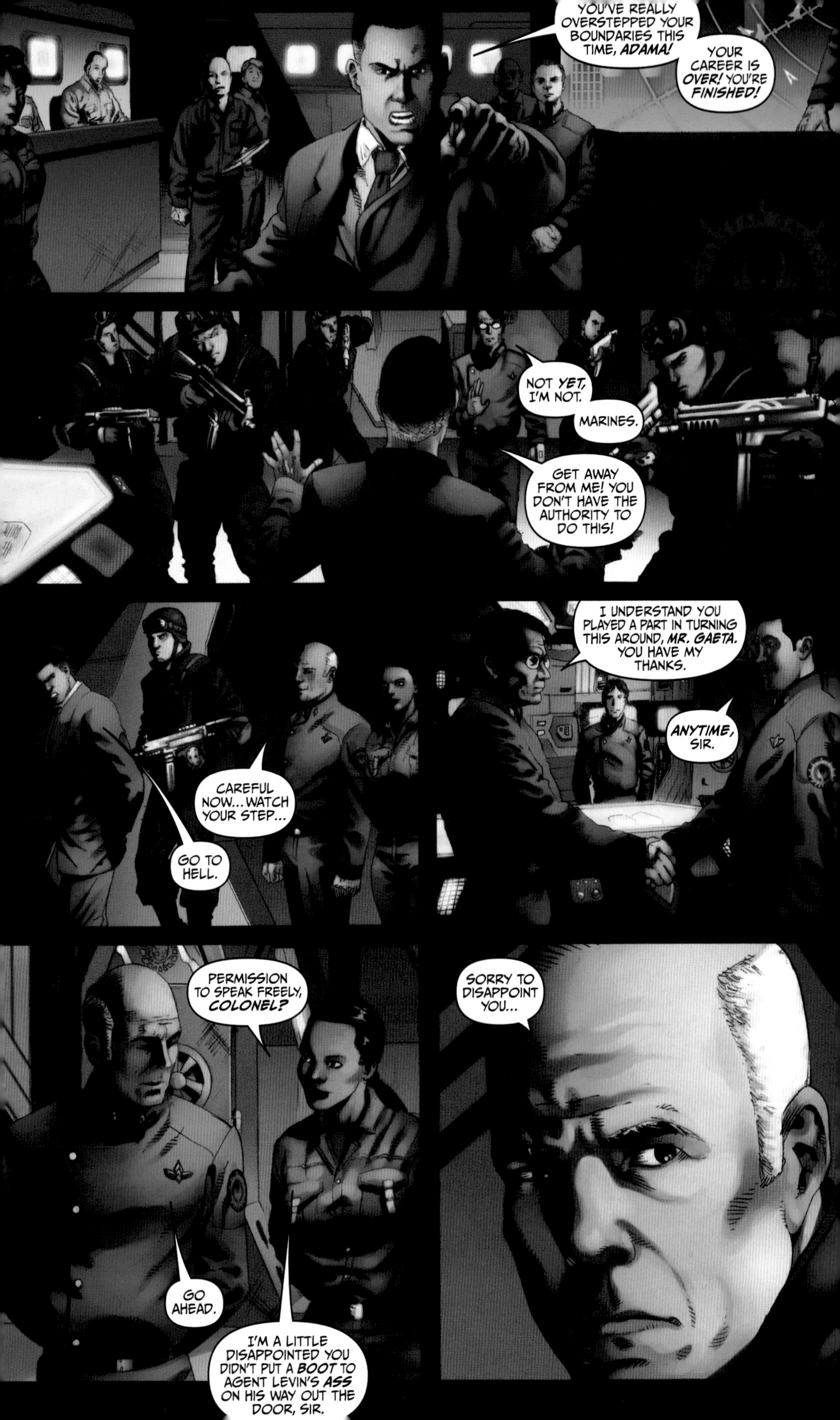
YOU'VE REALLY OVERSTEPPED YOUR BOUNDARIES THIS TIME, ADAMA!
YOUR CAREER IS OVER! YOU'RE FINISHED!
NOT YET, I'M NOT.
MARINES.
GET AWAY FROM ME! YOU DON'T HAVE THE AUTHORITY TO DO THIS!
CAREFUL NOW... WATCH YOUR STEP...
GO TO HELL.
I UNDERSTAND YOU PLAYED A PART IN TURNING THIS AROUND, MR. GAETA. YOU HAVE MY THANKS.
ANYTIME, SIR.
PERMISSION TO SPEAK FREELY, COLONEL?
GO AHEAD.
I'M A LITTLE DISAPPOINTED YOU DIDN'T PUT A BOOT TO AGENT LEVIN'S ASS ON HIS WAY OUT THE DOOR, SIR.
SORRY TO DISAPPOINT YOU...

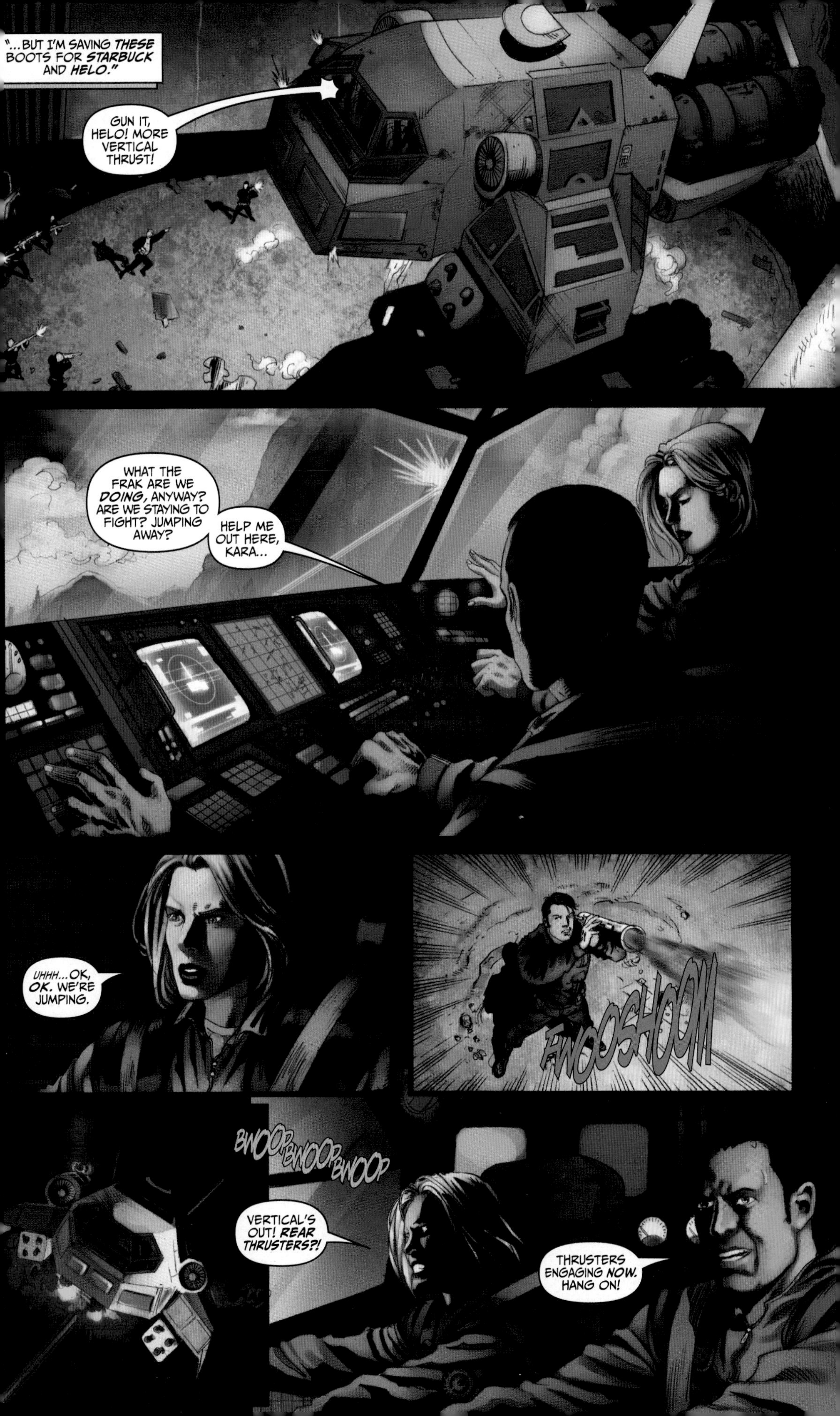
"...BUT I'M SAVING *THESE* BOOTS FOR *STARBUCK* AND *HELO*."
GUN IT, HELO! MORE VERTICAL THRUST!
WHAT THE FRAK ARE WE *DOING*, ANYWAY? ARE WE STAYING TO FIGHT? JUMPING AWAY?
HELP ME OUT HERE, KARA...
UHHH...OK, **OK.** WE'RE JUMPING.
FWOOSHOOM
BWOOP BWOOP BWOOP
VERTICAL'S OUT! *REAR THRUSTERS?!*
THRUSTERS ENGAGING *NOW*. HANG ON!

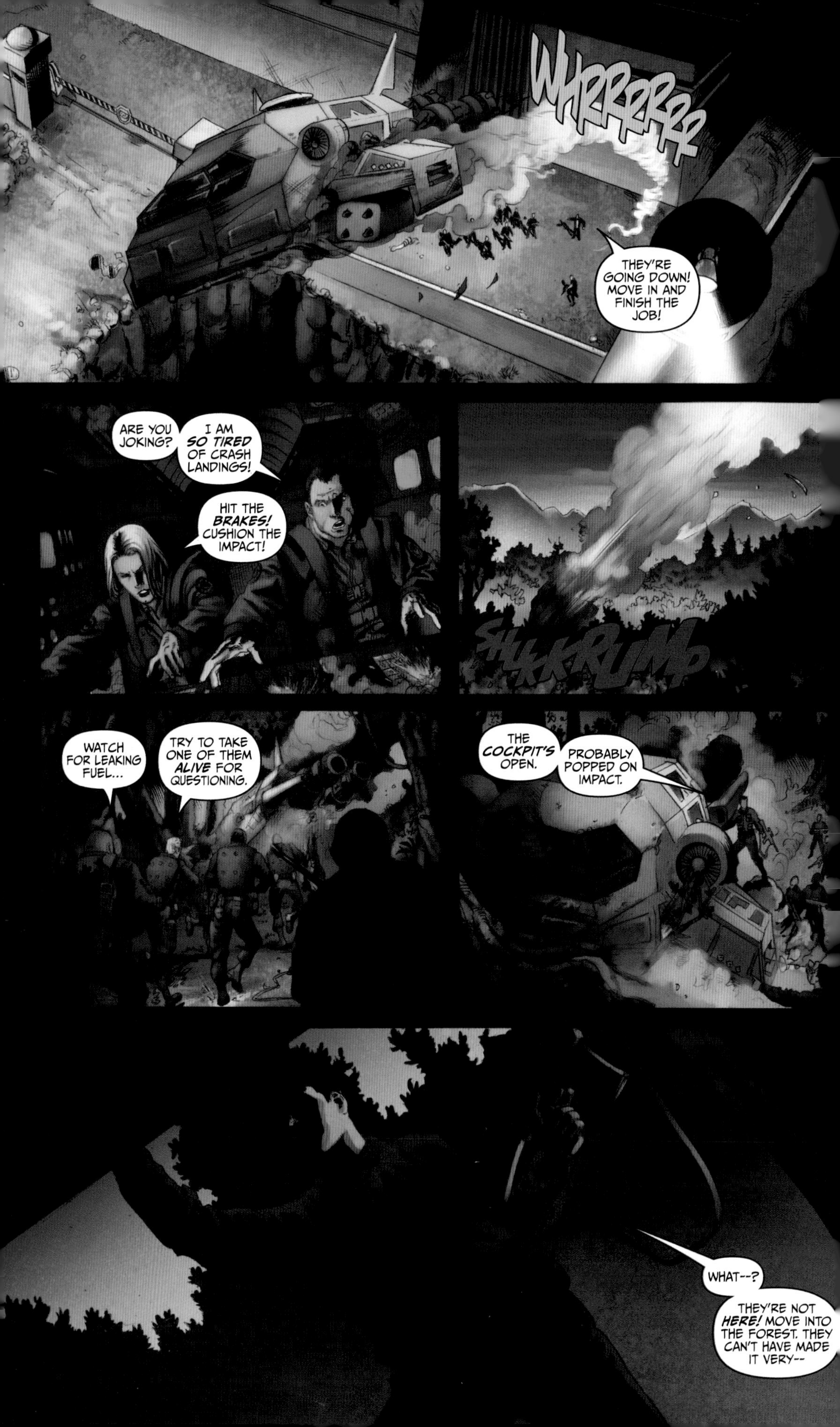
WHRRRRR
THEY'RE GOING DOWN! MOVE IN AND FINISH THE JOB!
ARE YOU JOKING?
I AM SO TIRED OF CRASH LANDINGS!
HIT THE BRAKES! CUSHION THE IMPACT!
SHKKRUMP
WATCH FOR LEAKING FUEL...
TRY TO TAKE ONE OF THEM ALIVE FOR QUESTIONING.
THE COCKPIT'S OPEN.
PROBABLY POPPED ON IMPACT.
WHAT--?
THEY'RE NOT HERE! MOVE INTO THE FOREST. THEY CAN'T HAVE MADE IT VERY--

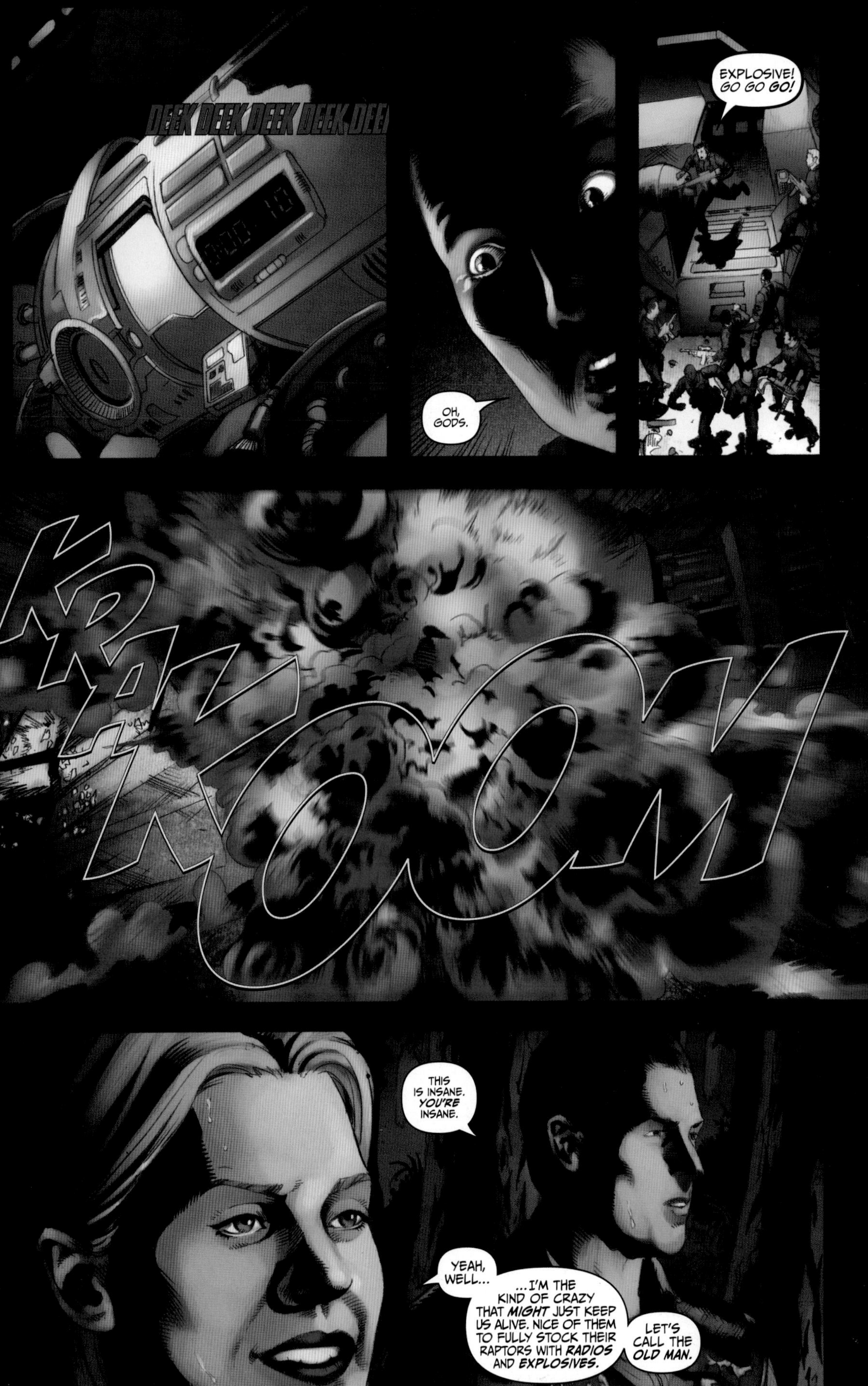
DEEK DEEK DEEK DEEK DEE
OH, GODS.
EXPLOSIVE! GO GO GO!
KRAKOOM
THIS IS INSANE. YOU'RE INSANE.
YEAH, WELL...
...I'M THE KIND OF CRAZY THAT MIGHT JUST KEEP US ALIVE. NICE OF THEM TO FULLY STOCK THEIR RAPTORS WITH RADIOS AND EXPLOSIVES.
LET'S CALL THE OLD MAN.

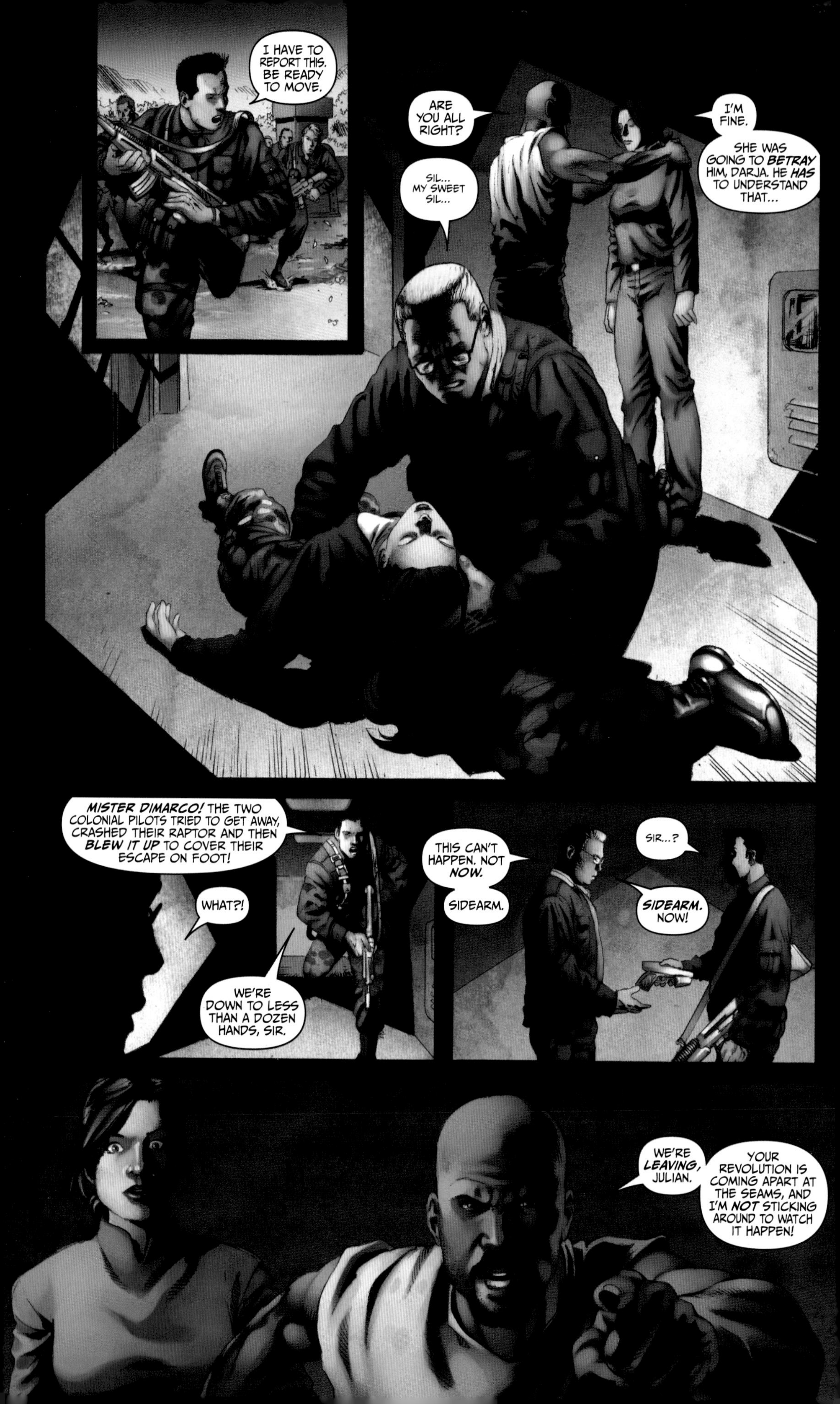
I HAVE TO REPORT THIS. BE READY TO MOVE.
ARE YOU ALL RIGHT?
I'M FINE.
SHE WAS GOING TO BETRAY HIM, DARJA. HE HAS TO UNDERSTAND THAT...
SIL... MY SWEET SIL...
MISTER DIMARCO! THE TWO COLONIAL PILOTS TRIED TO GET AWAY, CRASHED THEIR RAPTOR AND THEN BLEW IT UP TO COVER THEIR ESCAPE ON FOOT!
WHAT?!
WE'RE DOWN TO LESS THAN A DOZEN HANDS, SIR.
THIS CAN'T HAPPEN. NOT NOW.
SIDEARM.
SIR...?
SIDEARM. NOW!
WE'RE LEAVING, JULIAN.
YOUR REVOLUTION IS COMING APART AT THE SEAMS, AND I'M NOT STICKING AROUND TO WATCH IT HAPPEN!

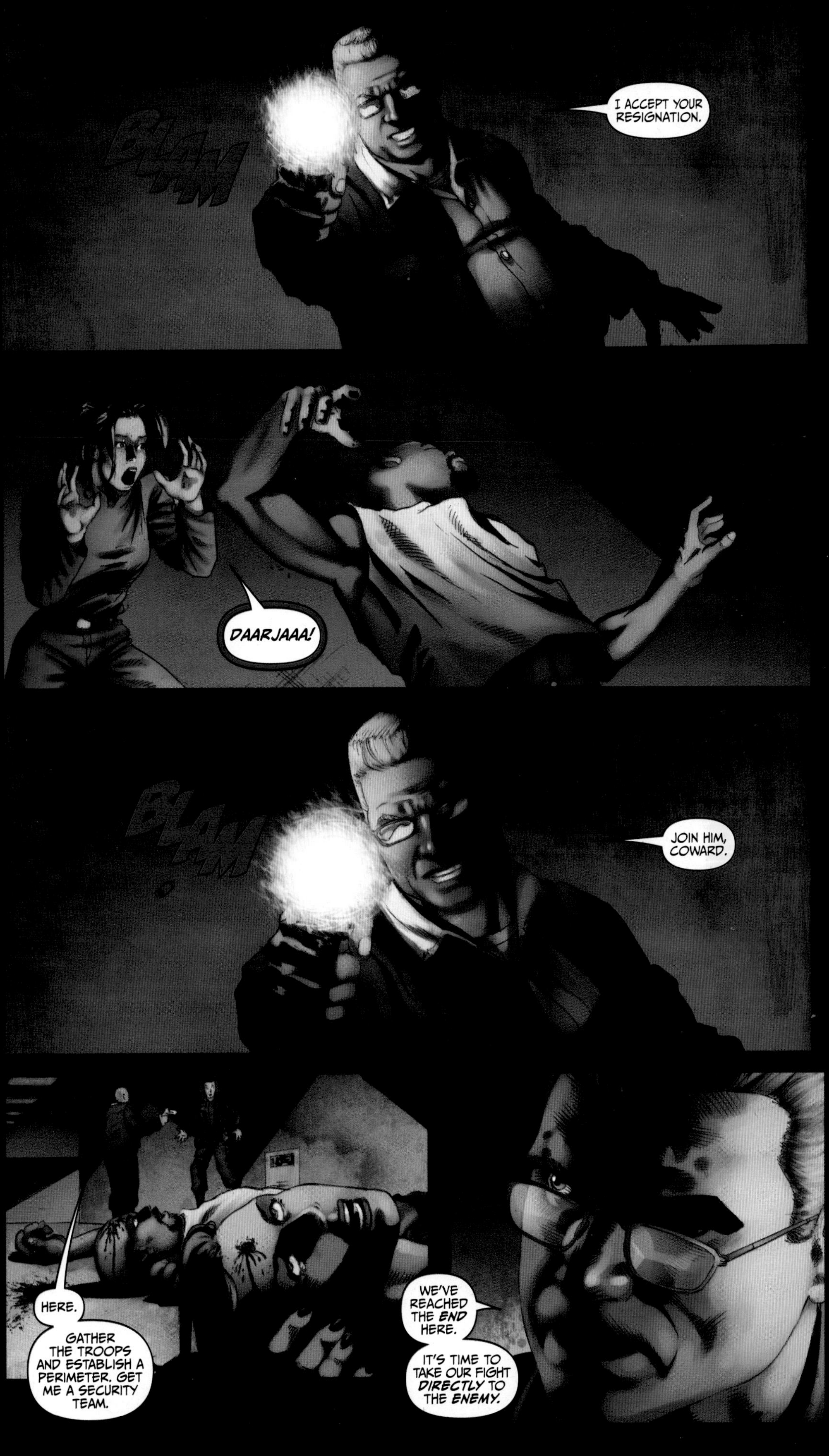
BLAM
I ACCEPT YOUR RESIGNATION.
DAARJAAA!
BLAM
JOIN HIM, COWARD.
HERE.
GATHER THE TROOPS AND ESTABLISH A PERIMETER. GET ME A SECURITY TEAM.
WE'VE REACHED THE END HERE.
IT'S TIME TO TAKE OUR FIGHT DIRECTLY TO THE ENEMY.

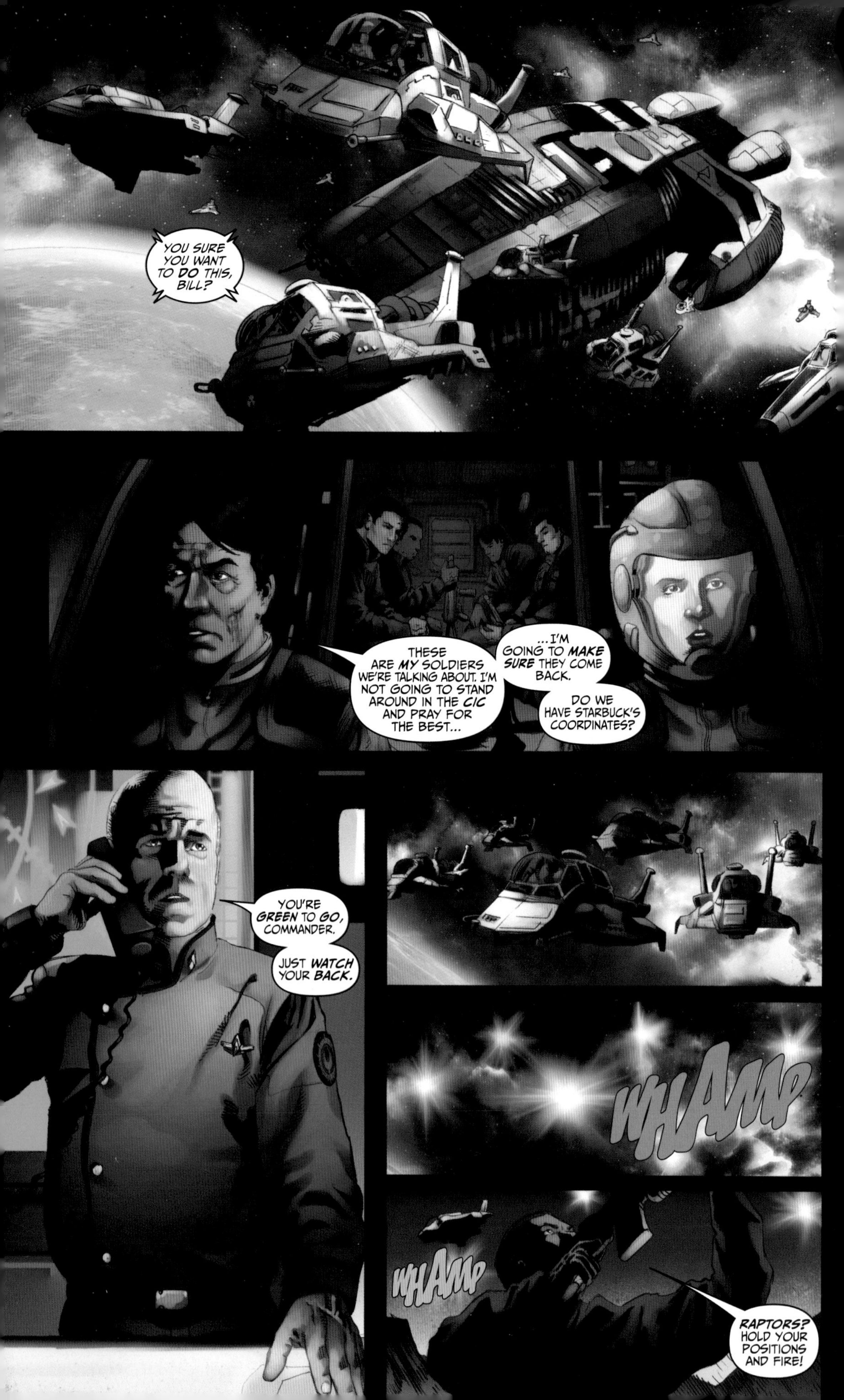
YOU SURE YOU WANT TO DO THIS, BILL?
THESE ARE MY SOLDIERS WE'RE TALKING ABOUT. I'M NOT GOING TO STAND AROUND IN THE CIC AND PRAY FOR THE BEST...
...I'M GOING TO MAKE SURE THEY COME BACK.
DO WE HAVE STARBUCK'S COORDINATES?
YOU'RE GREEN TO GO, COMMANDER.
JUST WATCH YOUR BACK.
WHAMP
WHAMP
RAPTORS? HOLD YOUR POSITIONS AND FIRE!

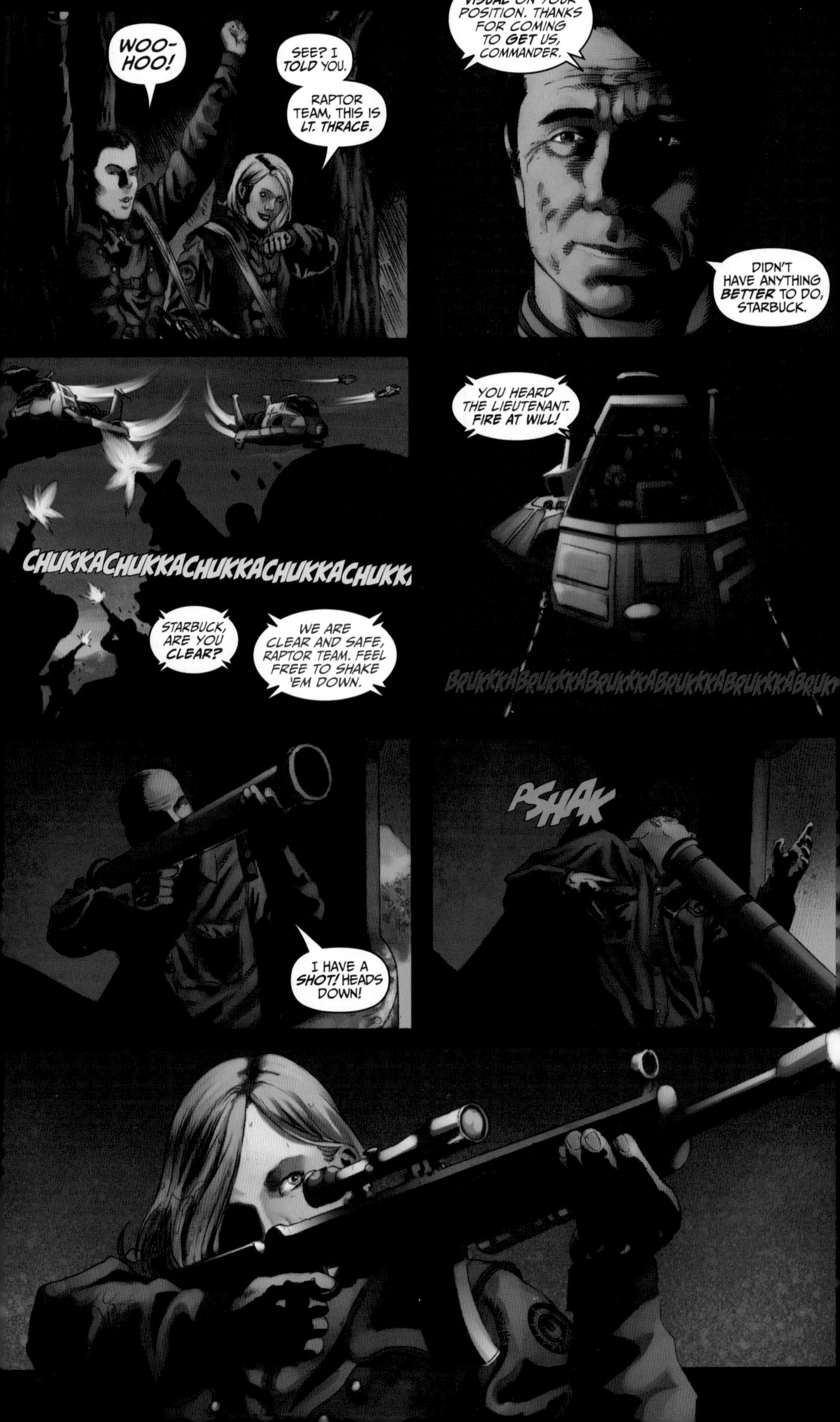
WOO-HOO!
SEE? I TOLD YOU.
RAPTOR TEAM, THIS IS LT. THRACE.
WE HAVE A VISUAL ON YOUR POSITION. THANKS FOR COMING TO GET US, COMMANDER.
DIDN'T HAVE ANYTHING BETTER TO DO, STARBUCK.
CHUKKACHUKKACHUKKACHUKKACHUKK
STARBUCK, ARE YOU CLEAR?
WE ARE CLEAR AND SAFE, RAPTOR TEAM. FEEL FREE TO SHAKE 'EM DOWN.
YOU HEARD THE LIEUTENANT. FIRE AT WILL!
BRUKKKABRUKKKABRUKKKABRUKKKABRUKKKABRUKK
I HAVE A SHOT! HEADS DOWN!
PSHAK

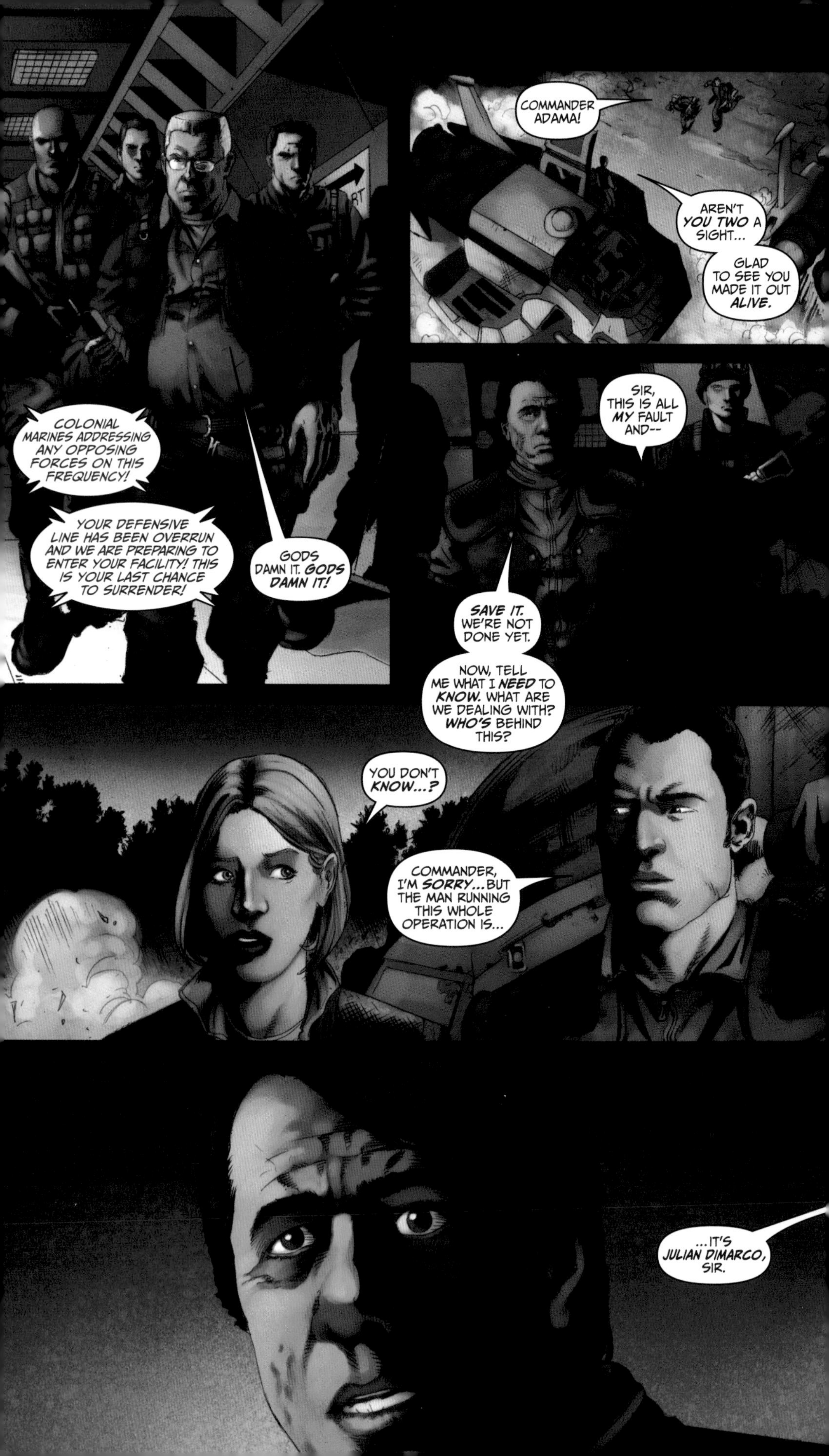
COMMANDER ADAMA!
AREN'T YOU TWO A SIGHT...
GLAD TO SEE YOU MADE IT OUT ALIVE.
COLONIAL MARINES ADDRESSING ANY OPPOSING FORCES ON THIS FREQUENCY!
YOUR DEFENSIVE LINE HAS BEEN OVERRUN AND WE ARE PREPARING TO ENTER YOUR FACILITY! THIS IS YOUR LAST CHANCE TO SURRENDER!
GODS DAMN IT. GODS DAMN IT!
SIR, THIS IS ALL MY FAULT AND--
SAVE IT. WE'RE NOT DONE YET.
NOW, TELL ME WHAT I NEED TO KNOW. WHAT ARE WE DEALING WITH? WHO'S BEHIND THIS?
YOU DON'T KNOW...?
COMMANDER, I'M SORRY... BUT THE MAN RUNNING THIS WHOLE OPERATION IS...
...IT'S JULIAN DIMARCO, SIR.

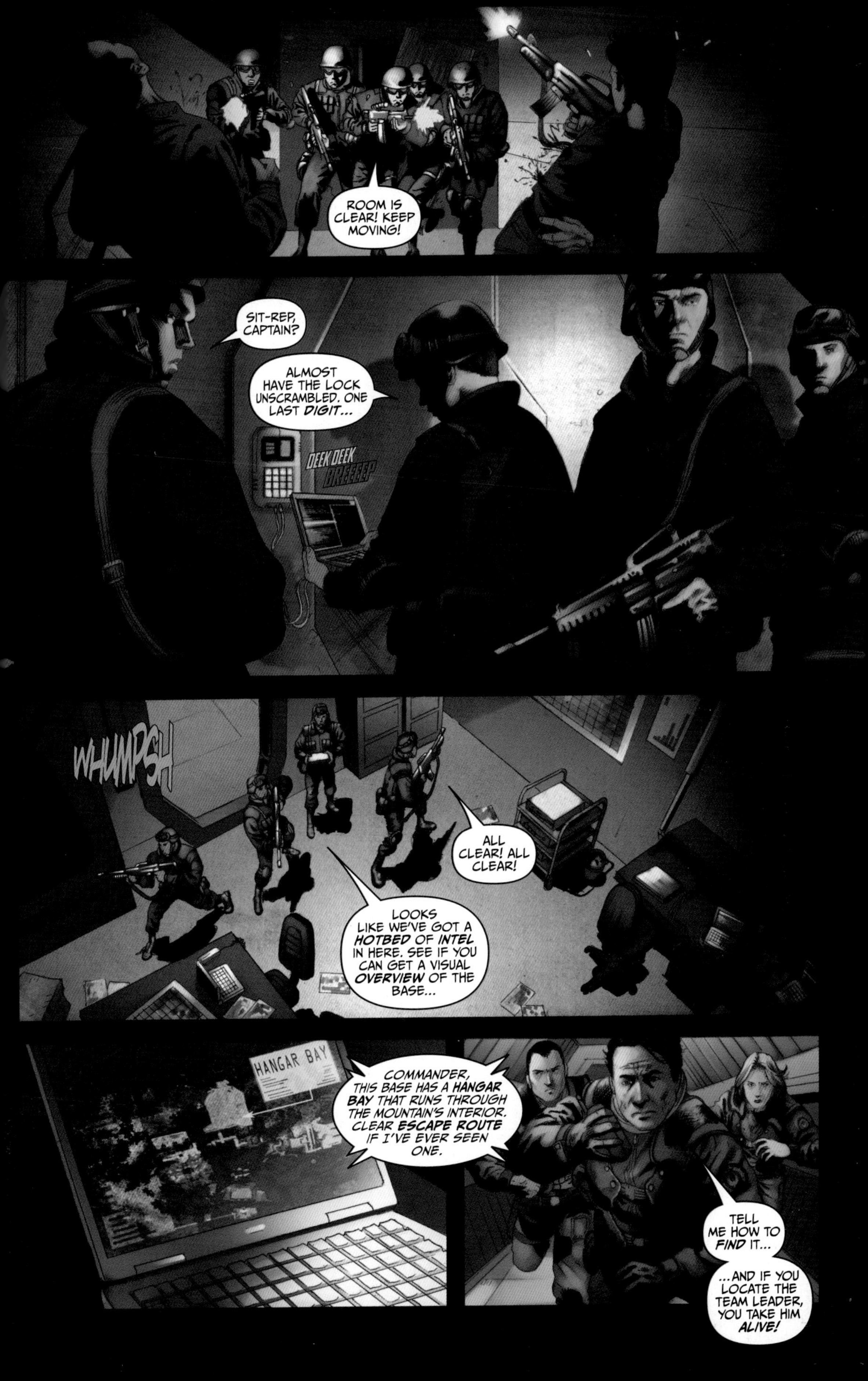
ROOM IS CLEAR! KEEP MOVING!
SIT-REP, CAPTAIN?
ALMOST HAVE THE LOCK UNSCRAMBLED. ONE LAST DIGIT...
DEEK DEEK BREEEEP
WHUMPSH
ALL CLEAR! ALL CLEAR!
LOOKS LIKE WE'VE GOT A HOTBED OF INTEL IN HERE. SEE IF YOU CAN GET A VISUAL OVERVIEW OF THE BASE...
HANGAR BAY
COMMANDER, THIS BASE HAS A HANGAR BAY THAT RUNS THROUGH THE MOUNTAIN'S INTERIOR. CLEAR ESCAPE ROUTE IF I'VE EVER SEEN ONE.
TELL ME HOW TO FIND IT...
...AND IF YOU LOCATE THE TEAM LEADER, YOU TAKE HIM ALIVE!

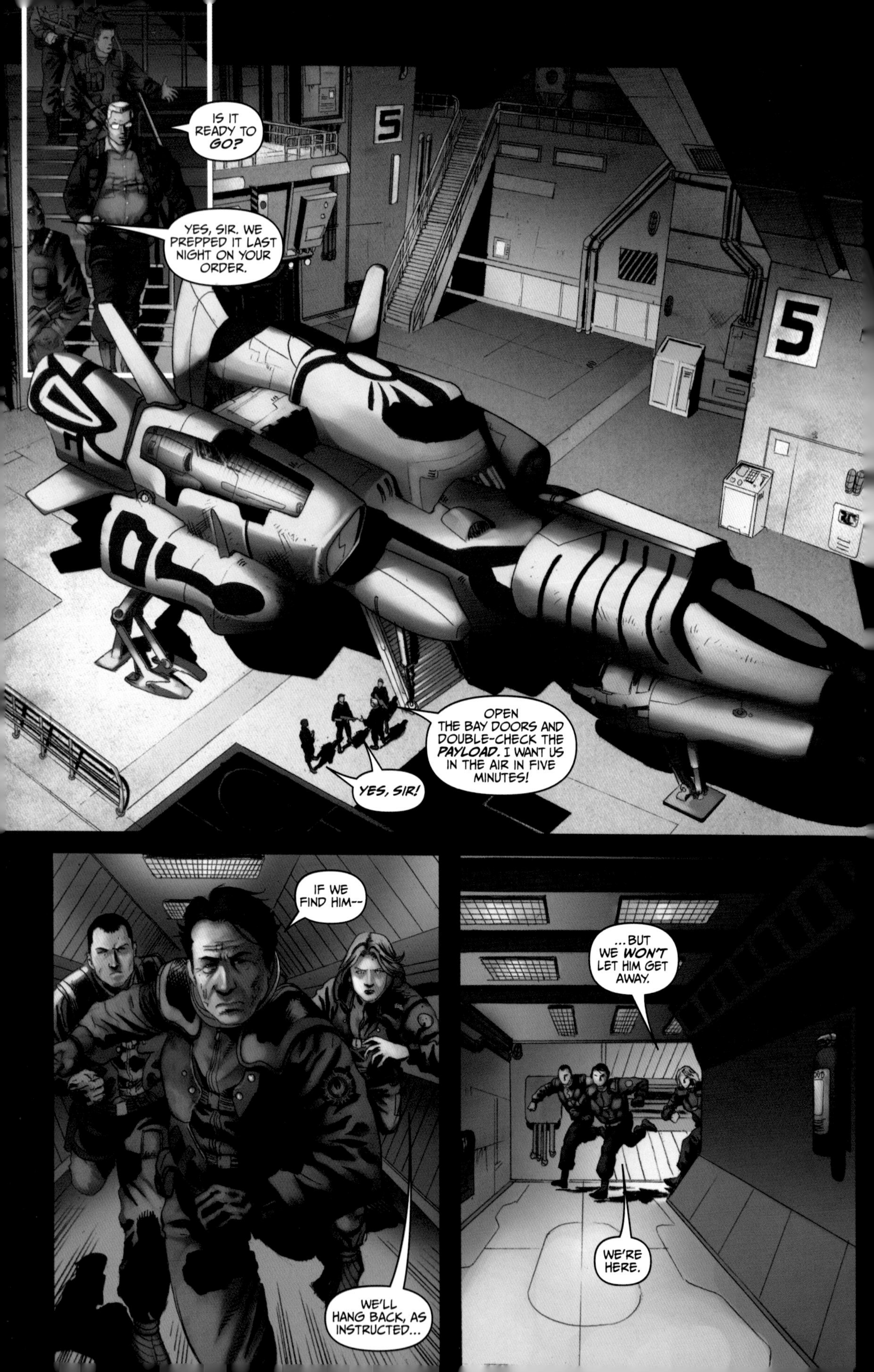
IS IT READY TO GO?
YES, SIR. WE PREPPED IT LAST NIGHT ON YOUR ORDER.
OPEN THE BAY DOORS AND DOUBLE-CHECK THE PAYLOAD. I WANT US IN THE AIR IN FIVE MINUTES!
YES, SIR!
IF WE FIND HIM--
WE'LL HANG BACK, AS INSTRUCTED...
...BUT WE WON'T LET HIM GET AWAY.
WE'RE HERE.

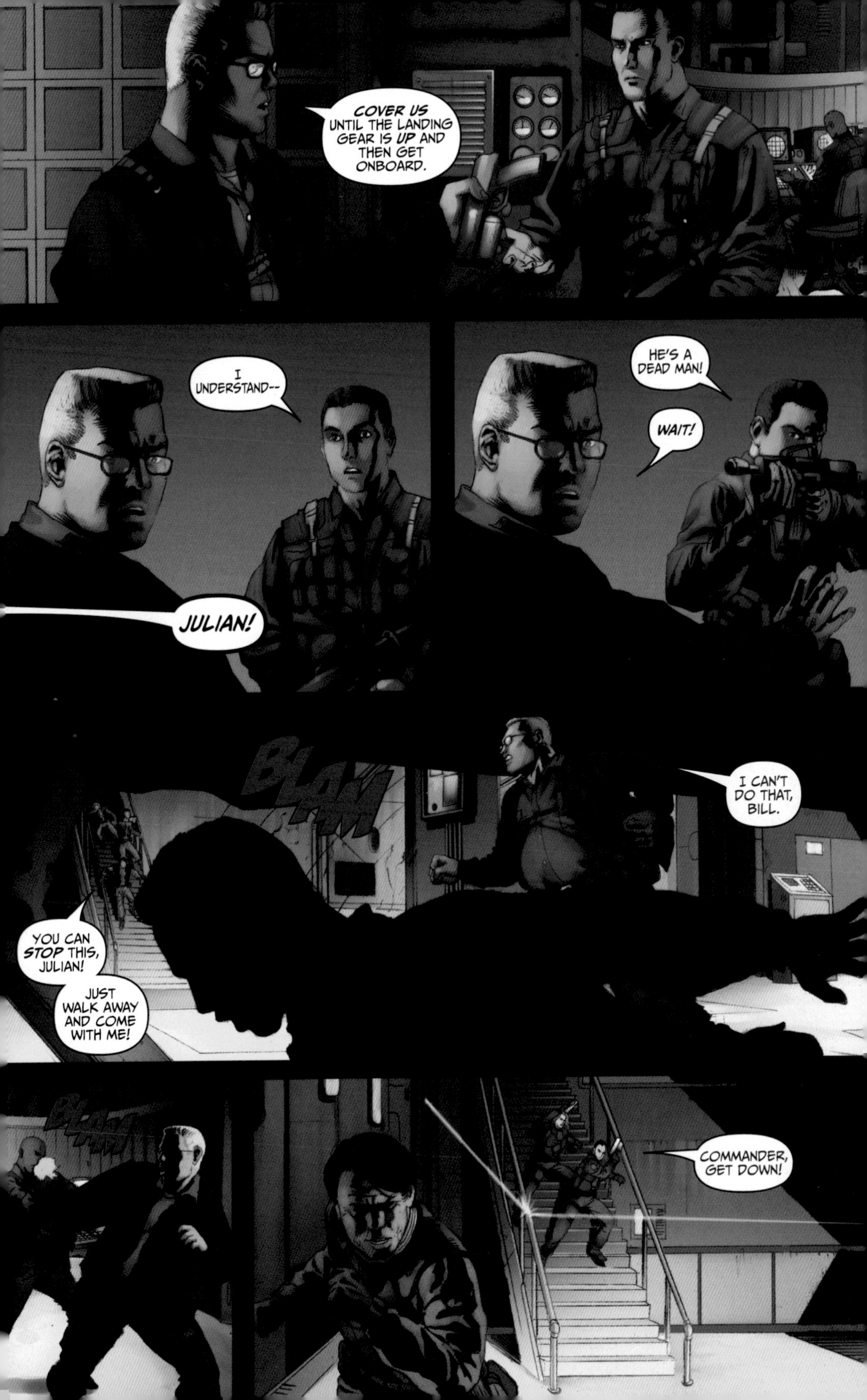

COVER US UNTIL THE LANDING GEAR IS UP AND THEN GET ONBOARD.
I UNDERSTAND--
JULIAN!
HE'S A DEAD MAN!
WAIT!
BLAM
I CAN'T DO THAT, BILL.
YOU CAN STOP THIS, JULIAN!
JUST WALK AWAY AND COME WITH ME!
COMMANDER, GET DOWN!

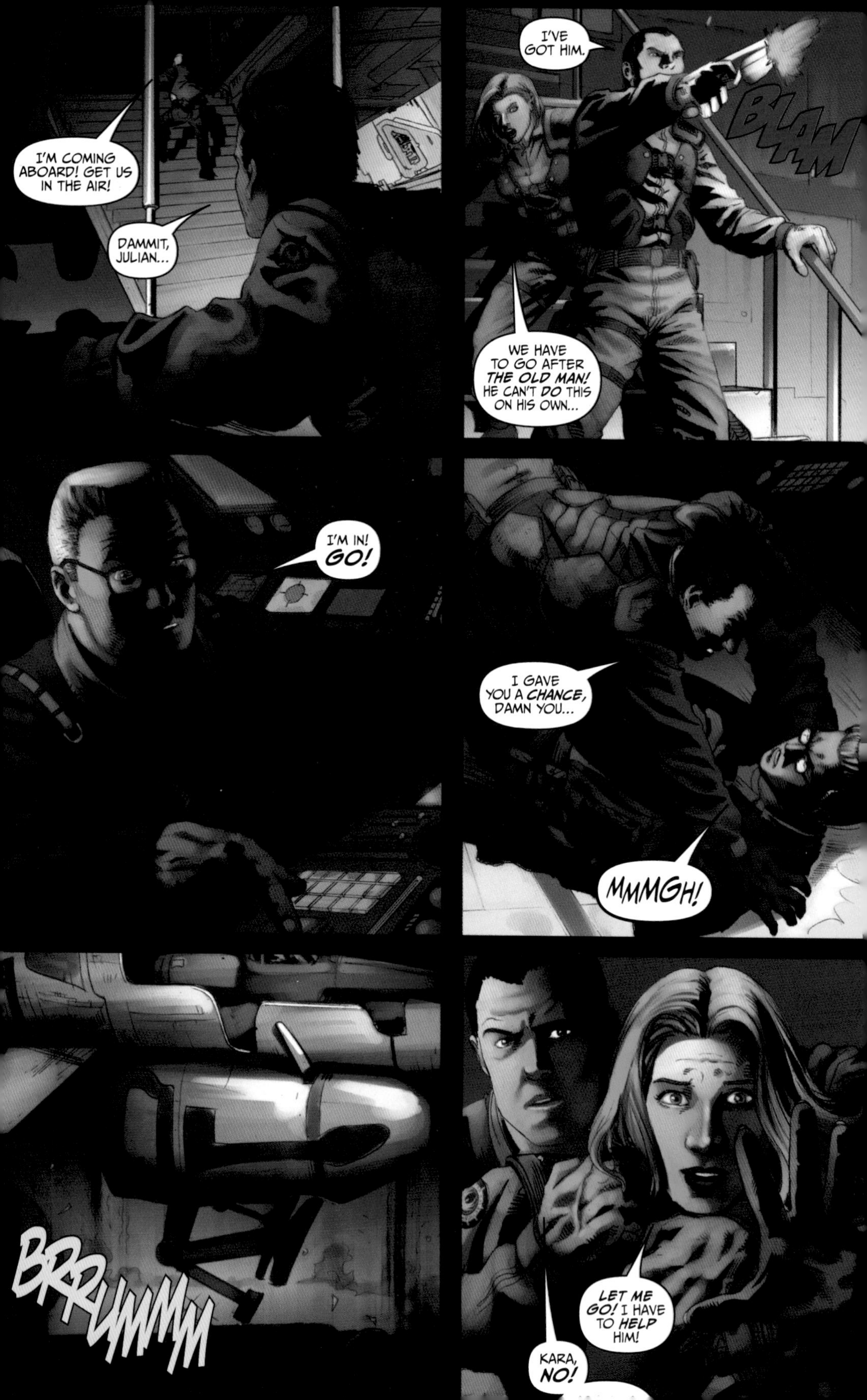
I'M COMING ABOARD! GET US IN THE AIR!
DAMMIT, JULIAN...
I'VE GOT HIM.
BLAM
WE HAVE TO GO AFTER *THE OLD MAN!* HE CAN'T *DO* THIS ON HIS OWN...
I'M IN! *GO!*
I GAVE YOU A *CHANCE,* DAMN YOU...
MMMGH!
BRRUMMM
LET ME GO! I HAVE TO *HELP* HIM!
KARA, *NO!*

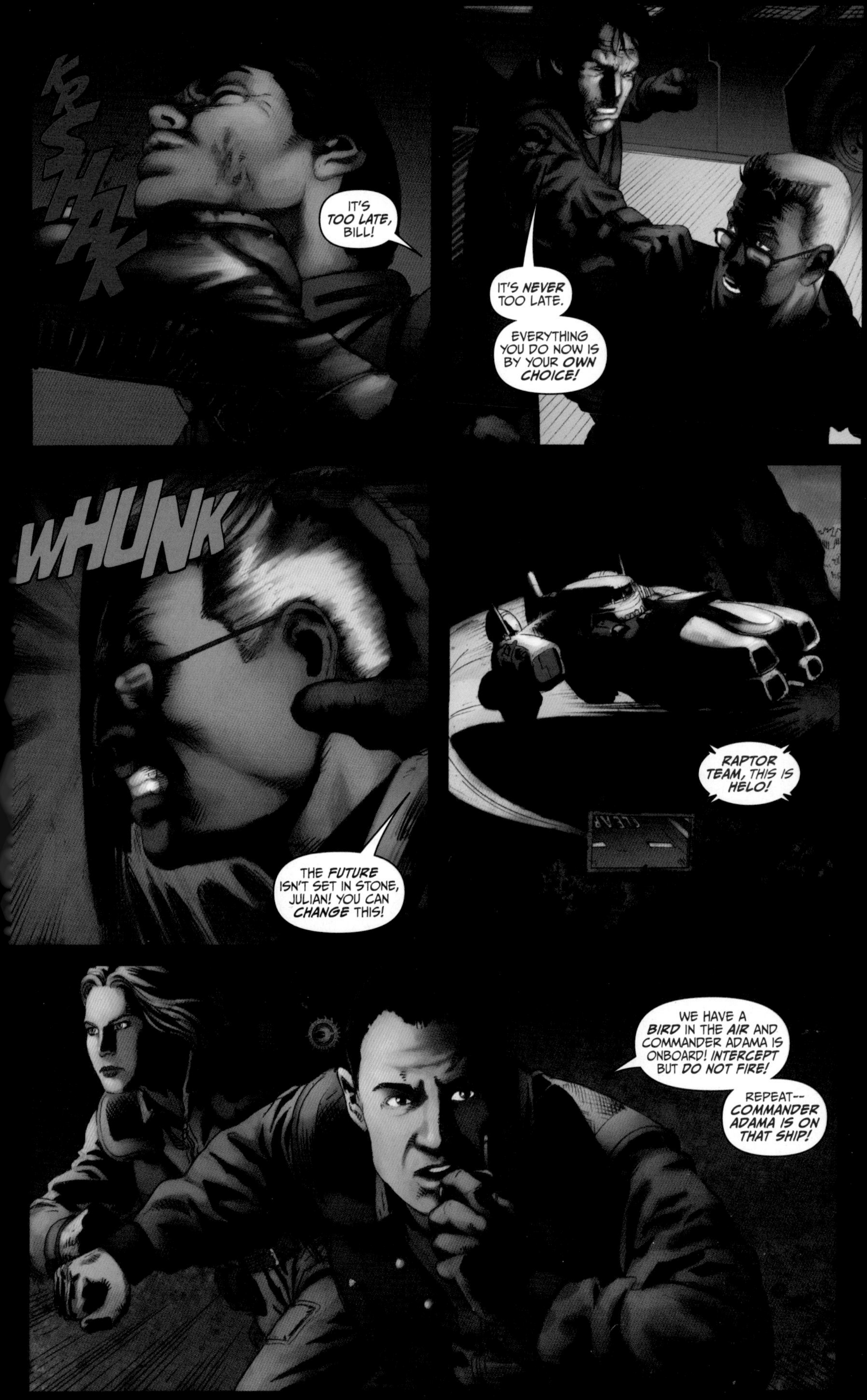
KRSHAK
IT'S TOO LATE, BILL!
IT'S NEVER TOO LATE.
EVERYTHING YOU DO NOW IS BY YOUR OWN CHOICE!
WHUNK
THE FUTURE ISN'T SET IN STONE, JULIAN! YOU CAN CHANGE THIS!
RAPTOR TEAM, THIS IS HELO!
WE HAVE A BIRD IN THE AIR AND COMMANDER ADAMA IS ONBOARD! INTERCEPT BUT DO NOT FIRE!
REPEAT-- COMMANDER ADAMA IS ON THAT SHIP!

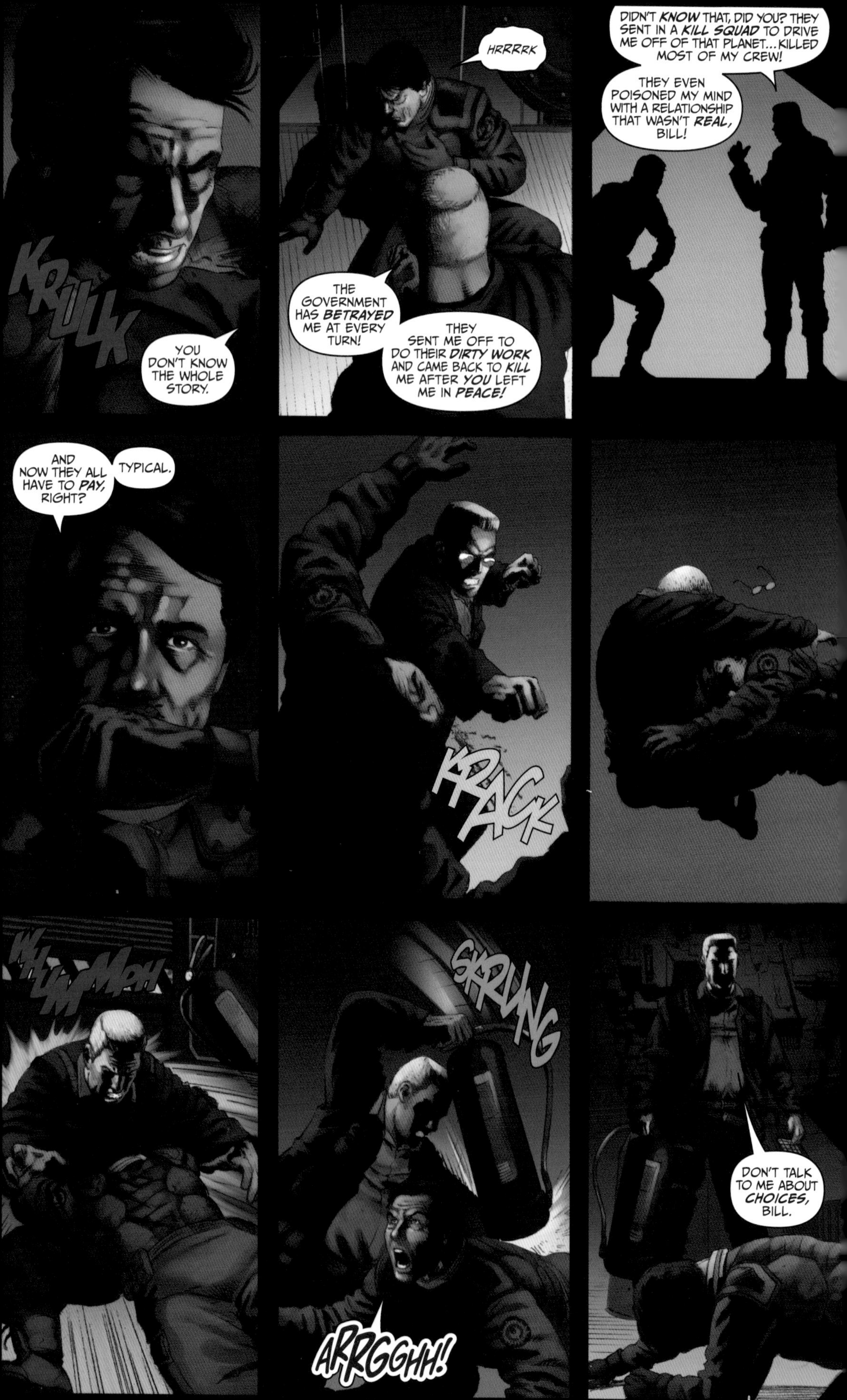
KRUNK
YOU DON'T KNOW THE WHOLE STORY.
HRRRRK
THE GOVERNMENT HAS BETRAYED ME AT EVERY TURN!
THEY SENT ME OFF TO DO THEIR DIRTY WORK AND CAME BACK TO KILL ME AFTER YOU LEFT ME IN PEACE!
DIDN'T KNOW THAT, DID YOU? THEY SENT IN A KILL SQUAD TO DRIVE ME OFF OF THAT PLANET...KILLED MOST OF MY CREW!
THEY EVEN POISONED MY MIND WITH A RELATIONSHIP THAT WASN'T REAL, BILL!
AND NOW THEY ALL HAVE TO PAY, RIGHT?
TYPICAL.
KRACK
WHUMMPH
SKRUNG
ARRGGHH!
DON'T TALK TO ME ABOUT CHOICES, BILL.

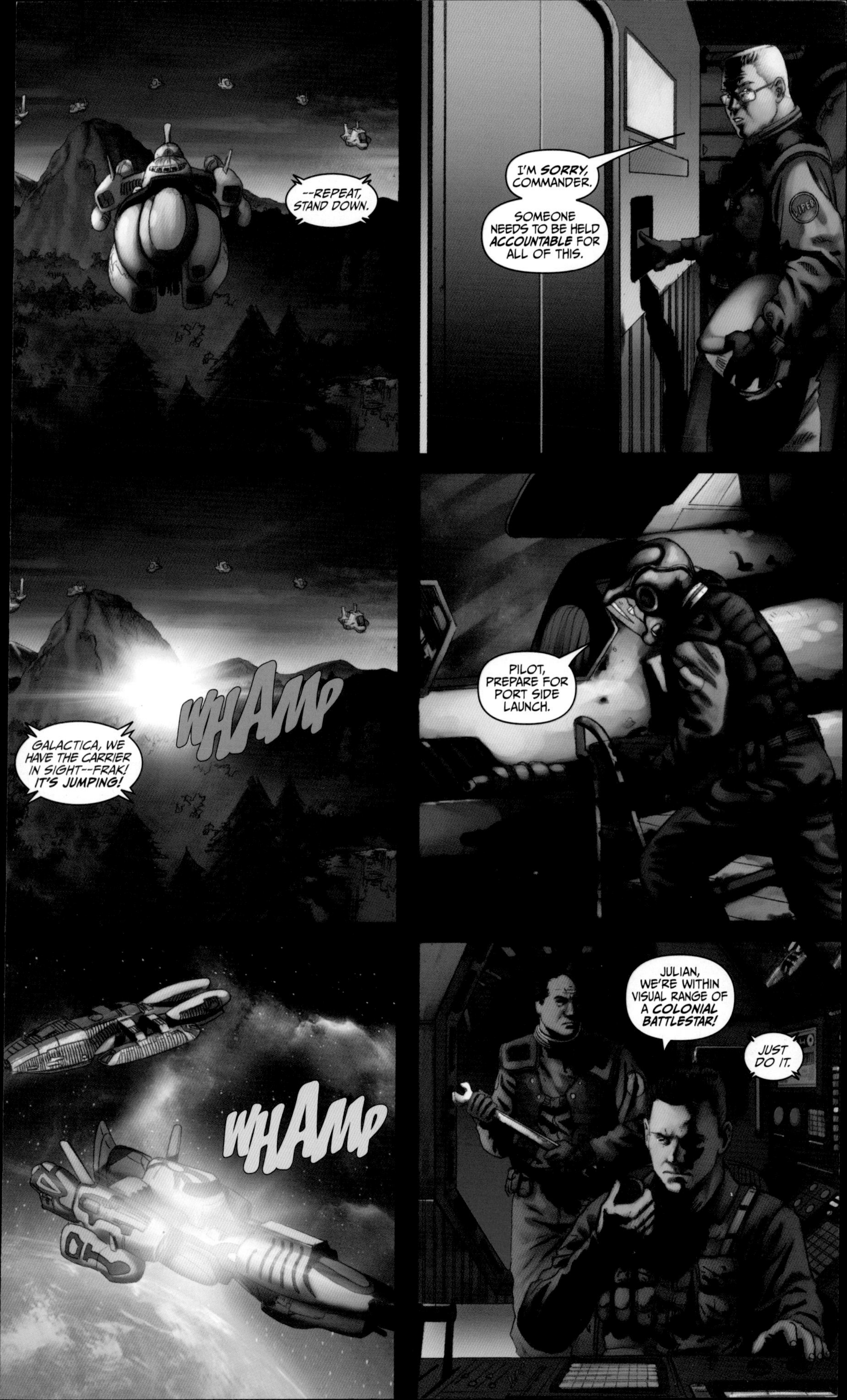
--REPEAT, STAND DOWN.
I'M SORRY, COMMANDER.
SOMEONE NEEDS TO BE HELD ACCOUNTABLE FOR ALL OF THIS.
VIPER
GALACTICA, WE HAVE THE CARRIER IN SIGHT--FRAK! IT'S JUMPING!
WHAMP
PILOT, PREPARE FOR PORT SIDE LAUNCH.
WHAMP
JULIAN, WE'RE WITHIN VISUAL RANGE OF A COLONIAL BATTLESTAR!
JUST DO IT.

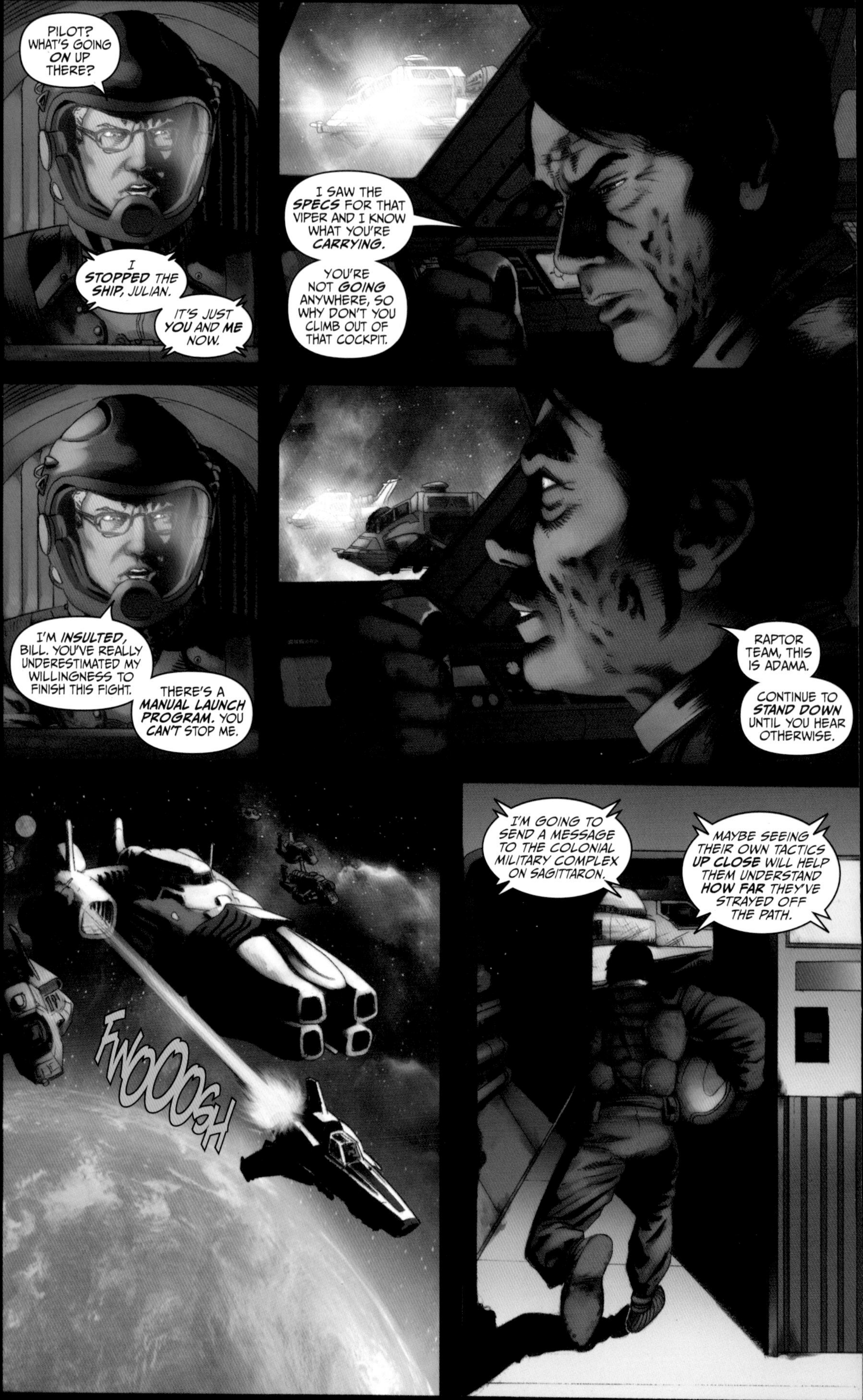
PILOT? WHAT'S GOING ON UP THERE?
I STOPPED THE SHIP, JULIAN.
IT'S JUST YOU AND ME NOW.
I SAW THE SPECS FOR THAT VIPER AND I KNOW WHAT YOU'RE CARRYING.
YOU'RE NOT GOING ANYWHERE, SO WHY DON'T YOU CLIMB OUT OF THAT COCKPIT.
I'M INSULTED, BILL. YOU'VE REALLY UNDERESTIMATED MY WILLINGNESS TO FINISH THIS FIGHT.
THERE'S A MANUAL LAUNCH PROGRAM. YOU CAN'T STOP ME.
RAPTOR TEAM, THIS IS ADAMA.
CONTINUE TO STAND DOWN UNTIL YOU HEAR OTHERWISE.
FWOOOSH
I'M GOING TO SEND A MESSAGE TO THE COLONIAL MILITARY COMPLEX ON SAGITTARON.
MAYBE SEEING THEIR OWN TACTICS UP CLOSE WILL HELP THEM UNDERSTAND HOW FAR THEY'VE STRAYED OFF THE PATH.

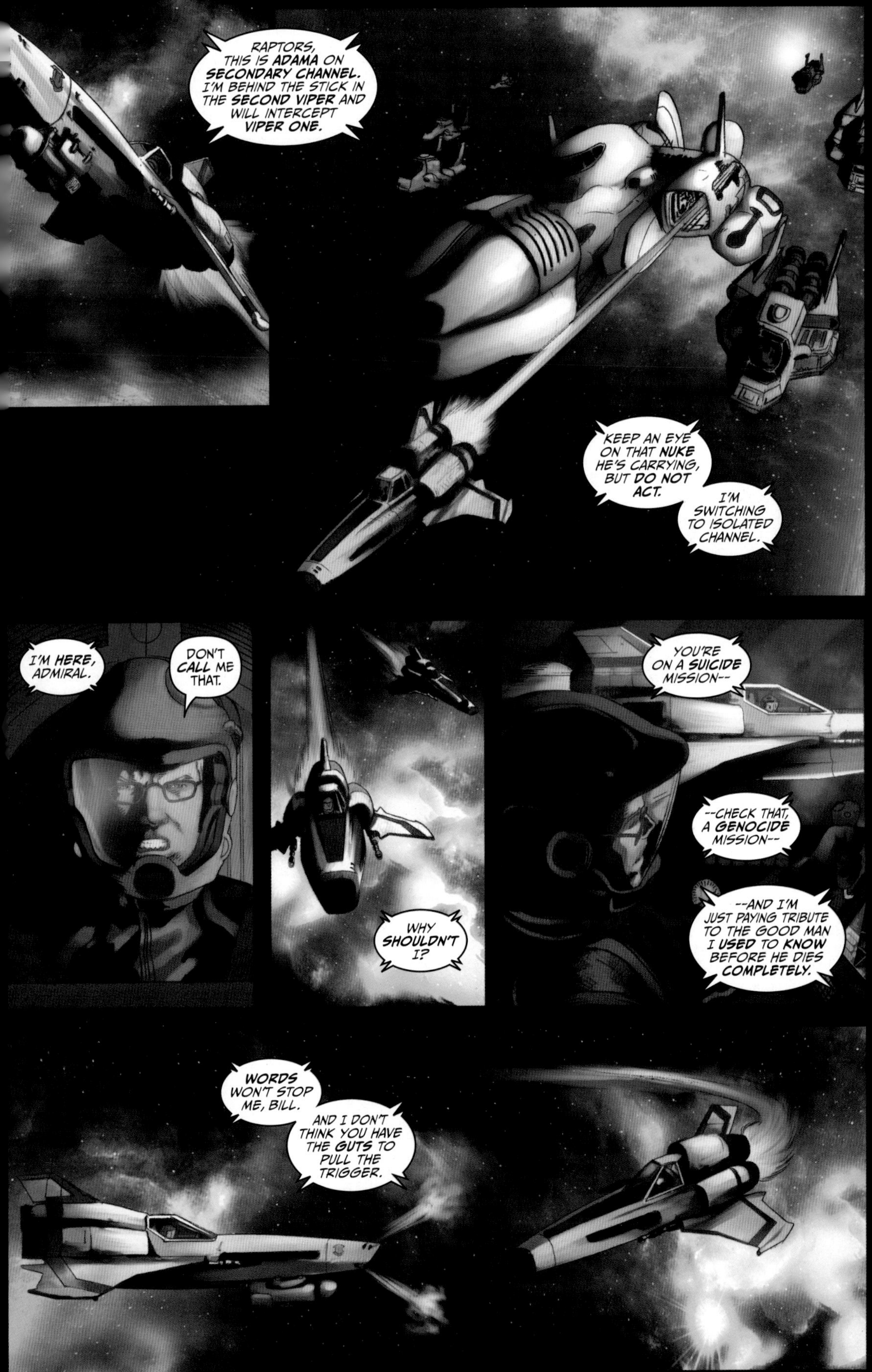
RAPTORS, THIS IS ADAMA ON SECONDARY CHANNEL. I'M BEHIND THE STICK IN THE SECOND VIPER AND WILL INTERCEPT VIPER ONE.
KEEP AN EYE ON THAT NUKE HE'S CARRYING, BUT DO NOT ACT.
I'M SWITCHING TO ISOLATED CHANNEL.
I'M HERE, ADMIRAL.
DON'T CALL ME THAT.
WHY SHOULDN'T I?
YOU'RE ON A SUICIDE MISSION--
--CHECK THAT, A GENOCIDE MISSION--
--AND I'M JUST PAYING TRIBUTE TO THE GOOD MAN I USED TO KNOW BEFORE HE DIES COMPLETELY.
WORDS WON'T STOP ME, BILL.
AND I DON'T THINK YOU HAVE THE GUTS TO PULL THE TRIGGER.

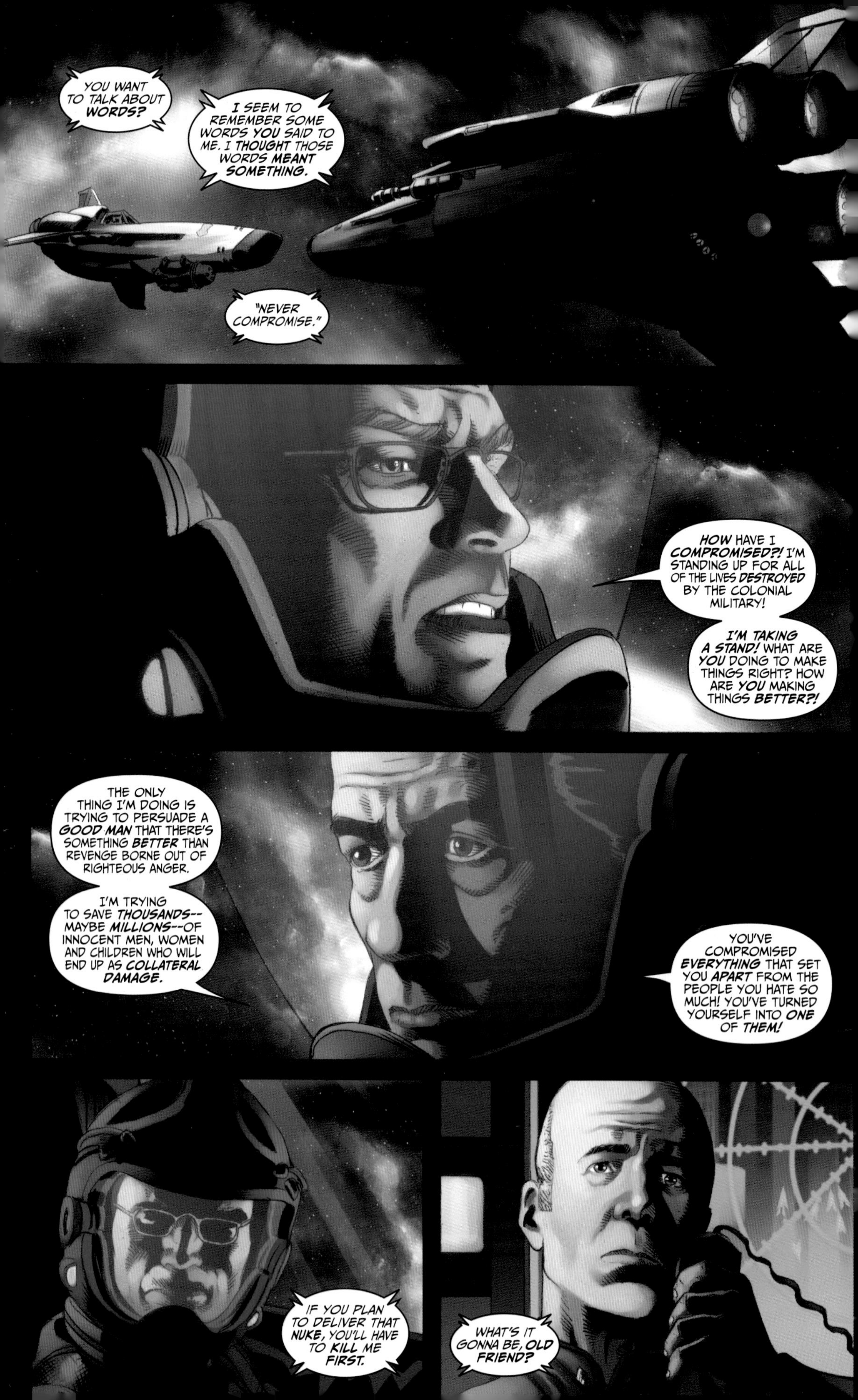
YOU WANT TO TALK ABOUT WORDS?
I SEEM TO REMEMBER SOME WORDS YOU SAID TO ME. I THOUGHT THOSE WORDS MEANT SOMETHING.
"NEVER COMPROMISE."
HOW HAVE I COMPROMISED?! I'M STANDING UP FOR ALL OF THE LIVES DESTROYED BY THE COLONIAL MILITARY!
I'M TAKING A STAND! WHAT ARE YOU DOING TO MAKE THINGS RIGHT? HOW ARE YOU MAKING THINGS BETTER?!
THE ONLY THING I'M DOING IS TRYING TO PERSUADE A GOOD MAN THAT THERE'S SOMETHING BETTER THAN REVENGE BORNE OUT OF RIGHTEOUS ANGER.
I'M TRYING TO SAVE THOUSANDS--MAYBE MILLIONS--OF INNOCENT MEN, WOMEN AND CHILDREN WHO WILL END UP AS COLLATERAL DAMAGE.
YOU'VE COMPROMISED EVERYTHING THAT SET YOU APART FROM THE PEOPLE YOU HATE SO MUCH! YOU'VE TURNED YOURSELF INTO ONE OF THEM!
IF YOU PLAN TO DELIVER THAT NUKE, YOU'LL HAVE TO KILL ME FIRST.
WHAT'S IT GONNA BE, OLD FRIEND?

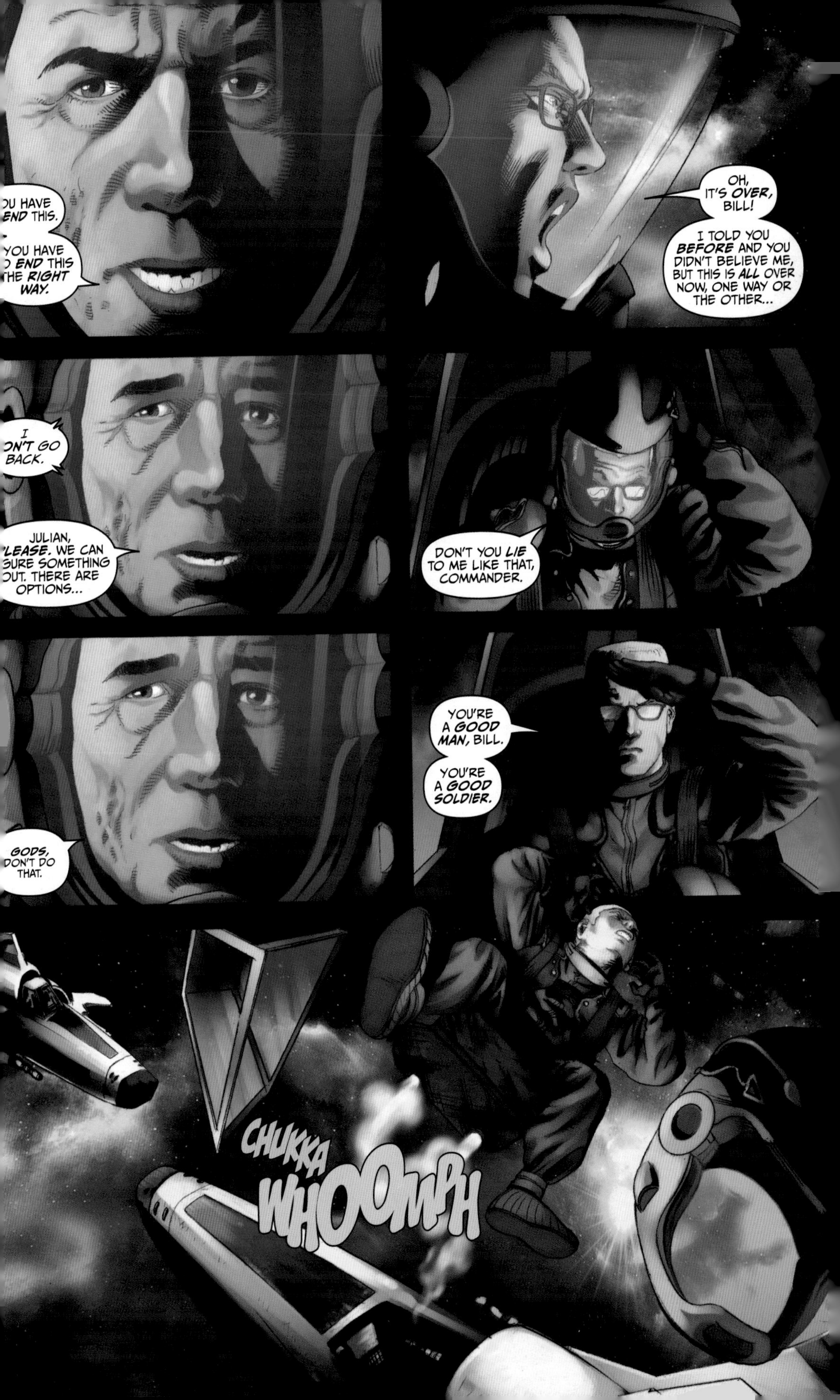

OU HAVE
END THIS.
YOU HAVE
O END THIS
THE RIGHT
WAY.
OH,
IT'S OVER,
BILL!
I TOLD YOU
BEFORE AND YOU
DIDN'T BELIEVE ME,
BUT THIS IS ALL OVER
NOW, ONE WAY OR
THE OTHER...
I
ON'T GO
BACK.
JULIAN,
PLEASE. WE CAN
GURE SOMETHING
OUT. THERE ARE
OPTIONS...
DON'T YOU LIE
TO ME LIKE THAT,
COMMANDER.
GODS,
DON'T DO
THAT.
YOU'RE
A GOOD
MAN, BILL.
YOU'RE
A GOOD
SOLDIER.
CHUKKA
WHOOOMPH

WHAT HAPPENS NOW?

TO YOU? PROBABLY NOTHING.

THANKS. WHAT ABOUT YOU?

HE WAS WRONG, YOU KNOW.

NO, HE WASN'T. THERE'S SOMETHING ROTTEN GOING ON AND I HAVE TO DO SOMETHING ABOUT IT.

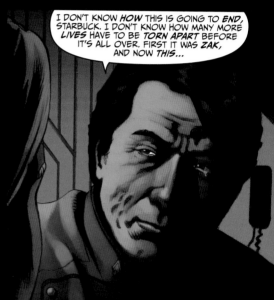

I DON'T KNOW HOW THIS IS GOING TO END, STARBUCK. I DON'T KNOW HOW MANY MORE LIVES HAVE TO BE TORN APART BEFORE IT'S ALL OVER. FIRST IT WAS ZAK, AND NOW THIS...

MAY I--?

WHAT?

DON'T LOSE FAITH, COMMANDER.

THAT'S AN ORDER.

THE END

COVER GALLERY

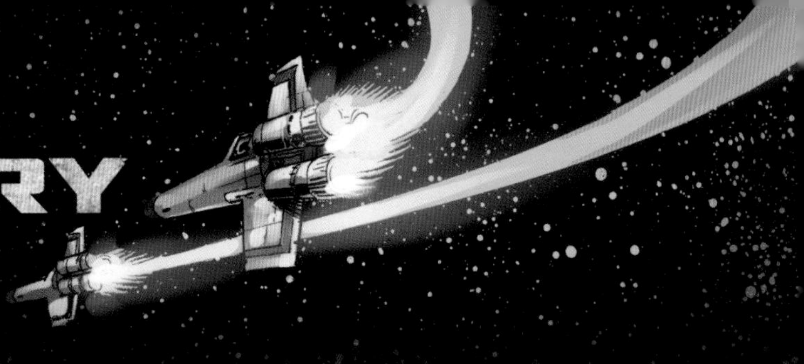

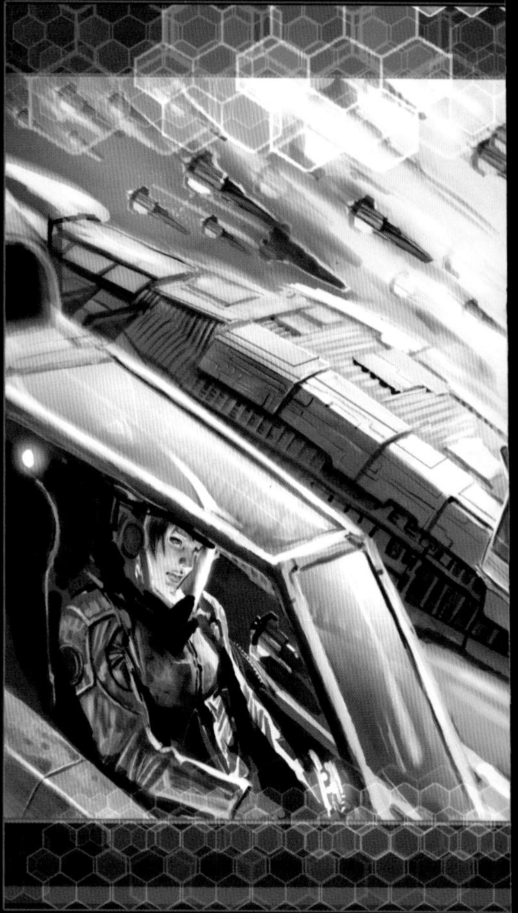

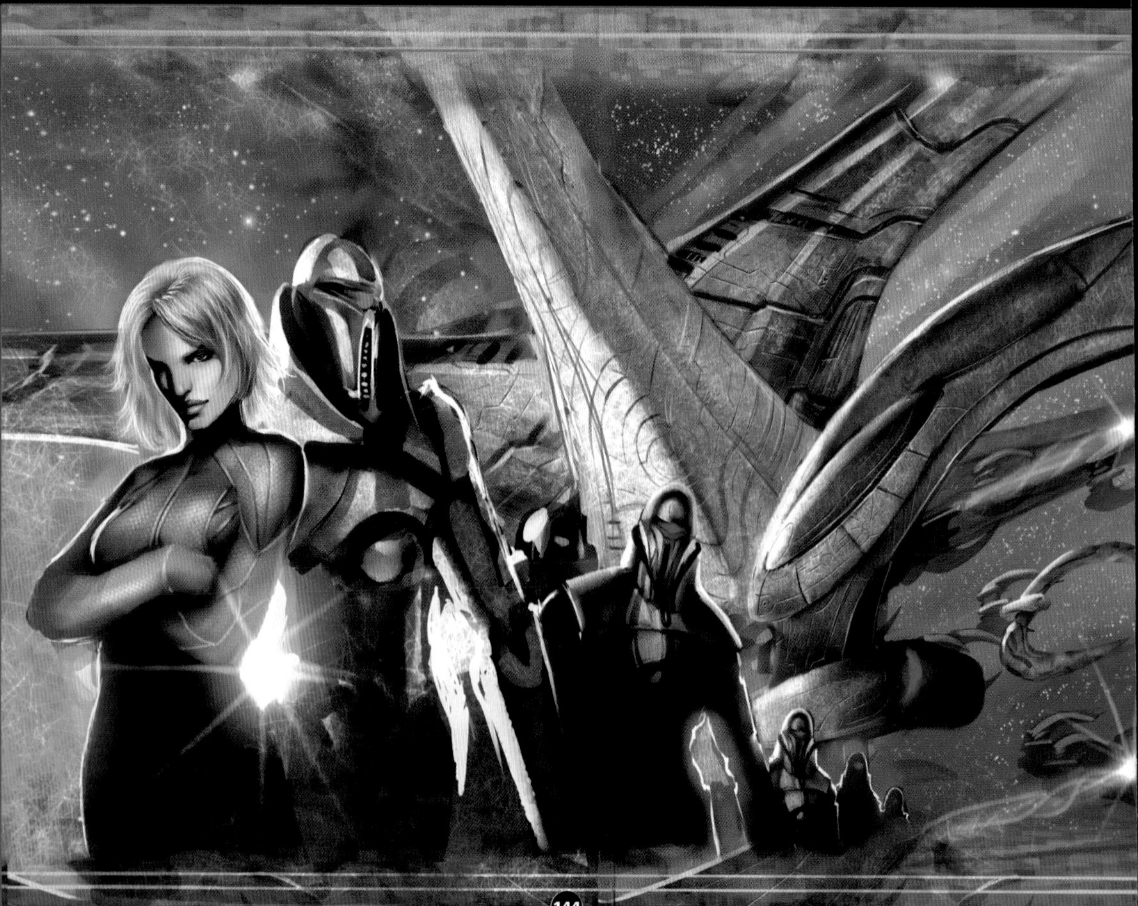

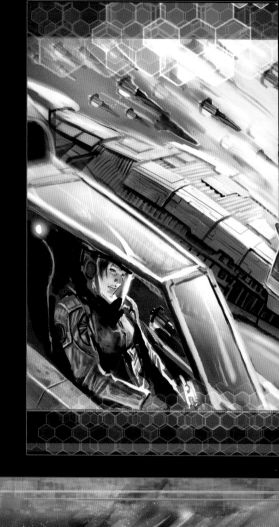

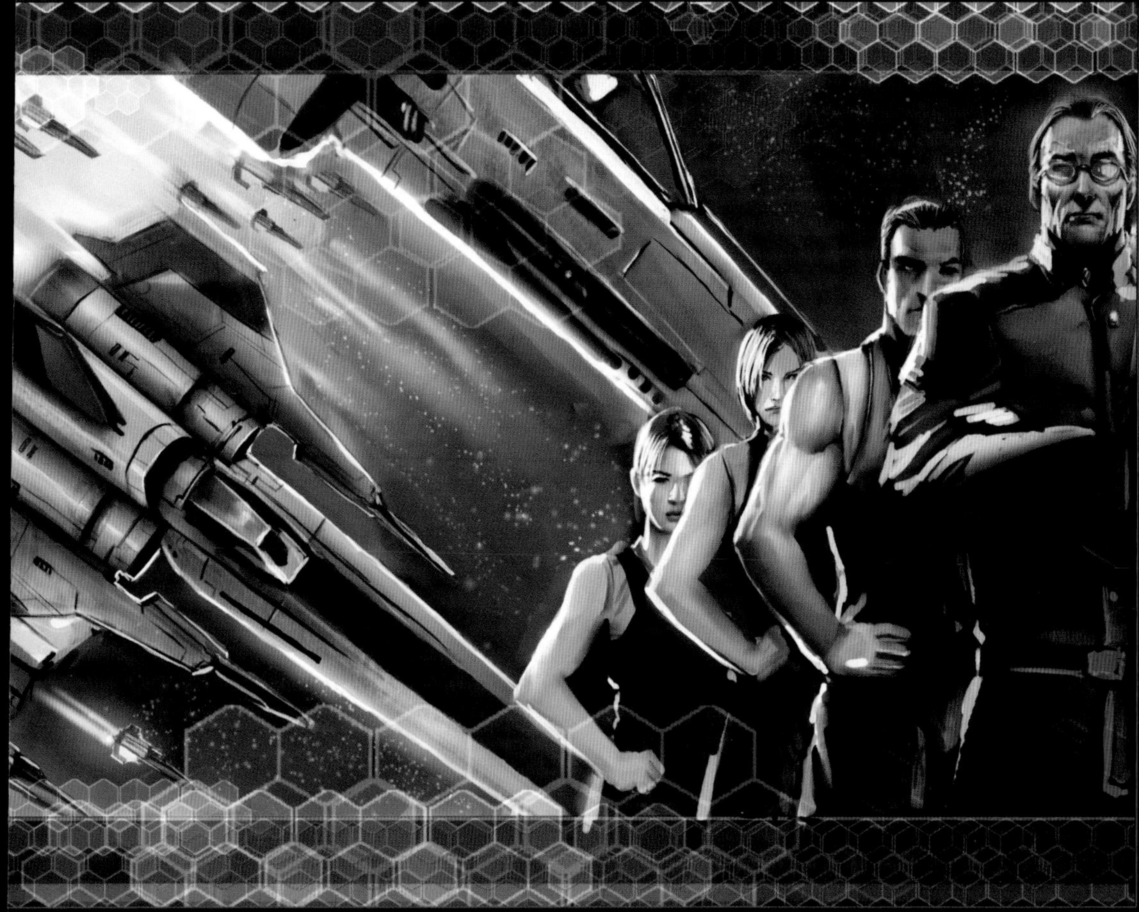

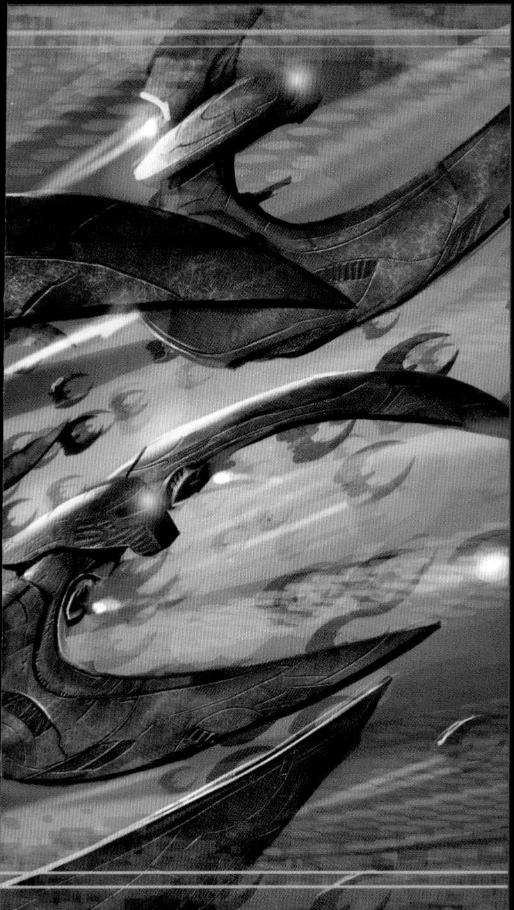

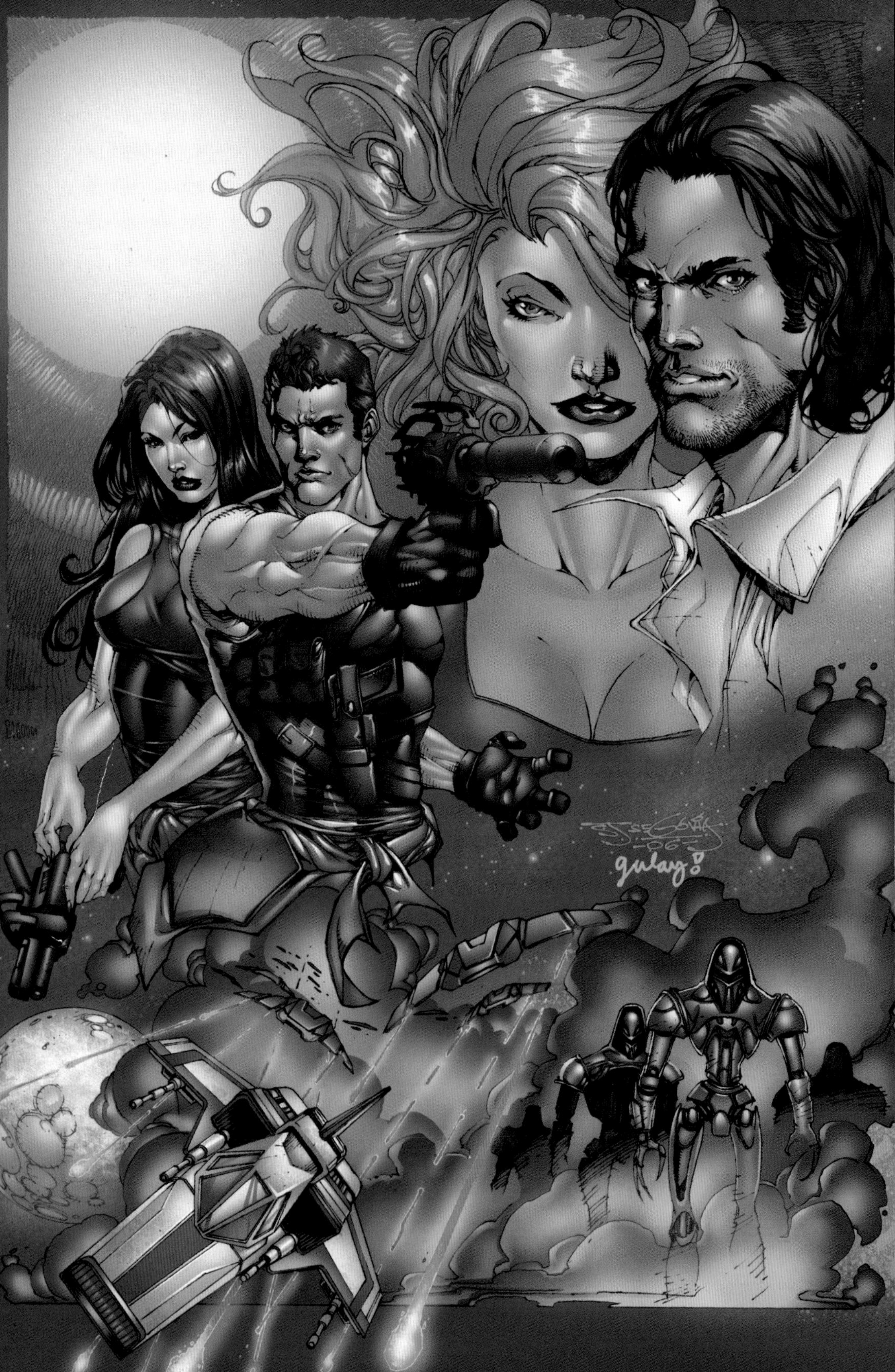

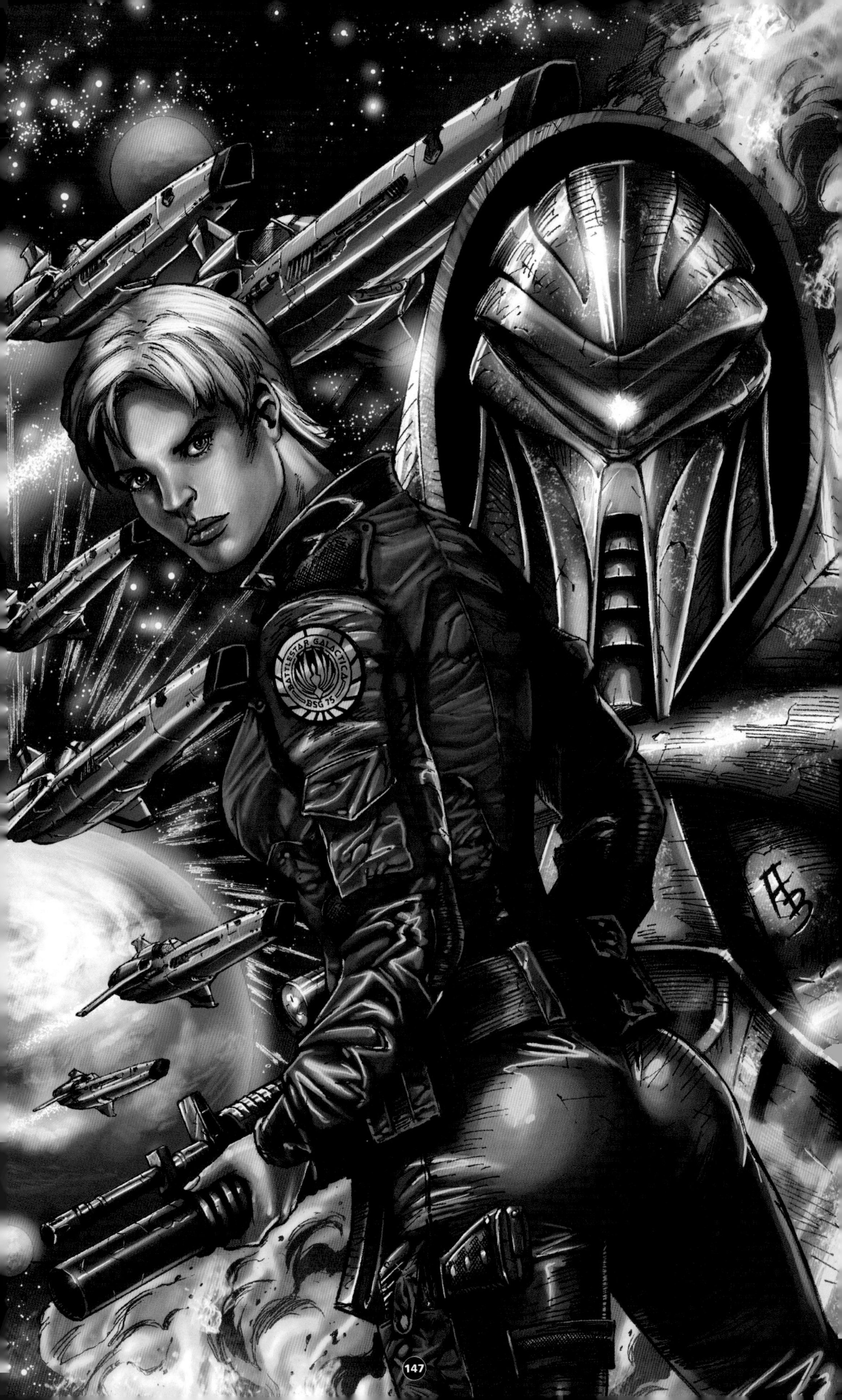
BATTLESTAR GALACTICA
BSG 75

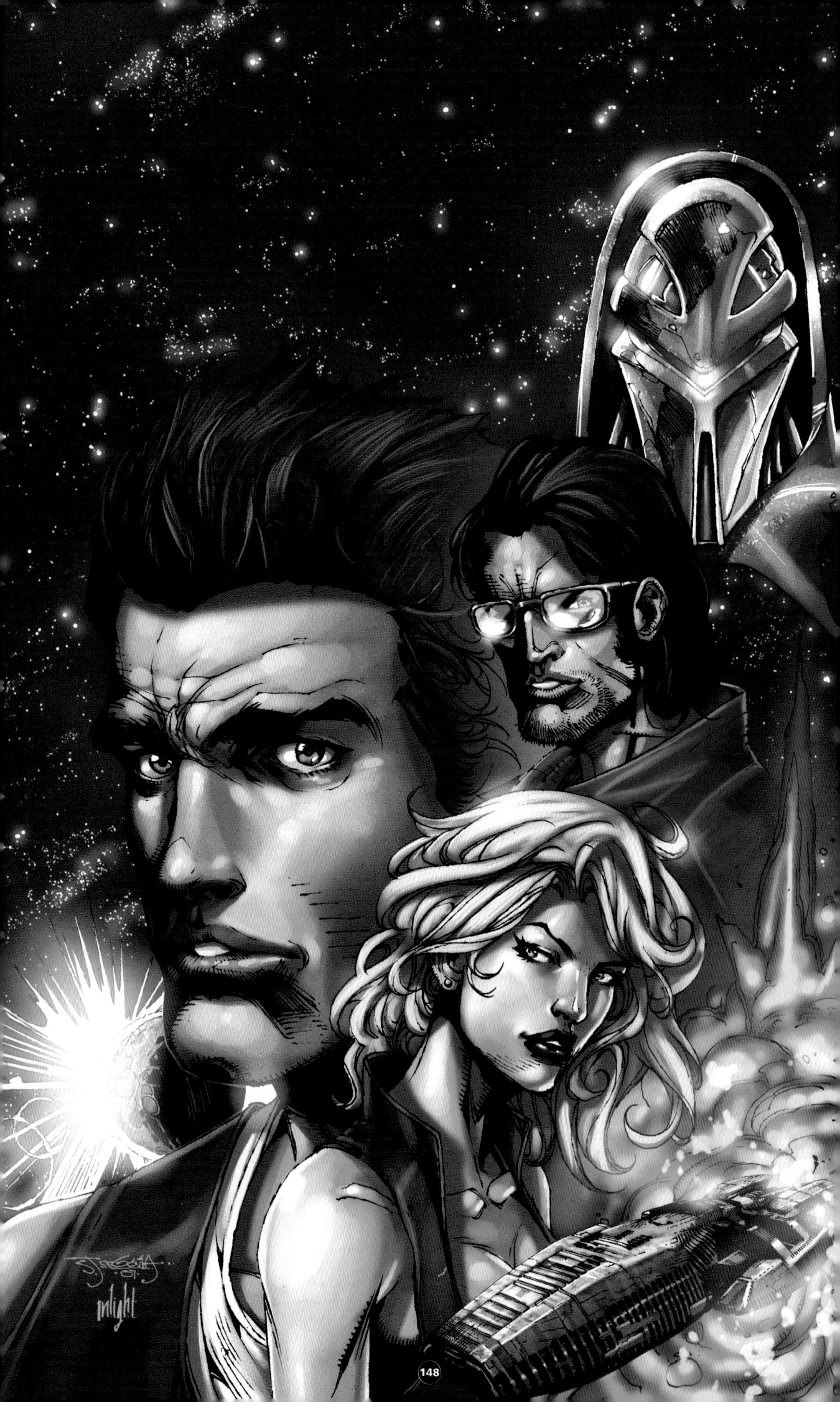

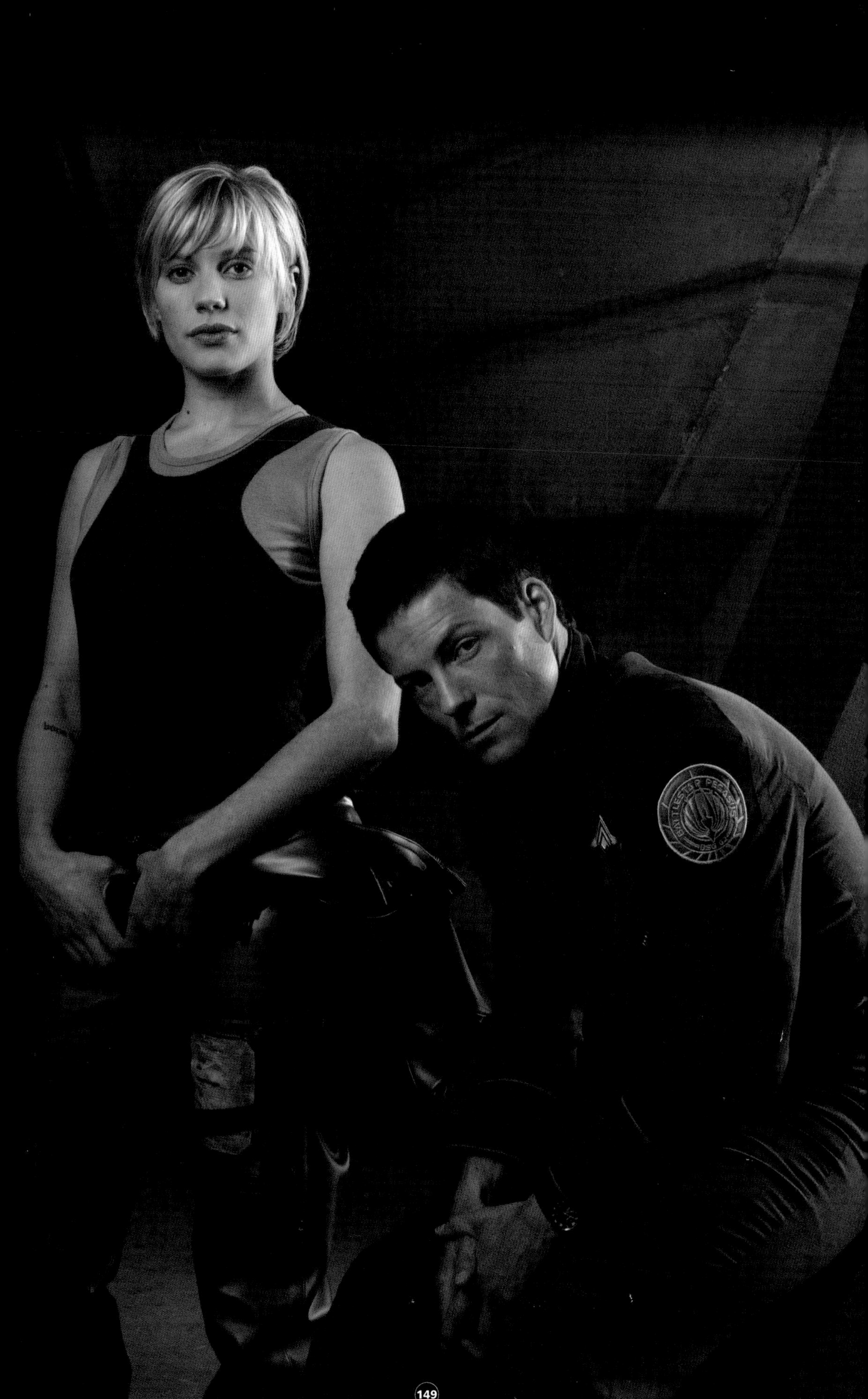
BATTLESTAR PEGASUS

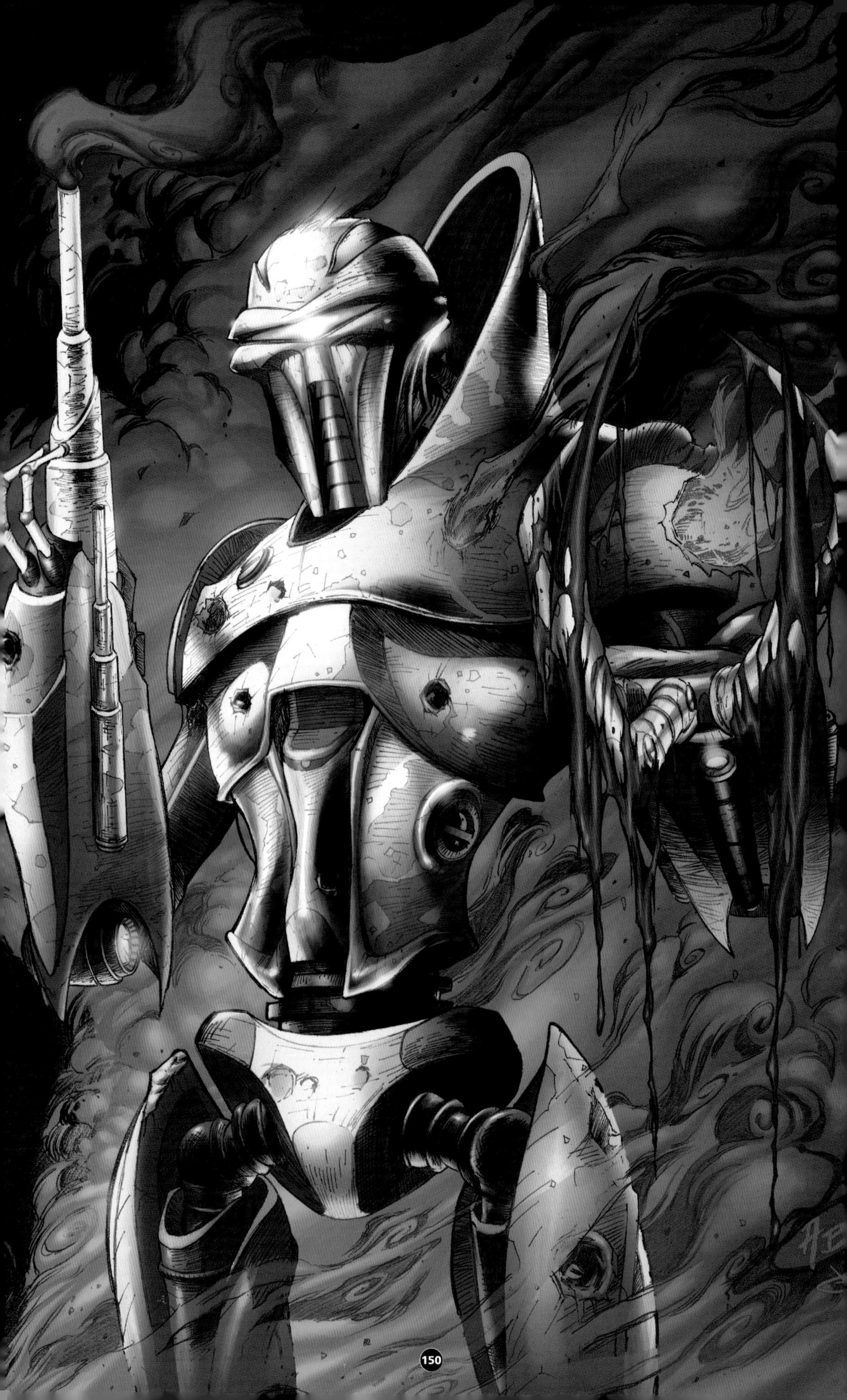

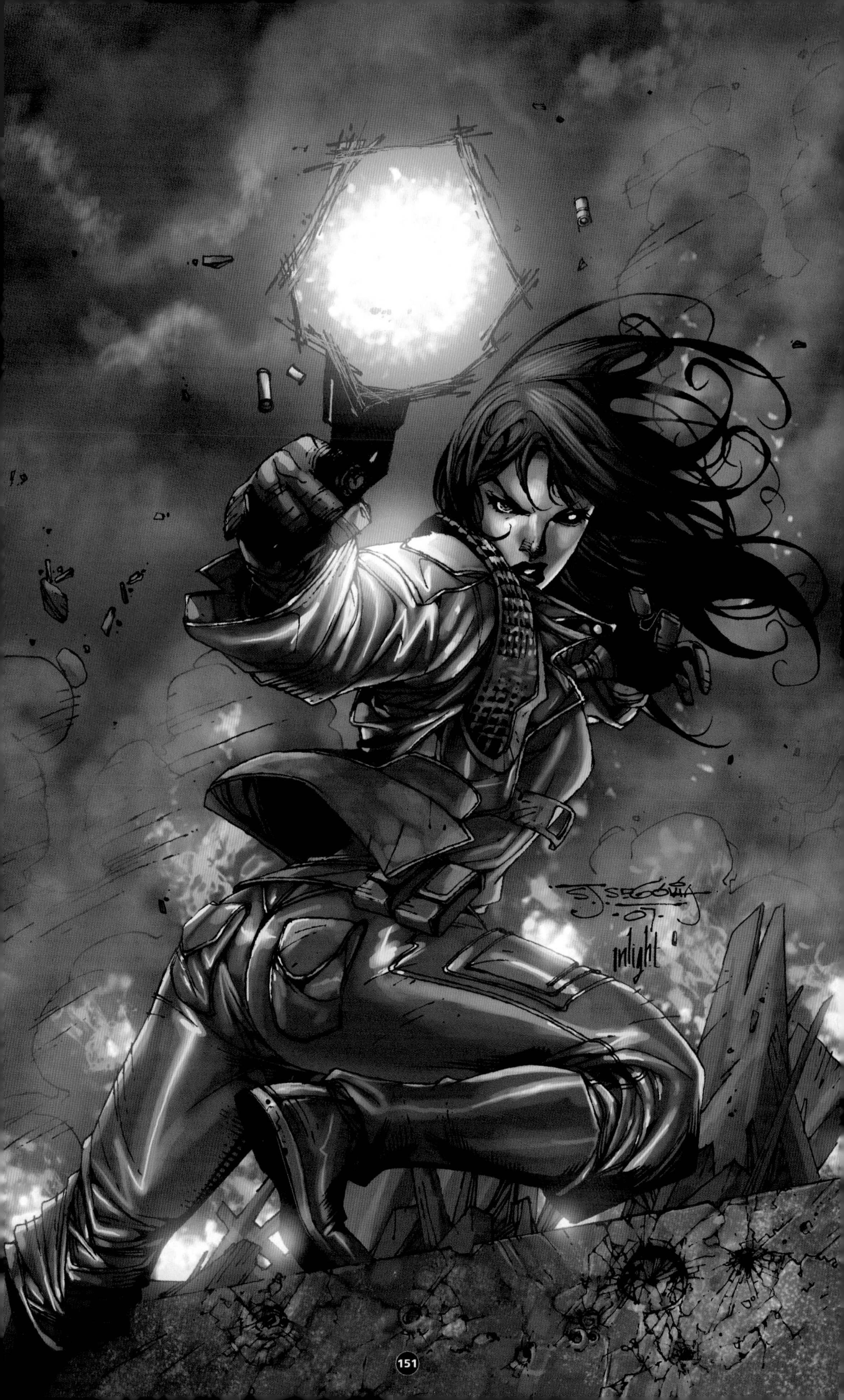

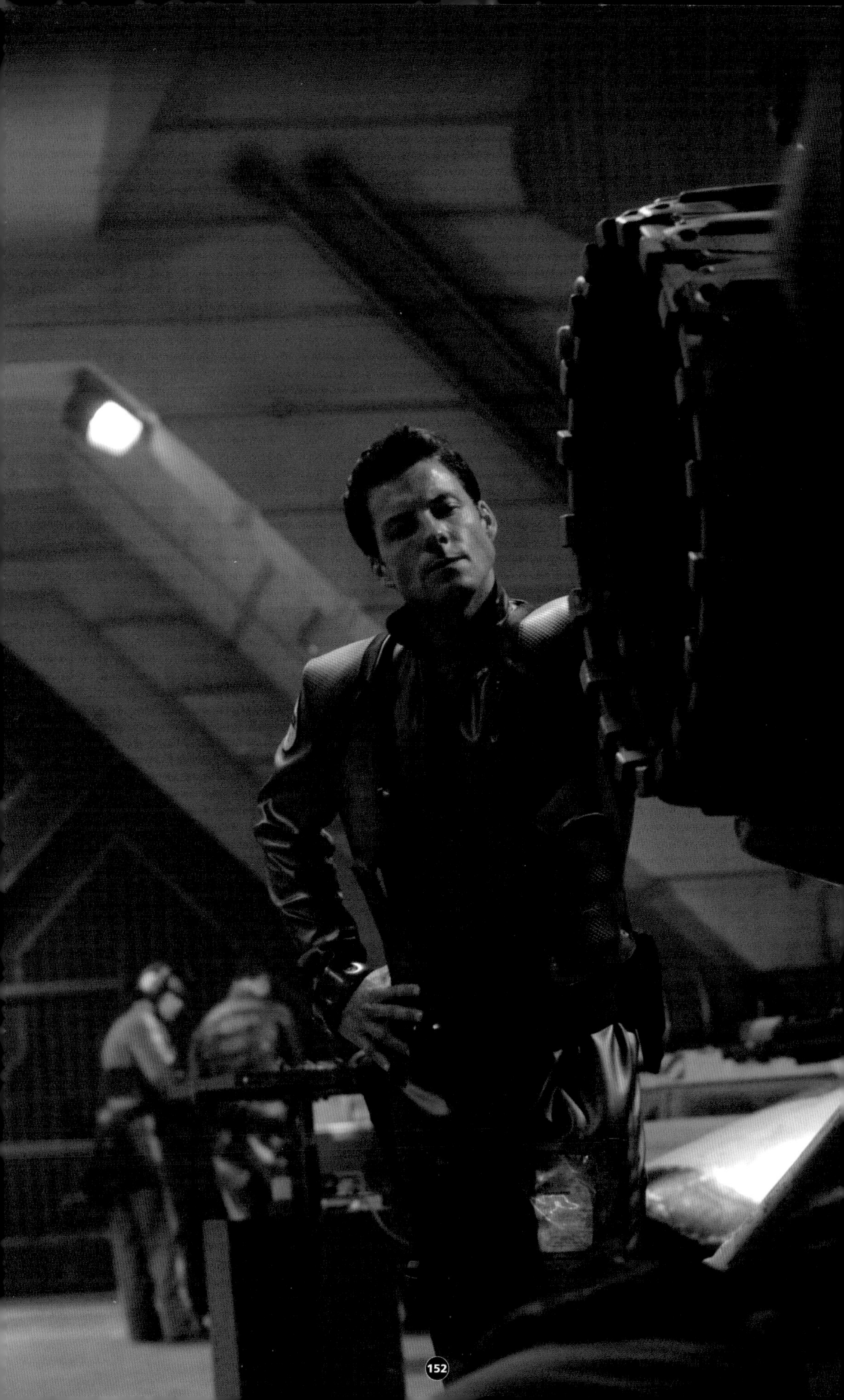

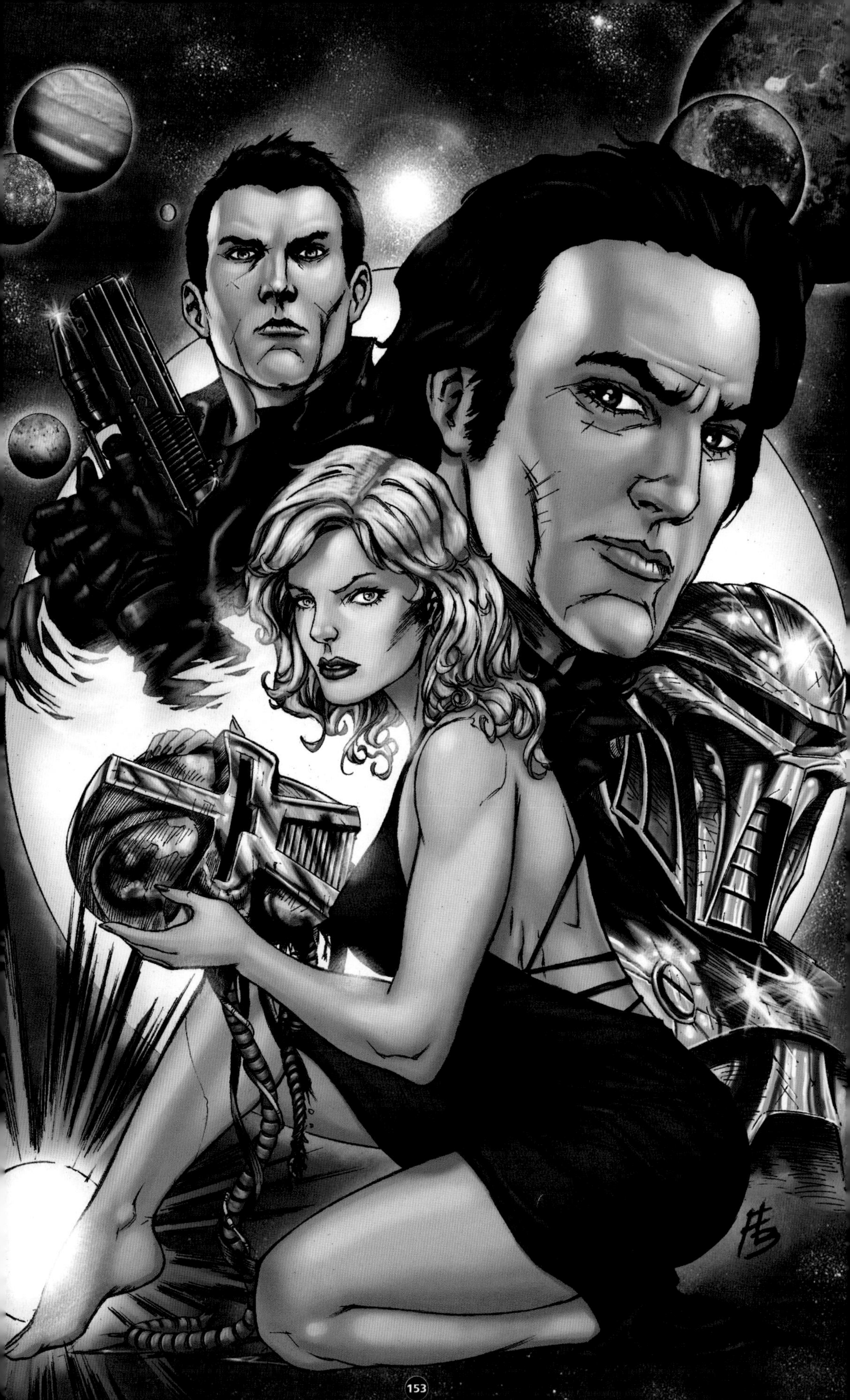

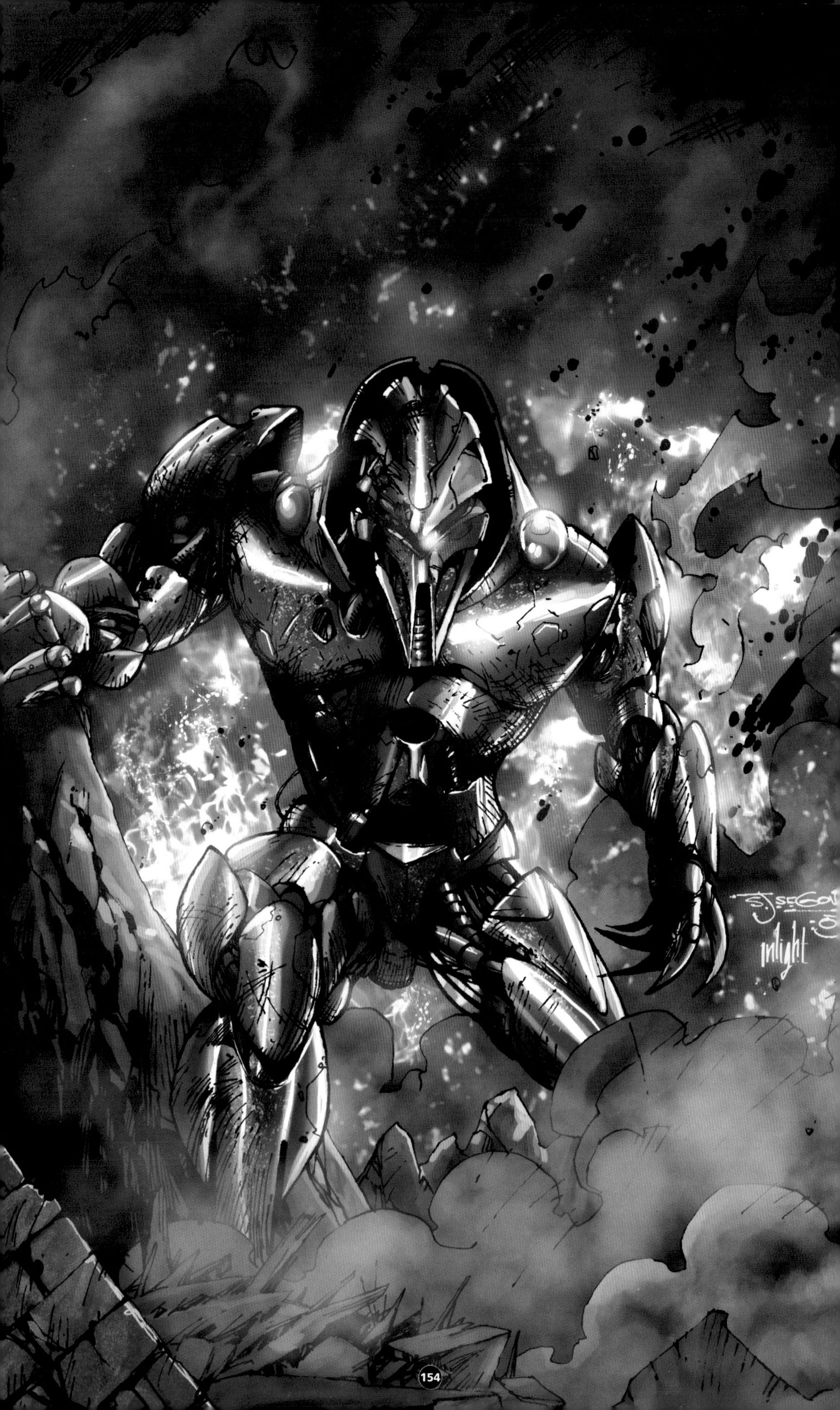

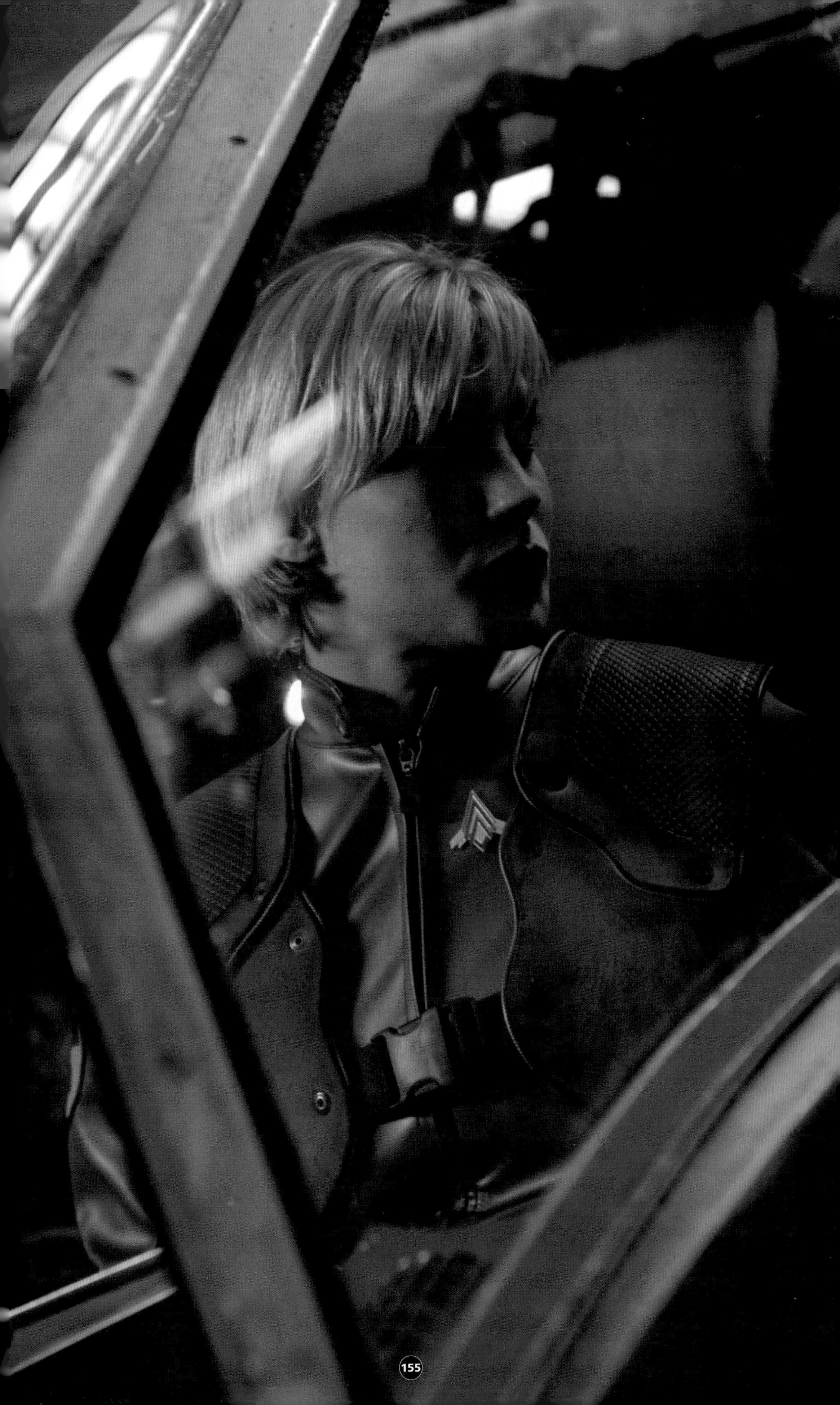

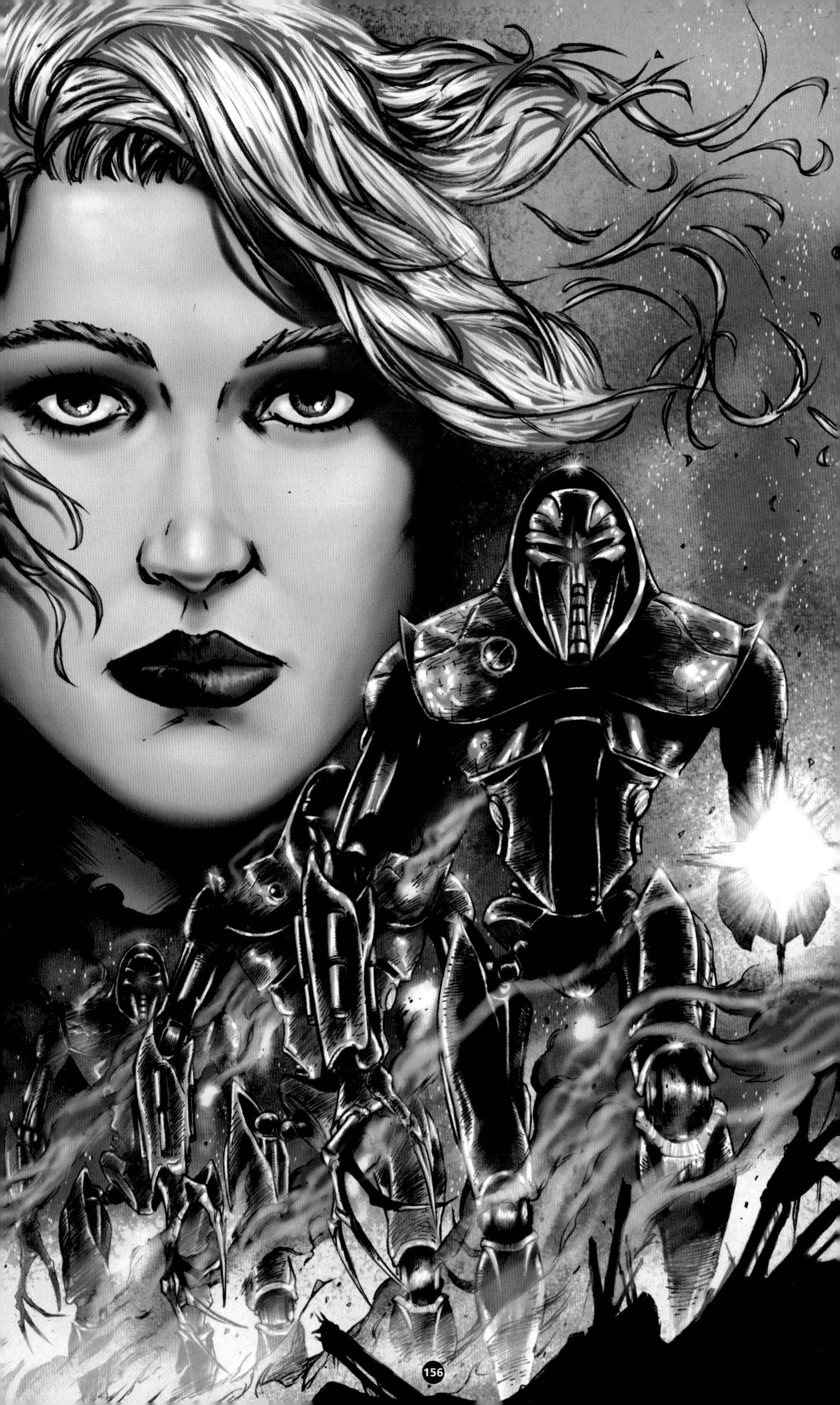

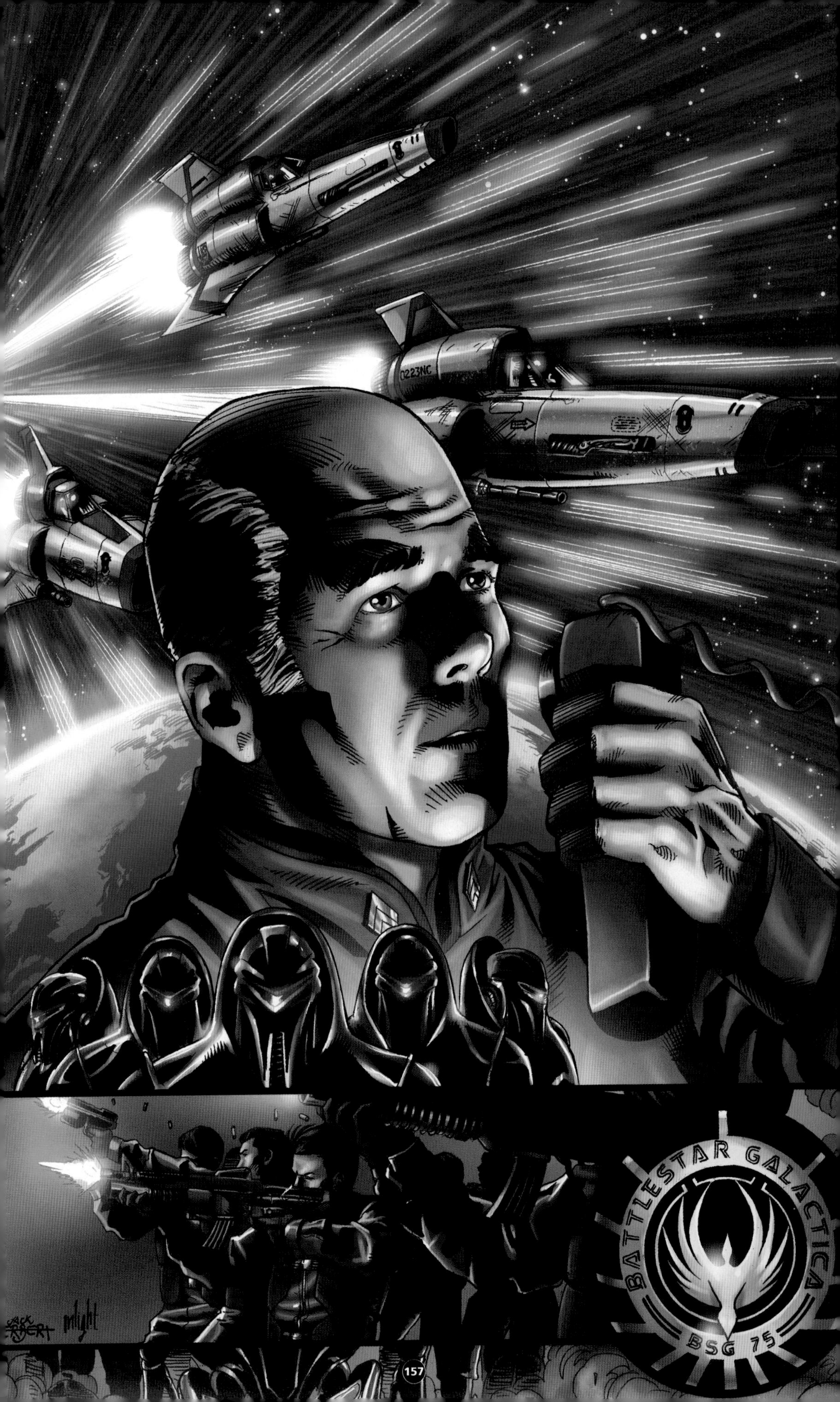
0223NC
BATTLESTAR GALACTICA
BSG 75

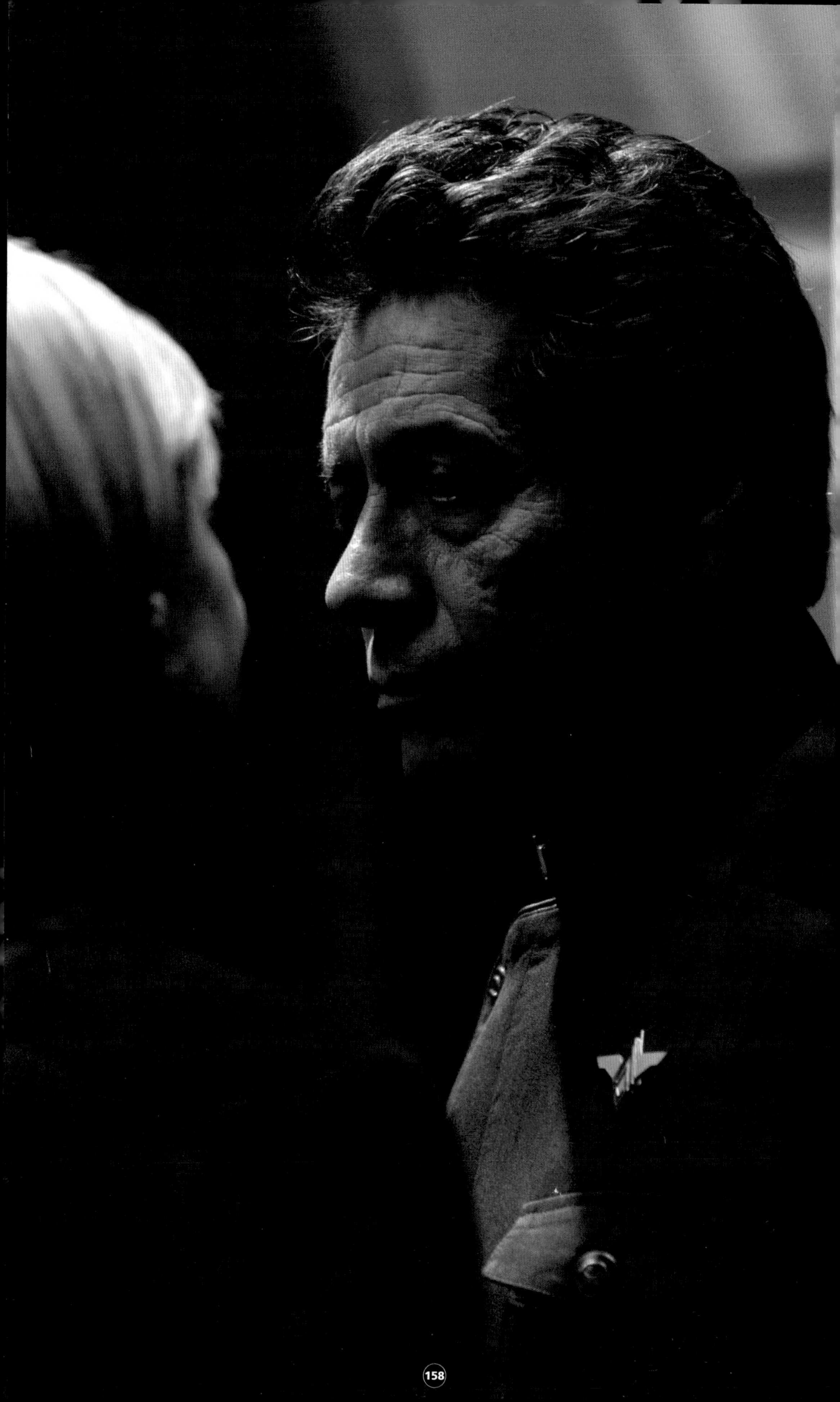

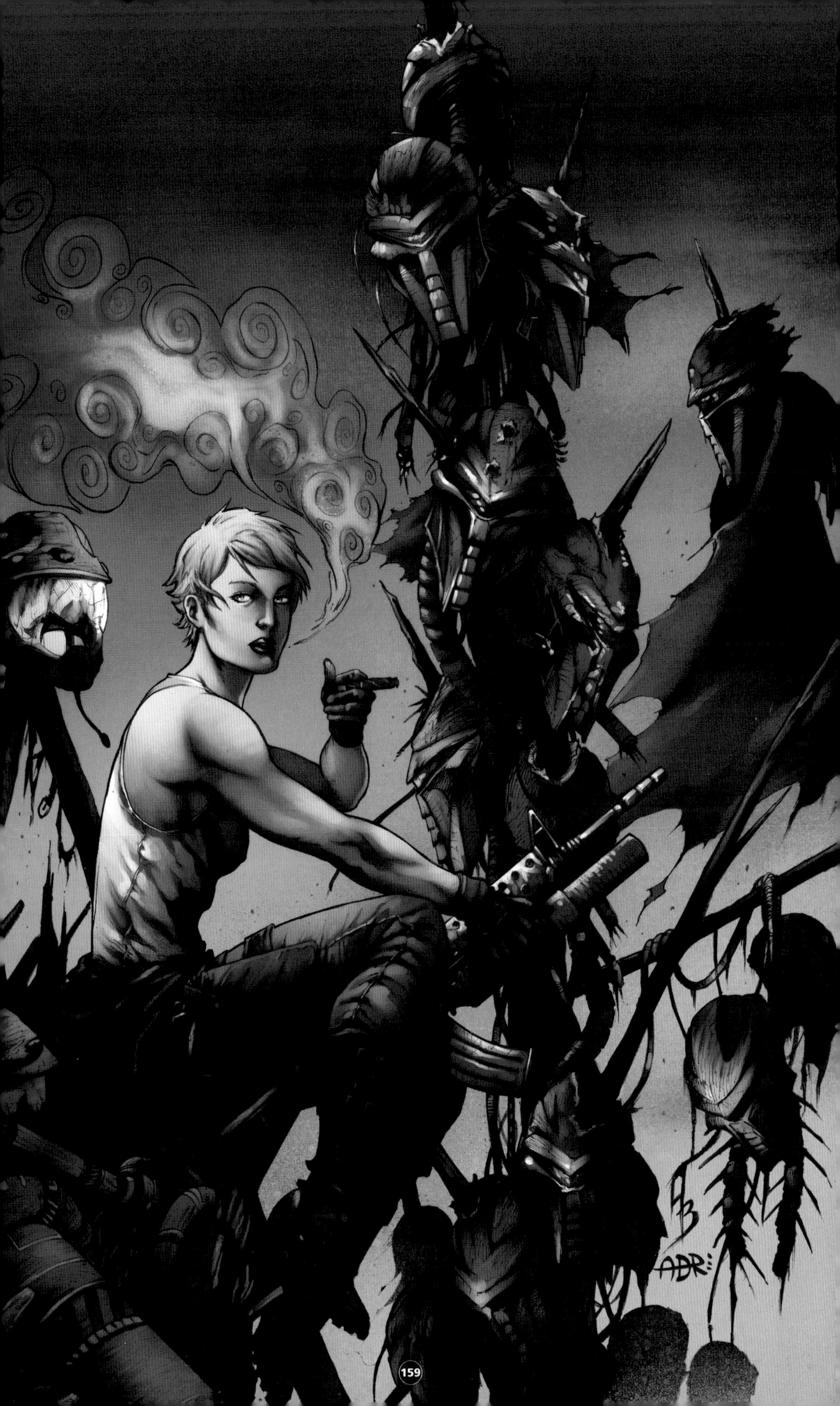

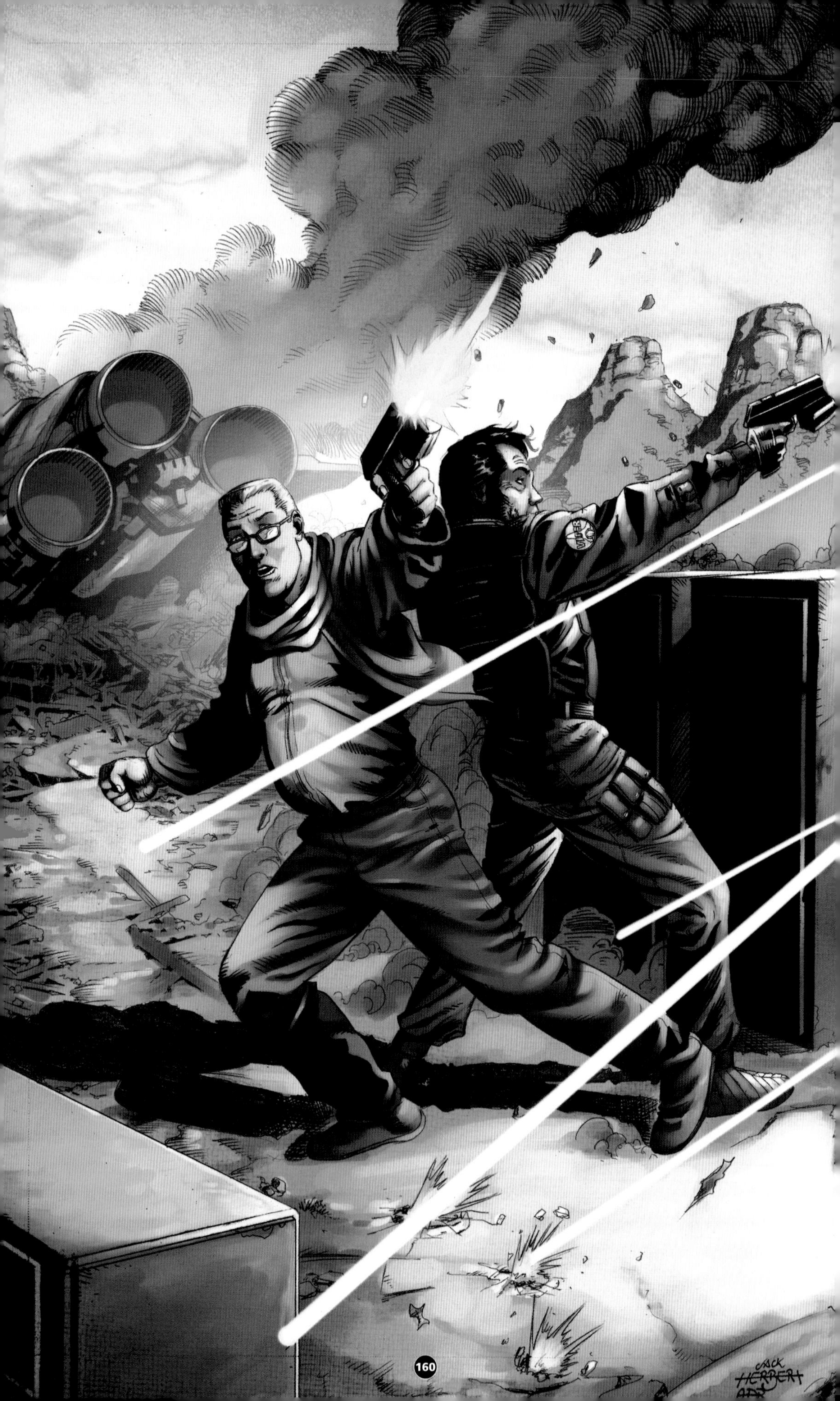
JACK HERBERT ART

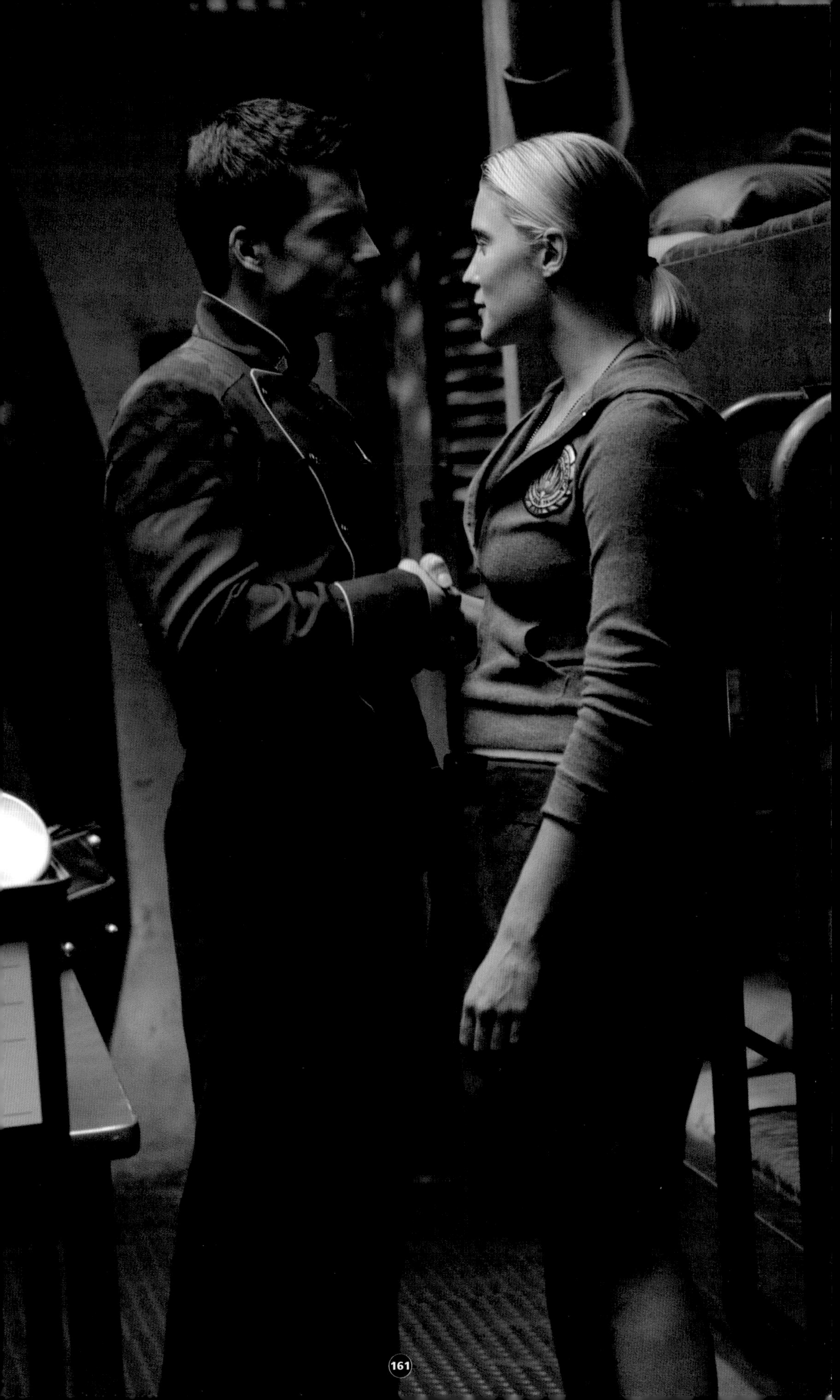

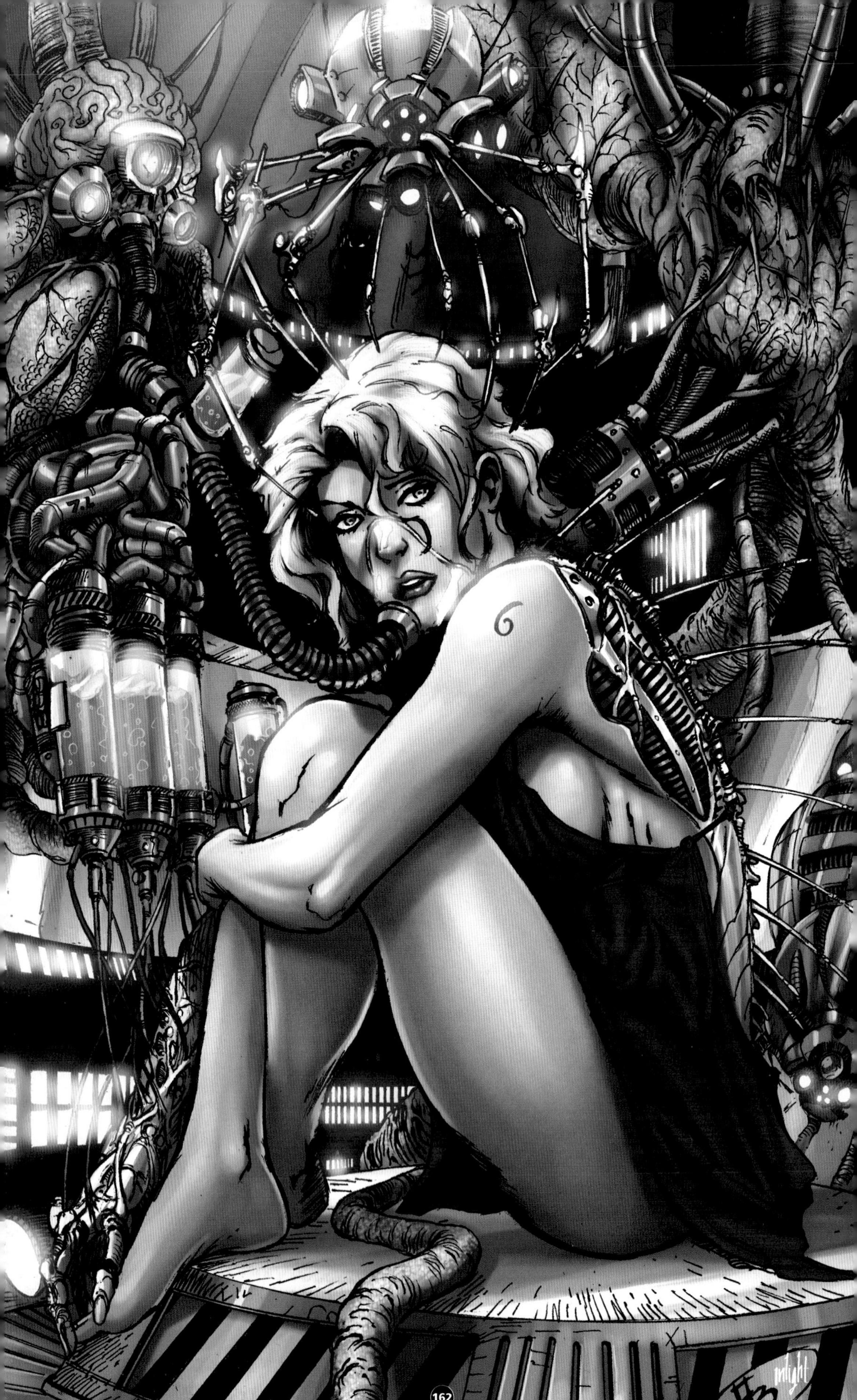

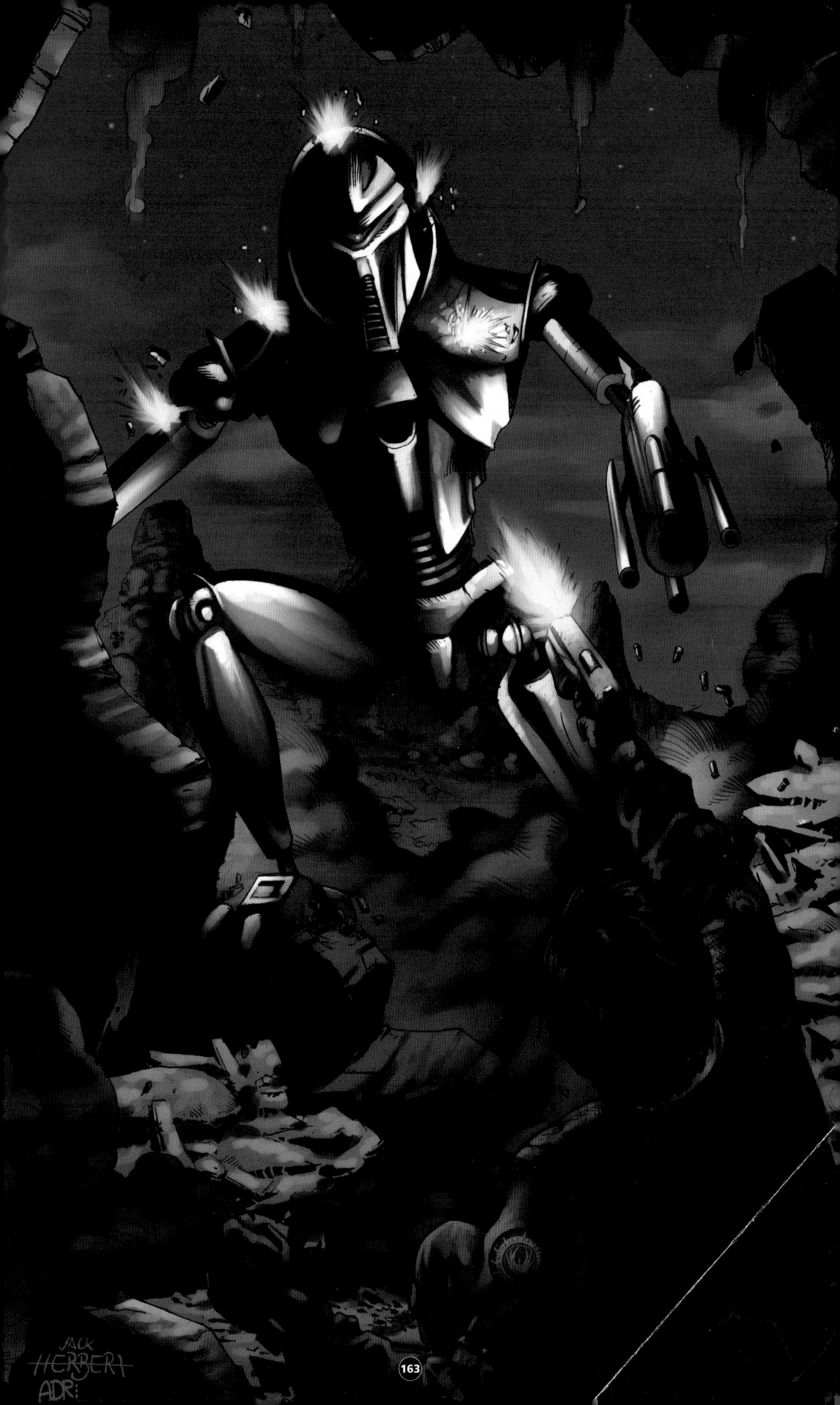
JACK
HERBERT
ADR

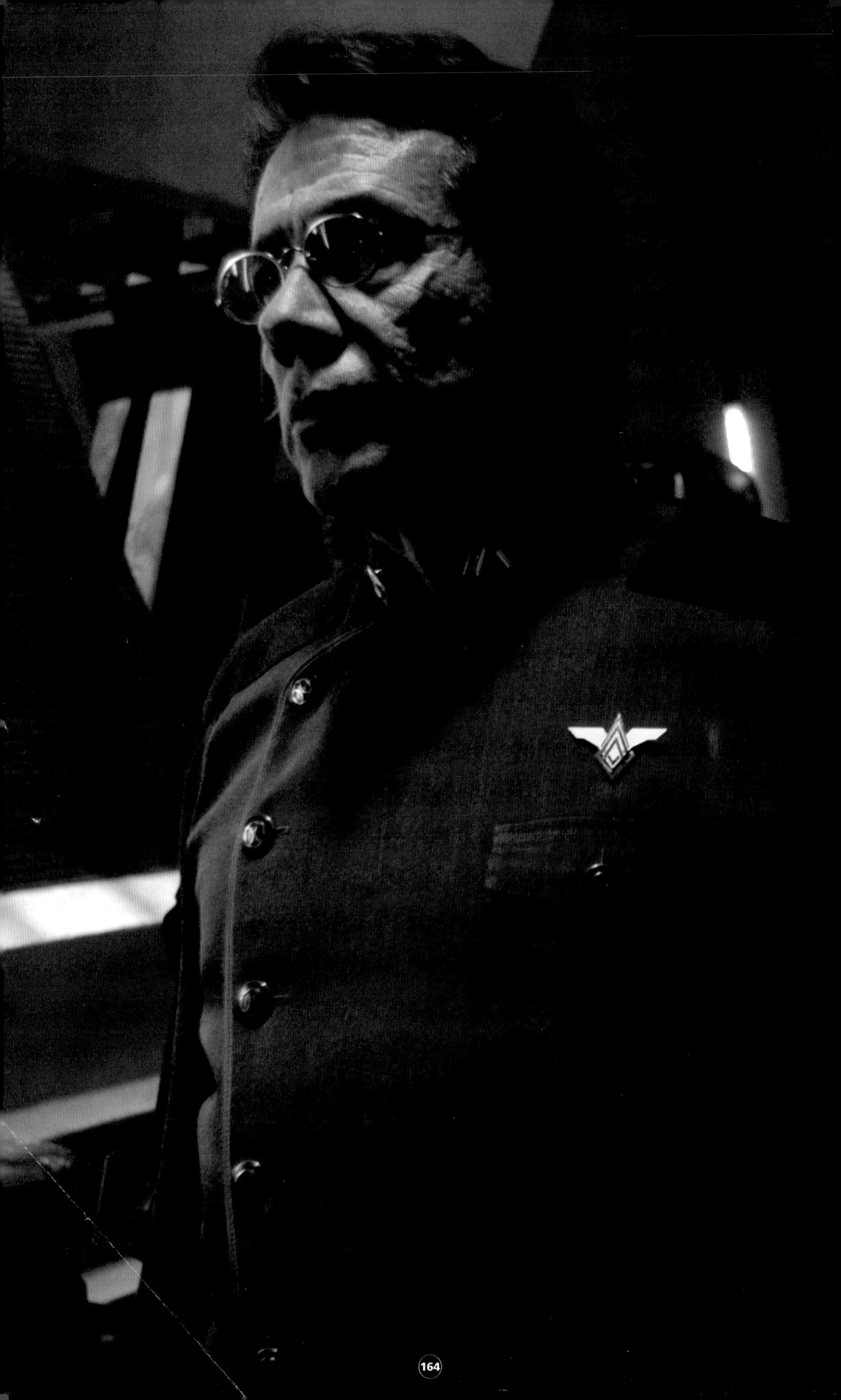

BATTLESTAR
GALACTICA™
SEASON ZERO

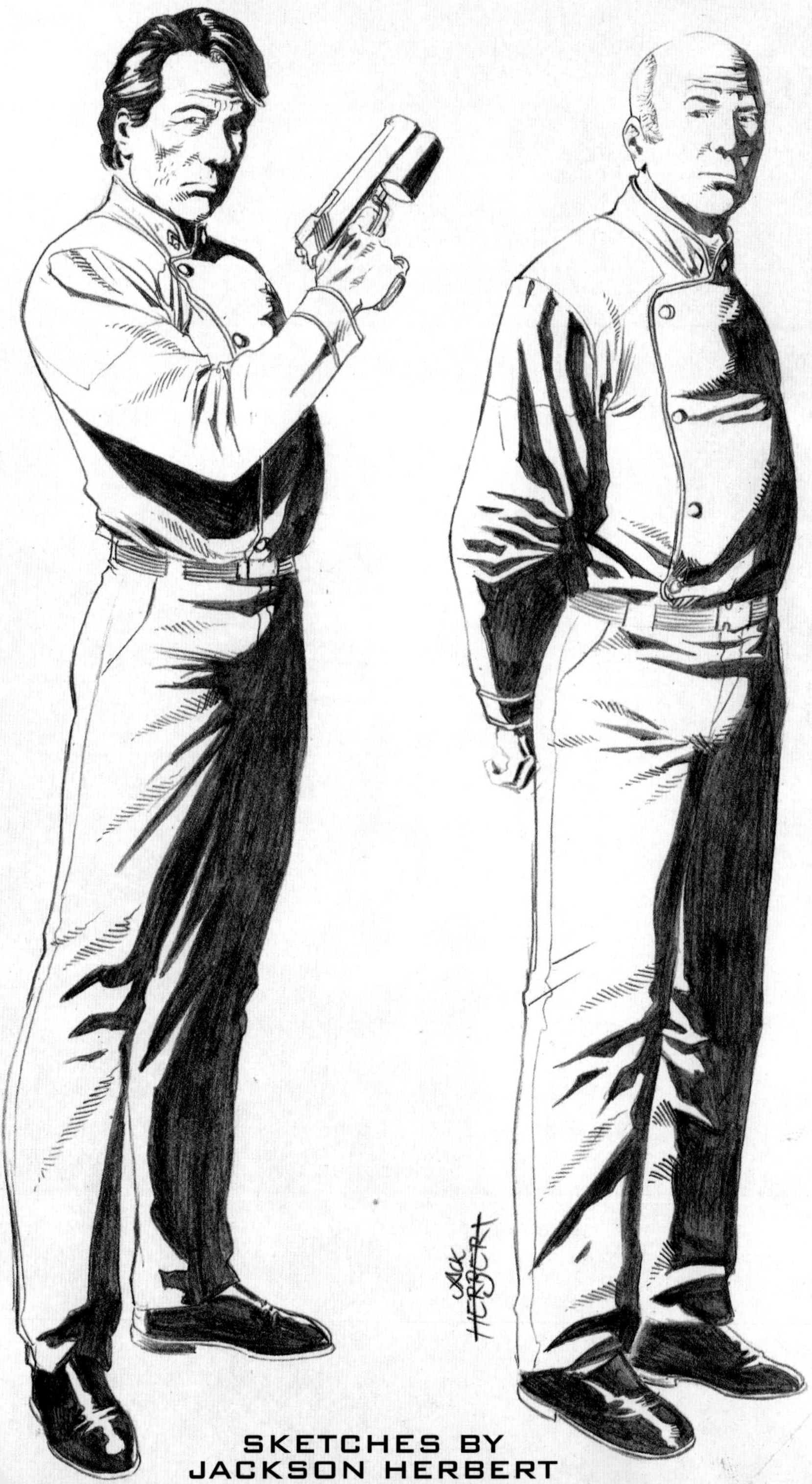
JACK HERBERT
JACK HERBERT

SKETCHES BY
JACKSON HERBERT

BATTLESTAR GALACTICA™
SEASON ZERO

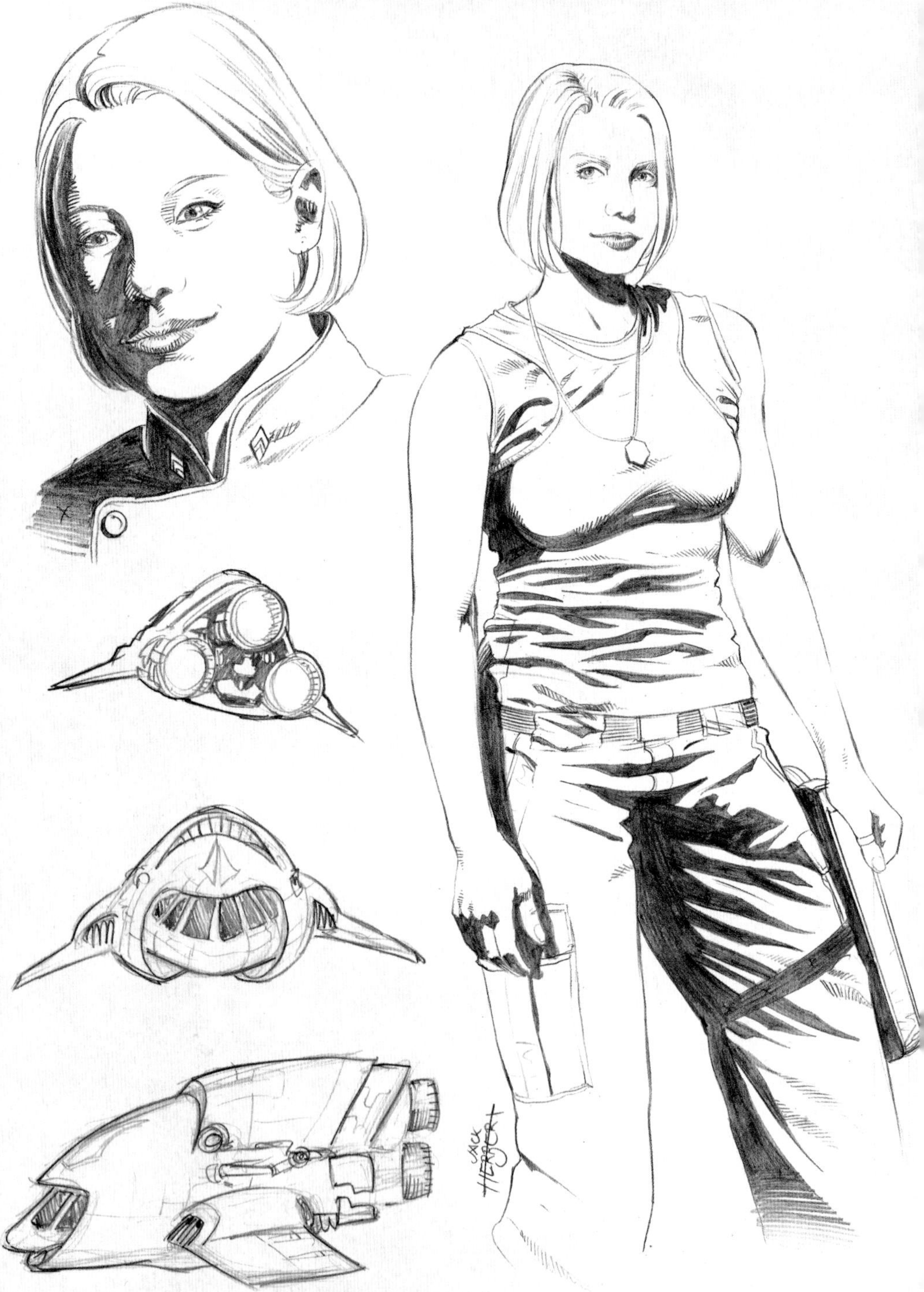
JACK HERBERT

SKETCHES BY
JACKSON HERBERT

BATTLESTAR GALACTICA™
SEASON ZERO

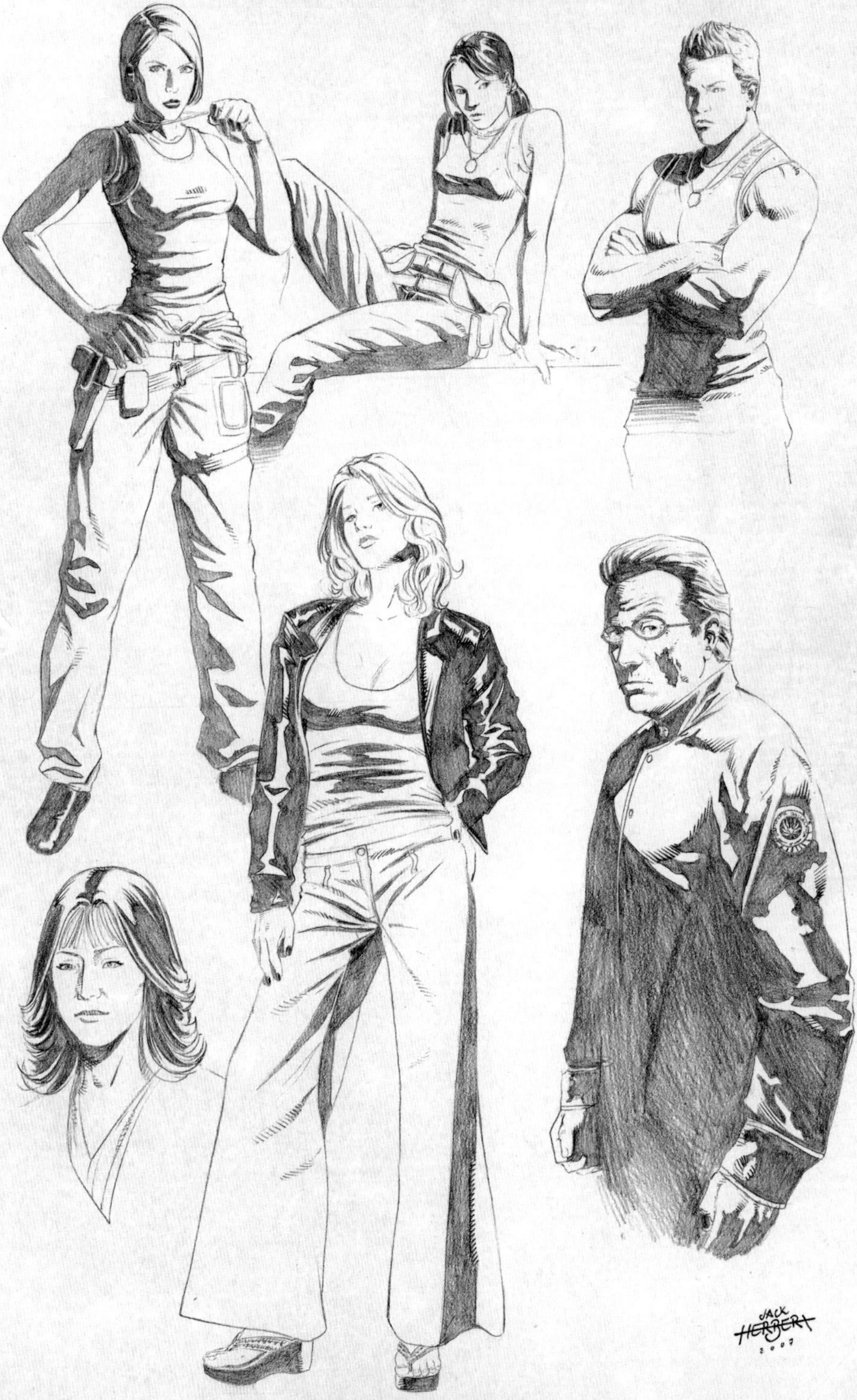
JACK HERBERT
2007

SKETCHES BY
JACKSON HERBERT

BATTLESTAR GALACTICA

BSG 75

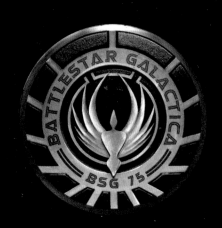